State, Nationalism, and the Jewish Communities of Modern Greece

Also available from Bloomsbury

The British and the Balkans: Forming Images of Foreign Lands, 1900-1950, by
Eugene Michail
Modern Greece: From the War of Independence to the Present, by Thomas W. Gallant
Nationalism, Identity and Statehood in Post-Yugoslav Montenegro, by
Kenneth Morrison

State, Nationalism, and the Jewish Communities of Modern Greece

Evdoxios Doxiadis

BLOOMSBURY ACADEMIC
LONDON · NEW YORK · OXFORD · NEW DELHI · SYDNEY

BLOOMSBURY ACADEMIC
Bloomsbury Publishing Plc
50 Bedford Square, London, WC1B 3DP, UK
1385 Broadway, New York, NY 10018, USA

BLOOMSBURY, BLOOMSBURY ACADEMIC and the Diana logo
are trademarks of Bloomsbury Publishing Plc

First published in Great Britain 2018
Paperback edition first published 2020

A catalogue record for this book is available from the British Library.

A catalog record for this book is available from the Library of Congress.

ISBN: HB: 978-1-4742-6346-7
PB: 978-1-3501-4376-0
ePDF: 978-1-4742-6347-4
eBook: 978-1-4742-6348-1

Typeset by Deanta Global Publishing Services, Chennai, India

To find out more about our authors and books visit
www.bloomsbury.com and sign up for our newsletters.

To Jennifer

Contents

List of Illustrations

Preface

This book begun over a decade ago while I was still a graduate student at UC Berkeley as a project for a course. What struck me at the time, and continues to amaze me, was how the history of Jews in Greece has not been problematized with regard to the convoluted paths of Greek nationalism since the creation of the modern Greek State and the variation of the Jewish communities themselves. Even today, when several excellent books on Greek Jewish history have been published and when more and more historians are shedding light on this part of Greek history, the focus rarely shifts away from the three decades between incorporation of the Jewish community of Thessaloniki (Salonica) to the Greek state during the Balkan Wars and its destruction during the Holocaust, nor look beyond the Salonica community, admittedly at least twice as large than all the other Greek Jewish communities combined. There are of course good reasons for all of this; availability of archival material, confrontation of long-held ideas in Greek historiography regarding the Holocaust, the significance of Salonica in Greek Jewish memory or Greek Jewish diaspora, and the simple fact that this is still a relatively new field in Greek historiography. But I believe that without exploring the development of the relationship between the Greek state and its Jewish communities, which by the time of the incorporation of Thessaloniki had almost a century's worth of history, we fail to capture the nuances of Greek state attitudes, policies, and perceptions with regard to Jews and other minorities.

The purpose of this book is not to discuss the history of modern Greece for which there are many excellent books available including a recent volume by Thomas Gallant,[1] nor to examine the history of Greek Jews for which Katherine Fleming produced a good history some years ago.[2] The aim of this book is to consider the interactions of the modern Greek State with its minorities, and explain its shifting policies, by focusing on the relationship between the modern Greek state and the different Jewish communities within its borders and beyond. In so doing I hope to shed more light into the complicated history of Greek nationalism and address questions of identity, especially with regard to the elites of modern Greece who formulated its policies and developed its policy aims and as a counterpoint to popular ideas and beliefs. I have deliberately tried to avoid discussing such popular views of Jews or anti-Semitism except when such ideas resulted in acts that forced the state to act. Although a comprehensive historical study of Greek anti-Semitism still awaits its author, the widespread presence of some form of anti-Semitism among the Greek public throughout Greek history is indisputable. What concerns this volume, however, is the place Jews had, if any, in Greek constructs of the nation and citizenship and how such perceptions contrasted with those reserved for other minorities. In short, I ask the question if Jews, and which Jews at that, were perceived as loyal Greek citizens, how and why this became possible, and how did the Jewish experience compare to that of other minorities in Greece.

To begin the discussion, I set the stage in Chapter 1 with a brief examination of the two millennia of history between Greeks and Jews, with a focus on the Byzantine and Ottoman Empires. Chapter 2 examines the Greek War of Independence, when the first attempts were made to define a Greek identity in terms of law and nationality, but which also saw horrific violence inflicted by all sides on the communities of the perceived enemy. Chapters 3 and 4 form the main body of my argument and investigation. They cover the period from the beginnings of the modern Greek state to the disastrous war in Asia Minor that shattered Greek dreams of creating a nation-state spanning both sides of the Aegean Sea. This is the period when the institutions of the Greek state were created, when concepts regarding citizenship, nationality, and ethnicity were developed and transformed, and when the modest state that emerged in 1830 purposefully expanded to essentially its current size. This was also the period when significant Jewish communities were incorporated to the Greek state alongside other minorities necessitating a readjustment of Greek internal policies and institutions. Chapter 5 examines the interwar period when the question of minorities in Europe was endlessly debated and was often the cause of friction between states including Greece and its neighbors. Chapter 6 concludes the discussion with a brief examination of the Holocaust in Greece and its aftermath in view of the preceding discussion and a glance into the relationship between Jews and Greece to the present.

Although ideas of the nation and nationalism stand at the core of this book, I have tried to avoid complicating the already complex historical circumstances with theoretical approaches to the question of nationalism. Instead I have opted for a brief overview of the ideas that have formulated my own understanding of the question that I hope will be useful in raising certain questions in the mind of the reader that will prove pertinent in the remaining chapters. Unfortunately a brief discussion of such a complex idea necessities gross simplification of the ideas of the scholars that I discuss. I simply want to present some of the arguments that have framed the discussion of nationalism and stress the difficulties in applying them to the Greek case.

Although nearly all theoretical approaches to nationalism stress its modern nature, it often appears that this is the only point scholars can agree upon. Theorists of nationalism have naturally focused on the development of nationalism in the various regions or periods they are particularly well versed in and thus have stressed different aspects of nationalism and its relation to modernity, which may be relevant in some cases but inapplicable to others. Despite the insights that these understandings of nationalism provide, in the Greek case one often finds that they fail to adequately explain the course of Greek nationalism. Ernest Gellner for instance makes a clear distinction between traditional and modern societies and offers the definition that "nationalism is primarily a political principle which holds that the political and the national unit should be congruent."[3] In his view, premodern, traditional societies had no incentive to impose a homogeneity on their people since diversity frequently provided greater benefits to ruling elites but modern, industrial societies strive for exactly the opposite as a new high culture infuses the whole society.[4] The role of the state is crucial for this development as it creates and maintains the necessary educational infrastructure.[5] However, Gellner sees nationalism as the product of industrial social organization, where labor migration and bureaucratic employment are important determinants for fostering the idea of the co-national. For him it is nationalism that generates nations, not the reverse.[6] Despite the appeal of Gellner's thoughts, it is hard to apply his model in Greece as others have noted[7] because it lacked industrial development and industrial employment until the end of the nineteenth, if not the early twentieth, century but with its highly influential, centralized bureaucracy and pioneering efforts toward mass education.

Most modernist theorists like John Breuilly link nationalism to the state and state power.[8] Breuilly too tied nationalism to modernization again identified primarily in economic terms that changed the economic order of society in the eighteenth and nineteenth centuries.[9] Breuilly stressed the idea of citizenship, the idea of the nation as a body of citizens, and although the conception of nationality in terms of the political rights of citizens dominated the eighteenth century,[10] many groups subsequently rejected this liberal understanding of the nation seeking a cultural understanding to nationality, the two often merging in a "sleight-of-hand ideology."[11] Those that pursued his thoughts further like Paul Bass saw literacy, media and mass communication, standardization of language, and schooling as the necessary factors to promote the necessary interclass communication.[12] Again, although there is much that seems to be useful in Breuilly and Bass' understanding of nationalism, Greece had neither the economic structures, literacy, or even standardization of language that their theory requires, Breuilly himself admitting that Greece was an anomaly to his theory.[13]

Eric Hobsbawm has been a great influence to Greek historiography so his understanding of nationalism is particularly pertinent. Hobsbawm believed that nations and nationalism are the result of a social engineering process where invented traditions play a crucial role in forging a necessary continuity with the past.[14] The nation is the most pervasive of these invented traditions with the period from 1870 to 1914 being the height of invented traditions, a period that also witnessed the emergence of mass politics.[15] Invented traditions were the primary means through which the ruling elites tried to counter the threat of mass democracy with a focus on primary education, public ceremonies, and public monuments,[16] Hobsbawm almost echoing Gellner in that "nations did not make states and nationalisms but the other way around."[17] Hobsbawm identified two basic stages of nationalism in European history, the first characterized by the democratic nationalism of the "great nations" infused with ideals of the French Revolution from 1830 to 1870, followed by the reactionary nationalism of the 1870s onwards of the so-called small nations mostly against the Ottoman, Habsburg, and Russian Empires.[18] Once again Greece ill fits Hobsbawm's description this time in a temporal sense since despite the obvious similarities of Greece with the "small nations," Greece emerged fully independent in 1830, and developed quickly a powerful nationalist agenda, yet she also does not seem to fit comfortably in his democratic nationalism of the "great nations."

One cannot discuss nationalism without mentioning Benedict Anderson whose understanding of nations as imagined communities has become ubiquitous in modern historiography. For Anderson, nationalism and nationality are cultural artifacts with nationalism emerging at the end of eighteenth century because of historical forces.[19] In a sense Anderson sees the nation in the same framework as religion or kinship and defines it as "an imagined political community—and imagined as both inherently limited and sovereign." The nation is imagined because members do not know the overwhelming majority of their fellow members yet "in their minds lives the image of their communion."[20] The factors that allowed these communities to emerge include according to Anderson the decline of the older religiously imagined communities, the exploration of the world by Europeans, the decline of Latin, the sacred language, and especially commercial book publishing or print-capitalism.[21] Print-capitalism created fields of communication in spoken vernaculars, fixed stable vernacular languages allowed the development of an image of antiquity crucial to the idea of the nation, and created different languages of power and authority, all leading to the creation of national consciousness.[22] Anderson's convincing formulation is nevertheless problematic in the case of Greece, not only because of the very different sacral language involved, but also due to the complex linguistic issues in Greece that were not resolved until 1974. Furthermore, the interaction of Greeks with the non-European world was quite different than the one Anderson describes while religion, as will be discussed in subsequent chapters, played a crucial role in the formulation of national consciousness in the region as others have criticized him with regard to the cases of Ireland, Poland, Armenia, or Israel.[23]

Miroslav Hroch has been more attuned to the peculiarities of nationalism in eastern Europe which is of great benefit to those who work in the region. Hroch tied nation-forming to the process of social transformation associated with capitalism but instead of focusing on the economic aspect he emphasized the social effects, especially the transformations with regard to mobility, communication, literacy and so on, all looked upon from an empirical lens.[24] For Hroch, the classical national movements had three demands: the development of a national culture based on the local language, to be used in education, administration, and economic transactions; the creation of their own social structure with their educated elites and economic classes; and the gaining of equal civil rights with some degree of political autonomy.[25] In a very structural way, Hroch then broke down the phases of a national movement and identified four separate types of national movements in Europe, the third, a mass movement already established in the old regime before the achievement of a constitutional order being confined to the Ottoman Balkans including Greece.[26] Unlike other theorists, Hroch considers the particularities of Easter Europe and the Balkans in his formulations and thus sees industrialization as one possible but not a necessary factor in successful nation building,[27] but his rather rigid structural approach often ignores political determinants.[28] He is also close to a primordialist understanding of the nation as exemplified by his rhetorical question of why nobody in the early nineteenth century thought to launch a campaign to convince the Irish that they were Germans and so on.[29] As we shall see, it did occur to some to try to convince Albanians, Slavs, and Vlachs that they were Greeks, often with remarkable success.

Anthony D. Smith comes from a different tradition representing ethnosymbolism which challenges the modernist approaches to nationalism examined above. He stressed the need for an analysis of identity over the span of centuries with an emphasis on the importance of continuity and the significance of preexisting ethnic communities (*ethnies*) in the formation of national identities.[30] Smith believed that to understand modern nations one needs to consider the preexisting ethnic components without which the process of nation building is highly problematic.[31] For Smith a nation is "a named human population sharing an historic territory, common myths and historical memories, a mass, public culture, a common economy and common legal rights and duties for all members."[32] Smith specifically addressed the Greek case in the early nineteenth century using the failure of the church hierarchy to respond to the emerging aspirations of the middle classes who then used secular ideological discourses to achieve their aims.[33] Smith identified two kinds of nationalism, a "territorial" and an "ethnic" version (roughly Western vs. Eastern), the latter seeming to fit Greek developments rather well.[34] Ethnosymbolists have been criticized for using such broad definitions of their terms as to make them useless, and that they fail to explore the differences between modern nations and earlier ethnic groups, essentially conflating the two terms. Malesevic accused Smith of "evolutionary historicism" based on determinism, fatalism, and finalism, with a view of history as having well-defined stages of development, and with historical evolution as a mission, that *ethnies* must become nations.[35]

Some recent approaches to nationalism have also made useful contributions. Michael Billig's banal nationalism made the excellent point that nationalism continues after the establishment of the political entity it demanded and becomes part of the environment of the homeland.[36] National identity is constantly reinforced and replicated in nation-states with politicians and newspapers playing a significant role in the reproduction of nationalism.[37] Partha Chatterjee made a crucial contribution to the field by focusing on the non-European world in a postcolonial approach showing the limits of the universalist claims of other theorists, challenging their understanding of nation and of the modern state.[38] Rogers Brubaker suggested that ethnic conflict should not be understood as conflict between ethnic groups nor should we uncritically use categories of ethnopolitical practice as our categories of social analysis. He stressed that the rhetoric of "ethnopolitical entrepreneurs" have a performative character seeking to call a group into being through invoking it.[39] Although I cannot say that I accept any of these formulations in their entirety, most have influenced my own understanding of nationalism and thus the discussion in the ensuing pages.

The question of nation building has been at the forefront of historical discussion of state structures and policies for the nineteenth and twentieth centuries at least since the groundbreaking volume by Eugen Weber on nation building in France forty years ago.[40] Weber's convincing argument for a much-delayed success at nation building in the most iconic nation-state in Europe, France, caused a reevaluation of previously accepted ideas about the effectiveness of nation building projects in the first half of the nineteenth century as well as with regard to the relationship of people to the nation-state. Inevitably that discussion led to the reexamination of the interactions between the state and those that did not identify with the dominant nation and the conflicts that often ensued but also the compromises achieved.

Unfortunately, such a discussion has not been sufficiently examined with regard to modern Greek history. Although Greece emerges as a nation-state remarkably early in 1829 and quickly builds all the institutions and trapping of a modern state, Greek historiography until very recently paid scant attention to the relationship of the state with the various ethnic, linguistic, and religious groups that populated it until the late nineteenth and twentieth century when Greek territorial expansion transformed it. In part this is because of an implicit assumption that the early Greek state was a homogenous entity that lacked minorities and thus did not have to confront such questions until the Balkan Wars of 1912–13.

It is nearly impossible, however, to discuss nationalism without at some level talking about the "other," those who do not belong to the nation or, even worse, are perceived as threats or enemies to the national goals. The idea that minorities, or nationalities as they were called in the nineteenth century, could be a threat to the state was not new as proven by the Wars of Religion in Early Modern Europe, and the persecution of threatening minorities such as the Moors of Spain, the Catholics in post-Reformation England, the Huguenots in France, and so on. However, the nineteenth and twentieth centuries heightened this fear as more and more "nationalities" demanded the right to maintain their difference, if not outright autonomy, challenging the assimilationist efforts of the new nation-states. If the "other" loomed large in the minds of nationalists, Jews had a prominent position as the ultimate national "other" in Europe.

Few authors that discuss nationalism and nation building in Europe fail to address the question of Jewish emancipation, persecution, exclusion, or inclusion to the national fold. The same, however, is not the case in Greece until the twentieth century when the Jewish question enters Greek historiography with the annexation of Thessaloniki and then disappears again following the Holocaust. Even in this context of the three decades from 1913 to 1943 the discussion is narrowly framed solely for the city of Thessaloniki, not only by nationalist historians but those who work on Greek Jewish history as well. In fact, most of Greek Jewish historiography has been focused on Thessaloniki/Salonica both in terms of its Ottoman past and in the transition to the modern Greek state.

Jewish Salonican historiography has a long pedigree but as Rika Benveniste noted it followed a parallel yet distinct path than the rest of Greek historiography. She identified three themes with regard to early-twentieth-century historiography: portraying the city as a haven for Jews under the Ottoman sultans, glorifying Sephardic supremacy in an implied juxtaposition to the Greek-speaking Romaniote Jews and to the Ashkenazi refugees from eastern Europe, and the idealization of migrant Jews as a unified group.[41] The focus was narrow, local, and almost unrelated to the rest of Greek history. Even later Greek Jewish historiography exhibited the same ethnocentrism and homogenization that one finds in Greek historiography in general.[42] The latter still fails to incorporate the Greek Jewish presence in the Greek historical narrative as Avdela and Benveniste noted, treating the "Jewish community of Salonica" as a trope that was challenged only recently for creating false dichotomies.[43] Although since the 1990s there has been some interest in Jewish history in Greece and increasingly more reflective works are being produced in both Greek and English,[44] the field has not broken free from the stranglehold that Salonica has exercised from the start, a rare exception being Fleming's general history of Greek Jews.[45] My objective here is to take a step toward integrating Jewish history into the history of the Greek state as an integral component of the evolution of the state, ideas about the nation, and national (or nationalist) policies from the nineteenth century through the twentieth.

Acknowledgments

I would like to briefly acknowledge those whose support, advice, and assistance made this book possible. I want to start with John Connelly my advisor at UC Berkeley so long ago for whom I wrote the paper that eventually evolved into this manuscript. He was also the first to urge me to turn it into a book even though it was not remotely connected to my dissertation research. I also want to thank my editor at Bloomsbury, Rhodri Mogford, who believed in the project and pushed me to finish it, and Thomas Gallant from UC San Diego, who introduced me to Rhodri and with whom I frequently discussed my ideas regarding this book. Several friends read and commented on parts or the entirety of this manuscript and I particularly want to mention Roxanne Panchasi, Aaron Windell, and Nicolas Kenny at Simon Fraser University, Giorgos Antoniou at the Aristotle University of Thessaloniki, Devin Naar at the University of Washington, and Takis Papas. I also want to thank Beatriz Lopez and Emma Goode at Bloomsbury, Alexandra Patrikiou at the Jewish Museum of Greece, Lambros Mpaltsiotis at Panteion University, and the directors and staff at the Historical Archive of the Ministry of Foreign Affairs in Greece and the National Library of Greece. Finally, I want to thank my partner Jennifer Groenewold for reading the ensuing chapters at various stages of development and providing me with honest feedback, and for tolerating my long absences to Greece while I was conducting research.

Note on Terms and Transliteration

One of the most difficult aspects of writing this book has been the appropriate use of terminology, even with regard to the most basic terms. The very word "Greek" is itself highly problematic in the context of this book. Modern Greeks do not call themselves that to begin with but use the word "Hellene," which is of course the word used in antiquity to describe those who belonged to the Hellenic culture. The word however was specifically chosen to associate modern Greeks with the ancients and it had at times taken other meanings. For most Christian subjects of the Eastern Roman Empire, what we often call Byzantium, up to the fifteenth century and beyond, the word "Hellene" was associated both with the ancients and with paganism, making it highly inappropriate to use except for some, often condemned, intellectuals like Georgios Plethon Gemistos. His own contemporaries like Gennadios Scholarios rejected the term in favor of the generic Christian.[46] A more appropriate term for the period from the late antiquity through the Ottoman period would have been "Roman," or *Romios*, which was also how the Ottomans identified Orthodox Christians in their empire (*Rum*). Some modern scholars have used the term "Romaic" to point to a strong identification with Orthodoxy especially in the context of the Ottoman Empire and the patriarchate of Constantinople but that identity is also unsatisfactory for my purposes since for much of the period under consideration it did not include only what today we consider as Greeks but also Bulgarians, Serbs, Albanians, Macedonians, Romanians, and even some Arabs. Medieval Europeans used the term "Greek" to refer to Greek-speaking Orthodox Christians, and a few Greeks did indeed appropriate it to refer specifically to what we call today Greeks (*Graikoi*) but it never achieved wide circulation. For these reasons I have tried to avoid the simple term "Greek" prior to the establishment of the modern Greek state and have used primarily composite words ("Greek-speaking" or *grecophone*, "Christian Greek," and so on).

The same problem exists for most ethnic groups of the region including the Ottomans who were often called Turks but that also had the meaning of Muslim almost up to the establishment of the Turkish Republic. Similarly, there are still heated debates about the use of the terms "Bulgarian" and "Macedonian," "Vlach," "Pomak," and so on. Greek sources frequently used terms that bestowed a nuanced identity such as *voulgarophonoi, alvanophonoi,* or *turkophonoi* (Bulgarian speakers, Albanian speakers, or Turkish speakers), *voulgarophronoi* or *tourkophronoi* (Bulgarian or Turkish-nationally minded), *roumanizontes* (Romanian nationally minded), and combinations of the above. But the meaning of the terms shifted overtime and per political calculations so that a *voulgarophone* (Bulgarian-speaker) could become a *slavophone* (Slavic-speaker) depending on the political circumstances.

For my purposes, the designation "Jew" is equally problematic, not only due to the ethnic and religious dichotomy, but also because of the existence of multiple Jewish communities in the area whose distinctive characteristics are crucial to this book. Once again I have tried to be specific when the distinction was important referring to the specific Jewish communities in question ("Romaniotes" "Sephardim") even though such terms were rarely used at the time or in the documents, especially the term "Romaniote." I have also tended to focus on the two main communities, the Greek-speaking Romaniotes and the Ladino-speaking Sephardim, but the reader should keep in mind that there were even more distinctive Jewish groups with smaller numbers including Italian Jews, Ashkenazi Jews, Karaites, and even some like the Dönme whose very Jewishness is a matter of debate. I would have rather used the terms used at the time (*hellenophone*—Greek-speaker, *ispanophone*—Spanish-speaker) but that would have diverged from the established terms now found in modern historiography.

As if that confusion was not enough, the way the "nation" was understood or even the word used to refer to it saw significant change over time, which is part of my story. There are several terms that can be used to refer to the Greek "nation" from the modern *ethnos*, to the older *genos*, and the more problematic *phyle* and the last two can also be used to mean race among other things. There were subtleties when authors chose to use *ethnos* over *genos* and vice versa, expanding or collapsing the breadth of the concept and thus the people included to their understanding of nation, which can be lost in translation. Some terms like *genos* can also have many interpretations (race, species, gender, breed, family, ilk, kin, etc.), and it and its derivatives *omogenos* (same-*genos*) and *allogenos* (other-*genos*) were frequently used from nationalist treatises to legal promulgations with significant impact on minorities.

A final difficulty regarding terminology involves concepts of what we call today ethnic violence, ethnic cleansing, and genocide. Modern understandings of genocide stem from the UN Convention on the Prevention and Punishment of the Crime of Genocide dating from 1948 which defined it as "any of the following acts committed with intent to destroy, in whole or in part, a national, ethnical, racial or religious group"[47] which listed the killing of the members of the group, causing serious bodily or mental harm to members of the group, imposing conditions of life calculated to result in the physical destruction of the group in whole or in part, imposing members intended to prevent births in the group, and forcibly transferring children of the group to another. Using that definition would be problematic when the concept of genocide had not yet been defined but the period I will examine includes most of these practices applied repeatedly to various groups. Some historians have raised objections to the use of the term "genocide" to describe such acts, even accusing those who do of violating historical principles and imposing modern concepts on the past. That is partly true especially with regard to what we would call today cultural genocide, which was widely practised by most states throughout Europe at the time. In many cases, however, the atrocities committed evoked responses from contemporaries that clearly show that such acts were deemed reprehensible. For example, although some Greek historians like Kremmydas have questioned the professionalism of those who have used the term "genocide" for the atrocities committed by Greek forces during the Greek War of Independence,[48] it is clear from the accounts of contemporaries that those acts were not within the norm of warfare. The contemporary, and philhellene, George Finlay described the atrocities committed by Christians and Muslims on each other as a war of "extermination," while even Greek commanders like Dimitrios Ypsilantis tried to avert the wholesale slaughter of prisoners or civilians.[49] Ottoman atrocities were in fact a crucial component in spurring some European states to intervene in the conflict in what some have called a humanitarian intervention. In my estimation, the use of such terms is quite appropriate and necessary to indicate the extent of violence inflicted upon communities based on their religious or ethnic composition.

Similar difficulties exist with names, place names, and even the transliteration of words into English. Transliteration from a different alphabet always involves choices and in the case of Greek the problem is greater because the standard transliteration method was developed for use with ancient Greek and to conform to Greek spelling rather than pronunciation. As a result, I have chosen to use the Library of Congress transliteration method for the most part with the exception of personal names which I have transliterated phonetically as they are most commonly used today.

The renaming of cities, villages, and regions is an old and effective policy of hegemonic cultural imposition seen throughout history and in the context of the nationalist conflicts. In the Balkans during the nineteenth and twentieth centuries, places repeatedly changed names which may confuse the reader. There is hardly a city that retained its name from Byzantine to Ottoman times and then to whatever Balkan nation-state that city ended up in and several may have had (and still have) different names based on the ethnicity of the speaker. Istanbul is still universally Konstantinoupolis (Constantinople) in Greece, Izmir is Smyrni, Edirne is Adrianoupolis (Adrianople), and so on. The choice of the word often implies a political stance and to avoid this I have chosen to use whatever name was officially or commonly used at the time. Thus, I use Salonica till 1913 and Thessaloniki from that point onwards, Philippoupolis till 1878 and Plovdiv afterward, and so on. Unfortunately, even that is not always effective since various authors and documents continue to refer to cities and areas in different ways. When I feared confusion, I often added in parenthesis the second (or third in some cases) name to be sure to avoid confusion.

1

Greeks and Jews from Antiquity to the Ottoman Empire

The interaction of Jews and Greeks dates back to antiquity with the conquests of Alexander the Great and the subsequent domination of the eastern Mediterranean by the Hellenistic kingdoms. This relationship was sometimes peaceful and productive but it was also frequently adversarial. The Jewish homeland was frequently rocked by revolts against Hellenistic, especially Seleucid, rule most notably in the Maccabean revolt of 167–160 BCE which is still celebrated today as Hanukkah. Conflicts also erupted periodically in areas where both Greeks and Jews had settled as in Alexandria. However, there was also close interaction between Greeks and Turks that led to the adoption of Hellenistic culture by many Jews, the first translation of the Hebrew Bible into Greek (the Septuagint), and the emergence of several Jewish scholars influenced by Greek philosophy like Philo.

The Roman conquest of the Mediterranean created a unified space where different peoples could interact, travel, and settle with relative ease. This was also the case for Jews, whose large communities continued to flourish in Egypt and elsewhere. The Jewish revolts and resulting Jewish-Roman Wars (66–73 CE, 115–117 CE, 132–136 CE) led to the devastation of Judea and many Jewish communities that had participated, such as those in Cyrenaica and Egypt. The ensuing diaspora of Jews saw the creation of numerous Jewish communities throughout the Mediterranean.[1]

The near simultaneous emergence of Christianity was a further blow to Judaism since most of the early converts to the Christian doctrine were Jews. Although the eventual success of Christianity did not impact Jews as much as pagans or heterodox Christian sects (Arians, Nestorians, Manichaeans, Donatists, Montanists, Gnostics, and many more) who were deemed heretical and were proscribed and persecuted, the standing of Jews in the now Christian empire was significantly diminished. Jewish refusal to convert to the dominant religion baffled and angered Christians who often vented their frustration with prosecutions and massacres such as their expulsion from Alexandria in 415ce following their dispute with Patriarch Cyril, famous for instigating the murder of the pagan mathematician and philosopher Hypatia by a Christian mob.[2]

As Orthodox Christianity came to dominate the empire, greater scrutiny was turned upon Jews and the perception that they harbored ill will toward Christians and the Roman state. Legislation restricting Jewish practices begun to find itself in Roman legal codes as in the *Codex Theodosianus* and the construction of new synagogues was often banned.[3] Jews were thought of as a disruptive element in society especially in the eastern provinces of the empire as evidenced in the historiographic and hagiographic texts of the time.[4] Some accounts portrayed Jews as perpetrators of atrocities against Christians most famously in the brutal murder and desecration of the body of the Patriarch of Antioch Anastasius II in 608/9 during an uprising,[5] while church fathers like John Chrysostom preached against Jews and deplored Christian-Jewish socialization.[6]

Jewish sources from late antiquity indicate an increasing Jewish anti-Roman attitude and the proliferation of polemics against Christianity.[7] Roman-Jewish tensions can, of course, be detected earlier from at least 303ce[8] but the Christianization of the Empire, especially of the still predominantly non-Christian "Holy Land" from Emperor Constantine onwards, intensified friction between Jews and Christian Romans.[9] The loyalty of Jews to the empire was questioned which could erupt into violence. For example, during the siege of the Roman town of Tella by the Sassanid Persians, the entire Jewish population was massacred after an accusation was made that they were constructing a tunnel from the synagogue to the walls to let the besiegers into the town.[10]

In the East, Jews had a potential ally against Roman persecution, the Sassanid empire that was the main rival to the Romans/Byzantines from 224ce to 651ce. Jews welcomed the Persian conquest of Palestine and Jerusalem in 614ce, which was supposedly followed by a massive slaughter of Christians and attacks on Christians in other cities like Ptolemais (Acre) and Tyre.[11] Support for the Sassanids backfired when Emperor Heraclius recovered Jerusalem in 629ce and proceeded to massacre the Jewish population.[12] Roman and Persian rivalry was also conducted by Christian and Hebrew proxies throughout the Arabian peninsula where the Hebrew kingdom of Himyar in today's Yemen was a Persian satellite opposed by the Roman satellite kingdom of Aksum in today's Ethiopia.[13]

Unsurprisingly this hostility between Christians and Jews facilitated the early Islamic conquests of the region. Although Muslim rule reduced both groups to second-class citizens, it also guaranteed basic rights of worship and property, famously under the so-called Pact of Umar. Though inferior to Muslims, Christians and Jews under Muslim rule were equal to each other and were more or less free to pursue their trades, religious practices, and customs as long as they paid an extra tax, the *jizya* (*cizya* in Turkish). In many ways the Christian Church and the three Patriarchates that came under Muslim rule (Alexandria, Jerusalem, Antioch) continued to function effectively while Jewish culture flourished from Spain to Persia.

The early crusades (1096–1291ce) disrupted that equilibrium. Crusaders and accompanying pilgrims targeted Jews even before they ever left Europe. Roused by Pope Urban II's appeals of 1095 that demonized Muslims, the crowds that gathered in 1096 fell upon the Jews of Cologne, the Rhineland, Moers, Regensburg, Trier, Mainz, Worms, Metz, Kerpen, and elsewhere massacring them indiscriminately or forcibly converting them as in Regensburg. On occasion the sources refer to the Jewish communities panic that led to mass suicides rather than face the brutality of the crusaders.[14] This violence continued and intensified when the crusaders reached the areas under Muslim control. Not only did the crusading armies slaughter Muslims and Jews indiscriminately when they captured cities, especially during the First crusade, but they also imposed their version of Roman Catholic Christianity on the local Eastern Orthodox Christians. The two churches had split over procedural, administrative, and theological issues in 1054, and the suspicions and hostility of each church toward the other turned into outright warfare with the Fourth Crusade of 1204, which instead of recovering Jerusalem or helping the struggling remnants of the crusader states sacked the Byzantine capital of Constantinople, ushering a sixty-year interregnum that fatally undermined the capacity of the Byzantines to resist the later onslaught of the Ottoman Turks.

"Byzantium" will be frequently encountered in this text, though the term is a scholarly construct to distinguish the later Eastern Roman Empire from its earlier manifestation. For the rulers and subjects of the empire they were always Romans carrying on from the founding of the empire until 1453 when the Ottoman sultan Mehmet II the Conqueror sacked Constantinople and turned it into the capital of the Ottoman Empire.[15] There were, however, some elements of the empire that justify a distinguishing characterization from the earlier Roman polity which allowed later Greek historians and nationalists to claim it as a Greek medieval state.[16] In the first case, increasingly the language of administration, church, and high culture was Greek, and as the borders of the empire shrunk under the pressure from Arabs, Slavs, Lombards, Normans, or Seljuks, the territories of the empire became concentrated in Greek-speaking regions. European contemporaries frequently referred to the Byzantines as Greeks, though for the Seljuk and Ottoman Turks the territory of the empire continued to be Rome (Rum).

The history of Jews in the Byzantine Empire has received some attention but there is still a lot to uncover. Jews certainly faced restrictions in Byzantium in terms of professions and interactions with non-Jews, but they generally did not face the persecutions and violence Jews faced in medieval Europe where they were regularly persecuted and murdered particularly at times of heightened religious fervor like the crusades. Western Jews were subjected to all sorts of legal restrictions that barred them from owning agricultural land, being employed in professions, and even engaging in certain mercantile functions. Jews were also frequently accused of all sorts of crimes and unholy practices. The ritual murder accusation, which we will encounter again in later chapters, was a common trope of the period starting from the first such accusation in Norwich in 1144 that linked Jewish rituals with the use of blood from sacrificed Christian children. Medieval monarchs habitually expelled Jews from their domains, often to seize their properties, as in England in 1290, France in 1306, Sicily and Lithuania in 1483, Spain in 1492, Brandenburg in 1510, the Papal States in 1569, and Bavaria in 1593. Jews were also victims of changing political circumstances as in the case of England and France following the French victory at Bouvines in 1214. In both states, Jews were expelled, while France and England developed new structures of taxation and governance, though in England Jews were expelled at the request of parliament over negotiations regarding taxation while in France the initiative rested with King Philip IV.[17] Even the generally tolerant Venice, which was willing to accept Muslims and later Protestants in its city, was only willing to accept Jews on the condition they remained segregated in their "ghetto."[18]

The Byzantine Empire had its own share of anti-Jewish monarchs, and there were occasions of violence especially in times of war as we saw with Heraclius, who in 630/1 may have launched a forced conversion policy. Forced conversions were rare but not unheard of throughout the Mediterranean from the early fifth-century onwards, and several Byzantine emperors entertained the idea of forced conversion or the expulsion of Jews.[19] As in the West, such policies frequently coincided with political or religious turmoil. Leo II, for example, pursued such a policy in the middle of the *iconomachy*, the dispute over the use of holy icons, while two notoriously anti-Jewish emperors, Basil I and Romanos I Lekapenos, were usurpers trying to establish their own dynasties. Recently scholars have challenged even the historicity of such forced conversions claiming that firm evidence exists only for the forced conversion of the Jews of Carthage under Heraclius.[20]

In general, however, the bureaucratic nature of the Byzantine state and its reliance on Roman law helped ameliorate potential outbursts by the authorities. In Byzantium Jews were probably threatened more by the mob in the not too infrequent urban riots of the empire or by the actions of churchmen as in the case of the expulsion of Jews from the city of Sparta, than from organized state oppression.[21] Furthermore, the relative control that the state had over the church ensured that the latter was not often the instigator of violence against Jews as was the case in the West. Though some emperors enacted discriminatory policies in specific regions and towns as in the case of Constantine X Doukas, who banished the Jews of Constantinople to the adjacent settlement of Pera, there was never an attempt to expel or forcibly convert the entire Jewish population of the empire, as was the case in many parts of Europe where as late as the end of the fifteenth century thousands of Spanish and Portuguese Jews were forced to convert after the Reconquista.[22] Byzantine emperors, even fanatically devout ones like Theodosius I, frequently protected Jews and punished those who attacked them, despite the political backlash of such actions. In Theodosius' case that backlash came from the bishop of Milan Ambrose, famous for excommunicating Theodosius over the massacre of the people of Thessaloniki and for forcing him to publicly repent. In the case of Jews, however, Ambrose forced Theodosius to retract the punishment of those who had looted a synagogue in Callinicum insisting that Jews were not protected by the law.[23] Byzantium had no uniform policy toward Jews and as Benjamin of Tudela, a twelfth-century Jewish traveler from Spain, reported Jews could be oppressed in some cities like Constantinople but enjoy freedoms and prosperity in others like Thebes.[24]

Despite this varied attitude toward Jews the Byzantine Empire inherited Rome's legislation which included restrictive policies toward Jews such as bans on circumcision and on Jewish settlement in Jerusalem and restrictions of certain religious practices and holidays.[25] Furthermore, Jews had been required to pay a special poll tax from 70ce onwards, while further legal impediments were enacted by late Roman emperors such as Theodosius I who banned polygamy, and Honorius, Valentinian III, Theodosius II, Justin, and Justinian who restricted Jewish employment in the bureaucracy and the army.[26] Jews were also forbidden from proselytizing while conversion of Jews to Christianity was legally encouraged with converts receiving various privileges and protection from disinheritance from their still Jewish parents.[27]

In addition to anti-Jewish legislation, Byzantine Jews were also the targets of lay and ecclesiastical literature that associated them with evil deeds. From the fourth century onwards prestigious theologians like Ephraem and John Chrysostom linked Jews with baseness and loose morals, and advanced the depiction of Jews as murderers, Christ killers, adulterers, and generally lawbreakers.[28] Although early Christianity made clear distinction between Jews and Christian heretics, over the centuries the line became blurred with pagans, Jews, and heretics being often seen in similar ways and thus subjected on occasion to similar repression. The characterization of the term "Jew and Judaizing," referring to Christian conversion to Judaism, was increasingly used as a label for heresy applied to a variety of sects such as the Bogomils, Paulicians, Athinganoi, and others, causing confusion.[29] Although the church itself was loth to accept the validity of forced conversions of Jews, unlike that of heretics, it certainly aimed at the ultimate conversion of Jews and through the banning of certain interactions between Jews and Christians instituted in Canon Law indirectly discriminated against Jews and their standing in a predominantly Christian society.[30] Conversion certainly carried great social and material benefits and was the only manner in which Jews could achieve positions of authority in the empire. A handful of such examples may indicate preferential treatment of such converts as in the case of Makarios who became an ecclesiastic and served both as confessor and as ambassador to Emperor Manuel II, while Philotheos Kokkinos, who was of Jewish origin, became patriarch.[31]

Finally, we should not ignore the significance of widespread popular anti-Semitism which took various form from the dumping of unclean water from the tanneries on the doorways of Jewish houses to "defile" them as Benjamin of Tudela reports[32] to violent outbursts as that in Callinicum discussed above. The existing hostility may have intensified with the arrival of the Western crusaders and the settlement of Catholic Christians in the empire in later centuries who were more strongly anti-Jewish in their attitude and who also saw the local Christian population as heretical.[33] On occasion Jews participated in the rather frequent urban riots of the empire as in 1042, and on rare occasions they even rose in revolt as they had done in earlier centuries but such acts could backfire. In Byzantine Bari, for example, Jews rose in revolt in 1051, which provoked the Christian population to retaliate by destroying the Jewish quarter of the city.[34]

Despite this, Jews were very involved in the economic life of the Byzantine Empire. Jews were employed in many professions including the vitally important silk manufacturing from as early as the seventh century in Constantinople, and the silk trade with Italy in the tenth century.[35] In urban settlements Jews worked in the tannery trade, the retail trade, cloth dyeing and manufacture, literary work and teaching, moneylending, and commerce.[36] Although most Jews lived in the cities of the empire there is also evidence of Jewish rural settlements. Benjamin of Tudela mentions 200 Jews engaged in agriculture on land they owned on Mt. Parnassus, and there is other evidence of Jews as farmers, manual laborers, and even peasants tied to monasteries.[37] As mentioned, Jews were legally barred from positions of authority including all military or bureaucratic posts,[38] but toward the end of the empire many Jews managed to circumvent many of the restrictions of Roman legislation by assuming privileged foreign status, usually Venetian of Genoese, which protected them from imperial taxation and imperial law.[39] That further fragmented the already diverse Byzantine Jewish communities and their legal status between local and foreign Jews who competed against each other.

Jewish diversity in the Byzantine Empire existed long before the decline of Byzantine power. Jews were divided in several sects with Rabbanite and Karaite Jews having communities throughout the empire including Constantinople, where prior to the fall of the city to the Fourth Crusade there were some 2,000 Rabbanite and 500 Karaite individuals or households.[40] The sectarian division was coupled with linguistic fragmentation. Even in Hellenistic and Roman times some Jewish communities had abandoned Hebrew and Aramaic and had become monolingual speakers of Greek as was the case in Alexandria.[41] Those living in Judea had maintained their languages but soon also adopted Arabic. Byzantine Jews on the other hand maintained the use of Greek in their daily lives but retained a knowledge of Hebrew as a scholarly language.[42] Karaites too were primarily Greek speakers and many Jews had even adopted Greek names.[43] Jewish communities in Greece were reported as early as the first century CE in Thessaly, Boeotia, Macedonia, Aetolia, Attica, Argos, Corinth, Peloponnese, Euboea, Cyprus and Crete, and in Byzantine times more Jewish communities were reported in Mantinea, Hermioni, Mani, Methoni, Koroni, and Aegina.[44] These Rabbanite Greek-speaking Jews will form the Romaniote community that I will be referring to in subsequent chapters. Relations between different Jewish communities were not amicable and were often in competition with each other. For example, when the Karaites fled the depredations of crusaders after the 1099 destruction of Jerusalem which was the center of their movement, they sought refuge in Byzantium. Their different culture and origins from formerly Islamic territory, however, was used against them by the Rabbanite Jews of the empire to arouse the suspicions of Byzantine authorities regarding their possible allegiances.[45] Similarly Byzantine Jews were often in conflict with the Italian Jews of later centuries and their claims to the privileges enjoyed by Venetian or Genoese merchants.[46]

It is also a curious circumstance that the final, and longest-lived, dynasty of Byzantium, the Paleologos dynasty, was perhaps the most philo-Semitic of all Byzantine dynasties. Although the Laskarids of Nicea cannot be considered philo-Semitic and Emperor John III Doukas Vatatzis supposedly ordered the forced conversion of all Jews, Michael VIII Paleologos, who sidelined, blinded, and imprisoned the last Laskarid emperor John IV, reversed that policy and gave Jews some privileges hoping to restore the empire to financial health.[47] Other emperors like Andronikos II issued decrees guaranteeing Jewish rights, a practice that was emulated by other Balkan rulers.[48] The weakness of the empire led later emperors to seek to subvert even their ecclesiastical autonomy to the pope in return for military aid, and spurred the emperors to a more liberal attitude toward non-Romans including Jews and Muslims. By the time the fiction of Roman independence ended with the fall of Constantinople in 1453, Byzantine Jews enjoyed the most extensive rights of all European Jews.

The relatively benevolent attitude of the Paleologue dynasty should not mask the fact that Jews were still second-class citizens and faced legal and social disadvantages and a hostile Christian population. Jews were seen at times as an existential threat or one tied to very real political challenges to the empire. Such attitudes varied over time as the early links between the political threat of Islam and the theological perils of Judaism subsided when Byzantium recovered and could hold its own against the Arab onslaught but were resumed from the fourteenth century onwards, when a new wave of anti-Jewish texts appeared tied to the new threat of the Ottoman Turks.[49] Even during the rather benevolent Paleologos period, and perhaps in reaction to imperial policies, the anti-Jewish rhetoric of the church intensified and several anti-Jewish diatribes were written including one by the deposed ex-emperor and usurper John VI Kantakouzenos from his retirement at the monastery of Mangana.[50] Patriarch Athanasios scolded Emperor Andronikos for his attitude toward Jews, Muslims, and Armenians, while when Byzantine officials supported Jewish claims they faced accusations of Judaizing as in the case of Chionios in Thessaloniki and Kokalas in Constantinople.[51]

At a time when the church felt threatened by the efforts of the emperors to seek military support against the Ottomans from the West in return for the subjugation of the Orthodox Church to the pope, attacks against Jews and Judaizing heresies helped to heighten the religious sensibilities of the Roman public and ultimately scuttle the proposed union with Rome. Although the two churches were supposedly unified in the Council of Florence (1438–45) under pressure from a desperate emperor John VIII who gave Rome control over the churches in the East, the eastern Orthodox people and clergy in their vast majority refused to accept the union. Instead of unifying Catholicism with Orthodoxy the 1439 Decree of Union divided the Byzantine public and church into unionists and anti-unionists and led to violent riots and political infighting that outweighed the meager aid that Byzantium received from the West. For many in Byzantium, Catholicism was a greater threat than Islam and the seemingly unstoppable Ottoman Turks and many had professed a preference for submission to a Muslim conqueror rather than a Catholic one.[52]

On May 29, 1453, the inevitable took place and the city of Constantinople, the Second Rome, fell after a brief siege to Mehmed II Sultan of the Ottomans. The last emperor, Constantine XI, died fighting and the much-diminished city was given to plunder. Mehmed II immediately moved his capital to the city and over the next few years subdued whatever Byzantine outposts remained in the Morea (Peloponnese) and Trebizond (Trabzon). Within a century the Ottomans would have built one of the largest empires of their time conquering the territories of the Mamluk empire in the Middle East, and of the Kingdom of Hungary in central Europe. Though often portrayed as a disaster in European and especially Greek historiography, ironically the Ottoman conquest also sheltered the Orthodox Church and gave it renewed authority in the East. While many Byzantines, and at least one Cretan Jew, lamented the fall in near apocalyptic language even some contemporaries who fought the Ottomans saw the conquest as the lesser of two evils, the worse outcome being Catholic domination.[53]

Greeks and Jews in the Ottoman Empire

The Ottoman conquests of the fourteenth and fifteenth centuries changed and retained the status of Jews in the region. On the one hand, Jews remained second-class citizens compared to Muslims and had to pay the tax assessed to all non-Muslims, called the *cizye.* On the other hand, they were now the equals of Christians who were still the majority of the population of the early Ottoman state particularly in the Balkans. Up to the reign of Mehmed II, Christians or converts from Balkan Christians continued to hold significant posts in the Ottoman administration, but in the sixteenth century Jews increasingly filled several positions in the Ottoman court and the diplomatic corps, until the seventeenth century.[54] As the Ottomans pushed further into Europe and were engaged in near constant warfare with European states like Hungary, Austria and Spain under the Habsburgs, Venice, and Poland, Jews served a useful role as intermediaries with Europe and other hostile states like Safavid Persia. Wealthy Jews dominated the money distribution networks of Constantinople and Adrianople in the sixteenth century, and later competed strongly with Greeks for government tax farms.[55]

The Ottomans already had long experience of ruling over a religiously and ethnically diverse population prior to 1453. Christians and Muslims had long interacted in Anatolia, especially during the Seljuk period when the ruling classes of the Byzantines and Seljuks, who were still going through the process of full conversion to Orthodox Islam, had crossed sides, converted, and apostatized, building familiarity with each other.[56] The image of early fourteenth-century Anatolia found in the account of the North African traveler Muhammad Ibn Battuta showed a region dominated by a multitude of small Turkish emirates, among which the Ottomans were hardly distinguishable, but in constant interaction between Christians, Armenians, Jews, Genoese, and Venetians.[57] Of all the emirates, the Ottomans had the greatest exposure to non-Muslims having rapidly expanded in the Balkans using Christians in their government, armies, and administration until the conquest of Constantinople by Mehmet II. Mehmet favored non-Turks in positions of authority including many members of the Paleologoi, the former Byzantine Imperial family, who converted to Islam like Has Murad Pasha, Mesih Pasha, and Huseyn Bey.[58]

The capture of Constantinople transformed the Ottomans and allowed the Ottoman sultans to legitimately claim the title of Roman Emperor. The Ottoman state became a stable, bureaucratic state, still rapidly expanding in all directions but with increasing need to standardize its administration and find effective ways to rule over a massive territory with diverse populations. For most of the sultans and the Ottoman elite, linguistic, religious, and cultural differences among the *reya* were not problems that needed to be addressed.[59] Drawing upon both Roman and Islamic traditions the Ottomans made religion a fundamental aspect of their system but they also formalized and institutionalized it to a previously unheard-of degree. This is the famous *millet* system which, although scholarship has challenged and problematized considerably since it was first suggested, is still a useful tool to summarize and simplify Ottoman administrative policies with regard to religious minorities.

The origin of the *millet* system was generally attributed to Mehmed II, who, immediately following the capture of Constantinople, sought out the renowned ecclesiastic Genadios Scholarius, who had been captured and enslaved, and named him the new patriarch of Constantinople.[60] The choice was politically astute since Genadios had been a prominent opponent of the union of the Eastern churches with the Catholic Church and the rapprochement attempted by the Paleologoi emperors with the West.[61] Under Genadios the Orthodox Church was guaranteed to repudiate the union and not undermine Ottoman rule. The sultans also saw the church as a source of income as recent scholarship has argued stressing of the Orthodox ecclesiastics as tax farmers and fiscal agents rather than leaders of the Orthodox Christians.[62] But Mehmed and the Ottoman sultans went further than simply appointing reliable churchmen to lead the Orthodox Church. The sultans duplicated the Byzantine emperors investiture of elected patriarchs and further enhanced their status by making them *millet-bashi*, the official heads of the Orthodox millet, making the patriarch of Constantinople and the church part of the Ottoman administrative structure.[63] In 1572, Jeremiah II received an official confirmation from Sultan Selim II in return for a significant payment which he had to repeat after the death of Selim and the elevation to the throne of his son Murad III.[64] Such payments were common for those seeking high office at the time and are indicative of the prestige of the position and the benefits, financial and otherwise, it carried with it. Like many viziers, patriarchs were frequently deposed, exiled, and even executed when they lost out in the power struggles of Istanbul (Constantinople). Patriarchs assumed responsibility for the behavior of its flock, and received great privileges and significant judicial authority over them. The Ottomans also elevated the patriarch of Constantinople above other ecclesiastics and over the course of centuries the patriarch was able to expand his authority even over the previously autocephalous Bulgarian and Serbian churches as the Ottoman government wanted reliable people in charge of such important offices.[65] The influence of the patriarchs was evident from the efforts exerted by various European ambassadors to influence their elections and policies, intrigues that contributed to the execution of four patriarchs.[66]

The arrangement with the Orthodox Church was duplicated to varying degree with other confessional groups such as the Armenians and the Rabbanite and Karaite Jews and later with Catholics and Protestants. In theory Jews were thus recognized as a separate *millet* and rabbis were given the same privileges and responsibilities that the Orthodox enjoyed, including some judicial authority over their flock. Unlike the Orthodox Church, however, the Jewish *millet* never managed to achieve the concentration of power and centralization that the patriarch of Constantinople did. Although there was a nominal head, the chief rabbi of Constantinople, every Jewish community was independent from the others. In part this fragmentation reflected the historical evolution of Jewish religion and organization as well as the diversity of Jews already seen in the Byzantine Empire, which became even more complex with the arrival of the Sephardic Jews from Spain at the end of the fifteenth and early sixteenth centuries.

Until the arrival of the Sephardim, the Jews of the Byzantine and then the Ottoman Empire were predominantly Greek-speaking, what scholarship calls today Romaniote Jews. Their numbers were not substantial and were predominantly concentrated in urban centers, many becoming prominent as tax farmers.[67] This situation was transformed by the expulsions of Jews from Iberia. On March 31, 1492, Queen Isabella I of Castile and King Ferdinand II of Aragon, the joint monarchs of Spain, issued the Alhambra Decree ordering the expulsion of all Jews who refused to convert by the 31st of July of the same year. Between half and two-thirds of the Jews in Spain chose to convert, though with varying degrees of sincerity, and the rest, perhaps as many as 100,000 were forced to leave. Many Sephardim settled in North Africa, and Portugal, but many accepted an invitation by Bayezid II to settle in the Ottoman Empire. The sultan saw an opportunity to gain the services of skillful craftsmen and merchants.[68] Over the ensuing years more Iberian Jews found themselves fleeing Iberia following the expulsion of Jews from Portugal by King Manuel I in 1496 and the establishment of the Inquisition in Spain, which targeted former Muslims and Jews whose conversion was deemed suspect.

The arrival of tens of thousands of Jews from Spain dramatically changed the character of the Jewish communities in the Ottoman Empire. Unlike common practice that had migrating Jews accept local Jewish customs and authority, the Spanish Jews outnumbers the local Romaniotes and were proud of their culture and language Ladino, a form of Castilian Spanish.[69] Thus in the European provinces of the empire two main and distinct Jewish communities coexisted from the sixteenth century onwards with the Sephardim gradually gaining a dominant position in Istanbul (Constantinople) although Romaniotes and Karaites resisted as much as they could.[70] The Sephardim formed the majority of Jews in Macedonia, Thrace, Crete, and the Aegean islands, while the Romaniotes were concentrated in southern and western Greece. The city of Salonica (Byzantine and Greek Thessaloniki, Selanik in Turkish) became the center of Sephardic Jewry. Salonica had been depopulated due to war and transfer of much of its remaining population to Istanbul by the Ottomans in their efforts to repopulate their new capital. Jews were also later moved by the Ottomans from Salonika to Rhodes.[71] So the Ottomans used the opportunity of the arrival of the Sephardim to rejuvenate the city turning it into an important component of the Mediterranean trade.[72] Jews soon comprised the largest segment of the population of the city maintaining this dominance for the duration of Ottoman rule over the city.[73]

The Sephardic diaspora also presented the Ottomans with an opportunity to access the networks developed by the dispersing Sephardim throughout Europe and to access the knowledge of these European Jews with regard to trade, diplomacy, and medicine. The presence of Sephardic communities throughout the Mediterranean and Europe, such as the Dutch provinces, allowed the Ottomans to have access to European markets, and provided them with people who knew European languages that could be used in diplomatic efforts. Thus, although up to 1492 the Ottoman-Italian trade used to be in the hands of Christian merchants (Greeks, Armenians, Ragusans), the Sephardim came to dominate trade in the sixteenth century.[74] Their influence was such that the Jews of the Ottoman Empire were able to impose an effective trade embargo on the papal port of Ancona following the anti-Jewish legislation of Pope Paul IV in 1555.[75]

Perhaps the most famed example of the prominence Jews attained in the Ottoman Empire was Joseph Nasi, portrayed at the time as an intimate counsellor of the sultans and an enemy to Christendom.[76] Originally from Portugal, he fled when the Inquisition begun to target the converted Jews known as Marranos. He first went to Antwerp, then to Louvain, where he briefly studied at the university, later to then France, Venice, and eventually he settled in the Ottoman Empire in 1554. Because of his European family connections Nasi was able to enter Ottoman service and became involved in the negotiations with Poland and later the Netherlands as well as the affairs in Moldavia and Wallachia. He built a fortune by securing a monopoly on the beeswax trade with Poland. When the Ottomans incorporated the Duchy of Naxos into their empire Nasi was named duke while the Duchy's status was still in flux, as a first step toward the full annexation of the island cluster.

Nasi's career, from a Jewish Portuguese refugee to one of the wealthiest and most influential men in the Ottoman Empire, was remarkable but other Jews and Christians also achieved great prominence in the empire. For Jews, however, the Ottoman Empire was perhaps the only place where such careers were possible. The Ottoman Empire was not simply a place of refuge but one where Jews could reassert practices that had been forbidden to them by Christian legislation, including the reintroduction of polygamy,[77] and a place where Jews could challenge Christian ideas of superiority that frequently associated Jews with "primitive" peoples.[78] In the Ottoman Empire Jews could, and did, own Christian slaves whom they often converted to Judaism—both forbidden practices since Roman times.[79]

The prominence of the Sephardic Jews meant the loss of influence for the older Romaniote community whose very presence declined in the main centers of the empire and slowly their communities were mostly absorbed by the more numerous Sephardic ones.[80] This was not always done easily and on occasion there were conflicts between the two communities as in Rhodes in 1523.[81] The Romaniotes continued to have a strong presence in western and southern Greece and especially in the city of Janina (Ioannina) which was their most numerous community but there were also significant communities in Patras, Tripolitsa (Tripolis), Negroponte (Chalkis), Preveza, and Arta.

Jewish ascendency in the Ottoman Empire reached its peak in the sixteenth century. In the seventeenth century, Jews were sidelined by the emergence of a new class of prominent Christian merchants and bureaucrats. The relative decline of Ottoman power and the benefits that Christian faith gave to Greeks, Armenian, and Slavs allowed the latter to supplant Jews in the trade between Europe and the Ottoman Empire, and gradually even in the Ottoman internal trade to a degree.[82] A few Christians even managed to break into the Ottoman state administration and assume positions of authority. These are collectively known as the Phanariots from the Istanbul neighborhood of Fanar where most of them resided and where the patriarchate of Constantinople was located. The rise of the Phanariots in the seventeenth century coincided with the end of the territorial expansion of the Ottomans and subsequent retrenchment. The Phanariots were perfectly placed to exploit the sudden need for negotiators familiar with Europe since many had studied in Europe and had a familiarity with European developments. They were thus able to enter the Ottoman structure of governance and despite retaining their religion integrate into the Ottoman system.[83] Starting as translators (*dragomans*) they soon gained a monopoly on certain posts in the Ottoman administration such as those of the Grand Dragoman, essentially the foreign minister, the Dragoman of the Fleet, and later, when the Ottomans sought reliable non-Muslims, they became *Voivodes* or rulers of the semiautonomous principalities of Wallachia and Moldavia. At the same time, the Phanariots became fabulously wealthy through trade, tax-farming, and banking activities, and even managed to gain some control over the appointments of patriarchs.[84] Although usually referred to as Greeks the Phanariots included among their ranks non-ethnically Greek Christians like the Albanian Ghikas family,[85] and were ultimately as Ottoman as any Muslim in the empire since their fortunes, positions, and power were tied to the Ottoman government. They did however create their own networks of patronage in the empire staffed by educated Christians of lesser status and employed numerous teachers, secretaries, and other functionaries that generated an intellectual environment that has been called the Greek Enlightenment. It is from this environment that the ideas for the future establishment of a Greek state would emerge.

In addition to the Phanariotes the eighteenth century also saw the emergence of a group of provincial Greek notables who were able to amass considerable land and wealth to become regionally influential. Their rise coincides with the emergence of a similar, though much more powerful, group of Muslim local powerbrokers, the *ayans,* who controlled vast areas and became semiautonomous though linked to the decentralized Ottoman government.[86] The most powerful of these like Ali Pasha of Janina, Osman Pasvanoglou of Vidin, or Muhammad Ali of Egypt are well known and well researched but there were scores of others less powerful but with local prominence who amassed considerable wealth and often little armies to defend their gains from other predatory *ayans*. These local Muslim *ayans* were able to build local networks of power and successfully confront the imperial commanders sent to their regions.[87] In some regions, as in Crete and Belgrade, these networks were closely tied to the local Janissaries, who were frequently involved in the worst cases of abuse and violence against the peasant population.[88] Christian notables were similar and often in alliance with the Muslim *ayans* of their regions, most famously in the Peloponnese where Muslim and Christian notables were divided into competing factions.[89] Similar notables also emerged in the Aegean islands though in their cases their source of wealth rested in trade and shipping which during the Napoleonic wars made fortunes for the notables of the tiny islands of Hydra, Spetses, and Psara.

From these groups, the local notables, the Phanariots, and the church, would emerge the leaders of the Greek War of Independence but it is important to recognize that within the Ottoman context and despite their support for local revolts and even foreign powers, notably Russia, these groups were fully integrated in the Ottoman fabric and functioned in very similar ways to comparable Muslim groups, which also frequently revolted or conspired against the state. They vied for personal gain as much with each other, as with Muslims, Jews, or Armenians and identified predominantly with the recognizable divisions of Ottoman society such as religion rather with any ethnic let alone national affiliation. However, the structural barriers that Karen Barkey argues made political action by the Ottoman peasants difficult in the seventeenth century, and the Ottoman legal system that acted as a release of grievances among the population[90] were weakened and undermined in the eighteenth century by the *ayans* and their networks to the detriment of the peasants who would respond by flocking to the standards of rebellion in 1821.

Religious affiliation and conversion in the Mediterranean

One aspect that has been hotly debated in recent decades has been the question of conversion and apostasy in the Ottoman world. Earlier accounts of Christian conversion to Islam such as Speros Vryonis' work in Anatolia saw conversion as a contemporaneous process of the conquest of the territory by the Muslim Turks with a focus on the policies of the Islamic state.[91] This does not apply in the Balkans where many conversions reach their high point long after the Ottoman conquest, in the sixteenth and even seventeenth centuries as in the case of the Vallahades and Pomaks.[92] The conversion process of the Balkans was not uniform nor sustained and the region remained predominantly Christian throughout the Ottoman period. There were areas and incidents of mass conversions as in Bosnia, Albania, the Rhodope mountains, and Crete but overall there was hardly an Ottoman policy of forced conversion with the exception of the infamous *devsirme*. This was the periodic recruitment drives from the fourteenth to the seventeenth centuries of young Christian boys to fill the ranks of the Janissaries which Balkan historiographies have painted in the most terrible light. However, the numbers involved were small, some 200,000 boys over the entire period, and recent evidence suggest that the recruitment of their sons was not always seen as a calamity by local Christians. Some parents bribed officials to have their sons recruited even as others bribed in order to keep their sons.[93] Certainly, there were many factors that influenced conversions from local circumstances such as the Bogomil heresy in Bosnia or the prolonged war on Crete, to the religious syncretism of certain Sufi orders and in particularly the Bektashi and Mevlevi ones, to economic considerations like the non-Muslim *cizye* tax, to social pressures especially among the nobility in the early phase of the empire.[94] Others have pointed out potential benefits to converts especially women and slaves when conversion could release them from bad marriages or bad owners.[95]

Jews also converted for a variety of reasons including Jewish women who wanted to divorce their husbands or retain their children after a divorce. There was at least one case of mass conversion that took place in Salonica in the seventeenth century. In 1666, Sabbatai Zevi, a Jewish religious leader who proclaimed himself the messiah and attracted a massive following in the Ottoman Empire and throughout Europe, suddenly converted to Islam in the presence of Sultan Mehmed IV rather than face execution for sedition. Sabbatai's conversion plunged his movement into turmoil and while most of his followers were disillusioned and returned to their homes, many chose to follow their leader and converted to Islam becoming known as the Dönme.[96] Settled in Salonica they formed their own unique society continuing many Jewish traditions as Muslims.[97] The proximity between the messianic disturbances caused by Zevi and the decline of influence of Jews in the Ottoman court from the seventeenth century onwards has led some to argue for a direct link between the two and the loss of trust of the Ottomans toward Jews.[98] The presence of foreign European Jews in Ottoman cities like Salonica who retained the protection of foreign states may also have further alienated the Ottomans, in a process strangely reminiscent of the settling of Italian Jews in the final centuries of Byzantium.[99]

Beyond the *devsirme* forced conversions were rare in the Ottoman Empire but have been given great prominence by the Orthodox Church and nationalist historiography which has celebrated the neomartyrs of the Ottoman period. Evidence however, seems to indicate that several of these neomartyrs may have been prepared for the role of martyr in monasteries as exemplars to fortify Christian sentiment and in any case their small numbers, 40–100 individuals over the course of several centuries, does not point to a deliberate Ottoman policy.[100] While some historians like Dennis Hupchick have made claims that the Ottomans pursued a deliberate policy of forced conversion in specific regions,[101] such claims have generally been debunked.[102]

Recent works have further problematized conversion in the Mediterranean world by presenting a much more fluid world than previously imagined.[103] In her recent dissertation Daphne Lappa linked conversion to mobility, whether voluntary or forced through captivity, with places of contact between the Muslim and Christian worlds such as the Venetian territories playing a prominent role in the process.[104] Christians and Jews from all over Europe sought their fortunes in the Ottoman Empire through conversion to Islam, but when their expectations were not met, or when better opportunities beckoned elsewhere, some had no qualms about reverting to their former religions. The same also happened with Muslims and Jews who converted to Christianity, and again the records reveal several examples of dubious conversions, or of individuals, particularly among the Iberian Marranos, who claimed different identities at different times and places. The trial of one such man, Abraham also called Righetto, who was investigated by the Venetian branch of the Inquisition reveals the complexity of religious identity in the Mediterranean. Brian Pullan in his investigation of the case repeats the definition given to this man in the records as "a Catholic without faith, and a Jew without knowledge, though a Jew by desire" but also points out that his trial was in part political rather than simply a case of apostasy.[105] Furthermore, the records themselves are inconsistent depicting him sometimes as "Enrique the Christian" and others as "Abraham the Jew" and his eventual escape from prison seems to have come as a relief to the authorities.[106] Even some of the most renowned figures like George Castriotes or Scanderbeg, the national Albanian hero, turned Ottoman only to revert to Christianity and become a bitter enemy of the Ottomans.[107]

That is not to say that conversion was taken upon lightly either by the individual in question or the states involved. Venice invested heavily as a government and as a society in providing proper religious instruction to converts, a quarter of whom were Jews, as well as the means to integrate in Venetian society.[108] In the Ottoman Empire distinctions between Muslims and non-Muslims were reinforced through regulations over dress, the flaunting of which could be perceived as treason. Even the learning of a European language by a Muslim could lead to his dismissal from the Ottoman court.[109] Although in both the Ottoman lands and Europe such sartorial regulations were not always enforced, in times of religious or political crisis they could be resurrected to galvanize the faithful and assert their superiority. It is no coincidence that Abraham/Enrique got into trouble at the time of Ottoman-Venetian conflict over Cyprus and the Battle of Lepanto. Political considerations were a crucial element in the complex question of conversion seen in conversions within a faith. The Ottomans certainly put a lot more effort in the conversion of the Shi'a Kizilbash in Anatolia than toward the conversion of Christians and Jews in view of their rivalry with the Safavids, and the papacy from the seventeenth century onwards devoted significant resources toward the conversion of Orthodox and Armenian Christians to Catholicism in faraway places like Aleppo.[110] However, religion did not divide groups as clearly as we often assume and there was a lot of space for individuals and states to negotiate. An excellent example was pointed out by Eyal Ginio in his examination of the Muslim Roma. Roma in the Ottoman Empire were assessed the *cizye* even if they were Muslim. Ginio also points out that this assessment by the Ottomans was justified on what seems to be ethnic rather than religious grounds and that Muslims Roma were also excluded from state institutions like the military.[111] Being Muslim may have been a necessary but not always a sufficient condition to achieve the highest levels of Ottoman society.

A final point regarding the changing demographic sectarian landscape of the Balkans involves the movement of populations. The Ottomans, like the Byzantines before them, engaged in forced transfers of populations as for example when Mehmet II repopulated Constantinople after 1453. Mehmet transferred Karaite Jews from Pravadi and Adrianople (Edirne) to his new capital in 1455, then Armenians from Anatolia in 1459, followed by Greeks and Armenians from Trebizond after its capture in 1461, Greeks from the island of Mytilene, and Muslims from Konya and Larende.[112] Some groups were forcibly moved because of their disloyalty and others to repopulated regions that had suffered population loss due to war or epidemics. There is no agreement among scholars regarding the numbers of Muslim immigration to the Balkans. Some scholars argue that Muslim migration to the Balkans was insufficient to affect the composition of the region while others argue for more impactful numbers. Even the most famous case of mass migration, the 1690 flight of Serbs under their patriarch Arsenije III from Kosovo to Habsburg territory due to their earlier support for the Austrians in a war and their subsequent replacement with Muslim Albanians is hotly disputed as far as the numbers are concerned. Serb nationalist historiography suggests the flight of some 400–500,000 people while other scholars bring down the number to 30–40,000.[113] Mass movements of population continued up to the early nineteenth century when perhaps a quarter of a million Bulgarians migrated to Wallachia, Moldavia, Bessarabia, and Russia between 1806 and the 1830s. There were many causes for this migration: war, taxation, banditry, and hope for better economic prospects, but it is also important to note that a significant portion of those who chose to migrate almost immediately returned to their original homeland when circumstances improved or when expectations were not met in their new place.[114]

Although most of the population in the Balkans remained Christian, it does not mean that conversions, and to a lesser degree migration of Muslims to the region, did not have a significant effect. Certain regions ended up with substantial Muslim populations, if not majorities like Bosnia, Crete, Albania, Rhodope, and Thrace. Although some Turkic speakers existed in the Balkans particularly in Thrace and Macedonia, many of these Muslims retained their ancestral languages, whether Greek in the cases of the Vallahades of Grevena and the Cretan Muslims, Slavic in the cases of Pomaks and Bosnian Muslims, or Albanian among Muslim Albanians. Throughout the Balkans many of the cities became predominantly Muslim and the remainder usually had significant Muslim and Jewish populations.[115] Furthermore, as much as half of the Christian populations of many Balkan cities such as Phillipoupolis (Plovdiv), Turnovo, or the Black Sea port towns Varna and Burgas were Greek-speaking while the surrounding countryside was Slavic.[116] Although Muslim and non-Muslim communities could work together and even protest together against abuses by officials as in the Cretan town of Chania, Athens and elsewhere,[117] sectarian violence was common from Lebanon to Serbia. Despite its fluidity religion was the most important marker of identity in the Ottoman state and conversions created divisions that often erupted in violence, not only from the Muslim side but also from Christians. In semiautonomous Montenegro for example, the Christian population massacred and expelled those that had converted to Islam in an incident celebrated in the most famous literary product of that nation *The Mountain Wreath* by Petar II Petrovic-Njegos.[118]

Before concluding this introductory discussion, I should mention that the Ottoman conquest did not encompass all Greek populated areas. Certain regions had been under Venetian rule since 1204 or had come under Venetian control in subsequent centuries, and although the Ottomans were able to conquer most of those in the fifteenth century, others remained under Venetian rule until the sixteenth (Cyprus) and seventeenth (Crete) centuries and the Ionian islands never came under Ottoman authority with the exception of Lefkada which experienced periods of Ottoman rule. The development of these regions was substantially different than that of the Ottoman Empire with Christianity maintaining a dominant position, although the rulers were for the most part Roman Catholics and the population Orthodox. Because of the Venetian preoccupation with trade several of these locales developed significant Jewish settlements especially in Corfu (Kerkyra) and Zante (Zakynthos). Venice itself had long-established Jewish communities, both Italian and later Sephardic ones, and had a complex history with the presence of Jews. Venice initiated the practice of isolating Jews in a specially defined space or "ghetto" in the city, and although the Venetian authorities frequently intervened to protect Jews from the violence urged by firebrand preachers,[119] they also tried to limit their economic power in trade and moneylending to the point that many Venetian Jews chose to immigrate from Venice to neighboring states.[120]

Corfu was an interesting mélange of Sephardic and Romaniotes containing two separate Jewish communities with their own synagogues and cemeteries. The two communities did not have amicable relations with each other,[121] the "Greek" community referring to themselves as "native" and insisting on special privileges over the "foreign" community. In response, the Sephardic and "Italian" communities frequently appealed to the Venetian authorities in order to be considered "old" inhabitants of Corfu, with the same privileges as the Romaniotes.[122] Relations with the local Orthodox population were far from amicable, and anti-Jewish violence was common. Corfu was also a significant ground of conversion to Christianity, as Lappa has shown, for Muslim captives or apostates from the Ottoman Empire but also for foreign and local Jews, many of the latter choosing to convert to the Greek Rite rather than the Latin one as almost all Muslim converts did.[123]

By the eighteenth century, Greek communities had spread beyond the Ottoman and Venetian territories throughout the Mediterranean, the Black Sea, and much of Europe similar to the Jewish diaspora. The Habsburg and Russian Empires welcomed the trade these predominantly merchant communities brought and gave them several privileges. The Habsburgs, who had already given privileges to the Serbs for their valuable frontier military services, extended religious and political rights to Greeks. Charles VI issued a patent in 1717 giving Ottoman Orthodox Christians the right to trade in Vienna; Empress Maria-Theresa issued in 1751 the Decree of Privileges for the Greeks and Illyrians of Trieste, while her son Joseph II gave in 1781 the right to Greeks and Serbs to build churches in various parts of Austria, Hungary, and Transylvania. Soon thereafter Greeks begun establishing their own schools in the Habsburg Empire.

The Habsburg state extended these privileges to Greeks in Transylvania, Hungary, and Vienna despite local opposition to Greek mercantile encroachment.[124] It is interesting to note, however, that while the Greek Patriarchs of Constantinople were solidifying their position in the Ottoman Empire by having the Slavic Balkan Patriarchates of Pec and Ochrid abolished in 1767, and thus creating a nominally unified Christian Orthodox body dominated by Greeks, the Habsburgs recognized the differences of the various "nations" of the Balkans. This was evident in Trieste where in 1781 the Austrian authorities recognized two distinct "nations," the Greek nation and the Illyric nation each given its own charter and administrators, although both were of the Greek Rite. The people themselves often confused the issue by self-identifying alternatively as Greek-Illyric, Greek, Oriental Greek, or Greek Rite, but for the Austrians at least the national divisions of the Ottoman Balkans were visible.[125]

For the Russians the Greek merchants did not bring only valuable trade, they were also a useful political tool in their constant struggles against the Ottoman Empire. Russia was the only independent Orthodox Christian state and from the seventeenth century onwards was growing in size and strength, though still mostly ignored by the rest of Europe. From the rule of Peter the Great onwards the Russians pushed against the Ottoman frontier seizing the Ottoman bits of the Ukraine and seeking to find an exit to the Black Sea. Following the 1768–74 war with the Ottomans their goal was realized in the Treaty of Küçük Kaynarca that ceded the Crimean Khanate to Russia. Although the Ottomans recovered Moldavia and Wallachia they were barred from stationing troops there, or appointing Muslim governors, and thus turned to Phanariot Voivodes to rule the principalities. More damaging still the Russians assumed the right to intervene in Ottoman affairs to protect the Orthodox, who also gained the right to fly the Russian flag on their ships. The Russians, who had instigated a revolt among the Christian populations of the Peloponnese and Crete only to leave them to their fate, thus assumed a paternalistic role over the Ottoman Orthodox and put some effort in cultivating ever closer ties by inviting Greek merchants to the new Russian ports of the Black Sea like Odessa and even utilizing prominent Greeks in their own administration. Their ultimate goal was to expel the Ottomans from Constantinople and Europe and take their place as the rightful heirs of the Byzantine Empire, a goal they would pursue on and off until the First World War.

When the French Revolution engulfed Europe in a series of devastating wars that would endure until the final defeat of Napoleon in 1815, the Greek-speaking Christians of the Ottoman Empire had been on the ascendant both within the political structure of the empire and in the Mediterranean and European mercantile networks for a century and a half. Greeks had established communities around Europe, many Greeks were being educated in Italy, France, Germany, and Austria, and some even rose to prominent ranks in European governments especially in Russia one of whose foreign ministers was Ioannis Kapodistrias, a Corfiote Greek. At the same time, conditions within the Ottoman Empire were deteriorating for the Christian peasant as the Ottoman government was increasingly unable to restrain the greed of the most powerful *ayans*. Ottoman efforts of reform, notably those by Selim III, failed at a time, when new revolutionary ideas coming from France were finding receptive ears among Western-educated Greeks.

My Enemy's Friend is my Enemy: Jews and the Greek War of Independence (1789–1830)

Nationalism, Revolution, and the Jewish question

Although some scholars, and many nationalists, have tried to push back the emergence of a "Greek" ethnic identity to the end of the Byzantine era,[1] most consider nationalism a modern phenomenon and assign the birth of Greek nationalism to the period following the French Revolution. Thus, it coincides with the first efforts to emancipate Jews and the subsequent rise of modern anti-Semitism. Although Joseph II with his 1782 Edict of Toleration allowed Jews to be naturalized in the Habsburg Empire, which was followed by the introduction of Jewish conscription in the army in 1788,[2] it was the French Republic that in 1793 became the first European state to fully emancipate its Jewish population. The French armies, either through emulation or opposition, also fermented the early stirrings of nationalism in much of Europe. For the first time Jews joined in significant numbers the European armies of the Napoleonic wars and for a brief moment, they saw the possibility of joining their Christian counterparts as equal members of their respective societies, as Hegel advocated.[3]

The French Revolution did not introduce but certainly popularized the idea of the nation. It also defined it as a "freely expressed will of the inhabitants,"[4] an idea that the French subsequently exported to other parts of Europe. This concept of self-determination for instance justified the inclusion of Corsica to France despite the linguistic differences since that was the wish of its people per Deputy Saliceti in 1789.[5] While this understanding worked for France which had several linguistic minorities, elsewhere in Europe, and especially in Germany, the national question was defined differently, in a call to unify the fragmented nation seen as a cultural and civilizational entity rather than a civic one. For Johan Gottfried Herder the barriers to the emergence of the German nation were religious, political, and class divisions, and the experience of the French Revolution gave hope that such barriers could be swept away.[6]

Even at this early stage Jews were faced with dilemmas. The French Revolution opened the possibility of Jews becoming full French citizens but the option came with strings attached. As was clearly stated as early as 1789, Jews as individuals could gain all rights available to French citizens but as a nation they could not even exist within a French nation-state. The unity of the nation could not tolerate the presence of a foreign body, and if Jews were unwilling to become fully French nationals, they would have to be expelled as some radical Jacobins suggested.[7] Similar arguments were made in Germany by influential figures such as Wilhelm von Humboldt and Johann Gottlieb Fichte, the latter referring to Jews as "a state within a state," a phrase often used in anti-Semitic diatribes from Voltaire onwards.[8] Even Hegel implied at first that Jews should not receive citizenship as long as they retained their religious difference.[9] Nor was the public always ready to accept the granting of full civic rights to Jews as the riots in Alsace indicate.[10] Apart from Prussia no German state was willing to emancipate its Jews until they were forced to do so by the French army.[11] As Poland shows, even the radicalization of the idea of the nation along republican lines, experienced after the 1794 Kosciuszko insurrection which aimed at the mobilization of the nation against external threats,[12] did little for Jews especially since the latter were often identified culturally with one of the main threats to the nation, Prussia. Nevertheless, Jews could briefly enjoy the hope that the French Revolution would introduce a new period in Europe where they could enjoy the same rights as everyone else.

Such hopes were soon dashed. As early as 1808, Napoleon with his "Infamous Decree" begun to reverse the earlier liberalism of the revolution. Jewish residence and economic rights were curtailed, loans to Jews were expunged, Jews were barred from hiring substitutes to serve in the army, and they were forbidden to settle in certain border regions.[13] Such retrenchment was later seen in other parts of Europe. In Prussia, Jewish veterans and war widows were denied the benefits, honors, positions, and pensions accorded to their Christian counterparts. Just as the hopes of many to transform the European society and overthrow the *Ancien Regime* were dashed following the Congress of Vienna and the restoration of the old dynasties, so was the conclusion of the Napoleonic wars a disaster for Jews. Their emancipation was reversed in almost every case.[14] Anticipated in Fichte's *Addresses to the German Nation* which included elements of ethnic exclusion,[15] anti-Semitic writings proliferated in post-restoration Germany often targeting Jewish emancipation as in the case of Christian Friedrich Rühs, Jakob Friedrich Fries, and others.[16] The anti-Semitic rhetoric was followed by a series of violent anti-Semitic actions in much of Germany known as the "Hep-Hep" riots, and further restrictions of Jewish rights.[17] Starting from Wurzburg in Bavaria in 1819 they spread to Munich, Bamberg, Bayreuth, Frankfurt, Heidelberg, Karlsruhe, Hamburg, and Copenhagen despite the efforts of the authorities to suppress them and even led Prince Metternich to issue an order for the deployment of the German confederation's troops though they were not needed in the end.[18] While the period leading to the French Revolution had been characterized by gradual tolerance toward Jews, the period following the defeat of Napoleon was noted for increased nationalist sentiments, radicalism, and a new anti-Semitism that was sometimes tied to revolutionary agitation. Thus, national uprisings in central and eastern Europe often coincided with anti-Semitic violence as in the case of Poland in 1830, and Alsace, Bohemia, and Slovakia in 1848, even though Jews outside the afflicted regions often supported such nationalist uprisings.[19] In some cases, as in Posen or Bohemia-Moravia, Jews were caught between competing nationalisms (German vs. Polish and German vs. Czech, respectively), and their cultural association with one group, usually the German, marked them as political enemies of the other.[20] Similarly, because emancipation had been achieved through a foreign imposition in Germany, Jews were mistrusted by nationalists despite Jewish close association with German culture.[21]

Worse still, the fear of revolutionary activity led governments to reexamine their citizenship and residency laws leading to legislation like the Prussian *Untertanengesetz* in the 1830s that was particularly restrictive toward Jews to ensure that only wealthy foreign Jews could become naturalized. Other German states, especially in the south, were even more restrictive either completely banning the naturalization of foreign Jews or preventing their settlement in communities without preexisting Jewish presence as in the cases of Bavaria and Baden respectively.[22] Jews were thus regularly placed outside of the emerging national identity, their religion excluding them from the national fold. Although the exclusion of Jews was not new and many highly influential European thinkers from Luther to Voltaire to Diderot and d'Holbach often saw Jews as a subversive and alien force with regard to European culture and society,[23] the overpowering significance of the nation in the nineteenth century would make such an exclusion particularly threatening. Even Herder, a self-proclaimed friend of Jews, rejected their emancipation in a unified Germany.[24]

The reestablishment of a conservative order throughout Europe in 1815 did not stifle the aspirations that had been raised by the French Revolution. The decade following the Congress of Vienna was one of revolutionary fervor especially around the Mediterranean. Revolts in Portugal, Spain, and Italy aimed at establishing liberal constitutional governments also had a clear nationalist tinge especially in Austrian-dominated Italy. Similar agitation was evident in central Europe especially in Poland where a brief period of autonomy under Napoleon had been followed by the redistribution of Polish lands to Prussia, Austria, and Russia. In Germany and Italy, the idea of unification was increasingly being heard while constitutionalism became a powerful force in the 1820s with the Cadiz Constitution of 1812 gaining widespread popularity from Latin America to the Mediterranean and beyond.[25] Even among liberal constitutionalists, however, and especially in the Mediterranean world, religious homogeneity was seen as a crucial component of the nation, whether the Catholic faith in Spain, Portugal, and Italy or Orthodoxy in Greece.[26]

Greek Proto-Nationalism and others

The Ottoman state had changed significantly by the end of the eighteenth century. Although past ideas about the decline of the Ottoman Empire have been reappraised, it was the case that the Ottoman Empire was not the military power that it had been through the sixteenth century. Though still able to stand up well against other empires like the Safavids or even the Habsburgs and Russians on an individual basis, the Ottomans often faced coalitions or multiple threats simultaneously and were barely able to hold on to their territory, suffering reverses and territorial losses like Hungary and the Crimea. The state was increasing unable to control the rising regional strongmen, the *ayans*, and the Janissaries who transformed from an elite military unit to a privileged and rapacious class that exploited the *reya* in the provinces and often disrupted the state with revolts that saw the demise of several sultans. By the end of the eighteenth century, there were as many as 400,000 Janissaries drawing a salary from the treasury but only a tenth of them were actually available for military units.[27]

The relative loss of control by the central government meant that local officials and *ayans* could exploit the peasant population ruthlessly and effectively. Throughout the seventeenth and eighteenth centuries, the tax burden on the peasantry increased, not only through greater demands by the state but also by increasing ecclesiastical taxes as the cost of gaining, and holding, ecclesiastical offices skyrocketed. Churchmen like Polykarpos bishop of Larisa were so corrupt that Ottoman officials complained to the patriarch of Constantinople that he and others like him used their ecclesiastical powers, including the power of excommunication, to extract funds that ruined the *reya*.[28] The sultans issued a series of, mostly ineffectual, *firmans* aimed at lessening the burdens of the *reya* but they were unable to stop the abuses, which included the transformation of the land into great estates (*ciftliks*) and the ruin of once vibrant communities like the Vlach trade town of Moschopolis which through the rapacity of local *ayans* was eventually completely abandoned.[29]

The difficulties faced by the Ottoman sultans in dealing with these *ayans* and troublesome Janissaries were exemplified by the events in the province of Belgrade that led to the first Serbian revolt of 1804. The sultan had dispatched Haci Mustafa Pasha to Belgrade to bring order to the region whose *reya* were greatly abused by the local Janissaries supported by the powerful *ayan* Osman Pasvanoglu of Vidin. Haci Mustafa had no private militia and was thus vulnerable to the attacks that the expelled Janissaries and Pasvanoglu launched from Vidin.[30] His solution, to arm the Christian peasantry, undermined his authority among Muslims and led to his overthrow and murder initiating a series of events that would end with a revolt by the Christian Serbs, initially against their local oppressors, but that later evolved into a general revolt against Ottoman rule.[31]

This weakness of the government in Istanbul in the latter half of the eighteenth century opened the space for local notables, Muslim and Christian alike, to assert themselves and build their own political networks. Although Christian notables could not rise to the heights of a Pasvanoglu or an Ali Pasha, they could amass power and wealth and through ties with Muslim notables wield real political influence. With the exclusion of Moldavia and Wallachia where the Christian Phanariotes nominally ruled, the Peloponnese was perhaps the one region where Christian notables were able to craft such networks and become engaged with their Muslim counterparts in power games that on occasion challenged even Ottoman rule over the region.[32] This is one reading of the 1770 rebellion in support of the Russian war effort against the Ottomans, as well as in the intrigues during the wars of the French Revolution and Napoleon, that led to the executions of several prominent notables and the formulation of a plan for the creation of an independent Peloponnese run jointly by Muslim and Christian notables.[33] The diminished authority of the Ottoman government in the region was further illustrated by the 1770 revolt during which the local governor Muhsinzade Mehmed had to hire Albanian mercenaries who subsequently refused to leave the area, preying on the local population. The governor was then forced to hire "local forces" through loans from the local notables to end the Albanian depredations.[34]

The Ottoman Balkans with their small urban centers, illiterate population, and simple agrarian structures would hardly be expected to prove an early hotbed of nationalism yet the revolutionary fervor of the Mediterranean facilitated the spread of such ideas especially among Greek-Ottoman merchants who had made fortunes during the Napoleonic wars.[35] As recent scholarship demonstrates, the revolutionaries and intellectuals of the Mediterranean, as well as the reactionaries, supported the causes of each other and frequently participated actively in the wars of the 1820s and 1830s.[36] Portuguese, Italians, Spanish, and Greek liberals formed a fluid Mediterranean network and were influenced by the developments of the region such as the Cadiz Constitution, which became a model for many constitutional movements from Portugal to Greece.[37] In many cases, national independence and political liberalism were simultaneous goals, with the former often trumping the latter.[38]

Even before the eruption of the revolts of the 1820s there were developments in the Ottoman-held Balkan lands that could be described as proto-nationalist. By the end of the eighteenth century, such a proto-nationalist identity was being formulated around the religious difference of Christian subjects and their Muslim rulers. There were different currents in this process, a populist one often centered around religious figures like the itinerant monk Kosmas Aitolos (the Aetolian), and more intellectual ones promoted by those who had been influenced by Western European Enlightenment ideas and the French Revolution. Although such currents appear to be quite different, they had an important common foundation in the fact that they did not draw their dividing lines based on ethnic or cultural affinities but stressed religious differences thus linking the evolving idea of the nation with religious affiliation from a very early moment.

The early manifestations of the religiously based populist current were expressed by monks and lower clergy through apocryphal writings and on occasion through small-scale revolts like that of the bishop of Trikala and Larisa Dionysios Skylosofos in 1611.[39] Although, as we saw in the previous chapter, the Orthodox Church had been given numerous privileges by the Ottoman sultans and the patriarch of Constantinople had assumed the role of the head of the entire Orthodox Christian flock in the empire, the lower clergy and, in particular, the monks often served as foci of popular resistance against authority as they had done during the Byzantine period. Early revolts against Ottoman rule were often led by such popular religious figures who were not part of the religious establishment in Constantinople. Many of these figures grounded their appeal on so-called prophesies like those of Agathaggelos about the imminent end of Muslim rule or the rebirth of a Christian empire.[40]

Though invariably unsuccessful, this agitation created fissures in Balkan Ottoman society and produced a genealogy of Christian neomartyrs, later talked about as "the first national heroes of Modern Hellenism."[41] They inspired Christian Ottoman subjects as the early Carbonari martyrs would inspire later Italian nationalists of the Risorgimento. The most notable of these was the aforementioned Kosmas Aitolos who advocated what can best be described as a Christian Orthodox revival. Contrary to similar figures like Dionysius Skylosofos who spearheaded revolts against the Ottomans, Kosmas did not lead or even urge armed uprisings. Quite the contrary he was careful to stress his submission to Ottoman authority in line with the official position of the Orthodox Church. His sermons, however, were subversive since they targeted those in power, and they inevitably led to his death in 1779. If Kosma's anti-Ottoman message was circumspect, however, his anti-Jewish rhetoric was quite explicit and Kosmas used such attacks on Jews as a safer trope to direct attacks on Ottoman rule. His "Lessons" (*didachai*) and "Prophesies" are peppered with anti-Jewish language calling Jews the "children of the Devil" and Christ killers, accusing them of murdering in the past "all the prophets and righteous teachers" and that during the siege of Jerusalem "fathers and mothers slaughtered their children and ate them," claiming that God has abandoned them to the Devil, that they engaged in the ritual murder of Christian children, that they befouled every food or drink they sold to Christians, and so on.[42] More than that, however, he also urged Christians to shun Jews and boycott their business:

> "Do I have eyes to see the Jew? And your Highness how can your heart hold to do business with the Jews? They do well and they foul us. They are ready at any time to do evil to the Christians. The Jew slaughters a sheep and the front half he keeps for himself and the rear he sells to the Christians to foul them. And if the Jew gives you wine or *raki*[43] it is impossible not to foul it first, and if he does not have time to urinate in it, he will spit in it. How does your heart stand to buy things from the Jews? . . . He who associates with the Jews, buys and sells—what does he reveal? He reveals and says that the Jews did well to kill the Prophets and the Just and that they do well to insult our Christ and our Virgin Mary. Therefore my Christians, nothing from them."[44]

Kosmas' reputation and influence soon spread throughout the southern and western parts of Greece and even European travelers were aware of him and his anti-Jewish sermons that may have included early, for the eastern Mediterranean, versions of the blood libel accusation:

> "(Kosmas) mainly talked against the Jews whom he accused of sticking needles in children to take their blood and so do their Sabbath sorceries and for many other imaginary crimes . . . he *xevaskane* [removed the evil eye from] many who had been bewitched by the Jews and as a new Apollonius gave light to a blind mule."[45]

His attacks on Jews may appear to be in the mold of old religious anti-Semitism that existed throughout the Byzantine period and was always present in church ideology and rhetoric but I believe that they represent something new and more ominous, especially when one considers Kosmas' main project, which was the revitalization of the Christian community. Jews were depicted as a foreign element and, worse still, one allied with the main obstacle to a Greek revival, the Ottomans. Jews were the implacable enemies of Christians at every level from the blood libel accusations, itself a new concept in the East though with a long history in Western Europe, to commercial rivalry. Kosmas openly identified Jews as his primary, and personal, enemies, writing to his brother Chrysanthos in 1779 that "ten thousand Christians love me and one hates me. A thousand Turks love me and one not so much. Thousands of Jews want my death and one does not."[46] Jews were an easier target to attack and a target that could serve to unify Christians, the first step toward the expected revival. His campaign against Jews was multifaceted. He urged Christians to boycott Jewish stores and avoid all contact with them. He tried to have market days moved to the Sabbath and thus disadvantage Jewish merchants and at least in Navpaktos (Lepanto) he seems to have been successful.[47] And he tried to link Jews with the Ottoman authorities by stressing the influence Jews had over Ottoman officials.

The latter point is particularly important for the events surrounding the Greek War of Independence. The local pasha Ali of Janina kept a court where Jews and Christians could rise to positions of authority and power.[48] The association of Jews with Ottoman officials was facilitated by the prominent positions certain Jews had held in the past like Joseph Nasi. However, by the end of the eighteenth century Jews were eclipsed by the rise of the Phanariots and other Christians who were much more influential with the Ottoman authorities in Istanbul. At the regional level in the areas that concern us, however, and despite the power of Christian notables, an association between Jews and Ottomans was credible because both were predominantly urban communities. Although by the eighteenth century Jewish influence in trade, banking, and government was eclipsed by Greeks and other Christians at the imperial level, Jews were still an important local component and part of an increasingly hostile relationship between the urban and rural components of Balkan society, competing with Christians for the local trade in towns like Arta (where Kosmas was active).[49] The link in the mind of Ottoman Christians between privilege, wealth, trade, and Jews was indicative by widespread popular belief that the inhabitants of Chios, a particularly privileged and prosperous island, were not Greeks but Jews.[50] The identification of Jews with the Ottoman State and Ottoman authorities was reinforced by the use of Jews and other minorities for unpleasant tasks which tended to generate hostility among the Christian population as the following account indicates:

> The Turks did not condescend to slaughter the Christian Greeks. They assigned this task to the Jews. A tall Jew executed the command of the bloodthirsty authority. I saw with my own eyes this Jew having the blade ready and the naked victim waiting, on his knees and tightly tied up, to lose his head.[51]

Although the validity of such accounts, or at least their frequency, is debatable, the imagery certainly played well with the rhetoric of people like Kosmas and fermented an atmosphere of antagonism between Christians and Jews.

Despite the strong religious roots of this "movement," the Greek Orthodox Church recognized and supported Ottoman rule until the very eruption of the Greek War of Independence in 1821 and beyond. The church loyally denounced and excommunicated every revolt and circulated letters urging its flock to remain loyal to the sultan.[52] The most famous of such proclamation was the one issued under the name of Anthimos patriarch of Jerusalem. It defended Ottoman rule as designed by God to protect Orthodox Christianity from Satan's agents represented by the Catholic Church and later the Enlightenment, and urged faithful Christians to eschew any revolutionary activity or corrupting ideas stemming from Europe and remain steadfastly loyal to the sultan as their God-appointed legitimate ruler.[53] The proclamation, titled "Paternal Instruction," was issued at a moment of crisis, while the French Revolution was raging. It was part of a broader effort by the church to diffuse any potential revolutionary activity and included the dispatch of prominent churchmen in Ottoman Greece to ensure the loyalty of the population to the sultan.[54]

Kosmas and others like him played a significant role in the process of what is often referred to as the "national revival" of Greece. Even after his death, Kosmas continued to be an influential voice, and a cult evolved around his person leading to his canonization by the Greek Orthodox Church in 1961. More importantly, his message of the exploited and abused Christian *reya* was well received among the Christian peasantry and his death merely reaffirmed the oppression inflicted by the Ottomans on the Christians as well as the hostility and duplicity of Jews. His sectarian message also helped forge a common cause for what would today be considered separate ethnic and social groups. Thus the Souliottes and many of the *Klefts* who were of ethnic Albanian origin found common cause with Greek and Vlach peasants, despite the frequent abuses of the former over the latter, and came to identify themselves as "Greek" in bitter opposition to the Muslim Greeks and Albanians with whom they shared a language and customs but not religion. Christian merchants, notables, warlords, and peasants found Kosmas' message appealing and a common ground despite their diverging interests.

This early anti-Ottoman and anti-Muslim current was exploited in the eighteenth century by Russia in its struggle with the Ottoman Empire. Under Catherine the Great Russian agents cultivated the hopes of the Orthodox populations in the Ottoman Empire that Russia, as the only independent Orthodox state in Europe, would expel the Ottomans and all Muslims from the territories that had belonged to the Byzantine Empire, restoring the former glory of Orthodoxy. Ottoman Christians were captivated by the vision of Russian armies sweeping the Ottomans from the Balkans and they rose in rebellion in 1770 when a Russian squadron arrived in the Aegean to foster unrest in the Ottoman provinces as part of a wider war between the Russian and Ottoman Empires. The revolt, which was centered around the Peloponnese (Morea) and Crete, was a complete failure and the local populations suffered greatly from irregular Albanian troops dispatched by the Ottoman government to suppress it.[55] However, after the otherwise successful for the Russians conflict, the Ottomans were forced to accept the humiliating treaty of Küçük Kaynarca that gave the Russian Empire the right to interfere in the internal affairs of the Ottoman state in defense of the interests and rights of the Orthodox population in the Ottoman Empire, a right it would often use and abuse.

Enlightenment, revolution, and a different kind of nationalism

The second pole of early Greek nationalism developed among the educated elites with ties to Europe and used different language and imagery. The main figures of this group were strongly influenced by the Enlightenment as well as by the ideas, rhetoric, and proclamations of the French Revolution and hoped to duplicate much of what that revolution had achieved in the context of the Ottoman Empire. They were also the heirs to a long tradition of intellectuals associated simultaneously with Western ideas and the Orthodox Church who had already engaged crucial questions regarding Greek language, identity, and education.[56] Although it is hard to consider these members of the "Greek Enlightenment" in nationalist terms, they are important for our purposes because they too promoted a "Hellenic" identity that excluded non-Christians. They also were the teachers and patrons of the next generation that would usher what an older, nationalist, historiography referred to as the "national awakening." From the seventeenth century onwards these men also produced tracts overtly or covertly attacking Jews. It is of note that the very first book published by the short-lived printing press in Constantinople, which was set up by the reformist Patriarch Kyrillos Loukaris, was the *Short Essay Against the Jews* written by the priest Nikodimos Metaxas in 1627.[57] More significant was the book by the powerful Grand Dragoman Alexandros Mavrokordatos, who penned a history of the Jews focusing on antiquity but used to surreptitiously target contemporary Jews in the Ottoman Empire.[58]

From the generation that lived through the American and French Revolutions, some had strong ties to the Phanariot "aristocracy" and the intellectual circles that developed around them, but although many were employed in the extended Phanariot households, they rarely held significant positions. Many had lived and often were educated outside of the Ottoman Empire, and others spent most of their lives in Europe, where it was safer to publish highly critical tracts against the Ottoman government or the Orthodox Church, though many did so anonymously especially in the antirevolutionary fervor following the Congress of Vienna. Rigas Phereos, or Velestinlis, stands out among this group both for his great influence over many of the later Greek revolutionaries and because he expressed an early program for the overthrow of Ottoman rule and the reconstruction of the Balkans along republican lines, and even attempted to establish a revolutionary organization. Rigas' writings were rooted in Enlightenment thought and heavily influenced by the early proclamations of the French Revolution especially the "Declaration of the Rights of Man and the Citizen." His own political writings borrowed heavily from that document especially his own "Rights of Humans"[59] and his "Political Constitution."

Like Kosmas, Rigas saw the Ottoman Empire in the Balkans as being composed of two main groups, the subjugated and abused Christians and the ruling Muslims, or Turks as he and many contemporaries called them. Unlike Kosmas, however, Rigas had a very specific political agenda and aimed to create a state that would embrace all races and religions under a regime of equality and justice. Although he believed in a "Hellenic" revival and the overthrow of the Muslim overlords, the new state would abide by his "Rights of Humans," which stipulated that "all the people, Christians and Turks, are by nature equal."[60] The concept of equality regardless of religion is peppered throughout Rigas' text from the first paragraph of his introduction to several later articles,[61] with a focus on the equality of Christians and Muslims but with only an offhand mention of Judaism when discussing the right of freedom of religion in Article 7, which affirmed an earlier statement in his "Revolutionary Proclamation" and again in his "Constitution."[62] Significantly when discussing the qualifications for citizenship to his model state Rigas made no distinctions based on religion, race, or ethnicity, but accorded special consideration to the knowledge of the Greek language for those born outside the state.[63] In essence Rigas was proposing the establishment of a multiethnic and multireligious Hellenic Balkan federation where Christians and Muslims, Greeks, Bulgarians, Serbs, and Vlachs would live as equals, in a democratic and liberal Ottoman state.[64] Greek would serve as the official state language as it had for the Orthodox Church during the Ottoman and late Byzantine periods.

Rigas' understanding of Ottoman society was not, however, only a sectarian one. He was primarily concerned with the abused Christian peasant and was thus quite willing to exclude the privileged high clergy and even the Christian notables from his oppressed group. Jews, being almost exclusively urban, were also de facto excluded from the oppressed, though not specifically mentioned. The idealist Rigas would never advocate the vicious language used by Kosmas nor would he consider Jews necessarily as enemies of all Christians. Nevertheless, while his poems meant to unite the oppressed people talk of "Bulgarians and Albanians, Serbs and Romans,"[65] and even referred to the oppression felt by "Christians and Turks,"[66] Jews were conspicuously absent. In his "Constitution" he specifically mentioned Greeks (Hellenes), Albanians, Vlachs, Armenians, and Turks as belonging to the "people" without distinctions based on religion or "dialect" but Jews were simply included to "and of all other kind of nations (*geneas*)."[67] Even Armenians, whose numbers were very small in the Balkans outside Istanbul, get separate references but not Jews, at least not in most surviving manuscripts.[68] Rigas probably shared the concept of Jews as a privileged group in Ottoman society and thus irrelevant, if not hostile, to his quest for a national and social awakening. Although his constitution, following the example of the revolutionary French, would accord them equal rights, Jews were not considered among those that would bring the new society about through a mass uprising. Despite his strong anti-ecclesiastical message and more nuanced social understanding of Ottoman society, Rigas created two sectarian groups locked in opposition to each other in which Jews were assigned to the hegemonic Muslim one, just as Kosmas had done.

This common ground between the thought of Kosmas and that of Rigas is more evident in the writing of a Rigas admirer who composed one of the first clearly articulated nationalist documents in modern Greek history, the "Ellenike Nomarchia" (Hellenic Rule of Law), under the pseudonym *Anonymou tou Ellenos* (the Anonymous Hellene). The anonymous author fiercely attacked the church as the great accomplice of Ottoman tyranny, and the bishop of Janina was particularly singled out for condemnation because he had excommunicated Kosmas. The author was a dedicated follower of Enlightenment ideas, and strongly believed in equality, the rule of law, and liberty, but he still could not avoid referring to the role of religion. The author claimed that the "people" (the Christian Greeks) suffered most in Salonica and Larisa compared to any other place in Greece "since almost every day two and three Christians are murdered."[69] Although he does not mention Jews explicitly, the choice of two of the most heavily Jewish cities as an example of oppression was indicative of his attitude, particularly if one considers Leake's statement about Larisa as noted above. In addition, he claimed that "the Jewish religion makes people misanthropic (*misanthropoi*),"[70] Islam makes people into automatons, while only Christianity makes them compassionate, hospitable, and likeable.[71] Thus, although the "Greek-Turkish" conflict was presented as one between tyranny and liberty, the underlying foundation was once again formulated on religious affiliation.

The most prolific and influential representative of the pre-independence intellectuals of Greece was Adamantios Korais, a scholar living in Paris and far removed from revolutionary activities in Greece. Unlike Rigas, Korais did not consider an immediate uprising to overthrow the sultan as a feasible option. Yet, he was probably the most fully developed "Greek" nationalist of his time in the sense that his understanding of the Greek nation was recognizably similar to modern Greek conceptualizations of the nation. Korais believed that the cultural state of Greeks was so far behind the great European nations that a process of rejuvenation through education and learning was required before any credible effort to establish an independent state was attempted. Although earlier authors of the Greek Enlightenment such as Athanasios Psalidas, Benjamin Lesvios, and some of his contemporaries like Grigorios Konstantas and Daniel Philippidis had expressed similar ideas of the need to "purify" the nation and link it to the glories of antiquity,[72] Korais was able to expose such developments in modern Greek thought to the rest of Europe through his participation in French intellectual circles and with his publications, most famously his "Report on the Present State of Civilization in Greece" in which he made an appeal to Europe to aid the enslaved Greece while attacking the conditions prevailing there including the ignorance of the Orthodox clergy.[73] Korais saw the Orthodox Church as a great impediment and penned a response to the "Paternal Instruction" of Anthimos titled "Brotherly Instruction" in which he defended the ideas of liberty as developed through the Enlightenment in Europe. The church was incensed and condemned and burned his essay.[74]

Before Rigas' plans could even begin to be implemented, he was captured by the Austrians in 1798 and extradited to the Ottoman authorities in Belgrade where he was executed for conspiring against the sultan. His ideas, however, lived on and inspired the creation of a secret organization, the *Philike Etaireia* (Society of Friends), which orchestrated the Greek revolt of 1821 that would eventually lead to the creation of the modern Greek state. The membership of the society covered nearly all sections of the Christian population of Greece, from bishops and scholars, to *Klefts*, notables, merchants, sailors, and peasants. The society deliberately appealed to all Balkan Christians and thus members were not exclusively Greek but included some Christian Albanians, Bulgarians, and Serbs, but significantly no Jews or Muslims.[75] The very oath of the participants limited the conspirators to those of the Christian faith. It extolled the members to:

> Do battle for your faith and country, hate, persecute and exterminate the enemies
> of the religion of the Nation and of your country.[76]

Although a later part of the oath included a short promise by the members to keep their faith without disrespecting other religions,[77] it is clear from the oath that neither Muslims nor Jews were conceived as possible members of the "Nation," the latter being understood solely on religious terms.

By the spring of 1821, the organization had grown to such an extent that its secrecy was threatened. The conflict of the Ottoman government with one of its most powerful pashas, Ali Pasha of Janina, provided an excellent opportunity to launch a revolt that was originally planned to take place throughout the Balkans, from Moldavia and Wallachia to the Peloponnese and Crete in southern Greece. The leadership of the *Philike Etaireia* under Alexander Ypsilantis who had lost an arm in the Napoleonic wars serving in the Russian army, was under no illusion that they could defeat the Ottoman forces on their own. The Serb revolts fifteen years earlier had shown that the Ottoman state was quite capable of suppressing internal dissent when not faced with external threats at the same time. However, the revolutionaries were hoping that Europe, and Russia in particular, would intervene on their behalf.

The Greek War of Independence

Alexander Ypsilantis crossed into the Danubian principalities and started a war that would last for almost a decade. His Revolutionary Proclamation of February 24, 1821, made it clear that unlike Rigas, he considered this conflict a "Greek" one. His text was filled with references to "Hellenes" and allusions to ancient Greek figures like Miltiades, Themistocles, Timoleon, Epameinondas, Thrasyvoulos, Armodios, and Aristogeiton, who had fought against the Persians at the battles of Marathon, Salamis, and Thermopylae, or who had overthrown tyrannies in Athens, Corinth, and Syracuse.[78] Although he made a short appeal to "friends and allies" like the Serbs and Souliotes, his proclamation was clearly aimed at "Greeks" even though it was published in what is today Romania. The audience of course was not the peasants who would not have recognized any of the references Ypsilantis used. The proclamation was meant for Europe whose assistance was explicitly solicited and it was written in a manner that was familiar to a public that had just emerged from the maelstrom of the French Revolution and the Napoleonic wars, and had been exposed to the writings of Korais but also those of Byron like *Childe Harolde's Pilgrimage* and *The Giaur* that presented Greece as a helpless woman abused by "Turks," images that would be continuously reproduced during the struggle by such iconic figures as Victor Hugo in his *Les Orientales*.[79] From the opening sentence with the exhortation "Fight for Faith and Fatherland!" to references of liberty, patriotism, despotism, tyranny, oppression, but significantly not of revolution, Ypsilantis' proclamation aimed to convince Europe to intervene on behalf of the Christian Greeks and end Ottoman rule in Europe.[80] Similar sentiments were reflected in other early proclamations. "The Revolutionary Directory of Patras," for example, in its announcement of the revolt, begun by identifying itself as "We, the Hellenic nation of Christians" who sought its freedom from the "Ottoman race (*genos*)," and appealed to the "Christian Kingdoms" for aid.[81]

Unfortunately for the rebels the Mediterranean was already in the grip of revolution with uprisings in Italy and Spain, that had forced the Great Powers to call a conference in Verona to coordinate a muscular response to these threats. The Greek revolt, therefore, was received within a climate of political agitation and Greek efforts to portray it in nationalist and religious terms were dismissed by the reactionary European governments under the direction of the Austrian chancellor Count Metternich. Thus the sought-after support from Europe and Russia failed to materialize, although the

European monarchies did not offer the Ottoman sultan active military aid as they did in the Italian and Spanish cases. Even without outside help, however, the Ottoman forces were able to deal with rebellion in the principalities and most of the Balkans. Only in southern Greece were the rebels able to establish a precarious foothold and endure despite Ottoman efforts to extinguish it. Nevertheless, if European governments did not come to the aid of the Greek cause, individual Europeans did. Philhellenism, as support for Greece was called, was for many an expression of opposition to the restored order of the Congress of Vienna while for others it became a celebrated cause that allowed the Romantic ideals of the time to be expressed in the arts, through economic support, and even through joining the war in Greece.[82] For others classical education and an admiration of antiquity and even religious sensibilities were determining factors in supporting the Greeks even when they held conservative political beliefs as expressed by Chateaubriand.[83]

The Greek War of Independence was thus concentrated in the areas where many of the Romaniote Jews lived, in southern and western Greece. As I mentioned, Jews lived primarily in the towns of the region as did many Muslims.[84] In cities like Navpaktos Jews could compose as much as 38 percent of the population with a similar number of Muslims, while half of Patras' population may have been non-Christian (33 percent Muslims and 17 percent Jewish).[85] In some towns like Athens, Muslims and Christians could coexist peacefully, while in other areas like Euboea there could be tensions.[86] Muslims could also be found in the countryside having their own villages in places like Lalla, Bardunia, or Karystos.[87] Despite a shared language with their Christian neighbors, however, Jews and Muslims became targets for the fury of the rebels who made no distinction between Muslims and Jews. Contemporaries were clear about the sectarian nature of the conflict throughout the war, the president of the 3rd National Assembly stating on the record on May 5, 1827:

> We fight the enemies of our Lord and we do not want any communion with them. . . . Our war is not offensive but defensive, it is a war of justice against injustice, [it is a war] of the Christian Religion against the Koran, of the being of reason against the irrational and beastly tyrant.[88]

The Greek War of Independence was in many respects a genocidal conflict or, as Finlay put it at the time, "a war of extermination," a sentiment echoed by John Comstock and others.[89] Contemporary Ottomans like Mir Yusuf el-Moravi also noted the "hatred of the Rum" toward Muslims, and felt that the "Greeks" had betrayed the prior peaceful relations that the Ottomans had allowed to exist.[90] The Ottoman feeling of betrayal by a privileged group resulted in the dismissal, and sometimes executions, of prominent Greeks in Ottoman service like the Grand Dragoman or the patriarch of Constantinople, the dismissal of all Greek sailors from the Ottoman fleet, and their replacement by Muslims.[91] Massacres of the Muslim population begun from the first days of the revolt in Moldavia and Wallachia, which in turn sparked massacres of Christians in many cities of the Ottoman Empire.[92]

The worst atrocities against Jews and Muslims took place in the areas where the Christian revolutionaries were most successful, in southern Greece and the

Peloponnese (Morea). On numerous occasions, even after the negotiated surrender of towns the Muslim population was massacred as was the case in Kalavryta, Kalamata, Gastouni, Pyrgos, Salona, Laconia, Livadia, Athens, Vrachori, Zapandou, Navarino, Acrocorinth, Stellida, and Tripolitza (Tripolis).[93] On many of these occasions, women and children were spared but only to be used as menial servants or "slaves" in the houses of Christians.[94] I will discuss the ramifications of conversion in the following chapter but it is important to note that many of these captives were also forcibly converted to Christianity and possibly the same happened to Jewish survivors.[95] On at least one occasion the Jews captured on a ship from Jaffa were not killed outright but were taken to the island of Kasos and forced to convert, remaining on the island until 1824, when Egyptian forces destroyed the island and freed them, enslaving in turn the Christian inhabitants.[96]

Massacres by the Christians rebels were answered by massacres of Christians in the areas firmly under Ottoman control such as Istanbul, Patras, Smyrna (Izmir), Adrianople (Edirne), Naousa, Salonica, Kos, Rhodes, Cyprus, Crete, Euboea, Pergamus, Kydonies (Ayvalik), and numerous other towns and regions of Asia Minor,[97] and particularly in areas recaptured by the Ottomans such as Chios, Psara, Kasos, and parts of the Peloponnese.[98] Thousands were killed and thousands of women and children were sold into slavery from Algiers to Trebizond.[99] Numerous atrocities including torture were perpetrated by both sides even against women, as in an infamous occasion during the siege of Tripolis that earned the Christian besiegers a reputation for cannibalism among the Ottoman defenders of the town, or in the case of the torture of the wives of the Greek chieftains Zaphiraki, Karatasos, and Gatsos, who were captured by Ottoman forces.[100] As Finlay put it:

> The Greeks entertained the project of exterminating the Mussulmans in European Turkey; the sultan and the Turks believed they could paralyze the movements of the Greeks by terrific cruelty. Both parties were partially successful.[101]

The Greek War of Independence would lead to the establishment of the Greek national state but it was a sectarian conflict pitting the Muslim population, often Greek, Albanian, and Slavic speaking,[102] against Orthodox Christian insurgents who in addition to Greek included Albanian, Vlach, and Slavic speakers.[103] Often religion was the only distinguishable element between the combatants who otherwise shared culture, language, and even dress with each other. Other sectarian groups found themselves in a precarious position. For example, the significant Catholic minority of the Aegean islands was not particularly keen to join the rebellion against the Ottomans and tried to stay neutral under French protection as I will discuss further below.

Acts of brutality by one side were used as justification for similar acts from the other and Jews were an integral part of the conflict sharing the fate of the Muslims as in the incident described by Alexander Kriezis, a leader of the revolution:

> I called my warlords to the ship, and told them that I would not help them anymore, unless they run to the fields after the Turks, since the enemy always come to us [from there], and so they started, once, twice, and many times, and

got used to it [fighting] and went to the fields, and set ambushes during the night, and one day, while they were in ambush, caught eleven Turks and a Jew alive; they caught them in the vineyards where they gathered *atsachia* [hay?] and other foodstuffs. . . . I recounted the impaling of Koukouvakos [a Greek soldier killed by the Ottomans] and that I wanted to avenge his blood with the eleven Turks and the Jew; . . . we had them strung from the armpits and immediately with three pulls [of the rope] we raised them; they began to shout Allah! Allah! except for the Jew, [and] plunging them in the sea, raising them and plunging them, we left them to hang.[104]

Especially during the first year of the Revolution, Greek sailors of the Revolutionary fleet habitually murdered Jews, along with Muslims, found in the ships that they captured.[105] The most brutal atrocities, however, occurred during the capture of cities with important Jewish communities like Tripolitsa.[106] The viciousness of the massacre of Tripolitsa, where a Greek man from the island of Hydra is said to have killed 90 "Turks" during that day,[107] was described by William Martin Leake:

For two days the town was given up to those horrors formerly common under such circumstances, . . . suffice it to say, that every kind of excess which wanton indulgence in cruelty and a thirst of plunder could suggest, was inflicted on the Turkish and Jewish inhabitants of this unhappy place; and that, when victims failed within the walls the Greeks proceeded to put to death a large body of defenseless inhabitants, who, having been allowed to remove from the town in consequence of the famine, still remained in the vicinity.[108]

Similar descriptions can be found in the memoirs of Greek Revolutionary leaders but in those the emphasis was on the massacres of the Muslim population and many like Konstantinos Koumas did not even mention the presence of Jews indicating how closely linked Jews and Muslims were in the eyes of the Christian insurgents.[109] When they did, it was frequently followed by the justifications for such massacres as in the example below, from the memoirs of the revolutionary leader Fotakos:

The Jews of Tripolitsa perished along with the Turks, and were killed with greater hostility, because the Greeks despised this Nation from ancestral tradition for the crucifixion of Jesus Christ and for their more recent insults to the Greeks in Constantinople, especially for the mockery of the body of the hanged Patriarch Gregory, and for other things that they did. In Koroni they committed ten thousand evils to the head priest of that place and his assistant, and after they killed them both, they threw the dead bodies outside the fortress from the top of the wall and with great contempt and mockery said to the besieging Greeks to take this meat if they have any need. In Navplion again, the local Jews, as I will recount later, harshly tortured the officer Anagnosti Kelperi who had been wounded and captured by the Turks. These are the Jews, incompatible with the Christians. Yet, despite all this, they did not harm the family of Hanam, a wealthy Jew, good and kind, but took them out of the city [Tripolitsa] the day before the attack through the intervention of Anagnosti Zafeiropoulou, friend of Kolokotronis, and in this action I too contributed. Kolokotronis also saved another Jew called Levi, also a wealthy and good person, after the attack.[110]

The Jews [of Navplion] in order to show to the Turks that they share their rage against the Greeks, dragged him [the captured Greek officer Kelperis] through the streets of the city and while he lived committed ten thousand tortures, mockeries and insults, and some of them even chewed [on] his ears, as if driven by an uncontrollable desire to please the Turks. After Kelperis died, they threw him in the sea.[111]

Fotakos repeated these claims in some of his other works,[112] while even more scholarly accounts as such by the contemporary historian Spyridon Trikoupis repeated the same justifications for the massacres of the Jews:

In addition, the Jews of Tripolitsa, because of the bad behavior of their coreligionists in Constantinople and elsewhere, were all destroyed, some by iron, others by fire, apart from those around Hane, known for his goodness . . . ten thousand Ottomans, Ottoman women, and Jews, of all ages, were lost.[113]

The stories of the Jewish perfidy go back to pre-Revolutionary times as in the case of Kosmas the Aitolos or the even earlier Dionysios Skylosofos, with frequent mentions of the role of Jews in the executions of Christians,[114] but were amplified by more recent events. Perhaps the one that caused the most anger among Christians was the execution of the patriarch of Constantinople Gregory V.[115] The order for his execution was given by the Ottoman Grand Vizier, but the story that circulated gave a prominent role to the Jews of Constantinople to whom his body was allegedly handed over and who proceeded to dump it in the sea.[116]

Three days the body was left hanging; on the fourth day the executioner took it down to throw it into the sea, since those executed by hanging or beheading at the orders of the Authority do not deserve burial. Then Jews came to the executioner, and with his permission and after bribing him, tied the legs of the body, dragged it from the Patriarchate to the coast of Fanar mocking and swearing, and threw it into the sea.[117]

The loyalty of Jews to the Ottoman authorities and hatred between Jews and Greeks were widely accepted even in foreign accounts,[118] and many more stories evolved around Jewish attitudes during the massacres of Christians in Istanbul, and Asia Minor, their loyalty to the Ottoman sultan and opposition to the Greek cause, or the behavior of Jews in Greek cities still in Ottoman hands like Navplion or Koroni.[119] Jews were reported "joyfully" watching the dumping of the bodies of the beheaded Christians after the massacre of Chios[120] or mocking, alongside Muslims, the persecuted Christians at Andrianople.[121] Jews were also widely reported to be implicated in the sale of Christians captured by the Ottomans from Patras, to Salonica, and Smyrna.[122] Furthermore, many accounts presented the Jewish population as fully engaged in the conflict as co-combatants of the Ottomans and torturers of Christians, especially in the suppression of the revolt in Macedonia.[123]

> The Israelites, as they were also implicated in the slaughters against the Christians, judging with good reason that there was no hope of salvation if the Greeks conquered the city [Salonica], offered their aid [to the Ottomans] which the commander accepted. And for the first time since the destruction of Jerusalem, Jews appeared in military guise. The nation without hearth or king united with the armies of Islam under the flag of Mohammed! Everything in this war was exceptional, and thus the nether forces allied against the Cross; the names Cain and Ahmet, Judas and Mustafa, Barouch and Idris, merged, as the ancient dislike of the circumcised nations; and the followers of Mohammed and of Moses prepared against the children of Jesus Christ. . . . The Turks, masters already of the field of battle, begun, followed by a flock of Jews, to collect heads, with whom they hurried to glorify their victorious entry in Thessaloniki. . . . Many Jews bought children [after the suppression of the revolution in Chalkidiki], some of whom they turned into Jews, while others. . . . I do not dare finish the sentence, while the moneylenders bought young Greek girls, whom they sent for sale to Smyrna, from where they were taken to Bengazi in the bay of Sidra in Africa which is inhabited by settlers descending from Macedonia.[124]

> [In Naoussa] A multitude of men, women, and children were slaughtered in front of his tent [pasha Adulubud who led the army that sacked the city] such was the number of the victims according to the indisputable evidence of an eyewitness from whom I received this information that 'I heard' he says 'some time after these massacres a Jew boasting that he beheaded in a single day sixty-four Christians!' This monster composed with similar men a body of six hundred executioners imbued with such horrible zeal that I rely on the judgement of the reader to calculate the number of murders that took place.[125]

> In order to satisfy the barbarous desires of his [Adulubud's] military mob addicted to slaughters, he extensively used the zeal of the Jews in his camp. . . . The hostages, whom the monks of Mt. Athos, had delivered to Adulubud pasha also died in agony from the beatings even though the Jews who tortured them tried with zeal to prolong [the suffering].[126]

> "Numerous Jews, armed and very thirsty for Christian blood, followed the Turkish army as voluntary executioners. Dragging the Christians outside the city [Naoussa] the Christians, they smashed their heads with clubs and as they fell to the ground, slaughtered them like oxen."[127]

The mobs in Salonica that pillaged Christian neighborhoods and killed some 3,000 Christians were invariably described as composed of Muslims and Jews, some historians even claiming that Catholic Levantines and Roma offered their support to the Ottomans.[128] The cause, according to some later historians, was the economic competition between the two groups, the war giving an opportunity to Jews to eliminate a dangerous rival in Salonica, Naousa, and elsewhere.[129]

Such stories, regardless of their veracity, placed Jews firmly within the enemy camp alongside the Muslim communities of the region who were equally devastated. However, while the Greek leadership of the revolution had reasons to limit the brutality of their soldiers against the Muslim communities, and especially their most prominent members who might serve as hostages for exchange with Greek prisoners and whose coreligionists might exact vengeance on Greek communities elsewhere, such considerations did not apply to Jews.[130] Once again Tripolitsa is a good example where prior to the capture of the city Greek and Albanian warlords reached an agreement to allow 2,000–4,000 Albanian Muslim soldiers to leave the town with their weapons, but when a Jewish leader attempted to negotiate on behalf of the Jews of the city for their safe passage, he was stripped of his gilded weapons by Kolokotronis, the most influential Greek commander, who considered it improper for a Jew to be armed and his offers were rejected.[131] Although the capture of the city degenerated into a chaotic massacre, local Muslims sought the aid of their former neighbors and regional allies, and many of the prominent ones survived as did nearly all the Albanians, but Jews were massacred almost in their entirety.[132] Few commanders bothered to contain the excesses of the Greek soldiers with regard to Jews whose communities were wiped out over the course of the war.[133] In some cases while some of the Muslims were spared, all Jews were massacred as in the case of Vrachori (or Vlochochori or Evraiochori, the latter meaning "village of Jews"[134]) modern-day Agrinion where the Muslim and Jewish inhabitants surrendered to the insurgents under negotiated terms. Some accounts claimed the Muslim population remained unharmed but "the Jews suffered the worst and most were killed without pity on the pretense that their coreligionists had dragged through the city of Constantinople the body of the Patriarch and denounced the hidden Christians."[135]

Later historians, including Jewish historians, downplayed the violence between Jews and Christians[136] and some have claimed that unlike the Sephardim, Romaniote Jews were sympathetic to the revolt and that some even actively participated on the Greek side as for instance the Crispi and Cohen families from Chalkis or a Jewish doctor in Macedonia.[137] Although some liberal European Jews were clearly in sympathy with the Greek cause which they perceived in terms of a struggle against despotism and tyranny,[138] as was also the case with the Polish revolt of 1830 which was also marked by anti-Jewish violence,[139] I have been unable to find in the revolutionary accounts any mention of local Jews fighting with the Greeks during the War of Independence. Furthermore, none of the accounts make any distinction between Greek- and Ladino-speaking Jews. Therefore, it is safe to assert that for the Christian rebels who fought against the Ottoman state, Jews were an enemy to be ruthlessly pursued as intently as the Muslims of the region.

We should not, however, automatically assume that the genocidal destruction of the Jewish communities of Greece was conducted under a master plan. On numerous occasions, the leaders of the revolt tried to limit the massacres, as did Dimitrios Ypsilantis for example.[140] On several occasions, surrenders were negotiated but the ability of commanders to enforce such agreements was limited as seen in the case of Monemvasia, where a quarter of the Muslim prisoners were not transported to Asia Minor as the terms dictated, and in turn sparked violent retribution by local Muslims on the Christians of Kisadasi. The same happened to the agreement in Navarino.[141] Furthermore, although the Greek "nation" was clearly understood in sectarian terms, there was an evolution in the terms in which citizenship was envisioned that, while not abandoning the strong religious associations evident throughout Europe, moved quite rapidly toward an understanding of citizenship that allowed non-Orthodox and even non-Christians to be conceived as Greek citizens even if they could not be considered members of the Greek nation.

The conclusion of the Greek War of Independence

By 1827, the Greek revolt was in its last gasps. The intervention of Muhammad Ali the pasha of Egypt and Ottoman vassal had resulted in a series of defeats for the rebels, the recapture of Crete, and most of southern Greece, and a renewed wave of atrocities at Kasos and Mesologi when thousands of captured women and children were sent to the slave markets of Egypt and North Africa. If the revolt faced its worst defeats in the battlefields, however, it managed to achieve a tremendous political success by internationalizing the conflict. Although both sides committed atrocities, and foreign consuls reported the massacres of Jews and Muslims by the insurgents,[142] the Ottoman massacres gained far more publicity and shocked Europe, partly because Ottoman commanders often boasted of their "exploits" and partly because foreign consuls, who were often ethnic Greeks, portrayed Greeks in a more positive light.[143] After six years of neutrality Britain, Russia, and France, under pressure from their philhellenic movements, were finally willing to break ranks with the Austrians and Prussians and apply pressure to the Ottomans to resolve the conflict.[144] They demanded a ceasefire and a negotiated settlement which the Greeks were quite willing to accept being on the verge of defeat. The Ottomans on the other hand had no reason to accept and the three Great Powers dispatched a fleet composed of a naval squadron from each state to apply pressure on the Ottomans. On October 20, 1827, the combined European fleet annihilated the Ottoman-Egyptian one and brought the three Great Powers into the conflict. A Russian army invaded the Ottoman Empire while a French expeditionary force was dispatched to expel the Egyptians from southern Greece. Faced with imminent disaster the Ottoman sultan was forced to admit defeat and let the fate of Greece in the hands of the European powers.

That same year, in 1827, while facing disaster on the battlefield, the Greek leadership finally decided to entrust the fate of the revolt to the hands of an experienced diplomat, electing Ioannis Kapodistrias, a Greek from Kerkyra and a former Russian foreign minister, as governor of Greece. Kapodistrias would lead Greece until his assassination on October 9, 1831, all the while attempting to sway the European governments to allocate as much territory as possible to Greece and to recognize Greece as an independent rather than simply autonomous state, as the early Treaty of London of 1827 envisioned.[145] Yet for the most part Greeks were relegated to the role of spectators over their fate. Their republican aspirations, expressed in three increasingly more progressive republican constitutions,[146] were utterly ignored and the three European powers decided that Greece was to be an independent kingdom under an absolute monarch. Although the three Powers had apparently broken ranks from Prussia and Austria by supporting a revolution against a legitimate monarch, none was willing to completely abandon the Concert of Europe established by the Congress of Vienna to contain the revolutionary movements of Europe. Greece was an aberration because a Christian people, and one with a classical pedigree no less, was subject to a Muslim ruler and thus the Great Powers could plausibly present their intervention in humanitarian and religious terms. By insisting upon an absolutist regime, it could be argued that their intervention conformed with the antirevolutionary principles of the Concert of Europe. Since Greece lacked a nobility the monarch was chosen from among the various royal houses of Europe the representatives of France, Britain, and Russia eventually settling on Otto of Wittlesbach, the second son of King Leopold of Bavaria. Because young Otto was still underage a Bavarian regency was selected to build the structures of the new state and to run his new kingdom until his maturity.

The three Great Powers were not blind to the task the young king and his regents would face. Not only was Greece utterly devastated after six years of brutal warfare, it was also bankrupt having defaulted in 1827 on two loans contracted a few years earlier in London. What little order Kapodistrias had managed to impose collapsed after his assassination. The state lacked any form of institutions, law courts, schools, tax authorities, a regular army, or police. In view of this situation, the three powers agreed in a convention in 1832 to provide a 60,000,000 franc loan that would help establish the necessary institutions, and to guarantee the independence of the nation and the recognition of its government becoming essentially its protective powers.[147] In 1832, the young king and his regents landed in Greece and set about creating a new state out of the debris of the war that had begun a decade earlier.

Citizenship, the state, and the nation

Among the myriad of problems the Greek state faced, the question of national identity would be a particularly difficult one to resolve. Although the rhetoric of the revolution had solidified the acceptance of the word "Hellene" for those who had taken arms against the Ottoman government, the term was used to describe the Albanian-speaking Souliotes and Hydriots, Serbs and Bulgarians, Vlachs, as well Greek speakers. The example of Hatzichristos that Eleonora Naxidou has investigated is indicative of the complexity of this issue. A Serb who had taken service with the Ottomans, he switched sides and joined the cause of Greek independence after he was captured at the siege of Tripolitsa.[148] He distinguished himself in the ensuing campaigns until he was captured again this time by the Egyptian forces of Ibrahim Pasha, and remained in captivity for three years refusing to switch sides again. Upon the establishment of Greece he settled there receiving the honorary title of Adjutant to King Otto and had some minor role in the ensuing political developments of the country. Greek accounts that mention him certainly recognize his ethnic difference though misidentifying his actual origins often call him Voulgaris (Bulgarian).[149] Memoirs from the war are peppered with references to "Bulgarians" who took part in both sides of the conflict, many fighting in their own units, others alongside other Christians.[150] It is significant to note, however, that the notion of the "Other" that Naxidou identifies in the writings of his contemporaries[151] does not extend to the state which recognized Hatzichristos as a national with full civic rights and honors. Nor was he a unique case. As Finlay noted as late as 1866, 200,000 "members of the Albanian race" lived in the Greek state and "even in the streets of Athens, though it has been for more than a quarter of a century the capital of the Greek kingdom, the Albanian language is still heard among the children playing in the streets near the temple of Theseus and the arch of Hadrian."[152]

The earliest documents to attempt to define Greek nationality unambiguously tied it to membership to the Greek Orthodox Church and Christianity.[153] Thus, in the first and second constitutions of Epidaurus in 1821 and Astros in 1823 the concept of Greek citizenship was reserved for Greek Orthodox Christians while Orthodox Christianity was recognized as the official state religion.[154] The 1823 constitution also explicitly forbade any utterance against the Christian religion.[155] On the other hand, the constitutions incorporated the ideas of religious tolerance and equality before the law by proclaiming that all other religions and their ceremonies could be performed without hindrance and that foreigners and Greeks were equal before the law.[156] The third constitution of Troezina in 1827 retained the clauses about state religion, freedom of religion, and the link between citizenship and Christianity, but weakened the latter by making it easier for "foreigners" to gain Greek citizenship. The new constitution removed explicit religious requirements from citizenship and one could even claim that it begun to separate the church and state by excluding lower clergy from public office.[157] Furthermore, the state oath was set in such terms as to make it palatable to Muslims and Jews by referring only to the Almighty.[158] Although the clause imposing respect for Christian principles was retained, the new constitution certainly made it clear that non-Christians could become citizens in the state to be.

The apparent contradictions of these constitutions can be understood through the circumstances and ideology of the people who drafted them. The influence of the French Revolution and the American constitution are clearly discernible throughout these documents, and especially in the final two, but the men who drafted them had the difficult task of trying to establish who should be included as citizen in this new state and who was not. Considering that the borders of the state were yet to be determined, Greece could end up with many people whose allegiance would be to the Ottoman Empire rather than her own, especially when one considers that Muslims and Jews composed more than 10 percent of the prewar population in the region. Not only had the overwhelming majority of Muslims resisted the insurgency, nearly all non-Orthodox Christian groups, including Catholics, had shown a hostile or at best a neutral attitude toward the revolt. Some had taken arms against it, others had fled the area, and some Catholic-dominated islands in the Aegean had declared themselves "neutral" by hoisting the French flag and seeking French protection for the duration of hostilities.[159] They had even continued to voluntarily pay Ottoman taxes, and involuntarily the Greek ones, over the course of the revolt.[160] The Orthodox and Catholic populations had anything but amicable relations even before the revolt as foreign travelers noted,[161] and such was the suspicion of the rebels toward the Catholics who were said to have secret contacts with the Ottomans and to have celebrated Greek defeats that Syros, an entirely Catholic island, was in danger of being sacked by an irregular force of Orthodox Greek soldiers and was only saved through the intervention of French warships, while in Naxos which experienced conflicts between the two communities the Orthodox bishop urged the extermination of the Catholics.[162] The Catholics of Syros were so alarmed that their island could be part of the independent Greek state that they dispatched the following petition to the pope on January 1, 1829:

Holy Father

The undersigned in the name of all the people of the island of Syra, have the honor to humbly submit at the feet of your holiness their wishes and their prayers, that you may deign to intercede on their behalf to the three allied powers.

The Greeks have revolted against their sovereign. Three Christian powers have decided to render independent a portion of the country of Greece, and we learn with the most vivid pain that our island is included in that part.

Holy Father, we have always remained faithful to our sovereign, following the precept of our holy religion; We have not shied from any sacrifice to accomplish this duty, and if it is true that fidelity is not a crime, why must we be counted by force among the rebels and submit to their law? In that case (that God keep that misfortune away from us), we will be forced to abandon our fatherland or change our rite in order to be able to live alongside a people so intolerant. But we lull ourselves with the hope that if the Christian powers have motives to support the Greek revolution, they would not want to constrain a poor people to become infidels against their will.

In the sweet expectation that, with the benevolent intercession of your Holiness, the allied powers will accord us the ability to live peacefully under the laws of our legitimate sovereign, we have the honor to humbly kiss the feet of your Holiness.

Syra 1 January 1829.[163]

The Greek authorities tried to ease the fears of Catholics, which could potentially involve French interference in Greek domestic affairs, by issuing a decree clearly stating that "nationality is not based on religious beliefs but in all those common elements of a nation, in the material and moral interests, which as other bonds hold together the entire nation" and reminded Catholics that even as members of the Latin Church they were "not Italians, nor French, nor Germans, but Hellenes."[164] Nevertheless, with such statements from the religious minorities in Greece on the eve of Greek independence, many Greek leaders believed that only the Orthodox Christian population could be reliable citizens of the state to be.[165] In a preview of things to come Orthodox refugees were settled in Catholic islands like Tinos and Syros that effectively transformed their sectarian character.[166] Language or culture were not good yardsticks in distinguishing between "Greeks" and "non-Greeks" and they could not separate between those who had fought for the revolution from their enemies. Contemporaries recognized a cultural affinity between Albanians and Greeks with regard to customs and stressed the significance of religious divides.[167] Romaniote Jews for instance were Greek speakers as were many Muslims in Greece or islands such as Crete. Many Albanian speakers, on the other hand, such as the Souliotes or the inhabitants of the island of Hydra had been among the most prominent fighters and commanders of the revolution, prompting many non-Albanians to adopt their style of dress, which endures to this day as the uniform of the Greek presidential guard, while Albanian speakers had also formed the bulk of the Ottoman armies that were trying to snuff out the revolt. If language, ethnicity, and culture could not serve as national markers, religion would have to and this led to the incorporation of the constitutional clauses ensuring a primary role for Orthodox Christianity in determining who was Greek and who was not. The obvious targets for exclusion were not necessarily Jews but rather the more numerous and potentially dangerous Muslims, but the result was to create an institutional definition of Greek nationality that could also be used to exclude Jews, among others.

There were of course liberal voices in Greece like Anastasios Polyzoidis, one of the most respected legal minds in the postindependence period. His 1825 treatise on government advocated a democratic parliamentary system of government, based upon full equality of all citizens and the recognition of basic freedoms including the freedom of religion.[168] It is significant that even the most "westernized" Greeks or critics of the Orthodox Church like Georgios Psyllas and Adamantios Korais, saw the utility of restricting full citizenship to the Christian population, at least in the short term.[169] In his commentary to the constitution of 1822 Korais approved of the general clause regarding religious tolerance but then proceeded to dissect the stipulation that only Christians could be "Greeks." He identified that as stated "Turks and Jews" were excluded from political rights "and correctly for the time being, not because they are not Greeks, nor because they do not believe in Christ, but for other reasons."[170] He believed that the article was poorly drafted because "Turks and Jews" who had been born in Greece for "generations and centuries" should have been dealt with in a separate clause. He accepted that Jews and Muslims were Greek by race (*genos*) and if Greeks excluded them from political rights then they would cohabit with two hostile nations (*ethne*) inviting rebellions and foreign interventions. The alternative, to expel them all, was a great injustice perpetrated only once in history, by Spain.[171] But to give them political rights immediately also invited danger because Muslims were accustomed to ruling over Greeks and they needed time to abandon their authoritarianism, while "the hatred of the Jews toward us, though born out of different causes, matches or rather surpasses the Turkish hatred. Their religion, holy and God-given at first, was transformed by their Rabbis in a superstitious religion, with implacable hatred toward all other religions, and especially the Christian, which they see not as the fulfillment but as the dissolution of their own."[172] He continued by saying that their hatred was increased due to the behavior of Christians who excluded them from the means to make a good living, persecuted, expelled, and slaughtered them. Jews hated eastern Christians even more since they had less cause to despise Jews being "co-slaves" under Muslim rule. Korais' conclusion was that to give political rights to Muslims and Jews was to invite strife. Instead he wanted a transitional period where Muslims and Jews would be given protection under the law and would be educated with regard to their rights and duties. This would be done through the Greek educational system so that those who graduated from the new Greek common schools would gain the right to vote, while the third generation would become full citizens.[173]

Korais' beliefs with regard to the desirability of accepting non-Christians as full citizens was not solely an outcome of the conflict or of prejudices among Greeks. Jeremy Bentham echoed Korais when he suggested to the Greek insurgents that if their constitution ensured a Christian majority in their parliament, only then could they allow for Muslim participation in the political life of the country.[174] As we saw at the start of the chapter, Jews were excluded from full civic rights from nearly all European states. Prejudice toward non-Christians was not only evident in the writings of contemporary Greeks but also in those of foreigners with long experience in the East like Pouqueville who referred to Jews as "a hideous race," suggested that Armenians were "used to selling even their own children," and that Turcomans were "strangers to any human emotion."[175] Korais in many ways was far more liberal than his contemporaries in Europe because he envisioned not only Jews but all Muslims as citizens of the Greek state in about two generations.

The physical destruction of non-Christians between 1821 and 1827 diminished the urgency to legally exclude those groups from the national fold, while the increasing reliance for the survival of Greece on foreign philhellenes and after 1827 on European governments tempered the explicit discrimination toward other religions and especially toward non-orthodox Christians. The award of Greek citizenship to those who had actively contributed to the Greek cause was a necessary recognition of the sacrifices so many philhellenes had made, as well as a means to retain individuals with skills the new state sorely needed. The elevation of Otto, a Catholic, to the Greek throne served to further weaken the link between Orthodoxy and citizenship especially since many of the highest members of new royal government of the Greek state were European Catholics and Protestants, including the regents appointed to run the state until the young king reached his maturity. New laws did not simply accept non-Orthodox Christians as naturalized citizens, they also opened Greece to the proselytizing efforts of foreign, particularly American, evangelical missionaries who set up missions and schools in the new kingdom, developing in the process a small Protestant Greek minority.

Although most Muslims and Jews had been killed or fled the Greek-held territories,[176] several fortress towns had never been captured by the Greeks and thus some non-Christians still remained. There was always a possibility that those who had fled would return like Yusuf Bei whom Kapodistrias appointed as a clerk and official translator of Ottoman documents.[177] Despite his acceptance of Yusuf, Kapodistrias was concerned about the possibility of a mass influx of Muslims and believed that a homogenous state was necessary for its survival and thus pushed for the complete separation of Muslims and Christians.[178] Prior to his election as governor, Kapodistrias had defined Greek nationality primarily in religious terms and tried to secure an exchange of populations that would leave Greece entirely homogenous in terms of religion. The first Protocol of Independence of March 1829, and the final Protocol of Independence of February 3, 1830, however, did not grant Kapodistrias his wish and guaranteed Muslims civic rights in the new state though there were provisions for the voluntary immigration of Christians and Muslims and compensation for their properties.[179] Jews were not mentioned but the acceptance of Muslims ensured that Jews would receive the same legal standing.

Despite his failure to force the removal of non-Christians from Greece, Kapodistrias was determined that Greece should honor its commitments and eschew policies that would force Muslims to leave. He instructed officials to give guarantees to the Muslims who expressed a wish to remain in Greece and to make sure they had the protection of the Greek government. Kapodistrias wanted to build the image of Greece as a state governed by the rule of law, while also normalizing relations with the Ottoman Empire.[180] The Ottoman Empire was after all both the closest and largest market for Greece and still had most Greek-speaking Christians as its subjects. It was for this purpose that Kapodistrias pursued a policy of prisoner exchange and the freeing of the women and children that had been captured or enslaved in the war, as well as cooperation with the Ottoman authorities over border security, banditry, extradition of criminals, and the control of Greek armed men who were aiding an Albanian revolt in the Ottoman Empire.[181]

Despite Kapodistrias' efforts the majority of the Muslim population that had survived the war chose to relocate to the Ottoman territories while Greece received thousands of Christian refugees from Crete, Chios, Psara, and other areas that had revolted but had not been assigned to the Greek state, despite the provisions in the treaties and protocols guaranteeing the safety of both. This movement of populations continued for decades up to the end of the reign of King Otto in the 1860s. Furthermore, thousands of Christians, especially women and children, had been enslaved during the war and they had been sold throughout the Balkans, Anatolia, Egypt, and the Levant. The numbers mentioned at the time were certainly exaggerated for effect, for example Pouqueville claimed that only from Chios 40,000 Greek slaves were sold in the market of Smyrna and that the price of a slave had dropped so dramatically that some slaves were killed by their captors to avoid the cost of feeding them,[182] but they certainly numbered in the tens of thousands. In the four years Kapodistrias was governor, the Greek state received over 3,000 requests for assistance in finding or ransoming captives. The Greek state through the assistance of the European powers attempted to create lists, an effort that proved effective mostly for those sold in Egypt. Through the assistance of the British consulate in Alexandria many were freed in 1828 and 1829 though some chose to remain as free residents in Alexandria.[183] For other regions, however, the process took decades. Unless they were important enough to be useful as hostages, or wealthy enough to be ransomed, adult males of all faiths rarely survived capture,[184] but the fate of the Muslim and Jewish women and children that were captured by the Greeks in the early years of the insurrection is a topic that has not been diligently researched.

It is clear from contemporary accounts that women and children were often spared in massacres like Tripolitsa. Fotakos, for example, claimed: "When we conquered Tripolitsan we found in it all sorts of foodstuff even good horses, and mules, and healthy and beautiful women, and young Turkish boys."[185] Many of these captives were taken to work the fields of the Christian notables, to serve in their houses, or even toil in public works,[186] and undoubtedly many were converted to Orthodoxy and as such they appear in various documents in postindependence Greece.[187] The legality of such conversions was suspect even at the time. Greek authorities from the early Peloponnesian Senate to the first national Greek government explicitly forbade the baptizing of prisoners even when the latter requested it, though partly out of suspicion for their motives. The minister for religion suggested in 1822 that it would be appropriate to baptize only Muslim boys under the age of 12 with their parents' approval and all girls and young women with permission by the senate. The debate continued with differing views from the legislative and executive branches in part because of disagreements about the status of these converts, and especially the male ones.[188] Kapodistrias seems to have showed a concern for those unfortunates as much for the enslaved Christians, but it is unknown if later governments showed similar concerns for the converts, although on occasion their presence created friction with the Ottoman authorities as we shall see.[189] Most Jews that survived the massacres probably chose to follow the exodus of the Muslim community relocating to cities with significant Jewish communities like Salonica, Corfu, Istanbul, Syrna, or Jerusalem, except for Chalkis, a city that had never fallen to the hands of the Greek rebels and thus had not experienced the persecution of Jews.[190] Thus the new state was born with a de facto Orthodox Christian foundation as far as its national identity was concerned.

At the same time, however, Greece became among the first modern European states to permanently emancipate Jews. The "monarchical constitution" of 1832 established the "Eastern Orthodox Church" as the "dominant" religion of Greece but also established the right for any individual to practice his or her religion freely and under the protection of the law as long as its "ceremonies were conducted openly and publicly."[191] Hellenes were defined as:

a. Those born in the territory of Greece "who believe in Christ."
b. Those born outside of the territory of Greece but of Greek parents, or of a Greek father and who followed their paternal religion.
c. Those who followed the dominant religion, of the same or different language who assisted Greece and fought with the local Greeks during the Greek War of Independence.
d. Those of the dominant religion who came to Greece a year earlier, had stable domicile in a community, lived by their craft and industry, and who had previously formally renounced the citizenship of another state.
e. Those of other nations believing in Christ who came and fought with the local Greeks for three years in the Greek War of Independence, had proof of their contribution and honest behavior, married a Greek woman or were established in Greece but those required to first abandon formally the citizenship and protection of any other state.
f. Those who from that point onwards became accepted as Greeks per the present laws.

All Greeks were to be registered in a "Racial" (*Phyletikon*) roster while those who attained the right to vote in the local municipalities were also registered in the "Political" roster of their community.[192] Although the provisions above clearly indicate an expectation that a "Greek" would also be a Christian, the last clause opened the possibility to non-Christians to be naturalized as Greek citizens.[193] Furthermore, once one was recognized as a citizen they faced no discrimination based upon their religion or race. The "constitution" stipulated that the heir to the throne had to be an Orthodox Christian[194] but being an Orthodox Christian was not a requirement toward any other post or office. In fact, it was explicitly stated that all citizens were equal before the law, could hold "all public professions, political as well as military," and were liable for military service.[195] Jews and Muslims therefore enjoyed the same rights as all other citizens, a fact that endured throughout the first century of modern Greek history. All professions and offices were open to Jews, who could vote and in theory at least be elected in municipal offices alongside the rest of the population. In the first decades of the new state, such liberties were more or less irrelevant since with the exception of Chalkis no other part of Greece had a significant Jewish community but that situation would change as Greece expanded over the course of the century and incorporated territories with established Jewish communities. Even accepting the official statistics of the new state, the Muslim population of what became Greece had dropped from 63,615 in 1821 to 11,450 in 1828 (no references to Jews) while by 1861 out of 1,096,810 people a mere 552 individuals were not Christians and of the remainder only 9,358 were non-Orthodox.[196] It would be reasonable to accept that most of these 552 people were Jews but their numbers were about to rise substantially with the incorporation of the Ionian islands and Thessaly.

What a Great Idea! National Identity and the Early Greek Kingdom (1830–62)

The Kingdom of the Hellenes

The new state that emerged from the Greek War of Independence was only a fraction of the state the rebels had envisioned and did not even contain all the territories that participated in the insurrection. The border was drawn by the Great Powers who dismissed ethnic and cultural considerations when making their allocations, assigning significant Albanian-speaking areas to the new kingdom while denying it Greek-speaking ones as contemporaries noted.[1] The Greeks were excluded from the deliberations carried out by the Great Powers and therefore had no input with respect to the future of their new state. Further, a Bavarian regency was imposed on Greece until the underage King Otto could assume direct governance as an absolute monarch, and the regency set about creating the institutions of the new kingdom. Although Kapodistrias had made an effort toward building the necessary institutions of a modern state, the anarchy following his assassination destroyed much of what he achieved and thus the regency had to start almost from scratch.

The Bavarian regency has a very poor image in Greek historiography but its achievements were in many respects quite remarkable. Within a few years, the regency created functioning systems of bureaucracy, law, education, and municipal government, that closely resembled those of Western Europe.[2] Furthermore, despite the authoritarian character of Kapodistrias, the regency and the early years of the reign of King Otto tried to get the Greek public to "buy in" to the various institutions they were creating, and implemented some progressive ideas of government and state services. The new justice system was quite open and affordable to the poor,[3] free elementary education was mandated for boys and girls,[4] and a system of public health, including a quarantine system, access to midwife services for all citizens regardless of wealth, and systems of control for venereal diseases and prostitution were introduced.[5]

The regency did not shy away from controversial policies and none was more controversial than its confrontation with the Orthodox Church and the patriarchate of Constantinople. The regency recognized the significance of Orthodoxy as a crucial part of modern Greek identity, perhaps the most crucial as contemporaries observed.[6] Priests held significant authority in their parishes, "substituting for an aristocracy" as Finlay noted,[7] and religious concepts and the language of Orthodoxy was being "reinterpreted" to provide the Greeks with a nationalist discourse that used familiar concepts like a national resurrection.[8] The church also held considerable land and wealth, controlling much of the education available at the time, and constituted the most literate segment of the population. The regency, however, recognized that the continuation of the dominance of the patriarchate of Constantinople over the church of now independent Greece was a potentially serious political and national threat, because of its influence over the population. The patriarchate was, after all, situated at the capital of the state from which Greece had just broken free after a particularly vicious war, and the patriarch was in thrall to the Ottoman sultan. Although individual members of the church had taken a prominent role in the Greek War of Independence including holding important government posts, the patriarchate consistently supported the Ottomans starting with the excommunication of Alexander Ypsilantis and the insurgents as we saw in the previous chapter. In response eight Greek bishops and a thousand priests signed a letter cursing the new patriarch Evgenios as a new Judas Iskariot, and ceased mentioning him in their services distancing themselves from the patriarchate.[9]

The solution to the quandary between the benefits of religion as a nation-building component and the threats of a church controlled from beyond the borders of the country was the creation of a national church as Thiersch had suggested.[10] Such discussions began as early as the Second National Assembly of Astros in 1825 and were deliberated under Kapodistrias but it was the regents who orchestrated the creation of an *autocephalus* (autonomous) Church of Greece headed by the Greek king, with its own Holy Synod and archbishop, which would be administratively separate from the patriarchate in the manner of the Russian Church.[11] This was not the first break of the "Orthodox Commonwealth" since Prince Milos Obrenovich had also begun to disentangle the Serbian Church from the patriarchate two years earlier, but the regency was more radical. It tried to transform the Greek Church into a part of the state bureaucratic machinery under the direct control of the Greek crown.[12] For the patriarch of Constantinople, this was a direct challenge to his authority as *ethnarch* (leader of the nation)[13] and led to the temporary break of relations between the two churches that endured until 1850. Despite the controversy, all Balkan states that would emerge from the Ottoman Empire would duplicate the Greek example creating national churches, in the case of Bulgaria even before the establishment of the state.[14]

An additional benefit expected from severing ties with the patriarchate was the diminution of Russian influence in Greece. Traditionally the influence of the Russian Czar over Orthodox Christians and the patriarchate of Constantinople was significant and Russian influence was already strong in the new state, the Czar already formulated plans to support Orthodoxy in Greece.[15] The establishment of the autonomous Church of Greece would buttress national independence and elevate the Greek king above the Czar in the hearts and minds of his subjects, or so it was hoped, and for this reason Czar opposed the autonomy of the Greek Church while the patriarch and many "traditionalists" sent petitions to the Czar hoping for his intervention.[16] If Otto had been Orthodox, this hope may have been realized easily but his Catholic faith made him a suspect to the eyes of many of his subjects, who continued to be devoted to the Czar, including numerous monks whom the regency distrusted.[17]

The regency further undermined the position of the church in the new state by seeking to remove education from its purview and by targeting the wealth of the Orthodox Church in Greece. Much of the land in Greece was controlled by hundreds of monasteries, many of which owned large tracks of lands inhabited by only a few monks. In 1833, a state ordinance closed all monasteries with fewer than six monks or nuns, amalgamating the monks of such monasteries with those of larger ones, and expropriating the properties of the now defunct institutions.[18] The number of monasteries in Greece was eventually reduced to 151 from between 453 and 563. Legal scholars, many of whom had studied in Europe, even challenged the supremacy of the church in such matters as marriage and divorce, arguing for the preeminence of the state and its right and duty to legislate and regulate family law.[19] Finally, the regents allowed foreign missionaries, mostly American and British Evangelical Protestants, to establish missions in Greece and open schools, and especially schools for girls, for the emerging Greek middle classes.[20]

All these were highly controversial policies and generated strong opposition within Greece. Secret societies were formed to defend what was perceived as an attack on Orthodoxy. Itinerant preacher-monks, the heirs of Kosmas discussed in the previous chapter, denounced the foreigners who attacked the traditions of the people, and occasionally small-scale revolts erupted in the countryside often led by such religious figures. Ottoman bishops toured Greece to advance the claims of the patriarchate, while Russia often supported many of these efforts.[21] This discontent was carried over to the first decade of the reign of King Otto, and found fertile ground among the Greek population as Otto, just like the regency before him, continued to rely on foreign ministers and advisors, particularly Germans, French, and expatriate Greeks.[22]

I should note that the Greek state as it emerged in 1830 was a remarkably homogenous one in terms of religious affiliation. Although significant minorities existed prior to the War of Independence, most Muslims and Jews had been massacred, converted to Orthodox Christianity, or fled to the Ottoman territories as discussed in the previous chapter. Even areas that had retained their minorities like Chalkis (Negroponte), because they had never been captured by the Greek rebels, saw a massive flight of the Muslim population in the years following independence. When Edmond About traveled through Greece he noted how rare Jews were and that the few Muslim families of Euboea left following the eruption of the Eastern Question.[23] The new state thus had only a small Catholic minority in some of the Cyclades, a tiny Jewish and Muslim minority mostly located in the town of Chalkis, and a small expatriate community many of whom had made use of Greek legislation giving citizenship to those who had taken part in the war. Despite the small numbers of these minorities, the Greek government was highly sensitive to questions of citizenship and strictly enforced residency requirements even among Balkan Orthodox veterans of the war as seen in the case of Bulgarians who had applied for Greek citizenship at the Greek consulate of Moldavia.[24] After all, even though Greece had few religious minorities much of its rural population was composed of Albanian, Vlach, and "Bulgarian" (Slavic) speakers.[25] Yet, as an interesting series of documents from 1834 indicates, the Greek government was not attempting to use this legislation to bar non-Christians from claiming Greek residency or citizenship.

On February 5, 1834, a group of Jews drafted a petition in the Greek consulate of the Cretan town of Chania addressed to the Greek foreign ministry. In it they claimed that they were born in the Peloponnese and "temporarily" fled to Crete during the War of Independence awaiting the restoration of order to return to their homes. Having learned of the arrival of the King and "his good governance and protection etc. that the people enjoy" they requested to have their Greek citizenship recognized and submitted with the petition a letter from merchants and honorable citizens verifying their claims. Some signed the letter in Greek and others in Hebrew.[26] Alexander Mavrokordatos, the former revolutionary leader who was both prime minister and foreign minister at the time, was clearly uncertain how to deal with this situation and forwarded the petition to the Ministry of the Interior as the one responsible for such matters with a note saying that the Greek consul in Chania believed that one of these Jews was from Tripoli (Tripolitsa) and that they wanted to register themselves in that municipality. Mavrokordatos asked the ministry to "act accordingly" and to keep him informed.[27] A few days earlier, Mavrokordatos sent a letter to the Greek consul in Crete informing him that if these individuals registered in one of the Greek municipalities and "fulfilled those [duties] due to them as members of the Greek society" they could indeed enjoy the protection of the Greek government.[28]

Although we do not know the outcome of the petition, we do know that some Jews returned to Greece following the conclusion of hostilities. For example, Misrel Barouch was born and raised in Patras and married his first wife there. After she died during the Greek War of Independence in 1823, Barouch fled to Ottoman-held territories. He returned in 1833, was naturalized as a Greek citizen, received a Greek passport in 1847, and although he later settled in Ottoman Janina (Ioannina), he never renounced his Greek citizenship.[29] There are several remarkable aspects exemplified by these cases. First of all, there was clearly a willingness by several members of the recently persecuted and devastated Jewish communities to return to Greece and this may be an indication that some Jewish communities, beyond the one that survived at Chalkis, likely reconstituted themselves within the first decades of the Greek state from Jewish survivors of the war. A new Jewish community slowly emerged in Athens despite About's belief that the violence of the Athenian mob dissuaded Jews from settling there.[30]

The second point of interest is the response of the Greek government, which was eminently bureaucratic. Although Mavrokordatos appeared surprised, his letter to the Ministry of the Interior gave no indication that he would want these Jews barred from achieving Greek citizenship, with the full benefits and obligations this entailed. Considering the restrictive policies regarding citizenship and even residency in much of Europe at the time, this was a remarkably liberal attitude for a state that had just emerged from a genocidal war. It is particularly surprising considering the controversies regarding religion and the state that Greece experienced throughout the 1830s and 1840s.

The horrific violence from both sides of the Greek War of Independence and the political infighting among the various factions of the insurgent Greeks often mask the fact that there was a strong liberal current at the time that wanted to establish a liberal state governed through a constitution that ensured individual rights and representation to the majority, if not all, the adult male population. Liberals like Mavrokordatos produced increasingly more democratic constitutions, tried to create a bureaucratic and centralized state based upon the idea of a nation, with legal structures and administration inspired from Western Europe.[31] As early as 1824, Mavrokordatos claimed in a letter:

> I want for the laws to govern and not to be at the discretion of a hundred despots to trample them. Because, if it is decided for Greece to be dragged at the feet of the military despotism of a Hydra, not with seven but with one hundred heads, I will not become neither the instrument nor the servant of these new tyrants[32]

These ideals were repeated to pacify the anxieties of the Catholic minority specifically decoupling religion as the sole criterion of nationality as a feature of "barbaric nations." The conservative and religious Kapodistrias may have retrenched from such positions but the regency resurrected them promoting secularization in addition to the decoupling of the Church of Greece from the patriarchate of Constantinople.[33]

Almost from the founding of modern Greece, Protestant missionaries begun to arrive and establish missions, schools, and even a printing house in Athens.[34] For Protestant missionaries Greece was in dire need of missions "for though nominal Christians, yet they pay an idolatrous regard to pictures, holy places, and saints. Their Clergy are ignorant in the extreme."[35] Such sentiments continued over the ensuing decades Protestant missionaries constantly refer to Greek superstition, bigotry, and ignorance in their reports.[36] Greece assumed particular importance in the Anglo-American missionary, movement being counted as one of the four most important efforts, the others being the "Mohammedan Countries," China, and Western Africa.[37] At first the Greek state did not object to their presence and even Kapodistrias was willing to receive them though he expressed a preference for the missions to provide financial aid to state schools rather than establish their own.[38] Three Protestant missions were set up by the American Board, the Episcopal Board, and the Baptist Board of Missions, which established several schools, some specifically for girls. Missionaries were also instrumental in translating scripture in modern Greek, and in providing thousands of books to state schools, some ordered by the Ministry of Ecclesiastical Affairs and Public Instruction and some donated by the missions, including translations of the New Testament, spelling books, and *The Elements of Moral Science* by the renowned Baptist Francis Wayland.[39] Although hundreds of students flocked to the missionary schools,[40] the missions only converted a handful of Greeks to Protestantism, even when their proselytizing efforts were unimpeded by the Greek authorities, and a few Greek converts went on to study in American Universities like Amherst College.[41]

Religious attitudes hardened over the first two decades after independence. The early liberal attitudes of the regency toward religious freedom sparked a conservative reaction among many segments of Greek society. Seen by many as a foreign imposition by the hated Catholics, the liberal policies sparked conspiracy theories regarding their ultimate aim. Missionaries also became associated with the policies and interests of the Great Powers and were thus targeted by politicians from rival parties.[42] The patriarchate of Constantinople Gregory VI launched a campaign against Protestant missionaries in 1836 not only in the Ottoman Empire but also in Greece and even the British protectorate of the Ionian islands.[43] Even during the early days of their mission, the missionaries were concerned with certain actions by Greek governments like the introduction of "pictures and idolatrous prayers" to the schools, and they directed those preparing manuals of instruction to "exercise a discreet tenderness for the national prejudices of the Greek people."[44] In 1842, an investigation was launched by the Holy Synod regarding the activities of John Hill and his wife Frances, who had founded a boarding school in Athens. The Hills were exonerated by the investigation thereby prompting the newspapers to attack the Synod for letting them off. Despite their acquittal, the Hills' school was temporarily suspended even though the Hills had the support of the government and were ultimately allowed to resume their work.

The ability of missionaries to function in Greece was dramatically restricted following the adoption of the 1844 Constitution which explicitly forbade proselytizing by all faiths other than the Orthodox Church. Jonas King, who alongside the Hills was among the most prominent Protestant missionaries in Athens, was excommunicated by the Synod in 1846 and 1847 and finally arrested and convicted to a fifteen-day prison sentence and exile for reviling the "God of the universe" and the "Greek religion" because he was teaching standard Calvinist doctrines. The supreme court of Greece, the *Areios Pagos* refused to reverse the conviction but King escaped the penalty of exile through the efforts of the American government and the personal intervention of King Otto.[45] Even before these events the Baptist Board of Missions decided to suspend their activities in Greece to the dismay of the missionaries on the ground who sent letters protesting the decision. Although admitting lack of success and a more hostile environment toward their missions compared to the past two decades, the missionaries stressed that Greece continued to be a much more open society than places like Italy or even the British-held Ionian islands, enjoying a free press and no restrictions whatsoever over the importation and distribution of books throughout the country. The missionaries claimed that these factors allowed them to function much more easily than elsewhere in the Mediterranean.[46] The missions did continue but with limited success and under much closer scrutiny by the state and the Greek Church.

Protestant missionaries were not the only ones to experience religious persecution, despite the constitutional guarantees. The most famous case was that of Theophilos Kairis, a Greek scholar, ordained priest, and participant in the Greek War of Independence. Kairis was among the most respected scholars in Greece and had at one time been offered the position of director of the newly established University of Athens by King Otto. He also established an orphanage for the many orphans of the war on the island of Andros. His writings, however, increasingly diverged from the established doctrine of the Orthodox Church becoming influenced by Protestantism and Deism.[47] Kairis was anathematized by the Synod of the patriarchate of Constantinople and was subsequently convicted by the Holy Synod of Greece in 1839. He was then imprisoned and died in jail in 1853 awaiting trial.[48]

Such cases were the outcome of a broader movement of religious revival that had multiple expressions, often political as well as religious. Kairis was vilified for his religious beliefs not only by the church but even by respected figures like general Makrygiannis who railed against all those whom he deemed as enemies of

Orthodoxy including the King, the Queen, Prime Minister Kolettis, Jonas King, the foreign ambassadors, and even the constitution.[49] Itinerant preachers galvanized the countryside against the Athenian, and foreign, elites, and the government they controlled, leading to frequent outbursts of violence and outright rebellion, most famously under the monk Papoulakos (Christophoros Panagiotopoulos) whose preaching attracted thousands of followers and required the dispatch of significant forces to restore order. Although the Holy Synod and the established church hierarchy did not support these popular movements, they also took a dim view against religious nonconformity, especially the influence that foreign missionaries supposedly wielded in Greece.[50]

The high point of this political and religious agitation was the emergence of the secret Philorthodox Society whose goals included the preservation of the Orthodox character of the new state, the expulsion of foreign influences, the liberation of fellow Christians from Ottoman rule, and perhaps even the overthrow of the Bavarian government and monarchy.[51] Many prominent members of Greek society, including notables and former leaders of the Greek War of Independence, became members and the society seems to have developed close links with Russia and her ambassador in Greece. Even the patriarchate was apparently in touch with the society.[52] The discovery of the secret society by the authorities in 1839 led to the arrest of Nikitas Stamatelopoulos (Nikitaras), one of the most renowned and admired leaders of the Greek War of Independence, and Georgios Kapodistrias, the brother of the former governor, while several other influential and respected members of Athenian society were suspected of involvement like Genaios Kolokotronis, son of the most renowned and effective military commander of the Greek War of Independence, Ioannis Mamouris, and Georgios Glarakis. The excitement generated by the arrests proved disappointing since the conspirators managed to destroy the most incriminating documents concerning their activities and at the ensuing trial they were acquitted. However, rumors were rampant that they had planned to abduct the king and force either his conversion to Orthodoxy or his abdication, while at the same time seeking the "liberation" of Macedonia, Epirus, and Thessaly. Despite their acquittals, and the doubts then and now about the very existence of the plot,[53] we should not easily dismiss the Philorthodox Society because its ideas at the very least represented a strong current in Greek society that aimed at religious homogeneity even through the use of force.[54] In 1841, on his return to Greece Mavrokordatos was concerned about the continued activity of the Philorthodox Society whose goals essentially became the goals of the nation after the events leading to the establishment of constitutional government in Greece in 1843.[55]

Conversion and its ramifications

As we have already seen, conversion was a complex issue in the eastern Mediterranean and the Ottoman Empire, and although I briefly discussed it in Chapter 2, I need to return to it because the parameters of conversion changed significantly in the nineteenth century. Traditionally the topic has been approached either through an examination of conversion to Islam during the Ottoman period or through the missionary activities of Protestant missionaries in the nineteenth century who targeted Ottoman Christians and particularly Armenians for conversion to Protestant churches. Both are, of course, important issues and they touch upon the discussions of nationalities and minorities but they often obscure other pressures including the conversions to Orthodoxy of Muslims and Jews in the emerging Balkan states.

Conversions to Islam had been occurring for centuries, often massively, as in Bosnia, Albania, or Crete during or in the aftermath of the conquest of these areas by the Ottomans as discussed in Chapter 2. In general, the Ottoman Empire did not actively pursue the conversion of its non-Muslim population. Non-Muslims, after all, had useful functions in the empire both as mediators for trade and diplomacy with hostile states like the Habsburgs, the Saffavids, or Russia and as a source of additional income as they had to pay an extra tax, the *harac*. In earlier centuries Christians were also the pool from which the best Ottoman soldiers, the Janissaries, could be recruited though that had ended long before the period that concerns us.

Conversion to the dominant religion of the state provided benefits not only in the Ottoman Empire but also the Russian Empire, Prussia, and elsewhere.[56] Conversion provided material benefits to non-Muslims, both financial in terms of lower taxes, access to restricted professions, or positions in the Ottoman administration, and social since Muslims had a legally recognized superior position in Ottoman society. Conversion to Islam in the Ottoman Empire could be a strategy for social or economic advancement just as conversion away from Islam can be a migration strategy today.[57] As a result, individual and even mass conversions continued throughout the existence of the Ottoman Empire even during the nineteenth century. At the same time, however, it represented a fundamental change of identity and frequently implied the abandonment of ties with the former religious community and often the family of the convert.[58] Because of the severe social implications, the Ottoman state had a duty to facilitate this transition once conversion took place and state and religious authorities were actively involved in the process. In the case of women, a quick marriage to a Muslim was often the outcome and perhaps also the cause of the conversion, which would secure against possible relapse, something that would stain the Muslim community and necessitate a response.

Historically conversion can be a complex topic especially in cases of mass conversion as occurred in Spain following the *Reconquista* when thousands of Jews and Muslims converted, often by force or threat, to Christianity. The same can be partly seen in the Ottoman Empire in the case of the Dönme, the Jewish sect that followed their leader Sabbatai Zevi and converted en masse in the seventeenth century. Their community remained separate from other Muslims in Salonica, keeping many of their Jewish customs, and they were viewed with suspicion by the rest of the Muslim population, a suspicion that became heightened in the age of nationalism and especially in the Republic of Turkey.[59] Muslim Albanians, Cretans, and Bosnians retained much of their former culture after conversion and their frequent associations with heterodox Sufi sects like the Bektashi often raised suspicions among the more Orthodox Muslims. Fundamentally, however, the conversion of unbelievers to Islam was a moment of validation for the Muslim community who frequently publicly celebrated such conversions that proved its superiority over the other faiths.

Starting from the eighteenth century, however, conversion begun to attract the attention of European states, several of which took upon themselves the role of defenders of certain minorities, a role subsequently recognized by the Ottomans. Thus, the Russian Empire become the defenders of Orthodox Christians, the French assumed that role for the Catholics, and so on. The conversion of non-Muslims to Islam, therefore, became a potential threat of confrontation with the European Great Powers especially when there were claims of conversions through the threat or use of force. Inevitably forced conversion narratives assumed renewed prominence in Europe, in the press and literature of the nineteenth century.

Cognizant of the threat and its own weakness, the Ottoman state embarked upon a widespread program of reform collectively referred to as the Tanzimat. Its purpose was to modernize and strengthen the state, but it also aimed to gain the loyalty of all subjects to the dynasty and the state through the creation of a common Ottoman identity. The legal restrictions to non-Muslims were lifted, the legal and educational systems reformed, and efforts were made to address the complaints of non-Muslims. Though in certain fields the reforms could be seen as successful, they failed to achieve their admittedly ambitious goals while arousing the enmity of the Muslim population whose superior status was undermined. A growing disconnection developed between the Ottoman reforming elite and local Muslim communities and conversion was one area where this disconnection was visible. While local communities celebrated, and supported the conversion of non-Muslims to Islam, the authorities were often uneasy, if not embarrassed, by such events especially when foreign delegates became involved as was often the case when the non-Muslim communities sought their intervention in cases of supposed forced conversions.[60] To make the position of Tanzimat officials even more difficult, on occasion non-Muslim communities intervened in the process forcefully, emboldened by the reforms and the meddling of foreign diplomats, which threatened widespread unrest. These problems continued even after the Tanzimat ended by the authoritarian regime of Abdulhamid II that spanned the last quarter of the nineteenth century. Under Abdulhamid II's reign numerous claims of forceful conversions were made especially in Armenia and in conjunction with the massacres of Armenians at the end of the century. However, there were also massive apostasies from Islam by supposedly crypto-Christians who used the opportunities by the legal changes regarding apostasy to assert a different identity for causes that have been debated ever since.[61]

At the same time when conversions to Islam were becoming contested, the Ottoman Empire experienced an influx of Protestant missionaries, who established themselves throughout the empire. Christian missionaries were not new in the East. The Jesuits had established Lazarist missions from as early as the seventeenth century targeting primary Orthodox, Armenian, Nestorian, and other Christian sects whose conversion to Catholicism was legal as opposed to that of Muslims. The Catholic Church continued its missionary activities in the Middle East and the Balkans throughout the nineteenth century targeting groups that were dissatisfied with the practices of the Orthodox Church under the direction of the Greek-dominated patriarchate of Constantinople. Thus, Lazarist and Uniate campaigns focused on the Vlachs, Albanians, and Bulgarians of the Balkans with various degrees of success.

Starting in the seventeenth century, but especially in the nineteenth, the Catholic Church faced competition by Protestant missionaries particularly from the United States and Britain. Benefiting from the development of a British empire in the Mediterranean and the presence of British forces, Protestant missionaries flooded the Ottoman Empire as well as newly independent states like Greece. By building schools and providing superior education to the local alternatives for the developing middle classes of the region, these Protestant missionaries were able to establish a considerable presence in the region that was quickly perceived as a threat to the local Armenian and Orthodox churches.[62] Complaints against the activities of the missionaries toward the Ottoman government were frequent and often favorably received because the presence of these missionaries was seen with suspicion by the state who feared missionary activities could undermine the state's efforts to create an Ottoman identity. Furthermore, these missionaries were often eye witnesses to the abuses inflicted upon non-Muslims in the Ottoman Empire such as the Bulgarian "horrors" or the Armenian massacres. The Protestant missionaries' accounts often found their way to the European press causing significant embarrassment, at the very least, to the Ottoman government.

In a rather similar way to the suspicions of the Ottoman government, the new Greek state government feared that the missionaries would undermine the "Hellenic" component of the Christian populations of the Ottoman Empire and thus disrupt their own nationalist proselytizing efforts. Greek consuls, as we shall see, monitored the activities of missionaries and supporters of other religious denominations and reported upon them to the Greek government in often alarmist tones. In such circumstances, the backlash against such missionaries within Greece discussed above takes a nationalistic meaning which helps us understand some of the policies of the Greek state in the nineteenth century.

Converts to Orthodoxy

The Greek state was called upon to deal with cases of former Muslims, especially women and children, who converted from Islam to Orthodoxy during the Greek War of Independence, often following request or complaints by surviving family members in the Ottoman Empire. For example, in the case of a twelve-year-old girl who was taken by a priest in Athens when she was two, her father, still living in Athens, demanded her return in 1831. The case was eventually resolved but only after the prolonged involvement of Greek and Ottoman authorities and the intervention of the Russian consul.[63] Cases could span decades, as was the case of a young boy named Abdul, who was captured by Dimitrios Zaimis from Kalavryta in 1821 after the death of his parents, baptized in 1822 under the name Ioannis, and raised as a Christian until his circumstances became a matter of scrutiny in 1842.[64] Most instances, however, involved women who were more likely to survive the onslaught of the violence of the Greek War of Independence as discussed in the previous chapter. In 1836, a permanent committee was established to deal with the properties of such women whom Ottoman law, recognized by the Greek state in 1830 as customary law for Muslims, stripped of their inheritances, but who vigorously defended their inheritance rights in Greek courts. The committee recognized an obligation of the state toward the well-being of these women who were in danger of being left without wealth. It conceived this problem as a question of "charity" and hinted that these women's Greek husbands may have married them because of their lands and could abandon them if those lands were taken away from them. The committee finally stated that it was willing to confront the Ottoman representatives and their demands since many of these women were "forced from the then circumstances to embrace the Christian religion."[65] This was a contentious issue throughout the 1830s and cases were still finding themselves in Greek courts thirty years later.[66] The Ottoman state submitted letters confirming that Islamic law disinherited apostates,[67] and the issue was significant enough that King Otto became personally involved in the deliberations.[68]

On occasion, conversions to Orthodoxy entangled the Greek government in other embarrassing situations. Certainly, many of the converts during the Greek War of Independence were converted to Orthodoxy by force and the Greek governments had to deal with accusations that such individuals were being held against their will. In 1838, for instance, the Greek government investigated the cases of two Ottoman children, one of whom had converted after the conclusion of the war, supposedly of his own free will though suspiciously at the age of fifteen making his conversion legitimate, as the investigation determined.[69] More problematic was a case in Chalkis in 1840 involving a Muslim family that was on the point of emigrating to the Ottoman Empire. The case of the family's daughter "Eleni" is particularly interesting because it ultimately involved nearly all the authorities of the Greek state from the local authorities and the police, to the Ministry of the Navy, the foreign ministry, the Greek courts, the church, and the Ottoman ambassador to Greece.

The case, as reconstructed from the internal correspondence of the Greek foreign ministry, involved a young Muslim girl who went missing on the eve of her family's emigration to the Ottoman Empire. Her father asked for the assistance of the police and the girl was discovered in a Christian house of the town. The young girl declared that she did not want to follow her family to the Ottoman Empire and wanted to convert to Christianity. The Greek war sloop "Argos" apparently transported the girl to Athens after she had presented herself in front of a Greek investigative prosecutor and a priest and had taken a vow in front of holy icons. The Ottoman ambassador demanded that she should declare her intention to convert freely in front of him and sent a letter to the Greek foreign minister making the accusation that the girl had been kidnapped and "enslaved." The drama took another twist immediately after Eleni became Christian, when she hired lawyers to contest her father's property. Eleni claimed her mother, who had remarried, had illegally appropriated her father's property for herself.[70] The case escalated as the Ottoman ambassador continued to protest to the Greek foreign ministry. The Ottoman ambassador, in a series of letters, revealed the case of another girl who was engaged to a Muslim man named Emin aga, but who had subsequently converted to Christianity and been married to a Christian. Her fiancé was then held in a jail in Chalkis. The Ottoman ambassador demanded the restitution of the girl to her family and the punishment of her Christian husband as well as the governor of Chalkis who had facilitated the whole thing.[71]

The Greek government was clearly embarrassed by these cases which had escalated to become diplomatic incidents. In September 1841, the Greek ambassador to the Ottoman Empire received a formal complaint by the Ottoman foreign minister regarding the forced conversions of these two Muslim girls.[72] To deflect the continuous demands of the Ottoman ambassador regarding the restitution of the girls, the Greek government found refuge behind the judicial system claiming that it was up to the courts to annul the marriages, and resolve the cases. At the same time, the Greek government investigated the circumstances of the two cases.[73] Two petitions by the Muslim inhabitants of Chalkis, however, indicate that there was a disconnect between the government in Athens and the local authorities in Chalkis. The petitions claimed that Greek soldiers had attacked the house of the widow Carpouzade Ahmed-aga and abducted her daughter and that these actions had the support of the governor of Euboea who refused to return the girl to her mother. Furthermore, the petition claimed that the Muslims of the region were constantly harassed by Greek soldiers. The same governor had also forcibly baptized a Muslim girl against the wishes of the previous Greek foreign minister Mr. Paico who had ordered her return to her parents.[74]

These were not isolated instances nor the only cases that caused friction between the Greek and Ottoman governments. The government in Athens took considerable pains to investigate and address such incidents. The government asked the governor of Achaia to report on the case of a brother and sister who had converted to Christianity following yet another complaint by the Ottoman ambassador.[75] The minister of the interior notified the foreign ministry regarding a couple of converted Muslim girls in Athens by forwarding letters of the governor of Attica, the chief of police in Athens, and the mayor of Athens, all of whom were involved.[76] The Ministry of the Interior also undertook to investigate the Chalkis cases as it informed the foreign ministry. The Ministry of the Interior appointed a state councilor, Mr. Rigas Palamidis, to go to Chalkis and determine the circumstances of the conversions and the validity of the complaints of the Muslim population and, if found to be accurate, to attempt to redress them.[77]

The local authorities, however, clearly had a different agenda and were not cowed by the Athenian government. The governor of Euboea Anagnostopoulos sent a harsh reply to the "unfounded" complaints of the Ottoman ambassador accusing him of fanaticism, of spreading unsubstantiated lies and slanders, and even criticizing the Greek government in Athens of adopting the Ottoman position and thus making the situation worse.[78] The government eventually removed the girls from Chalkis and brought them to Athens delivering them to the mayor of the city to personally protect them from "all religious suggestion,"[79] but the Ottoman government continued to file letters of protest. The case was further complicated by the discovery that the man who had married one of the girls was a Greek officer and as such needed royal permission in order to marry in the first place, which conceivably made the marriage invalid. The internal correspondence shows the quandary of the Greek government which on the one hand more or less saw the validity of the Ottoman complaints that such acts were "an insult to the honor, the religion, and the property of the Ottomans in Greece" but feared that if they returned the girls to their families, and especially if the latter relocated to the Ottoman Empire, they would be forced to convert back to Islam. The government feared the impact such an outcome would have in Greek society and the problems it could generate. The issue was taken up by the council of ministers. Subsequent letters reveal the involvement of prominent political figures in the conversions of the Muslim girls, such as general Kriezotis in whose house one of the conversions apparently took place.[80] Inevitably the Greek government dithered as the Ottoman ambassador fumed.[81] Although the officer who married one of the converted girls without permission was initially dismissed from the army, the King subsequently pardoned him and the war ministry asked the foreign ministry to inquire if the Ottoman ambassador objected to his reappointment to the army. This was a remarkable request, a state asking a foreign power for permission to reinstate one of its officers, indicating that the dismissal had been due to the protests and effective pressure of the Ottoman Empire.[82]

Ten years later the council of ministers was once more embroiled in a controversy over the conversion to Christianity of Ayse, who changed her name to Marigo in remarkably similar circumstances. Similarly, the family of Ayse was emigrating to the Ottoman Empire but the boat they had chartered was forced to dock at Karystos, a coastal town of Euboea, due to the weather. Ayse used the opportunity to seek refuge to the house of a Christian resident of that town and declared her intention to become Christian. The local authorities, including the prosecutor and port and police functionaries, transferred her to the home of the army captain Eleftherios Hatzikonstanti, where she was promptly baptized. Her parents appealed to the French consul Mr. Benois to intervene but she was apparently set in her decision to become Christian. After a few days the prefect of Euboea, the mayor, and other officials attempted to return her to her parents by force but she protested that she did not want to stay with them. When her parents apparently threatened her with physical harm, the state functionaries once more removed her from her parents' house and she was permitted to write a formal appeal to the government in Athens.[83] Alexander Mavrokordatos, then minister of the interior, directed the prefect of Euboea to take care and protect "her personality" and to make sure that "her freedom of conscience is not forced in the least, as it is protected through our legislation."[84] This case took over a year to resolve and involved repeated interventions by French and British diplomats who complained that the local authorities were ignoring the directives of the Athenian government to return the woman to her parents.[85] The prosecutor of Chalkis also became involved as did the Minister of Justice, who reported that her conversion was irregular since she had been baptized a mere three days after her request thus not allowing for the mandatory catechism nor the required ecclesiastical license.[86] The case ended up in the Greek courts where the mayor, police and military personnel, and other locals were accused of physical violence against Muslims, while Ayse, now Maria, and her new Christian husband Damianos Gierotis were accused of voluntary abduction, a crime under the Penal Code.[87] This case naturally brought about the involvement of the war ministry, the Ottoman embassy, and even the Greek embassy in Istanbul which applied for a *fatwa* from the *sheikh-ul-Islam* regarding the age of maturity for Muslim women and forwarded it to the court.[88] Throughout this period the state undertook the support of Ayse and King Otto and Queen Amalia, on at least two separate occasions, authorized substantial funds for her maintenance.[89]

It was not only Muslims, however, who faced pressure to convert and who sought the assistance of the Ottoman government to prevent or reverse such conversions. In 1845, the Ottoman ambassador in Athens sent a letter to the Greek foreign ministry regarding the case of Riza Mizdrahi, a Jewish woman and a native of Smyrna (Izmir) who worked as a servant to a Christian Athenian called Dimitrios Boghazianos. According to the ambassador, Boghazianos baptized Riza's six-year-old daughter without her mother's permission or consent and when Riza, accompanied by her son-in-law Haim Solomon and other Jews, went to demand the return of her daughter from Boghazianos, they were confronted by a "crowd of fanatics" who encircled Boghazianos' house and threatened to "exterminate" Riza and her coreligionists if they attempted to remove the child. "Terrified," the mother had to abandon her child and flee Athens for Chalkis. From Chalkis she sought the intervention of the Ottoman authorities, who requested the return of the child to the imperial legation.[90]

The government sought to find out what had happened from the Athenian police, who reported that "Rika" had notified the police on January 15 that she was a servant of Dimitrios Grigoriou and had a child by him who had been baptized as an Orthodox Christian in accordance to her own wishes and had "placed it with her own hands in the arms of the priest" who baptized it. The priest, however, would not also baptize Rika as she wanted until after five or six months had passed, presumably in order to provide her with the required catechism. Rika had then changed her mind and did not want to be baptized after all and wanted her daughter back. The police asked Dimitrios Grigoriou and his wife Eleni to explain themselves and to produce the child. They proceeded to state the same story but refused to hand over the girl who, as was reported, did not want to go with her mother. The police, unsure how to proceed, had sent the case to the prosecutor who informed them that he would give them his opinion the next day. The next day, however, Rika, her son-in-law, and her son informed the police that they would leave the girl with Dimitrios and receiving their passports departed for Chalkis.[91] The prosecutor of the Appeals Court of Athens Diomidis Moriakos, in a separate document, provided a slightly different version of the story. He claimed that Rika had "given" her daughter to the childless couple of Dimitrios Grigoriou and his wife who baptized it with the mother's consent, and she would have been baptized as well but changed her mind under pressure from her relatives and wanted to reverse her daughter's conversion and take her back. Dimitrios refused but eventually they compromised and Rika received some money and departed for Chalkis. The prosecutor then expanded upon the legal issues involved, stated that the applicable law was not the law of the place of residence but that of nationality, meaning the laws of the Ottoman Empire, but he was ignorant of Ottoman laws and the rights they bestowed upon the mother. According to Roman law, he continued, only the father had authority over children but in the absence of a father the mother enjoyed such rights. However, according to the laws of Greece a "heretic" (*airetikos*) could not be considered as guardian of a Christian child. Thus Rika could not initiate a court case on behalf of the child but only another Christian appointed by the court the child's guardian.[92]

These reports were forwarded to the Ottoman ambassador,[93] who formally responded that the justifications supplied contradicted international law and the "private law of all civilized nations."[94] The Greek ministers of Justice, Ecclesiastical

Affairs, and Foreign Affairs commented on the Ottoman ambassador's response, passing the case from one to the other. Then the Ottoman ambassador received, and forwarded to the Greek government, a further note, in Greek, from Michail Mizdralim, a Jew from Smyrna (Izmir) who claimed he was the husband of Rika and father of the girl Dama that Dimitrios Grigoriou Bogazianos was keeping illegally. Michail claimed that while he was away to Jerusalem, a great fire destroyed much of Smyrna and without his knowledge his wife had relocated to Greece with his son Solomon and his three daughters, one of whom was married in Chalkis to a man called Malakia Ferizi. When he returned to Smyrna and found what had happened, he went to Chalkis to find his family. He claimed that Grigoriou lied that he had adopted his daughter from his wife since there were no adoption papers nor did she have the right to agree to such a thing in the first place while he was alive.[95] In the end the Ministry of Religious Affairs and Public Education once again dodged the responsibility of resolving the problem and determined that the Greek government could not interfere in a judicial matter since the adoptive father enjoyed the rights of a free Greek citizen. The natural father could seek his rights through the appropriate Greek courts if he so desired and it would be up to the courts to resolve the case.[96] Based upon this recommendation the council of ministers rejected the demands of the Ottoman ambassador.[97]

These cases reveal the attitude of the Greek state toward minorities and religion. First of all, it is evident that Chalkis, the one part of the Greek state that retained its religious minorities after the genocidal conflict of the Greek War of Independence, was the center of minority religious conflict in Greece, both for Muslims and for Jews, and perhaps somewhat of a haven for non-Christians. It was a precarious haven, however, since the Greek state tried to dilute the religious composition of the region by settling refugees from Samos in Euboea as Muslims and Jews protested. The latter requested certain privileges including the establishment of a separate municipality and exemption from military service which were denied by the Greek government.[98] I should note that Euboea was the scene of atrocities committed against Christians as late as 1831,[99] while many of the refugees fleeing to Greece were armed and retained their weapons after their resettlement.[100] Second, it is also clear that not only Muslims but Jews as well saw the Ottoman Empire as a protector for their rights and well-being in Greece, and that the Ottoman state was quite willing to undertake that role, just as Greece was willing to act this way for Orthodox Christians beyond its borders. Finally, we see that the Athenian government was very reluctant to get involved in such cases and its ministers repeatedly sought to pass along responsibility for dealing with such matters from one to the other and ultimately to the Greek judicial system. I have no doubts that Greek ministers of the time had little sympathy for the plight of Muslims or Jews in Greece, but these cases presented a particularly thorny problem for them.

These cases threatened the international reputation of the Greek state, a state that was trying very hard, and with little success, to present itself as a modern, European polity. Furthermore, it disrupted relations with a power, the Ottoman Empire, that had ruled Greece less than two decades ago and which was still considered the greatest threat to Greek independence and existence. Finally, they threatened to undermine Greek arguments for the expansion of the borders of the Greek state, an expansion that would inevitably bring significant non-Christian populations under Greek authority.

Thus, in terms of international politics the Greek government had every incentive to resolve these cases quickly and with fairness. Such a course however ran counter to the demands of local politics. A government already mistrusted by the population on religious matters for reasons discussed above could not be perceived to be taking an anti-Orthodox stance especially when local sensibilities were at stake. These cases make it quite clear that regional communities and even municipal and local authorities appointed by the government supported or even forced the conversion of non-Orthodox and were willing to stand up to the government in Athens over such issues. The royal government was therefore in a very precarious predicament and its perplexing espousal of Orthodox causes beyond the borders of the Greek state as in the example of the Kingdom of Two Sicilies discussed below may have been meant as a foil to the mounting pressures over religious policies in Greece itself.

The constitutional monarchy and the Great Idea

The goodwill with which King Otto was received by the Greek population was quickly dissipated by the efforts of the regency and later the King to impose a centralized government and to place foreigners, or expatriate Greeks, in positions of authority. The severe efforts to reduce expenditures, due to the inability of the Greek state to meet its debt payments, and the subsequent default, led to further popular disaffection with King Otto's rule.[101] Otto also failed to support a new uprising in Crete in 1841 which attempted to utilize the confusion of the Eastern Crisis and the conflict between the Ottoman Empire and Egypt which was effectively suppressed by Ottoman troops.[102] These events eventually resulted in a bloodless coup in 1843 which forced the young monarch to promise his subjects a new constitution and a representative government. The coup brought together disparate forces, from the army, the common people, wealthy landowners, and former leaders of the Greek War of Independence. The coup probably had the backing, or at least the acquiescence, of the ambassadors of the three powers that stood as surety over the Greek state. The King was forced to dismiss his foreign advisors and call a constitutional assembly which began deliberations the following year.

The debates of the constitutional assembly raised, among others, the fundamental questions of what constituted the Greek nation, who could be a Greek citizen, what the relationship of the "unredeemed" Greeks to the fledgling state should be, and what was the "mission" of the Greek state, none of which had an easy answer. These questions were obviously interrelated and different answers presented very different visions with regard to the Greek state and nation. The heart of these debates reflected the widely held idea that the Greek War of Independence had not been an unmitigated success and had ultimately failed to achieve its goals. Rather than the culmination of the national aspirations of Greeks, the Greek War of Independence had simply been a first step toward national realization and independence that was yet to be fully achieved.

One of the most fraught questions was what constituted the nation. This was still a time when German Romantic nationalism had not yet achieved its later overwhelming influence in central and eastern Europe. It was competing with ideas stemming from the French and even American revolutions promoting a civic identity that had already been partly expressed in the first decade of Greek existence when numerous foreigners, refugees, and expatriates had been naturalized as Greek citizens. A new, better-defined idea of the nation was needed, a cultural construct for sure but one whose parts were hotly debated. Language, for example, was a crucial factor in these debates and the linguistic question would plague modern Greece for the next century and more.[103] This debate dated from the Ottoman period and pitted those who supported the use of colloquial Greek (*demotic*) against those who wanted a revival of ancient Greek or a "purified" form of modern Greek known as *katharevousa*. The debate was not solely one of linguistics but involved a question of history and links to the past, especially the classical past, which was increasingly embraced by the state.

This association between modern Greece and antiquity was again evident in the works of prerevolutionary Greek authors like Adamantios Korais but it found a new expression with the founding of the modern Greek state which immediately became the custodian of the Greek past. The modern Greek state founded the first archaeological service in Europe and gave it far-reaching powers. The state passed legislation that made the relics of the past the property of the entire Greek nation,[104] and actively promoted the link between modern Greece and its ancient past through education and commemorations. The formulation of a Greek historical identity, however, was still in flux with an emphasis on classical antiquity but with ambiguous positions over later periods. One of the most popular textbooks of the 1850s for example, "Gerostathis" by Leon Melas, was quite critical of the ancient Macedonian conquest of the Greek city states, let alone the Byzantine period, both crucial components of the later idea of Greek historical continuity.[105]

Language and history, therefore, despite their significance, were not the sole or even the most significant markers of Greekness in the eyes of many contemporaries. As we have seen in the previous chapter, the Greek War of Independence had been fought on religious rather than ethnic lines, and many of the heroes of the war, several of whom were still alive and politically active in 1844, spoke predominantly Albanian dialects. In this context religion seemed a stronger and clearer marker of ethnicity and the three revolutionary constitutions had already established a strong link between membership to the Greek Orthodox Church and Greek citizenship.[106] But religion was also entangled with problems. First, there were Orthodox Christians that were patently not "Greek" notably the Russians who harbored their own designs upon the Ottoman Empire in possible competition with the Greek nationalist goals and it should be noted that religion was also playing a crucial role in the formulation of "Official Nationality" in Russia at the time.[107] Other Balkan peoples, Romanians, Serbs, Bulgarians, Albanians, were also partly or predominantly Orthodox and were increasingly developing their own national aspirations, again often in competition to Greece as future chapters will discuss. Finally, by 1844 the Greek Kingdom had disassociated itself from its ties to the patriarchate of Constantinople by establishing an autocephalous church which the patriarchate refused to recognize and had in fact issued an interdict against the Greek Church. Although that breach was temporary and relations would be patched up in 1850, assisted by the fact that the new constitution transformed the King from leader of the Greek Church to its protector,[108] but a rather ambivalent relationship between the Greek state and the patriarchate would continue and the patriarchate resisted nationalist divisions and remained more or less loyal to the Ottoman state and to a universalist Christian mission.

To complicate matters further, the political debates over the question of nationality were enmeshed in a real power struggle between those who had been born in the areas that were included in the independent state of Greece in 1830 (*autochthones*) and those that had settled there from other regions that remained part of the Ottoman Empire (*eterochthones*). Many of those *eterochtones* achieved significant political power both during the Greek War of Independence and in the ensuing years like Alexandros Mavrokordatos and Ioannis Kolettis, both of whom served as ministers and prime ministers. *Autochones* particularly resented the fact that most government posts and bureaucratic appointments were given to *eterochthones,* or worst still foreigners, in part because of their superior education but also because of the distrust and distaste that early governments starting from Kapodistrias had for local elites whom they considered fickle, corrupt, and unreliable.[109]

At first it appeared that the *autochthones* won the debate at the drafting of the constitution by stipulating that only those born in the kingdom could hold positions of authority.[110] Although foreigners and many *eterochthones* were removed from the Greek bureaucracy following the establishment of the new constitution, this provision was subsequently ignored.[111] In the end, it was the *eterochthones* who ultimately won the debate by establishing the principle that a "Greek" was not solely an inhabitant of the Greek state but rather that the Greek nation was a vague, ill-defined but recognizable group that in its majority lived beyond the confines of the Greek state in the lands of the Ottoman Empire. Kapodistrias had first mentioned the concept behind the *Megali Idea* in 1827,[112] and Prime Minister Ioannis Kolettis coined the term in the constitutional debates of 1844 as a duty of the modern Greek state to act as a conduit of Western civilization to the East.[113] Although at first some mocked the concept even as a foreign import,[114] over the following decade and especially after 1864 and the union of the Ionian islands to Greece, the concept was expanded and transformed as the duty of the new state to ensure that those members of the Greek nation that still lived under Ottoman rule were brought in the fold of Greece through a process of territorial expansion, and endured in more or less that form until 1923.[115]

Nationalism was a powerful force even before the adoption of the irredentist rhetoric of the *Megali Idea* as evidenced by the abrupt end to the political career of Konstantinos Zografos who had dared in 1839 to be the first Greek foreign minister to visit Istanbul where he signed a commercial treaty between Greece and the Ottoman Empire.[116] After 1844, the *Megali Idea* would absolutely dominate Greek politics for the next century, although there were inevitably high points of fervor followed by periods of relative calm. Its impact and all-pervasiveness is perhaps the most important characteristic of nineteenth-century Greek society and would color nearly every policy and debate over the ensuing century. At the same time, the specifics of this nationalist undertaking were left quite vague and open to multiple interpretations. Greek nationalists deliberately avoided providing details regarding the precise territorial aspirations of the *Megali Idea*, although nearly everyone accepted that Constantinople was to be the capital of the eventual Greek state.[117] It was understood that the new state would expand into the Balkans and Anatolia but the areas to be claimed as part of Greece varied significantly in the writings of Greek nationalists. For example, as late as 1901 a Greek schoolbook included Palestine among the regions waiting to be liberated from the Ottoman yoke alongside the more commonly claimed regions of Macedonia, Thrace, Asia Minor, Crete, and Cyprus.[118] Increasingly Greek historians took a leading role in the formulation of the *Megali Idea* and its development in the imagination of modern Greeks and in the process laid the foundation for the formation of the identity of the modern Greek nation.

Starting with Spyridon Zambellios, who reformulated Greek perceptions regarding Byzantium, but especially with Konstantinos Paparrigopoulos, Greek historians developed the concept of an unbroken historical narrative of the Greek nation stretching from antiquity to the present.[119] In order to achieve this, they transformed the Byzantine Empire from a decadent and declining phase of the Roman Empire that was so alien to "Hellenism" that Antonios Miaoulis in his account of the naval battles of the Greek War of Independence referred to the Ottoman fleet as "Byzantine,"[120] to a vibrant, Christian, and Hellenized state of the Middle Ages that compared favorably to contemporary European medieval entities. This construction allowed Greek nationalists to present a continuous Greek history spanning millennia, but also a historical claim to the territories of the Byzantine Empire at its perceived height, the Macedonian and Komnenoi dynasties as the poet Alexandros Soutsos suggested as early as 1843.[121] It also allowed them to foil perceived ideological threats such as the Fallmerayer's thesis that seemed to threaten the very existence of a Greek, or rather Hellenic, nation. In fact, much of the historiography of Paparrigopoulos and other Greek historians of the time was spurred by the perceived threat of Fallmereyer's thesis regarding the descent of modern Greeks.[122]

Jakob Philipp Fallmerayer was a distinguished medievalist and among the first serious scholars of Byzantine history.[123] His 1830 controversial thesis, published just as the modern Greek state was being born, claimed that the ancient Hellenes had been essentially wiped out by the Slavic invasions of the early middle ages and thus the current Christian population of the Balkans, even those who spoke Greek, were the descendants of Slavic tribes and Anatolian settlers.[124] Fallmerayer did not deny the existence of the modern Greeks but he considered them descendants of Byzantine settlers from Asia Minor and Hellenized Slavs, who over the centuries had lost their language and culture just like the Slavs of Brandenburg, Pomerania, Silesia, Saxony, or Mecklenburg in Germany.[125] Although many in Greece have associated Fallmerayer with Panslavism, his thesis was more complex than that and significantly Fallmerayer was a German nationalist who saw Panslavism as a threat to the German nation and Europe.[126] His thesis was a warning to Germans and an argument in favor of the efforts toward German unification of which he was a great supporter.

Greeks of course saw Fallmerayer's thesis as a dangerous threat to their national identity, especially since his book was filled with statements guaranteed to rile Greeks, for example when he called Athens an Albanian city.[127] Greek studies of folklore emerge as a result of Fallmerayer's thesis,[128] but those that spearheaded the effort to disprove his thesis and prove the continuity of modern and ancient Greeks were historians led by Paparrigopoulos. The pinnacle of this effort was Paparigopoulos'

History of the Greek Nation, a six-volume survey of Greek history from antiquity to the Greek War of Independence published between 1860 and 1877. The *History of a Greek Nation* became almost immediately the unassailable basis for national historiography in Greece.[129] Paparrigopoulos and other contemporary Greek historians established a strong Greek claim not only toward antiquity but also with regard to the Byzantine period. Although this claim was not unchallenged at the time by Romanian historians like Nikolae Iorga who also claimed the heritage of the Roman and Byzantine empires,[130] within Greek historiography Paparigopoulos' narrative achieved hegemonic status.

Historical consciousness therefore joined religion as a fundamental aspect of Greek national identity, and at the same time a sense of genetic continuity that linked Ancient and Modern Greeks begun to take hold in popular consciousness. The incorporation of Byzantium into the Greek national narrative also allowed the resolution of the tension that had existed since the Enlightenment between "Hellenism" and Christianity into a "Helleno-Christian Civilization." Byzantium allowed the two concepts to be connected and these efforts also had the effect of giving "Hellenism" an "ethnic content" as Effi Gazi has stated, directly linking it to the Greek nation.[131] This fusion was, in many respects, an even stronger rejection of the work by Fallmerayer for whom the values of Byzantium and ancient Greece were fundamentally opposed to each other.[132]

Alongside the debates and the forging of a new national identity and territorial claims, there were heated policy debates about how the *Megali Idea* was going to be realized. Although the use of force was not discounted, a simple military conquest was generally not seen as a viable policy. After all, the tiny Kingdom of Greece could not hope to match the military strength of the Ottoman Empire, even if the latter was in decline. Although on occasion some reckless Greek politicians would push for direct confrontation with the Ottoman Empire, there was a general understanding that the goals of the Greek state would only be realized with the acquiescence, if not direct support, of the European Great Powers. This meant that Greece throughout the nineteenth century had to present its territorial claims in terms that would be acceptable to European governments and the European public. In the era of nationalism where the major political questions in Europe were the German and Italian unifications, Greek claims were presented as the demands of a subjugated people striving to achieve its unification with its nation-state.

In some regions like Crete this was an easy argument to make. A significant part of the population identified with the evolving Greek nation since the time of the Greek War of Independence. Christian Cretans continued to periodically rebel against Ottoman rule demanding union (*enosis*) with Greece. In other areas, however, the Greek state had to work harder to encourage local rebellions through the use of irregular armed bands that would cause disturbances, provoke revolts and the inevitable reprisals, and hopefully attract the attention of the European public and European governments. This policy was repeatedly put into effect, especially in times when the Ottoman Empire faced other threats or rebellions such as the Crimean War, the Cretan Revolts of 1841, 1866, 1878, and 1897, or the Russian-Ottoman war of 1877. These small bands were not expected to defeat the Ottoman forces, but to lay a claim to those territories and convince the Great Powers through subsequent diplomatic efforts to accept those claims.

Minorities and the *Megali Idea*

In the early decades of the Greek state, minorities in general, and Jews in particular, did not feature in these policies. This was due, in part, that Greece was the only independent Balkan state. The only other Balkan states with some degree of autonomy, Serbia, Moldavia, Wallachia, and Montenegro, did not compete over the immediate targets of Greek nationalist aspirations. Thus, the Greek state had no incentive to seriously tackle the question of minorities either internally or in the regions it sought to acquire. Greek constitutions in 1844 and 1863 included liberal provisions of freedom of belief, religion and so on,[133] and bestowed full civic rights and obligations to the few Jews and Muslims that remained in the kingdom. Even certain restrictions regarding other religions, such as the ban on proselytizing, were aimed at the perceived threat of foreign Protestant missionaries rather than the indigenous religious minorities.[134] The restoration of order and the enactment of the constitutions created an environment that allowed some Jews to either seek to return to their former places of residence or even emigrate to Greece from other parts of Europe and the Mediterranean. Some new communities were reconstituted or, as in Athens, emerged for the first time, and although they were miniscule, they were fully integrated into Greek society.[135] Greek governments only concerned themselves with the question of minorities when it interfered with the image the state tried to cultivate abroad and hinder their efforts toward the *Megali Idea*.

Before examining Greek irredentist policies however, it should be noted that Greece stood at the forefront of the states that bestowed religious minorities full civic rights. France had emancipated religious minorities including Jews in 1791 but most European states still imposed legal impediments on their Jewish subjects. Even Jewish authors like Heinrich Heine had ambivalent stances on Jewish emancipation, often railing against Jewish bankers and merchants.[136] In France, efforts were made after the Restoration to return Judaism to its inferior status but the charter of Louis XVIII was rather similar to the Greek constitution in setting Catholicism as the state religion while guaranteeing freedom of worship to all other faiths.[137] Greece and France have many similarities with regard to their Jewish populations, both having very small minorities with regard to their population and concentrated in a few cities.[138] Greece and France also followed similar policies with regard to Jewish conscription as seen in the decision of the Greek state to reject the request of the Jews of Chalkis for an exemption which in some ways mirrors French attitudes during the Revolutionary and Napoleonic periods.[139] This progressive legal framework of the Greek state should be kept in mind as we discuss the interactions of the Greek state with minorities within and beyond the borders of the state.

As we have seen in the early decades of the Greek state, significant pressure was exerted by local communities and local authorities on remaining Muslims to convert or immigrate.[140] These pressures can hardly be considered state policy, and in fact the Greek governments as described above, were often embarrassed by such incidents which they could neither denounce due to domestic political considerations nor embrace since they caused diplomatic incidents with the Ottoman Empire and the European Great Powers. At the same time the Greek consuls in the Ottoman Empire began to monitor and comment upon the conditions of various ethnic groups of the regions that the Greek state hoped to incorporate. The Greek consuls also commented on the activities of the various ethnic groups of the region as well as referencing of the attitude of such groups, including the Jewish communities, toward the Greek state or the Greek Orthodox community.

Macedonia in general, and Salonica in particular, were especially problematic from the point of view of the Greek consuls, and would become even more contested over the course of the nineteenth century as we will see in the following chapter. The commercial significance of Salonica meant that it was one of the first areas to have a Greek representative whose reports to the Greek government often show a city riven by sectarian divisions despite much of modern historiography that tends to emphasize coexistence among many different ethnic and religious groups.[141] The reports mention the persecution of Christians by Muslims,[142] but the consuls stressed particularly the conflicts between Christians and Jews in the city. As early as 1835 a report blamed the Jewish population of the city for a "new" violent event between Greek sailors and Ottomans. According to the report the conflict resulted from

> the intrigues of the Jews who never cease to foster in every way the displeasure of the Ottomans against the Greeks. The dispute was initially limited between Greeks and Jews [but] the Jews in order to cause harm to the Greeks appealed to the local garrison which immediately came to their aid and instead of containing the commotion, in a manner unworthy of a regular force begun to strike with its bayonets the unfortunate Greeks one of whom was forced to attack the regular [soldiers] wounding one and disarming three."[143]

Such claims of Jewish hostility were repeated over the next decades in a variety of occasions, for instance when two Christian and Muslim bandits were hanged by the Ottoman authorities:

> The Jews rushed in numbers only to the two gates where the two Christians were hanging and with pleasure watched the miserable spectacle of the hanged men. But at the gate where the Ottoman criminal was hanging nobody dared to show up being afraid to provoke the wrath of the Turks.[144]

The hostility of the Greek consuls toward the Jewish community in Salonica was palpable even before the anti-Greek riot of 1852, which was described in detail over multiple reports. According to Konstantinos Ramfos, the consul at the time, 5,000 Jews gathered at the marketplace and attacked Christians with knives and clubs who were going to the market or their homes. The attacks killed three and injured many without reaction from the authorities. Konstantinos Ramfos, alongside the consuls of Britain and Russia, lodged protests with the Ottoman authorities, and made a particular point in his report that "the Jews besides the murders and the injuries also stripped the victims (of their valuables)."[145] From the numerous reports the consul dispatched to Athens, it appears that the cause of the riot was the murder of a Jewish butcher, an event the consul disputed, and that the Ottoman authorities instead of protecting the Christians imprisoned the victims of the riot on the charge of murder and even threatened to exile the Orthodox bishop. The consul openly accused the Jewish notables and chief rabbi of protecting the perpetrators of the murders of the Christians and that they had threatened to repeat the violence. Thus, according to Ramfos, Christians and Jews were walking around the town armed.[146] The consul insisted that the Ottoman press had distorted the events and that "the Jewish treasury has performed a miracle on this occasion," while accusing an unnamed Jewish merchant and banker of leading the riot during which shouts of "strike, kill, and the common (treasury) will pay" were heard.[147] The consul was fearful for the safety of Christians since the city had 35,000 Jews and only 25,000 Muslims and Christians combined, and so he wanted a naval demonstration by Greek and other European warships to restore order.[148]

From such reports it was evident that the consuls identified Salonica's Jews as inherently hostile to Christians and by extension to the Greek state which acted as their patron and defender. Despite the evident bias of these reports their assessment was probably correct. Jews filed complaints against the Greek consuls almost from the moment they were established,[149] while even when the Greek consuls attempted to carry favor with the leading Jews of the city by hiring two of their relatives the chief rabbi essentially forced their dismissal.[150] The image of Salonica after the establishment of the Greek Kingdom is one of tension between the Jewish and Christian communities in which the Greek state assumed the role of representing and defending the latter.

The reports from Macedonia stand in stark contrast to those from Epirus and Albania, another region where Greece had claims. The primary concern of the Greek consuls in Epirus was the attitude of the population with respect to the Ottoman authorities, and the persistent disturbances and lawlessness of the region. They were interested in the religious breakdown of Albania,[151] Albanian uprisings and banditry,[152] and the occasional Greek involvement in the general disorder, especially during the Crimean War when Greek officers and soldiers in uniform apparently entered Ottoman territory.[153] Jews were barely mentioned, and when they were, it was often only as an afterthought, for example when the consuls reported the gathering of "Christians, Ottomans, and Jews" to hear proclamations,[154] or when a provincial council "composed of six Christians, six Turks, and one Jew" was created.[155] Furthermore, unlike the reports from Salonica, the reports from Epirus were not explicitly hostile to Jews but were instead, rather indifferent.

This does not mean that there were no conflicts between Jews and Christians in the region. The Greek consul reported in 1851 a case of religious fervor over the discovery of the foundations of an ancient monastery by a young shepherd "inspired according to the belief of the people by the Virgin Mary." The location became the site of a pilgrimage where many Christians and Muslims flocked and the shepherd, who according to the consul suffered from "religious fervor" (*theovlaveia*) was preaching and prophesizing unmolested by the Ottoman authorities. The shepherd was railing against social or commercial interactions with Jews and the latter complained to the authorities and, as the report mentioned, bribed them to arrest the shepherd. This "assault" against the monastery and the "instrument of the Virgin Mary" intensified the religious fanaticism of the people of Epirus, even among Muslims, because of the many miracles that had taken place. The consul included a letter by the bishop and Christian notables reiterating the events though with a less critical stance and accepting the supposed Marian instruction to avoid contact with Jews.[156]

The specific events may have unsettled relations between Jews and Christians but it is worth noting that the preaching of the shepherd was remarkably similar, if not identical, to other popular holy men like Kosmas who was discussed in the previous chapter. Furthermore, it was evident that relations between Jews and Christians had been deteriorating long before the arrest of the self-proclaimed prophet. A few months earlier the Jews of Janina had been the victims of a deadly riot quite reminiscent of the Salonica riot of 1853 but with roles reversed. According to the Greek consul during Easter some Jews insulted the cantor of the Church of St. Nicholas who was leading a religious procession through the Jewish quarter, overturned the baptismal urn and spit in it.[157] This enraged the Christians of the city and of the surrounding villages and while the bishop and the notables met to demand satisfaction, a crowd of Christians attacked any Jew they could find in the marketplace killing at least one man. This murder further inflamed the Christian crowd who armed themselves with daggers and at the funeral of the victim pelted the body with stones and filth. Even the presence of a military detachment failed to disperse the crowd. The Christian notables insisted that the Ottoman authorities should "punish the Jews" for their sacrilege and refused to surrender the murderer. A Greek citizen had apparently taken an active role in the disturbances and the consul placed him under house arrest for a while. The consul also took the lead along with the bishop and notables in directing the authorities to take measures against the Jews to pacify the crowd. Although the Ottoman commander rightly considered the Jews to be the victims, in a manner similar to the events in Salonica he imprisoned four Jews as responsible for the sacrilegious act that had sparked the riot. Nevertheless, spirits in the city remained tense as the consul reported with the Jewish community offering a reward for the discovery of the man who had murdered the unfortunate Jew during the riot.[158]

These reports indicate that relations between Christians and Jews in Janina were hardly any better than in Salonica, though the circumstances were reversed since at Janina Christians outnumbered Jews. Unlike Salonica, however, the reports of the consul are much more matter of fact, less prone toward negative characterizations, and despite his personal involvement they appear more objective. Clearly the consul did not consider Jews to be a threat either toward the Christian community of the city or toward Greek interests in general, unlike his counterpart in Salonica who identified Jews as a greater threat than Muslims.

I do not want to give the impression, however, that Jews were the foremost concern of Greek diplomats, even in Salonica. For the Greek consuls, the greatest threat to Greek interests was Panslavism and Russian machinations, the brief friendly interlude of the Crimean War notwithstanding, this concern mirrors concerns that were voiced at the time in Greece.[159] The concern with Panslavism is not surprising because, as we shall see in the next chapter, Macedonia and Epirus would become a contested region between Greece and Balkan Slavic states notably, Serbia and Bulgaria. Although the conflict over Macedonia would reach its peak in the twentieth century, the emergence of Bulgarian nationalism takes place in this period, in part, as a movement to oppose Greek dominance of the Orthodox Church in the Ottoman Empire.[160] For the Greek authorities, this opposition was fostered and directed by Russia particularly in the period following the conclusion of the Crimean War. The consul of Salonica, for instance, described a conflict between "Greeks" and "Bulgarians" in which an ethnic Bulgarian bishop donated various "Russian" hieratic vestments to the churches of the region of Polyani. This caused local concern as it was perceived as an attempt to turn the population toward the "Western dogma." The consul did not believe that it was Catholic propaganda but rather "another unseen but active power that promotes these divisions to support Bulgarism," clearly referring to Russia.[161] Other reports were more blatant describing the activities of Russian agents and consuls and specifically linking them to Panslavism. Some focused on the proselytizing efforts of Russians specifically aimed against Greek interests,[162] efforts by Russian consuls to combat "Hellenism" in Thessaly and Macedonia in order to foster Panslavism,[163] or efforts to promote the Uniate Church, referred to as the Bulgarian-Catholic dogma (*voulgarokatholiko dogma*), among Slavs by promising the building of new churches where the liturgy would be in the "Slavonic" language.[164]

The Greek embassy in Constantinople also focused on the Panslavic propaganda of the region monitoring newspapers that were considered pro-Bulgarian and anti-Greek like the *Courrier de' Orient*, or the role of churchmen that were seen as hostile to the Greek-dominated patriarchate of Constantinople.[165] Similar reports came from the Greek embassy at St. Petersburg which dispatched two memoranda on the "Bulgarian issue" published by the Russian government in support of Bulgarian demands supposedly to counter the successes of Catholicism and conversion to the "western dogma."[166] Ironically some reports also mention the hostility of the British consuls toward Greek interests alongside the denunciations of Russian policies.[167] Britain, of course, was at this time a supporter of the integrity of the Ottoman Empire while Russia's goals were the opposite, but both opposed Greek aspirations which threatened the territorial integrity of the Ottoman state but in opposition to Russian interests. Thus, Greece under King Otto often found herself enmeshed in Great Power politics and frequently isolated in the international arena. Questions of ethnicity were already being considered by Greek state authorities and impacting Greek policies though Jews were of minor significance at this point or seen as a further obstacle especially in Salonica.

The Greek state as defender of Orthodox Christianity

The Great Powers in the nineteenth century often used religion to advance their interests and nowhere was this rivalry more obvious than in the Ottoman Empire. Russia traditionally presented itself as the defender of Orthodox Christianity and had been joined by France who acted as a patron of Catholics while Britain also, on occasion, picked up the cause of the few Protestant converts helping them become a separate millet.[168] It was perhaps surprising that the Greek state would seek to rival these Great Powers, and in particular Russia by presenting itself as a bastion and defender of Orthodoxy and Greek Christian communities both within, but also beyond, its borders. However, this was a logical outcome of the confluence of the *Megali Idea* and the incorporation of religion into the Greek nationalist construct. Greek consuls throughout the Mediterranean monitored activities that they considered were aimed against Orthodox Christians and their interests and reported them to the Greek government.[169] Greek diplomats repeatedly intervened with Ottoman authorities in cases of Islamic conversion of Orthodox *reya*. The Greek diplomats kept the Greek government appraised of the progress of such cases that could involve Ottoman subjects and often children, though on occasion cases involved Greek subjects usually young sailors.[170] Letters from the consuls indicate that on occasion the conversion of a Christian was used to intimidate Christians, as for instance in 1855 when a young man named Panagiotis Prasinelis was "forcibly" converted to Islam. After his conversion, he was paraded through the streets at the head of a Muslim mob brandishing swords, shields, and banners which frightened the remaining Christians to such a degree that many fled the town.[171] Most cases of conversion reported to the Greek government involved young women marrying Muslim men as in the case of Lemonia and Husein in Chios.[172]

Christian communities in the Ottoman Empire frequently voiced concerns to the authorities about the way conversions, especially those of children or women, were carried out. These complaints placed the Ottoman authorities in a difficult position since they risked offending either the Muslim or the non-Muslim local communities.[173] The frequent involvement of the patriarch of Constantinople or that of foreign consuls and diplomats further complicated such cases for the Ottomans as did the fact that many of these conversions could develop in cases of apostasy from Islam if the new convert was convinced to return to her or his original faith.[174] In this context Greece could intervene on behalf of Christians in order to assert her role as the defender of Orthodox Christians and claim them as members of the Greek nation. The Ottomans were not unaware of the challenge the Greek state made to their authority over Ottoman Christians and thus Greek interventions could escalate into serious diplomatic incidents. One such occasion took place in Varna and involved a thirteen- or fourteen-year-old daughter of a Greek subject who was "seduced" and transported to an Ottoman house "by force or subterfuge" where she was held in order to embrace Islam. Both the local Greek consul and the Greek ambassador to Istanbul got involved and successfully requested the intervention of other foreign dignitaries like the Russian consul and the Spanish ambassador. The escalation of a local issue to an international incident provoked the ire of the Ottoman government and a rather extensive diplomatic correspondence with Athens that led to an Ottoman request for the recall of the Greek consul in Varna.[175]

Greek consuls were also concerned with the fate of the so-called Muslim-Christians (*Islamochristianon*) or crypto-Christians, some of whom were formerly captured Christians that had nominally converted to Islam but continued to practice Christian rites secretly. Often entire communities practiced hybrid forms of Christianity and Islam and were known by a variety of names throughout the empire.[176] When such individuals tried to declare their return to Christianity openly in the context of the Tanzimat, they became apostates from Islam and were thus liable to face persecution.[177] One such occasion in Crete was revealed when the wife of an Ottoman treasurer fled to the house of the British consul with her daughter and son-in-law to escape the fury of her husband when the latter discovered that she was still practicing Christianity alongside her daughter and her son-in-law.[178] The Greek consul returned to the issue of these crypto-Christians in another letter reporting that Veli pasha was touring Crete to bring the "discovered Muslim-Christians" to the Ottoman fold.[179] The Tanzimat had created an environment where such apostasies could be contemplated and entire communities like the Kromlides or Istavri declared their Christianity in the 1850s and 1860s.[180] Although I have not examined diplomatic correspondence dealing with the larger crypto-Christian groups that abandoned Islam en masse in the nineteenth century, since their cases were beyond the geographical focus of my research, it is likely that Greek diplomats were also involved with their cases since as Deringil noted, foreign consuls regularly reported on such cases and the patriarchate of Constantinople was often involved in counseling and on occasion, recognizing them as Christians.[181] Greek nationalist narrative has consistently assigned membership of crypto-Christians to the Greek nation as part of the Christian neomartyr narrative discussed in the earlier chapter.[182]

The significance the Greek government attached to its role as defender of Orthodox communities is best exemplified by the fact that Greek consuls and the Greek government did not limit themselves in defending Orthodox Christians in the Ottoman Empire against the threat of Islamic conversion but perceived their role in much wider terms. Greek consuls investigated reports about the rape of a young Ottoman Christian boy by the drunk commandant of Naousa Murat bey.[183] The Greek consul in Cairo refused to notarize a dowry contract between a Greek citizen and a young Catholic woman because a clause stipulated that the offspring of the marriage would be raised in the Catholic faith.[184] He also reported on the "religious fanaticism of the *ulema* and the mob" in cases of anti-Christian violence.[185] In Herakleio (Candia), the consul kept the government informed about Muslims in Crete who wanted to convert to Orthodoxy as well as about Christians who converted to Islam.[186]

The significance Greek governments placed on religion as a component of their political mind-set, however, is best exemplified by the concern that Greece attached to events in the Kingdom of Two Sicilies in 1843. The Greek government monitored the actions of the government of the southern Italian kingdom and objected strenuously to its decision to dismiss the Orthodox priests and replace them with Catholics particularly in the cities of Messina and Barletta where the Orthodox churches were seized and transferred to the Catholic Church. King Otto instructed the Greek embassy in France to act with regard to the freedom of worship of the Orthodox in the Kingdom of Two Sicilies. He insisted that the Orthodox should enjoy the same rights as Catholics mentioning that his government had already sent numerous letters to the government of the Kingdom of Two Sicilies following complaints from the Orthodox communities in Messina and Barletta.[187] Nor was this an isolated incident. As early as 1833 numerous Orthodox inhabitants of Ancona applied for Greek citizenship in order to secure Greek protection from religious discrimination by local authorities.[188] The fact that the Orthodox communities of southern Italy would see the Greek government, a decade after the creation of the tiny Greek Kingdom, as a possible protector is indeed remarkable considering the traditional role of Russia as the protector of Orthodoxy. I should also note that the Greek government adroitly used an opportunity to supplant the traditional role of the "Ecumenical" patriarchate of Constantinople after the 1840 deposition of Gregory VI following intense pressure by the British government and its foreign minister Lord Palmerston over the patriarch's meddling in the religious affairs of the Ionian islands.[189] Despite the continuing influence of Russia in Greece itself, the Greek Kingdom had already emerged as a possible rival to the role that Russia enjoyed at least since the Treaty of Küçük Kaynarja. This challenge may cast a new light on Russian concerns and responses such as the establishment by Britain of an Anglican bishop in Jerusalem in 1841 or the founding of a Catholic patriarchate there in 1846 which caused significant concern to Russian authorities,[190] the controversy over the control of places of worship in Jerusalem that led to the Crimean War, and Russian policies in the Balkans in the second half of the nineteenth century that appear to be explicitly directed against Greek national interests. It also explains Greek concerns about the role of Russia in Macedonia and Panslavism in general.

The Don Pacifico affair

Like most of Europe, Greece in the nineteenth century was a deeply anti-Semitic society especially at the popular level. Despite the virtual absence of Jews in Greek society, anti-Semitism was deeply rooted, as we saw in earlier chapter, and expressed in local customs particularly during Easter, a time of increased anti-Semitic violence that was often reported in the European press.[191] The state did not endorse such acts and in fact it tried to limit the bad press that anti-Semitic acts generated in Europe. Such efforts, however, could backfire as the most famous anti-Semitic event in nineteenth-century Athens, the Don Pacifico riot, exemplifies.

The riot took place in 1847 and may have been the outcome of the convergence of long-standing anti-Semitic traditions, modern European-inspired anti-Semitism, and popular reaction against the perceived role of foreigners in Greece. Athenians, like many other Greek Orthodox communities, practiced the burning of the Judas effigy in Easter, a public spectacle following the Holy Thursday Mass which makes frequent references to the "*genos* of Jews" and their culpability for the crucifixion of Christ. [192] In 1847, the Orthodox Easter coincided with a visit by Baron James Mayer de Rothschild, who represented the British bondholders of Greek debt, which the Greek government had suspended. Baron Rothschild was hoping to negotiate a resumption of payments which would have allowed the Greek government to resume borrowing, and the government, hoping to avoid offending the distinguished guest, issued an ordinance banning the offensive custom of the burning of Judas. This act gave an opportunity to certain political factions to stage a violent protest, a rather common phenomenon in Greek politics, and a small crowd attacked the house of Don Pacifico, caused extensive damage, and made off with jewelry and other household items. The police did not intervene, perhaps due to the presence of the son of the Minister of War among the rioters, according to statements made later by Don Pacifico. [193] Don Pacifico was of Portuguese origin but a British citizen, and he appealed to the British ambassador Sir Edmund Lyons demanding compensation from the Greek government. Although serious, Don Pacifico's claim was not the only dispute between British subjects and the

Greek government. George Finlay for example, a philhellene and author of a history of the Greek War of Independence, settled in Greece and engaged extensively in land speculation in Athens. Some of his lands were subsequently expropriated to form the Royal Gardens. Finlay was in litigation with the Greek government with regard to his compensation. Similarly, other British merchants and subjects, some of them Greeks from the British-held Ionian islands, had a variety of disputes with Greece. [194] Furthermore, the British and Greek government disputed ownership of two tiny islands Cervi (Elafonissi) and Sapienza, over which Palmerston had directed the British Ionian authorities to assert British sovereignty in 1849 though no action ensued. [195] The Greek government, however, quickly recognized the significance of the Don Pacifico case and tried to appease the British and in particular to disassociate the event with any accusation of anti-Semitism.

In a letter dated 16/28 July 1848, to Sir Edmond Lyons the Greek foreign minister Konstantinos Kolokotronis attempted to explain the Greek government's position. Kolokotronis reported that the Greek government immediately began a judicial investigation over the incident and expressed his surprise that Don Pacifico had not waited for its conclusion before seeking the aid of the British government, noting that Don Pacifico had not assisted in the investigation. He rejected the British accusation that Don Pacifico would have been exposed again to "the fury of a population incensed and superstitious" claiming that:

> There have always been Jews, and there still are in many parts of Greece, where they freely practice their trade without any serious complaint, as far as I am aware, that has been presented to the Royal government, nor to those that preceded it, of violent and barbaric acts committed by Greeks against the Israelites.

Kolokotronis concluded his letter by mentioning that Don Pacifico lived for years in Athens without incident and tried to shift the case away from anti-Semitism toward one of legal jurisdiction stating that the government could not give a foreign subject more rights than those it recognized toward its own citizens. [196]

This was a remarkable response by the Greek government considering the events of the Greek War of Independence but it reflected accurately the position and convictions of the Greek cabinet. A similar response was delivered in 1852 to the US minister in Istanbul George Marsh when he attempted to intervene on behalf of the missionary Jonas King which stressed the great degree of religious toleration in Greece specifically mentioning Catholics, Protestants, "Mohammedans" and Jews. [197] In the letters of Minister Glarakis there was clear confusion why Don Pacifico did not seek redress through the courts in Greece, "as would have been the case in any other European state," and indicated the difficult position the British demands placed on the Greek government since they were in essence asking the government to intervene in a judicial matter, undermining the independence of the judiciary in Greece. Furthermore, Glarakis again disputed that anti-Semitism was behind the actions of the mob "because, I repeat, fanaticism does not exist in the customs or the laws of Greece that tolerate and protect the practice of all religions." [198]

While the Greek government repeatedly tried to disassociate the events from anti-Semitism, Don Pacifico always linked the two in his letters. He claimed that he attempted to follow the legal path but failed to find justice and only then did he resort to the British government. Furthermore, he held the Greek government politically responsible by drawing parallels to similar cases in Ithaca, then under British authority, where the British government had forced the local community to compensate the victim with £20,000, and to a case in Portugal where a similar resolution had been achieved, even though in both cases the governments themselves were not at fault. In his case, however, the Greek government was culpable because:

> Trying to carry favor with Mr. Karolos [*sic*] Rothschild who was in Athens in April 1847, it had forbidden to the churches of Athens the burning of the Judas without accompanying this prohibition with the necessary means to ensure its compliance and the people thought that Pacifico had instigated the prohibition.

Don Pacifico also thought that the government did not want to lose its popularity on his account "acquiescing to the superstitions of the Athenians." He stated that after the events he went repeatedly to the prosecutor denouncing the presence of the sons of General Tzavellas among the mob and even naming the houses that contained some of his stolen articles but no action was taken, and concluded that as a Jew and a foreigner he did not enjoy the same rights as Greek citizens since "prejudice weighs me and my religion to which all Greeks in general and without exception adhere to."[199]

Internal reports by the Ministry of Justice and the prefecture of Athens and Boeotia substantiate, to some degree, Pacifico's claims. The investigation did find evidence that the episode was orchestrated by "intriguers" naming specifically a man called Hatzas Athanasios Tsamtsis who "exploited the boundless superstition of the small mob of the lowest class that used to burn the image of a Jew on that day." They also mentioned rumors that had been circulated to the effect that Don Pacifico tried through bribes to prohibit the burning of Judas. However, despite this information, the lower courts had suspended the investigation without filling charges citing lack of evidence.[200]

It is interesting to note that despite the fact that Pacifico named the sons of Minister Tzavellas as taking part in the attack on his house, a story corroborated by general Makrygiannis, and *The Economist* stressed the point further,[201] neither the Greek documents, nor the British ones that I have seen, drew connections to the fact that following the death of Prime Minister Kolettis, General Tzavellas became prime minister in September of 1847 until March 1848, during which the relations between Greece and Britain rapidly deteriorated over this issue. Lyons bombarded the Greek government with letters and demands and the refusal of the Greek government to satisfy the substantial claims of Don Pacifico led Lord Palmerston in 1849 to dispatch a British naval squadron to Greece with orders that in the event the Greek government refused the British demands the squadron was to seize the Greek navy, blockade the Greek ports, and take any other action deemed necessary. The Greek government appealed for support to France and Russia and receiving it rejected the British ultimatum. The British carried through their threats by seizing several Greek warships and imposing a blockade on the main Greek ports that lasted for forty-two days. They also sequestered several merchant ships as surety toward their claims against the Greek government.[202] These actions provoked a mass of protests by the representatives of various European states including France, Russia, Prussia, and Austria, and sparked a political crisis in Britain itself where the conservative opposition seized the opportunity to unite the fractured party and question the foreign policy of the British government.[203] Many conservative politicians essentially reiterated the Greek government position that Palmerston was flouting international law by not giving time to the local legal system to examine the cases of the plaintiffs.[204] Lord Stanley introduced a motion in the House of Lords to censure the government over the issue and the great liberal Richard Cobden also criticized the actions of the British government.[205] In a brilliant speech, the beleaguered Palmerstone defended his policies both in the particular case of Don Pacifico, specifically referring to Pacifico's Jewish heritage, as well as the broader principles of British intervention comparing British policy to the *Pax Romana* of antiquity:

> As if because a man was poor he might be bastinadoed and tortured with impunity, as if a man who was born in Scotland might be robbed without redress, or, because a man is of the Jewish persuasion, he is fair game for any outrage. . . . Whether the principles on which the foreign policy of Her Majesty's Government has been conducted, and the sense of duty which led us to think ourselves bound to afford protection to our fellow subjects abroad, are proper and fitting guides for those who are charged with the Government of England and whether, as the Roman, in days of old, held himself free from indignity, when he could say, *Civis Romanussum*; so also a British subject, in whatever land he may be, shall feel confident that the watchful eye and the strong arm of England, will protect him against injustice and wrong.[206]

Palmerstone's speech won him the support of parliament and he was subsequently able to appease the French by having the dispute referred to an arbitration commission approved by Britain, Greece, and France.[207] It also catapulted his career and he begun being mentioned as a possible prime minister.[208]

Although the selection of Don Pacifico as a target for the mob's violence was indisputably due to his Jewish origins, it is a problematic event to use as an exemplar of Greek anti-Semitism as other scholars have also noted.[209] To begin with, Don Pacifico was a British national at a time when relations between Greece and Britain were strained in part due to Greek defaults on debt held to a large extent by British investors, and in part due to a perceived tendency of the Greek government to favor Russia over the other Great Powers that had guaranteed Greek independence—Britain and France. As *The Economist* noted at the time, Pacifico was targeted due to "popular prejudice" and "because he was a Jew and an English subject."[210] In similar fashion in the riots following the overthrow of Bavarian-born King Otto in 1862, several houses of Germans were pillaged by the mob.[211] The Don Pacifico case was essentially magnified by the British government in order to apply pressure on the Greek government, despite the prevalence of British anti-Semitic prejudices of the time to which *The Economist* alluded to.[212] Significantly the Greek government did not perceive the case in terms of anti-Semitism, or even as a question of minority rights, but rather as a case of the rights of foreign nationals, extraterritoriality, and the jurisdiction of the Greek government and Greek courts of law, as the exchange of the Greek foreign ministry and the British ambassador Sir Edmund Lyons indicates.[213] The issue at hand was the right of the Greek courts to determine the compensation, if any, that Don Pacifico was entitled to as opposed to the assertions of the British government regarding Don Pacifico's claims. The diplomatic support the Greek government received by other European governments and the eventual settlement that was brought about through the intervention of the French government are a clear indication that there was an element of Great Power politics involved as Disraeli, then in opposition, suspected all along.[214]

The case rightly is more noted in Greek historiography as an example of gunboat diplomacy than a case of anti-Semitism.[215] After all, although Palmerson had been an early supporter of Greek claims to Crete by 1840, he reversed course and even threatened Greece with military intervention if she continued to support the rebels on the island, in part because of the influence of Russia in Greece.[216] Furthermore, Britain experienced two rebellions on the Ionian island of Cephalonia in 1848 and 1849 and some rebels sought refuge to Greece, and demanded the recall of the local consul Chourmouziadis in 1848 for collaborating with nationalist radicals.[217] The origins of the case, however, the mob violence and the anti-Semitic custom of Judas burning in Easter, should not be ignored nor should the attitude of the Greek government which attempted to suppress the custom in order to facilitate other, unrelated, national issues, and the fact that the government accepted the principle regarding compensation but disputed the size of the claim and the right of the British government to interfere in a Greek judicial matter. For a better example on how the Greek state dealt with questions of anti-Semitism and how it perceived its Jewish citizens we must go to the last decade of the nineteenth century and look at the question of the blood libel accusations in Greece and especially the Kerkyra (Corfu) pogrom that will be discussed in the following chapter. Ironically the whole Don Pacifico incident restored the popularity of King Otto and his government and even contributed to the mending of relations with the patriarchate of Constantinople which eventually recognized the autonomy of the Church of Greece under certain conditions.[218]

The constitutional reign of King Otto was a turbulent period marked by domestic and foreign crises that eventually led to his deposition and exile in 1862 after yet another revolt. Otto was unable to accept his role as a constitutional monarch and attempted to use the extensive powers given to the crown by the constitution of 1844 to control the government and parliament. That naturally created resentment against his person since government failures would often correctly be ascribed to the King. Although mid-nineteenth-century Greece was plagued by numerous problems including perennial fiscal difficulties, a corrupt political system based on patronage, practically nonexistent industrial development, a lack of infrastructure, the greatest crises involved external matters and almost all were tied to the pursuit of the *Megali Idea*.

Ironically, the Bavarian-born Otto became a strong supporter of Greek nationalism and would remain so even after his exile until his death. Despite the strongly nationalist policies of the Greek governments throughout the 1840s and 1850s, the armed forces and especially the army were surprisingly neglected. Logic and the experiences of the Greek War of Independence had convinced the Greek leadership that direct confrontation with the Ottoman Empire was a suicidal course. If territorial gains were to be achieved Greece needed to get the European Great Powers to agree to them and force the Ottomans to comply, as had occurred at the end of the Greek War of Independence. Unfortunately for the Greeks, this was the time when the so-called Eastern Question preoccupied the Great Powers, the apparent weakness of the Ottoman Empire and the fear that Russia would exploit this weakness to expand its borders southwards into the Mediterranean. Most European governments, therefore, strove to preserve rather than undermine the Ottoman state, and the one power that wanted to weaken the Ottomans, Russia, had no interest in doing so for the benefit of Greece.

This did not necessarily dissuade Greek nationalists. After all, the second lesson from the Greek War of Independence was that in time, and under the right circumstances, the European public could exert its influence and force its governments to change their policies. Thus, the unstated policy of the Greek government was to foster, and even orchestrate, revolts in the Ottoman territories bordering the Greek state, which regardless of their success could involve the European powers and in such circumstances Greece might convince them to cede those areas to her. The primary target of this policy was Crete, the island that had participated in the Greek War of Independence but had not been awarded to Greece, as well as territories on the borders between Greece and the Ottoman Empire in Epirus, Thessaly, and Macedonia.

In Crete the Greek governments did not have to try hard to instigate revolts. Christian Cretans repeatedly rose in rebellion in the nineteenth century and the atrocities of the Muslim inhabitants in response were often reported in the foreign press.[219] The strategic location of the island, however, ensured that the Great Powers in general and Britain in particular did not support the radical transformation of the status of the island. If anything, as we shall see in the next chapter Cretan Revolts disrupted Greek politics by forcing Greek governments to either confront Greek public opinion which was demanding Greek intervention, or to risk war with the Ottomans against the wishes of the Great Powers.

On the mainland, the situation was quite different. The Greek-Ottoman border spanned a mountainous and sparsely populated region that neither government was able to control effectively. That allowed the proliferation of banditry as was the case in many similar circumstances throughout the Mediterranean, as well as insurgents from either side who often found refuge by crossing the border as did Albanian and Greek rebels.[220] Early on both Greek and Ottoman governments allowed local authorities to manage the fluid border in a spirit of cooperation[221] but the rise of the *Megali Idea* transformed the situation. The Greek governments recognized a valuable political tool in the bands of outlaws that plagued the region. Such bands could become the seeds for "popular" uprisings in the Ottoman provinces bordering the Greek state. Reaching back to the tradition of the *Kleftes*, a tradition that had been embellished and sanitized by nationalist historians, these bandits could be rebranded as *andartes* (guerillas) and used to promote Greek claims to the region. This was a dangerous policy, however, in part because the bands were not under the effective direct control of Athens, and because, as in Crete, the Greek government could face unbearable pressure by the public to intervene openly in favor of such revolts risking war with the Ottomans.

Although incidents occurred throughout the 1840s, the perils of this nationalist policy materialized during the Crimean War which gave the opportunity to the Greek government to deploy such bands to foster widespread rebellions in Macedonia, Thessaly, and Epirus.[222] The Ottomans enjoyed the support of France and Britain who had grown increasingly alarmed by Russian expansion and even Piedmont whose policies and aspirations were not that much different with respect to Italy than Greece's were with the Ottoman Empire and whose ambassador in Istanbul tried to warn Greece against agitation in the Balkans.[223] Greek pro-Russian policies and agitation provoked a severing of diplomatic relations with the Ottoman Empire and despite warnings from France and Britain to remain neutral, Greece seemed on the verge of entering the fray against the Ottomans amassing troops at the border. Although such actions succeeded in temporarily convincing Russia, until then the greatest opponent to the *Megali Idea*, to support Greek claims to Ottoman territory, the Crimean War was a miscalculation. The "volunteers" and rebels were easily suppressed by the Ottoman forces, and British and French squadrons blockaded Greek ports and occupied Piraeus provoking a cholera outbreak that claimed 30,000 lives.[224] The entire war was a great humiliation for Greece and Otto and the conclusion of the Crimean War found Greece with the same borders and with its main ports under occupation.

As with the Pacifico case, this disastrous policy temporarily boosted the popularity of the King but deteriorated the already dismal economic situation in Greece.[225] Otto had forfeited the trust of two of Greece's protective powers without succeeding to aid Russia in any substantial way. To make matters worse the open embrace by Russia of Panslavism in the aftermath of the Crimean War directly threatened Greek interests in the Balkans. Otto also alienated the Greek public with his stance regarding Italian unification which most Greek supported, some even volunteering to join Garibaldi in his campaigns.[226] With nothing to show for three decades on the Greek throne, Otto's credentials as a nationalist leader had evaporated while his political meddling, disastrous economic policy, and general insensitivity toward the mood of the Greek public led to a second revolt against his rule in 1862 that forced his abdication and exile from Greece.

Competing Nationalisms: New Territories, Nationalist Aspirations, and Jews (1862–1923)

The overthrow of King Otto produced yet another constitutional crisis in Greece. The Great Powers once again were involved in selecting the next king, this time the younger son of the king of Denmark who became George I King of the Hellenes under a new more democratic constitution that nevertheless still gave wide powers to the crown. George I would prove a much savvier monarch than Otto but he too would come to embrace Greek nationalism and the *Megali Idea*. He married a Russian Grand Duchess, raised his children in the Greek Orthodox faith, and named his eldest son Constantine with clear allusions to the last emperor of Byzantium. He was also intelligent enough to accept limitations to his authority and give greater power to the Greek politicians thus retaining his throne and, to a large degree, his influence especially over military and foreign affairs.

In the second half of the nineteenth century, Greece saw certain significant transformations with regard to state institutions, citizenship, and how Greek elites viewed themselves and their aspirations. The new constitution was both more democratic and guaranteed the equal treatment of all, including Jews.[1] Although in 1863 and then 1881 the addition of several Jewish communities increased the numbers of Jews in the Greek state significantly, they remained a small minority overall and were nearly invisible in the capital Athens, forming an official community only in 1890.[2] Even though Jews appeared nearly invisible in the capital, they had been attending and graduating from the University of Athens from the 1870s, were conscripted in the army, and participating in Greek society fully.[3]

In the last decades of the nineteenth century, Greece developed a more stable political scene with the emergence of more coherent political affiliations that evolved into modern political parties, more or less. Those coalesced into two main political grouping. Both groups were highly nationalistic and supported the *Megali Idea* but as was the case in the preceding period, they differed in their policies in pursuit of that goal. One camp, exemplified by the reforming Prime Minister Harilaos Trikoupis emphasized economic development and fostering of alliances and diplomatic ties to the Great Powers. These close ties would supposedly allow Greece to build up the strength to confront the Ottoman Empire while maintaining good relations with the Great Powers, whose support was seen as absolutely necessary. The second group exemplified by the firebrand politician Theodoros Deliyiannis wanted to plunge right ahead toward the expansion of Greece by supporting or instigating revolts in the Ottoman Empire. The political rotation of these groups in power did not allow for a consistent policy. The lack of consistent policy coupled with the financial costs of either public infrastructure expenditure to dubious projects or the costs of armaments and mobilizations put enormous strains on the fragile Greek state's finances. The situation was further complicated by the fact that Greece was no longer the only nation-state with claims to the European provinces of the Ottoman Empire.

Over the course of the nineteenth century several other Balkan states had emerged on the map with their independence from the Ottoman Empire. Greece was joined by Serbia (which had already achieved a degree of autonomy in the early nineteenth century), Romania, Montenegro, and eventually Bulgaria, all with irredentist claims of their own against the Ottoman and Austro-Hungarian empires. Inevitably these claims clashed with each other particularly in Macedonia and Epirus. None of these states were powerful enough to contemplate independent action against the Ottomans, so they each sought to attach themselves to one of the European Great Powers, especially France, Russia, Austria-Hungary, and later Germany. The Great Powers intervened continuously to support the Ottoman Empire or the various Balkan states, and to oppose projects that were seen to be against their interests.

Nationalism was not a Balkan prerogative of course, and the two great nationalist projects of Europe in the nineteenth century were the German and Italian unifications. Both had come to fruition between 1864 and 1871 creating two new European Great Powers formed around two smaller core states, Piedmont and Prussia. This was the model Greece and the other Balkan states hoped to emulate. Some nationalist projects had been fully or partially achieved (Belgium, Hungary), while others were in revolutionary fervor (Poland, Ireland). Increasingly the surviving multinational empires of Europe, in particular Austria-Hungary, viewed nationalism as a threat to their existence but that did not stop them from attempting to exploit nationalist fervor for their own purposes.

The case of Bulgaria is a good example. We have already seen in the previous chapter that Greek diplomats were concerned by the emergence of Panslavism and the Russian policy of promoting Bulgarian nationalism in the aftermath of the Crimean War.[4] Between 1876 and 1877, a series of revolts in Bosnia and Bulgaria against Ottoman rule embroiled the whole region in turmoil drawing in Serbia and Montenegro who also had claims on these territories. The Ottomans were able to suppress the revolt but the irregular troops they used committed numerous atrocities on the Christian population of Bulgaria, as had the rebels on the Muslim population. The atrocities by the Ottomans, however, received widespread publicity in Europe and became famous as the "Bulgarian Horrors" in a manner reminiscent of the Greek War of Independence. This gave the Russians an opportunity to declare war on the Ottomans, ostensibly to defend the Orthodox Christians, and after a surprisingly difficult campaign the Russian forces were able to force the Ottomans to accept a peace treaty that in essence created a Great Bulgaria in much of what is today Bulgaria, Macedonia, and Northern Greece, under the effective control of Russia.

Predictably the remaining Balkan states and the other European Great Powers erupted in protest and thus the Treaty of San Stefano as it is known was never implemented.[5] Instead a European Great Power Congress was convened in Berlin where the terms of the San Stefano treaty were radically modified. Bulgaria was substantially reduced in size and split in two distinct entities, Bulgaria and Eastern Rumelia. Much of the territory that was previously assigned to Bulgaria was returned to Ottoman control. Austria-Hungary took over Bosnia-Herzegovina as a protectorate, while Britain acquired Cyprus. Serbia, Romania, and Montenegro were all recognized as fully independent states, while Bulgaria was made an autonomous state under nominal Ottoman suzerainty. The Treaty of Berlin was thus a significant humiliation to Russia, a great disappointment to Bulgaria, but also a disappointment to the Balkan states, especially Greece who did not receive any territorial compensation at the time and who now had a new rival over Macedonia.

Greece was further disappointed because it also failed to gain control of the island of Crete which had been in constant turmoil since the Greek War of Independence. Crete is also an excellent example of the complexities the Balkan states had to navigate to achieve their irredentist goals. The circumstances of the island were simpler than in Macedonia pitting a Christian majority against a Muslim minority, but the strategic location of the island and fears regarding the integrity of the Ottoman state led many of the Great Powers to oppose Greek plans for annexation settling instead for a form of autonomy. Sectarian violence intensified through the 1860s to the 1880s with Muslims fleeing the countryside while Christians were subjected to attacks in the cities. The increasing violence forced further involvement by the Great Powers who were still unwilling to accept Greek demands. The island experienced continuous violence and became the cause for a war between Greece and the Ottoman Empire in 1897 that neither side desired, yet Greece was unable to annex it until 1912.[6]

The Treaty of Berlin and the Treaty of San Stefano are interesting for an additional reason, the inclusion of clauses dealing with the duties of these new Balkan states with regard to the ethnic and religious minorities that were being added to their states. Article IV and Article XI of the Treaty of San Stefano dealt with the question of the property rights of Muslims in Serbia and Bulgaria,[7] but it was the Treaty of Berlin that specifically addressed the rights of interests of minorities in the context of the formulation of the Bulgarian constitution or Organic Law (Article IV), specifically mentioning the right of worship, civil and political rights, public employment, functions, and honors, in Bulgaria (Article V), Montenegro (Article XXVII), Serbia (Article XXXV), and Romania (Article XLIV) as well as in the Ottoman Empire with particular mention of Armenians (Articles LXI, LXII).[8] Although these treaties obliged the newly recognized states to respect the rights of their minorities, there was a clear recognition that minorities may be unwilling to remain in the new nation-states.[9] This minority protection was tied explicitly to the recognition of the new nation-states by the rest of Europe even though the same rights were not accorded to minorities in the West like the Irish, Bretons, Basques, or Corsicans, nor was Greece a signee, although in 1881 with the Convention of Constantinople that ceded Thessaly to Greece the latter undertook similar obligations including the obligation not to disarm the Muslim population of Thessaly.[10]

The Treaty of Berlin did not resolve any of the Balkan controversies. Four years later in 1885, Bulgaria took a step toward resurrecting the Greater Bulgaria of San

Stefano by annexing Eastern Rumelia which sparked a brief war with Serbia that Bulgaria, surprising everyone, won. The annexation of Eastern Rumelia with its significant Greek population in urban centers like Philippoupolis (Plovdiv) was a blow to Greek nationalism. Where the Treaty of Berlin failed most spectacularly was with regard to the rights of minorities despite the language of its terms. In the Ottoman Empire, the imposition of the authoritarian regime of Abdulhamid II after only a brief constitutional period resulted in the persecutions and massacres of thousands of Armenians in eastern Anatolia despite the specific obligations undertaken by the Empire in the Treaty of Berlin. In Serbia, Albanians were discriminated against and harassed forcing their flight toward Ottoman-held territories.[11] In Romania, Jews were regularly blamed for all the ills of Romanian society and were disenfranchised and discriminated against.[12] In Serbia, Jews had been barred from settling or trading in 1839, and although these restrictions were reversed with the 1869 constitution, Jews could not become officers in the army until 1888. Serbia was essentially forced to give civil and political rights to Jews in 1878 following the Treaty of Berlin.[13] Even in Thessaly, where the Greek government tried hard to retain the Muslim population in order to sustain the valuable agricultural productive capacity of the region, the annexation of the region to Greece was followed by a steady exodus of Muslims, who chose to emigrate to the Ottoman Empire rather than remain under Greek rule. Out of 35,000–45,000 Muslims in 1881, only 3,000 were left in 1911 and the same process was evidenced in Crete whose Muslim population fell from 73,000 in 1881 to 27,850 in 1911, and those fled en masse to the towns of the island after 1889, even though the island technically remained under Ottoman sovereignty. Similar exodi can be seen in other areas.[14] Bulgarians and Armenians often fled to the Russian Empire, although some evidence suggests that on occasion this was temporary.[15]

The Ottoman Empire received a great number of refugees in the latter half of the nineteenth century. The Russian expansion into the Crimea in the late eighteenth century was followed by further incursions along the Black Sea coast and into the Caucasus. Despite the fierce resistance of local Muslim peoples, the Russians slowly and with great brutality pushed into the Caucasus toward the Ottoman frontier.[16] The Russian advance caused massive waves of Muslim refugees starting with the Crimean Tatars and continuing with Chechens, Dagestanis, and especially Circassians. The Muslim refugee crisis was exacerbated by the conflicts of 1876–78 when Muslims, including Circassians and Tatars recently settled in Bulgaria, fled ahead of the Russian armies and the expanding borders of the Balkan states.[17] The Ottomans tried to settle these groups in Anatolia and the Balkans but the numbers and the experiences of these refugees caused significant unrest. The Ottomans also used them as irregular soldiers, similar to the way Russians used Cossacks, and like the Cossacks, these irregulars often committed atrocities especially when used against Christian insurgents as was the case in Bulgaria in 1876 or in Anatolia against Armenians.[18]

In addition to these Muslim refugees the Ottoman Empire was also the recipient of thousands of Jews fleeing a new way of anti-Semitic violence in central and eastern Europe. Although many Jews chose to emigrate to France or the United States, others settled in Ottoman cities, especially in the Balkans like Salonica, Istanbul, Smyrna (Izmir) or Adrianople (Edirne).[19] In 1891 and 1892, the Greek foreign ministry received several letters from its embassy and consulates in the Ottoman Empire and from the Ottoman government regarding the transportation of Jewish refugees from Russia, many of whom were carried on Greek ships. The Ottoman government demanded that the Greek ships not allow the disembarkation of the refugees in Ottoman ports. Consular reports stressed that the great numbers of the refugees could change the "national" (*ethnologiko*) character of certain cities like Smyrna in the future. The Ottoman consuls asked the Greek government to take measures to oppose the settlement of Jews there.[20] These Jewish refugees, like the Muslim ones, harbored deep mistrust toward Christian states and were highly suspicious of the Balkan nationalistic projects. They naturally felt some sympathy toward the Ottoman Empire, framing an understanding of the empire in general, and Salonica in particular, as a safe haven for Jews over the centuries, beginning from the Spanish expulsion of 1492 but incorporating other Jewish refugees such as Hungarian Jews following the eviction of the Ottomans from that country and more recent East European and Balkan arrivals.[21] Jews feared that the territories where they settled would be annexed to one Balkan state or another and would mean new dislocation and exile. With the emergence of new anti-Semitism throughout Europe, including anti-Semitic rhetoric and violence in the Balkans, such fears were given additional credence especially as far as Greece was concerned.

Despite the political setbacks of the Greek irredentist project entailed by the emergence of rival nationalisms and states in the Balkans, the period from 1863 to 1881 saw the first additions to the Greek state, both achieved through negotiated settlements. In 1863, on the occasion of the ascension of the new king George I to the throne, Britain ceded the Ionian Islands to Greece, satisfying a long-standing demand of the local Orthodox population that had included revolts and conspiracies. Then in 1881 Greece received the region of Thessaly as well as some territories in southern Epirus from the Ottoman Empire. Both additions significantly transformed the composition of the Greek state since both introduced substantial minorities to an otherwise rather homogenous state. The Ionian islands had several Jewish communities mostly in Kerkyra (Corfu) as well as a small Catholic population. Thessaly originally had a significant Muslim population as well as a number of smaller Jewish communities. Although nearly all the Muslims of Thessaly and many Jews soon departed for the Ottoman Empire despite the best efforts of the Greek governments to retain them and their agricultural expertise, most of the Jews in Thessaly remained, as did those in the Ionian islands. More than that, Jews in several Epirote, Thessalian, and Ionian cities welcomed Greek annexation and Greek officials often made a point of visiting the main synagogues or Jewish schools of the towns as King George did in Larisa and Arta.[22]

The Ionian islands had not essentially experienced Ottoman rule but remained under Venetian rule until the Republic was dissolved by France following the French Revolution. France briefly occupied the islands but was expelled by the Russians and Ottomans and eventually the islands were given to Britain to administer as a protectorate. Thus, the islands had a long period of association with Italy and developed along somewhat similar lines with a landowning aristocracy, a destitute peasantry, and small urban centers where most Jews and Catholics lived. The original Greek-speaking Jews that predated Venetian rule were augmented over the years with Italian and Sephardic Jews, victims of the expulsions from Italy in the late middle ages and the early modern period so that by the nineteenth century there were two distinct Jewish communities, an Italian-speaking one and a Greek-speaking one, circumstances seen in other Greek cities as well.[23]

Unlike the Ottoman Empire the experience of Jews in the Ionian islands closely resembled that of Western European Jews. Anti-Semitism was commonplace and prone to violent outbursts. There is evidence of cases of possible forced conversion of Jews to Orthodoxy from the Venetian period,[24] The Venetian Senate had intervened on several occasions to negotiate between the Christian and Jewish communities (1406, 1408, 1524, 1546) especially with regard to Jewish settlements which the Christian population wanted to be constrained, and outrageous demands by the local population such as the right to stone Jews.[25] Such incidents were common enough to be commented upon by foreign travelers before and during the British occupation and the violence usually peaked at times of religious celebration like Easter when the Judas effigy was burned and the Jewish district stoned. Jews that were encountered in the streets at such times were pelted with crockery and harassed or worse. For their own safety Jews lived within ghettos that isolated and to some degree protected them from the Orthodox Christian mob, although this was not a legal requirement as in other European cities.[26]

When the British took control of the islands, they were horrified by the violence they encountered, not only that directed against Jews but also among the Orthodox population. Establishing order was therefore a priority for the British. British administrators considered Greeks, like the Irish, as barely civilized. Even the landholding aristocracy was looked down upon despite the fact that many, including the highest officials of the church, collaborated with the British authorities and helped them control the islands through the periodic peasant disturbances.[27] Some of these, like the 1849 uprising, were significant enough to result in the execution of twenty-one individuals, the flogging of hundreds more, and numerous imprisonments, and exiles.[28]

The addition of the islands to Greece was a shock to that insular society. Greece lacked the rigid class structure of the Ionian islands, and its past constitutions had explicitly forbidden aristocratic ranks and honorifics. Greece had a vibrant and pluralistic political life with universal manhood suffrage, a free press, and the potential for great social mobility. The incorporation of the islands to Greece also meant the emancipation of the Jews of the islands who had been politically excluded by the 1852 law that made the Christian religion a requirement for the right to vote despite unsuccessful efforts in 1861 to change the requirement.[29] Similarly, Jews had been excluded from the legal profession, from the commercial tribunal, and so on.[30] All these issues presented a challenge to the established elites of the islands and they responded by reinforcing the existing patronage networks while seeking to divert the potential social conflict by promoting nationalist causes and demonizing the non-Orthodox minorities, especially the Jews. Thus, the already-considerable anti-Semitic sentiments of the Ionian population were deliberately stoked by local politicians for their own political benefit, creating circumstances where a violent outburst was a very real possibility.

The acquisition of Thessaly was very different than that of the Ionian islands. Thessaly had been under Ottoman rule from the fourteenth century and had a significant Muslim population that controlled most of the uniquely fertile land. Thessaly had a number of urban centers, with small Jewish communities, though only Larissa was of significant size. Thessaly had a fairly complex social structure and, like the Ionian islands, was dominated by a few wealthy landowners who held most of the land.

Unlike the Ionian islands, Thessaly had potential to be a significant productive asset to Greece and produce much needed agricultural goods and exports for a state that was only just emerging from decades of crushing debt and defaults. From the start, the Greek government recognized that the incorporation of the region required an understanding with the Muslim and Jewish minorities. The government of Greece went to great efforts in order to assure both Muslims and Jews that their rights and properties would be respected and some Muslims of Thessaly were elected to the Greek parliament.[31] In part this was necessary in order to convince the Muslim landowners to remain in Thessaly and provide the expertise needed to make the incorporation of Thessaly into the Greek economy a success, but it also reflected an understanding by the Greek government that the incorporation of Thessaly in Greece was an audition for future acquisitions. An easy transition would be a strong argument for similar territorial expansion in Crete, Epirus, and Macedonia. A violent or chaotic transfer would provide Greece's detractors with ammunition to block the fulfillment of the *Megali Idea*.

Despite the efforts of the Greek government, within a few years most of the 35,000–45,000 Muslims of Thessaly had left for the Ottoman Empire spreading stories of persecution.[32] As a result, agricultural production of Thessaly fell substantially in the first years of Greek rule, and the Muslim landowners were replaced by a few Christian ones who bought the properties of Muslims at bargain prices.[33] The social inequities generated by this transfer were quite unlike the circumstances in the rest of Greece and these new Greek landowners became known pejoratively by the Ottoman term *tsiflikades* (from *ciftlik*). Thessaly would become a hotbed of social agitation between landless peasants and wealthy landowners who were not above using armed bands to impose their will, in a manner surprisingly similar to the circumstances of the Ionian islands under the British and immediate post-British periods when the aristocratic landowners used bands of *bravi* to enforce their will.

The blood libel accusation

There is often a distinction made between older forms of anti-Semitism from the middle ages to the early modern period and a modern anti-Semitism that emerges after the French Revolution with the rise of nationalism and questions of race, emancipation, and citizenship. Old Western European anti-Semitism was intimately tied to religion and Jews were despised as the "murderers of Christ," as heretics who refused to accept the savior, and as outcasts from society, partly because medieval laws deliberately marginalized Jews in terms of the professions they could have, the properties they could own, the dress they could wear, and even where they could live.[34] In addition to these legal disadvantages, Jews also faced popular anti-Semitism based upon the same religious prejudice. One of the most common popular beliefs was that Jews required the blood of Christian children in order to bake their matzo bread and throughout Europe disappearances or murders of children were often followed by anti-Semitic violence and trials of wrongfully accused Jews on the so-called blood libel accusation. Many such accusations occurred in the middle ages and early modern Western Europe, most famously in the blood libel case of Trent in 1475, but by the sixteenth century the practice had begun to die out.[35]

Religious anti-Semitism was replaced by nationalist and cultural anti-Semitism tied to questions of emancipation and citizenship as discussed in earlier chapters. For many their religion barred Jews from full legal equality and most importantly citizenship in the modern European states in part because their difference set them aside from the rest of the nation. Only through the abandonment of Judaism could Jews join the nation as full members with equal rights and obligations, though not necessarily through conversion to Christianity since many, though not all, of the same authors also wanted a separation of church and state. Many nationalists who stressed the significance of a common historical experience for the nation also viewed Jews with suspicion because of their different experience, while later in the nineteenth century the issue of race would emerge as yet another obstacle to Jewish participation in the nation. Jews who had positions of authority in the new nation-states were viewed with particular suspicion. Jews could also be useful scapegoats as the infamous case of the French officer Dreyfus exemplifies.

Jews were also associated with corruption in society and moral degeneration. From France to Russia, Jews were seen as intimately involved with prostitution and the "white slave trade" often portrayed as a worldwide conspiracy.[36] Jews were associated with social disorder, a danger to Christian culture, a threat to masculinity itself, while ironically also feared for their supposed sexual vitality.[37] Similar perceptions became widespread in the Ottoman Empire as many refugees from Russia ended up in the underworld or brothels of the port cities of the empire.[38] The increasing popularity of eugenics elevated the moral fear to one of "racial hygiene" where Jews were seen as a racial threat to the health of the nation.[39] Such ideas became particularly prominent in Romania, although some proponents of eugenics saw little threat from Jews who remained socially isolated and did not intermarry compared to other undesirable groups like the Roma and Sinti.[40]

From a different perspective, Jews also faced hostility from the unlikely source of the revolutionary left and Marxists who frequently associated Jews with capitalism, finance and banking, and urban industrial interests. This association of Jews with money predates the modern period but the explicit association of Jews with capitalism is found in many writings from the revolutionary left and even Marx himself. Like nationalists many socialists often saw the abandonment of Judaism as a prerequisite for full Jewish emancipation, not in a legal but in a social sense. Thus, anti-Semitic assertions are not rare in the writings of Jules Michelet, Pierre-Joseph Proudhon, Charles Fourier, Alphonse Toussenel, or Edouard Adolphe Drumont.[41] Ironically the presence of many Jews among socialist and revolutionary circles also gave fodder to anti-Semites on the right to associate Jews with radicalism and revolution at the same time that they were being tied to money and capitalism, sometimes in the very same texts. Nationalists also used the supposed Jewish association with capitalism to associate them with hostile nations, Michelet with England, and Heinrich von Treitschke with France.[42]

The situation was different in eastern and southeastern Europe. To begin with the numbers of Jews during the middle ages were small and thus Jews were often not burdened with the same legal handicaps seen in Western Europe. As a result, Jews often migrated to central Europe, Poland, and the Ottoman Empire when they were expelled as was the case in England (1290), France (1306), Spain (1492), Portugal (1497), Germany (1510), the Papal States (1569), Italy, and Bavaria (1593). By the nineteenth century, the majority of European Jews lived in central and eastern Europe and especially in Russia, Austria-Hungary, and the Ottoman Empire. Perhaps as a result of the expulsions of Jews from Western and central Europe to the East and southeast the blood libel accusation migrated there and experienced a revival with some seventy-nine cases in the 1890s, including in the United States.[43] While absent in eastern Europe or the eastern Mediterranean until the eighteenth and nineteenth centuries, as the blood libel begun to fade in Western Europe it found new life in the East starting with the infamous Damascus case of 1840.[44]

The blood libel accusation found particularly fertile ground in the Russian Empire where one of the most famous cases, the 1912 trial of Mendel Beilis took place. Russia had not experienced such accusations until the nineteenth century when a number of cases emerged in Velizh in the 1820s and 1830s, Saratov in the 1850s, and in Georgia in 1879. As Weinberg suggests, the rise of nationalist, anti-Semitic groups like the Union of Russian People or the Union of Archangel Michael led the authorities to sacrifice the needs of justice in order to carry favor with such popular organizations, even if such anti-Semitic policies and actions were a target of criticism by foreign governments.[45] The Beilis case, like the Dreyfus affair in France, painted Jews as malicious conspirators aiming to dominate society through their economic, political, and cultural influence and threats to society.[46] In both Russia and France, the authorities were implicated in the framing of an innocent man. In Russia, the conspiracy extended from the prosecutor to the government itself which was more concerned to prove the reality of the ritual murder than to convict the specific individual to justify the regime's harsh treatment of Jews.[47] Indeed, the jury accepted that a ritual murder had occurred but split on the guilt of Beilis.[48]

In eastern Europe and the Mediterranean, there was a fusion of the modern anti-Semitic concepts with a continuation of an older, regressive, religiously based anti-Semitism. Certainly, the Orthodox Church maintained anti-Semitic rhetoric throughout this period, and often to this day, as did the Catholic clergy in central and eastern Europe. Times of heightened religious awareness, like Easter for Orthodox Christians, invariably led to heightened tensions between Jews and Christians as we saw in the last chapter and continued throughout the nineteenth and into the twentieth centuries. Much of Central and eastern europe witnessed violent pogroms against Jewish communities on a variety of pretexts such as during the 1848 uprisings against the Habsburg monarchy, the assassination of Tsar Alexander II in 1881, which led to 169 pogroms mostly in southern Russia, the Odessa pogrom of 1871, or those between 1903 and 1906 conducted with the collusion of the imperial government, and the Hungarian pogroms of 1882 following the Tiszaeszlar blood libel case while Bohemia experienced a blood libel case in 1899.[49] East European anti-Semitism, including Greek anti-Semitism, changed significantly in the nineteenth century with the importation of new ideas regarding Jewish roles in modern society but also through the importation of old but previously unknown anti-Semitic prejudices such as the blood libel, as did the violence directed against Jewish communities forcing the wave of emigration mentioned above.

In Greece, attacks on Jews during Easter were common,[50] and blood libel accusations as the one in Volos in 1889 were popularized and given particular prominence by newspaper and literary accounts from anti-Semites like the early feminist Maria Michanidou whose works *The Jewish pseudo-priest* (1886), *Human Sacrifice by the Jews* (1891), and *Jewish Harmony* (1893) gave it great publicity.[51] The late nineteenth century saw the publication of many works in Greece dealing with the Jewish question, some original, others translations, most of which were overtly anti-Semitic as the *Of Jewish Things* (1861) by the monk Neophytos Kavsokalyvitis,[52] *Blood, Jews, Talmud* (1891) by Petros Kasimatis,[53] *The Devil in Turkey* (1862) by Stefanos Xenos,[54] or *The Conquest of the World by the Jews* (1874) by Kibrilzi Zade Osman bey.[55] While some like Osman's book replicate more modern anti-Semitic ideas focusing on the supposed Jewish materialism, Jewish dominance of banking and capital, with references to the infamous *Protocols of the Elders of Zion*, or their social revolutionary tendencies,[56] others like the editor of the volume by Neophytos, Sergios Raphtanis, focused on the blood libel recounting in his introduction several supposed cases of blood libel in Greek areas from 1712 to 1859.[57] While serious Greek scholars like Spyridon Papageorgiou and even ecclesiastics like the Metropolitan of Zakynthos Dionysios Latas publicly refuted such accusations with historical evidence,[58] the blood libel accusation slowly became ingrained in nineteenth-century Greek popular consciousness.

Kerkyra, where the greatest pogrom against Jews in nineteenth-century Greece would take place, was in many respects unique. Unlike the rest of Greece, the Ionian islands and Kerkyra in particular had a significant Jewish community of some five to six thousand people composed of Romaniote, Sephardim, and Italian Jews.[59] Jews had historically been institutionally discriminated against and were frequently the target of the local peasantry, especially in Easter as was documented by foreign visitors even prior to the incorporation of the island to the Greek state.[60] The British had even issued an order restricting the movement of Jews outside their neighborhood from Good Friday to the Tuesday following Easter to limit the chances of violence.[61] Religion was also closely tied to nationalist trends on the islands and the local clergy played an active role in nationalist demonstrations.[62] Finally, Kerkyra, as a Venetian colony, was exposed to Western anti-Semitism much earlier than the rest of Greece. For example, as early as 1554 the Talmud was publicly burned in the city by order Pope Julius III.[63] Sakis Gekas has argued that overt anti-Semitic acts by the population declined over the period of the British Protectorate despite the imagery one gets from contemporary accounts and foreign publications.[64] However, Kerkyra experienced several anti-Semitic acts during the Greek War of Independence and afterwards, including the desecration of the Jewish cemetery in 1861. When reforms were instituted in 1852 to allow some local representation, Jews were disenfranchised and adherence to Christianity became a prerequisite for the right to vote. A subsequent attempt to change the law in 1861 failed to pass; Jews were emancipated only upon the islands' incorporation to Greece.[65] Greece did not simply inherit an island with a significant Jewish minority but also one where tensions between Christian and Jewish communities that were palpable. This tension was recognized three decades later by the Athenian newspaper *Estia*, which believed the Jews of Kerkyra were being intimidated by local political factions and the Orthodox public.[66] And yet the newspaper *Efemeris* published in 1891 an article deploring the rise of anti-Semitism in the world but described Greece as a haven.[67]

That same year the death of a child became the excuse for the eruption of one of the most violent anti-Semitic riots in modern Greek history. Despite the fact that the child was Jewish, the occasion was used by local politicians and newspapers to stir the public against the Jewish community literally laying siege to the Jewish ghetto of the town. The local authorities and police proved incapable or unwilling to restore order while the unrest was constantly fueled by opposition politicians and newspapers in Athens.[68] Despite the reprehensible stance of the local police chief and the inaction of the mayor of Kerkyra, Greece's judicial, military, and state authorities eventually responded decisively as the riots spread to the neighboring island of Zakynthos and troops were dispatched to restore order.[69] Even the local metropolitan intervened after a request by the chief rabbi of the city to rein in the violence.[70] In the aftermath of the riots, as many as 2,000 Jews, especially those of poorer means, chose to abandon Kerkyra and move to Athens or emigrate to Europe and the United States, many establishing themselves nearby in Trieste or in Alexandria.[71]

Historians have seen this event in various ways with one recent examination assigning the pogrom to nationalism and irredentism that aimed to deny Jews equality and rights to citizenship.[72] There is, however, a tendency in historiography to project such attitudes to the state rather the local level. For example, through the emancipation granted by the Greek constitution, Jews were elected to the municipal council for the first time which may have caused tensions but such tensions were local. There are strong parallels between the reaction of Ionian Christians following the emancipation of Jews and similar outbursts throughout Europe on similar occasions discussed in earlier chapters or the reaction of Ottoman Muslims following the Tanzimat reforms that emancipated, to some degree, Christians and Jews. The interventions by the government in Athens may have exacerbated tensions as when the government insisted upon the exclusion of non-Greeks who had not opted for Greek citizenship in 1864 from a newly founded worker's fraternity which targeted one-third of the fraternity, mostly Jews.[73] Similarly, only those Jews who wished to become Greek citizens were registered and thus gained the right to be included in the Electoral List.[74] The pogrom itself was often blamed on a few fanatics, but this ignores the history of violence against Jews on the islands, the eager involvement of all segments of the Christian population in the attacks on the Jewish community, and the continuing economic boycott of Jews after the Athenian government had sent troops to restore order.[75] As Sakis Gekas has shown, the local press cultivated an anti-Semitic discourse from the 1880s by portraying Jews as undeserving of the rights they had received in 1864.[76] It is important to stress however, the novelty of Jewish rights applied only to the Jews of the Ionian islands and not to the rest of Greece where Jews had enjoyed them for decades.

The reaction of the Athenian government, as opposed to the local authorities, merits some attention. The Greek government was forced to dispatch troops to protect the Jewish community or risk losing its authority in Greece and abroad, but its actions went beyond simply reestablishing order. It conducted a thorough investigation that resulted in the removal of certain officials and in the prosecution of those deemed responsible for fostering anti-Semitic actions. The government even brought charges against those it considered as morally complicit to the riots including anti-Semitic agitators who had never left Athens. One such was the abovementioned Petros Kasimatis whose 1891 volume rehashed ideas found in Henri Desportes' *Le Mystere du Sang* (1890) regarding the accusation of the blood libel.[77] In his book, Kasimatis recounted other cases of supposed blood libel based on Greek newspaper stories in Kerkyra (1812, 1815) and Volos (1889), and proposed the remarkable claim that Greece, and especially Athens, had become the preferred sanctuary of Jews. As proof, he recounted an incident in 1890 where the police had supposedly beaten up certain Christians following a complaint by a rabbi.[78] His prosecution, however, along with that of Maria Michanidou, the far more established author also mentioned above, failed to bring a conviction as the magistrate's court (*plemeleiodikeio*) it deemed itself incompetent to rule on the question of slander of the Jewish faith which was the accusation.

Similar to the case of Don Pacifico, there was a clear link of these events to political machinations. Two leading opposition figures on the island, Iakovos Polylas, author, literary critic, publisher, and politician, and Georgios Theotokis, who would go on to become prime minister four times between 1899 and 1909, led the anti-Semitic campaign with speeches and articles in newspapers and magazines and were rewarded with an electoral victory a couple of months later in the municipal elections of July 1891.[79] They were able to utilize deep-seated anti-Semitic sentiments in the local population regarding the supposed "privileges" of the Jewish community with respect to exceptions from military conscription and their supposed electoral influence, themes that we will encounter again in a different context a generation later.[80] Ironically, an outcome of the riots was the ban by the Holy Synod of Greece on April 12, 1891 the custom of burning the Judas effigy that had been the instigation of the Pacifico Affair.[81] Greek intellectuals were perturbed by the events and contemplated the issue of anti-Semitism in works like *Aktis Photos* by Georgios Zavitsianos, *Rachel* by Grigorios Xenopoulos, or the *Entyposeis ek Thessalonikis, Evraios Vasileias tes Kypros*, and *Sten Demiourgia Ethnikes Estias tou Periousiou Laou tou Israel* by Christos Christovasilis.[82] But the pogrom was not an isolated incident and in 1906 there would be new, less extensive, disturbances in Kerkyra, again during Easter and again with the support of local elites like Polylas.[83] A mere four years after the pogrom a local author and supporter of the "Philorthodox Society" that had opposed British rule and their Ionian Code as contrary to the traditions and teachings of the Orthodox Church, could describe Jews as "ungrateful," "ignorant," "impassive," "corrupt," and "self-interested."[84]

The pogrom in Kerkyra was another example of the contrast between intense anti-Semitism at the local level and more "progressive" official state policy that pervades modern Greek history. Although anti-Semitic acts were not rare in Greece, those acts did not enjoy the support or even toleration of the Greek government which frequently intervened in such cases. A remarkable example took place in Romania where Greek diplomats extended their protection over numerous Jews and monitored the frequent anti-Semitic outbursts there with concern. During a pogrom in 1868, the consul in Galati reported that sixty Jews were under Greek protection in the city and that "thankfully nothing had happened to them."[85] The foreign minister commended the consul for protecting them and the Jewish community of the city also sent him a letter of thanks.[86] Romania objected to Greek interference, claiming that Jews used Greek protection to evade conscription and taxes, a claim rejected by the consul in Bucharest who stated that the 200 Jews in the city who enjoyed Greek protection fully complied with their other obligations using Greek protection only to avoid "unjust assaults."[87] Romanian pressure apparently led the Greek government to eventually withdraw its protection despite a desperate letter by the Jewish community of Galati, which saw this as "a new punishment that fate reserved for the unfortunate Jewish people," pleading to be allowed to keep the protection of Greece "the cosmopolitan teacher, the world's instructor, the saint of humanism and of enlightenment."[88] These exchanges indicate the willingness of the Athenian government to take a principled stance, but also a willingness to abandon it in the face of political cost. The strong reaction of the Greek government to the Kerkyra pogrom may have been partly due to the negative publicity for Greece and Orthodoxy that the pogrom generated abroad. Responding to this publicity, the Greek ambassador in London Ioannis Gennadios published an article in the Daily News blaming the local Ionians for anti-Semitism as opposed to the rest of Greece, an article that provoked a furious response by Polylas.[89] Athenian elites believed that such acts were due to the backwardness and ignorance of the peasant mob,[90] and were detrimental to the pursuit of the *Megali Idea,* which required the support of the Great Powers and meant the addition of further minorities to the state.

Nationalist competition in Macedonia

The Kerkyra pogrom erupted at a time when tensions were rising in the Balkan provinces of the Ottoman Empire, especially in Macedonia following the Bulgarian annexation of Eastern Rumelia in 1885.[91] Two years after the Kerkyra pogrom, in 1893, the Internal Macedonian Revolutionary Organization (IMRO) was founded in Salonica to seek the establishment of an independent Macedonia or its incorporation to Bulgaria depending upon the faction. Greece and Serbia responded by forming their own clandestine nationalist organizations and were later joined in the melee by Vlach and Albanian organizations. The aim of these groups was to convince the multiethnic and multiconfessional population of Macedonia to support their claims over the region. In part their campaign was conducted through peaceful means such as the establishment of schools and cultural associations, and churches, but increasingly these organizations turned to the use of violence and terror targeting each other as often as the Ottoman authorities who were the nominal masters of the region and in the process substituted the Ottomans (Turks) with the Bulgarians as the main foes of Hellenism.[92] Thousands were murdered or tortured in the two ensuing decades as these organizations killed each other's agents, especially teachers, notables, and priests, while the Ottoman authorities conducted an ineffective counterterrorism campaign against all of them.[93]

This rivalry over the hearts and minds of the populations of Macedonia and Epirus forced a reexamination of the way the nation was perceived but also a rethinking of the strategy that Greece had pursued with regard to its *Megali Idea*. Although loath to abandon the religious component of the Greek identity since it allowed Greece to claim as conationals many non-Greek speakers, Greek governments recognized that even if they succeeded to incorporate the territories they claimed they would be adding to their state tens, possibly hundreds of thousands of individuals who did not identify themselves as Greeks especially since efforts to promote Greek nationalism in predominantly Slavic northern Macedonia had not been.[94] This presented many difficulties, most significantly the possible violent opposition of such groups to their incorporation to the Greek state. The increasing proliferation of arms in the region ensured that any such opposition would quickly turn violent. Furthermore, any border change in the Balkans was bound to involve and require the acquiescence of the Great Powers, and potential opposition by hostile minorities to Greek rule could have significant diplomatic repercussions, or used by rival states to derail Greek plans. On the other hand, these minorities, if convinced that the eviction of the Ottomans from the region was a foregone conclusion, could shift their allegiance to one of the claimants of the territories giving it additional diplomatic weapons in the struggle against its competitors. There were several such stateless groups in Macedonia and Epirus such as the Albanians, who had, however, already begun to agitate for their own state, the Vlachs, the various Muslim communities (Turks, Pomaks, Roma, Gagauz, Tatars, Circassians, etc.), and of course the Romaniote and Sephardic Jews. Greece, along with Serbia and Bulgaria, tried hard to build bridges with some or all of these groups and claim them to their national cause.

This situation was further complicated by the activities of the Great Powers themselves, several of which had interest and claims in these areas. Russia, as we saw in the last chapter, had been actively engaged promoting what the Greek government officials called a Panslavic agenda since the mid-century and continued to do so in this period by primarily supporting the interests of Bulgaria though ostensibly also worried about Catholic and even Protestant penetration in the region, in particular with regard to Vlach and Bulgarian converts.[95] The Vlach population of the region found support in Romania but also in Austrian consular authorities and the Catholic Church.[96] Greek consuls would at times assign anti-Greek sentiments and policies to nearly all foreign powers in Epirus from Italy and Austria-Hungary, to Great Britain and Russia.[97] The continuing close associations between the Greek state and the patriarchate of Constantinople are evident in the correspondence of the Greek consular authorities, but there was also an increased concern about language and its impact on the national agenda of Greece. Mackridge identified a renewed urgency in the linguistic debate between the proponents of *demotic* and *katharevousa* in Greece in the last decades of the nineteenth century, which culminated in the gospel riots of 1901 over the translation of the Bible into modern Greek.[98] As Carabott pointed out, the riots were about more than a translation and were closely connected to developments in Macedonia and Greek irredentism.[99] As far back as 1867, before even the establishment of the Bulgarian Exarchate, the Greek state was concerned with the mandatory teaching of the Greek language in the seminaries in Bulgaria, and the strengthening of "slavism" and the Bulgarian language through the efforts of Russia.[100] The Greek foreign minister instructed Greek consuls in 1871 to help establish schools with funds from educational and philanthropic organizations and the Greek government.[101] By the 1890s, Greek professors from the University of Athens were producing linguistic maps of the Ottoman regions sending students to gather data regarding the language and religion of the population.[102] Greek efforts on the linguistic and educational front were significant enough to alarm other nationalisms to the point where Apostolos Margaritis, the main figure of the Vlach movement, and the Lazarist abbot of Bitola Faverial issued a proclamation not to the Vlachs but to the Albanian nation stressing the danger that the 3,000 Greek teachers in the region represented as well as the effects of the various Greek scholarships and institutions presented to Albanians, 300 of whom studied at the University of Athens.[103] Greece invested heavily in the region with 176 educational and philanthropic associations set up between 1870 and 1880 in Macedonia.[104] Greek efforts, however, may have lagged behind those of Bulgaria in Macedonia whose 353 schools, 516 teachers, and 18,315 students in 1887 had risen to 1,196 schools, 2,096 teachers, and 70,000 students by 1912.[105]

It is within this context that we begin to see the Greek state's viewpoint of the stratification of the various communities in the Balkans. For example, although Muslim Albanians were perceived as the primary threat to Greek territorial expansion in Epirus, Christian Albanians, and especially Orthodox Albanians, were seen as potential allies under the right circumstances.[106] Albanians and Vlachs (and Roma) were seen as nationally indistinguishable from Greeks by the Greek consuls, sometimes a different "tribe" but belonging to the Greek nation and state or as possessing a "fluid national consciousness."[107] From the time of the Italian Risorgimento, traditionally seen as tied to the Albanian national project, Greece sought close ties to the Albanian populations of Epirus, seen as absolutely necessary for a successful uprising in the Balkans, in collaboration with Serbia.[108] Through its educational efforts there was considerable Hellenization of the Albanian populations especially in the Pashalik of Janina, where a significant percentage of the Albanian population was Orthodox Christian.[109] Similarly, the acquiescence of Muslims to Greek rule in Macedonia was seen as possible because of the attacks by IMRO on Ottoman authorities and Muslim communities which Greek authorities expected to make them fearful of a possible annexation by Bulgaria.[110] Vlachs who were Orthodox were seen as the easiest to bring into the fold of Greek nationalism if only Romania would cease its agitation.[111] The Jewish communities, however, presented a unique case and could cause particular difficulties and opportunities to the Greek plans.

Without a doubt the most significant Jewish community in the region was the Sephardic community of Salonica, the largest, and most important city in all of Ottoman Macedonia. As Christovasilis put it in his letter in 1894 when he visited the city:

Jews in front of me, Jews behind me, Jews on my right, Jews on my left, Jews over there, Jews over here! Jews everywhere![112]

Already numerous, the community had increased further with the arrival of refugees over the course of the nineteenth century from Greece as well as other Orthodox countries, especially Russia, and thus had developed a strong distrust toward Orthodox states.[113] Greek authorities recognized the dominant position of the Jewish community in the city but relations between Jews and the Orthodox inhabitants of the city were often confrontational as we have already seen, especially in times of crisis between the Greek and the Ottoman states.[114] In such times of tension, it was the Jewish community that often took the initiative to confront the Orthodox one. We already discussed the 1852 violent anti-Greek riot when a crowd of some 5,000 Jews attacked the Christians found in the streets following the fatal stabbing of a Jewish butcher with knives and cudgels.[115] A similar event took place in 1874, a time when the Orthodox community was in the midst of a divisive religious conflict,[116] when a Jewish watchmaker was found drowned and a Jewish mob vented its anger on Christian homes and individuals.[117] The Jews of Salonica steadfastly supported the Ottoman Empire in its disputes with Greece, again taking to the streets against the uprisings in Crete in 1866, and organizing boycotts against Greek products and businesses, who reciprocated by boycotting Jewish stores throughout Macedonia.[118] Greek prisoners of war during the 1897 conflict between Greece and the Ottoman Empire were set upon by Jewish youths in the train station at Salonica, an incident widely reported in the Athenian press.[119] Such incidents tended to arouse the suspicions of Greek nationalists toward the attitudes of Jews with regard to the Greek nationalist project, not only in those territories that formed the *terra irredenta* of Greece, but also with respect to Greek Jewish citizens.[120] At the same time, it was clear that there were contacts and connections between the Jewish community and the Greek state evidenced by the presence of numerous Jewish names in the Salonica and Kavalla consular courts, some of whom were Greek citizens but many belonging to other nationalities.[121]

The second largest Jewish community of Macedonia and Epirus lived in the city of Janina. The Jews of Janina were Greek-speaking Romaniotes and were decidedly a minority in the city which was dominated by the Orthodox and Muslim communities. The Jews of Janina were also loyal to the Ottoman state and like their Salonica brethren found themselves caught between competing nationalist claims, in this case between Albanian demands for independence and Greek demands for union with Greece. Unlike the Jews of Salonica however, the Romaniotes of Janina did not have the numbers to assert themselves and were often the victims at the hands of the Christians as in the case of the 1851 riot.[122]

In both cities, therefore, relations between Orthodox Greeks and Jews were tense and on occasion violent. But in the circumstances of the struggle for Macedonia and Epirus the Greek state quickly perceived the value of trying to build bridges to the Jewish communities who were not nationalist rivals. When the city of Arta was handed to Greece in 1881, the chief rabbi of the town was included in the celebrations commemorating the event alongside the mayor of the city and the Orthodox bishop while King George I made a point to visit the Jewish school of the city on his first official visit later that year. The state recognized the community, alongside all other Jewish communities, as a legal entity and dispatched a state-paid teacher of Greek for the Jewish school.[123] Similar events took place in Larisa, which was also incorporated into Greece in 1881, and again King George made a point of visiting the synagogue of the city.[124] The same year the first Greek Jewish public school was founded there which, in addition to the normal Greek curriculum, taught Jewish religion and history.[125]

The contrast between the responses of the Muslim and Jewish communities to the efforts of the Greek state to incorporate them is indicative of the different perceptions of the two groups with regard to the Greek state. In Arta, the Muslim community whose religious and cultural autonomy was also recognized shrunk from 800 individuals in 1878 to 45 in 1881 and then 6 in 1907, most settling across the border in the Ottoman Empire.[126] The 617 Romaniote Jewish population on the other hand did not begin to emigrate until the years 1907–14 and they did so mostly to the United States for economic reasons as did many Christian Greeks at the time.[127] For the Greek state the incorporation of the Jewish communities in 1881 was a success and served as a model for the future.

The Greek foreign ministry kept a very careful note of the relations between the various ethnicities of Macedonia and Epirus, and despite significant concern over the activities of Bulgarian, Vlach, and Albanian nationalists, the documents indicate no animosity toward the Zionist movement, though the ministry was concerned about the links between Jews and foreign powers and international organizations such as the *Alliance Israelite Universelle* which in some ways resembled the Greek nationalist societies being set up.[128] There were, however, differences in how the Greek state perceived the various Jewish communities of the region. Consular accounts barely mentioned the Romaniotes of Janina despite the increased nationalist agitation of the region, but carefully detailed the actions of the Sephardic community of Salonica. Differences between the various communities and linguistic factors, which were crucial in the rise of Albanian nationalism despite the best efforts of the Greek state to appeal to Christian Albanians, were beginning to influence the perceptions of the Greek authorities and set up the stage for the policies the Greek state would pursue in the early twentieth century. Furthermore, as Devin Naar demonstrated, Jewish intellectuals in Salonica had by the late nineteenth century begun to fashion the idea of the city as the "mother of Israel" (*madre de Israel*) tying the history of the Salonica Jews to that of the Ottoman Empire.[129] These efforts may have further helped separate the two communities in the eyes of Greek authorities by emphasizing the different historical trajectories of the two groups to individuals for whom history was a crucial component in their irredentist claims to the region.

Historians of Greece and Greek Jewish history have not given particular consideration to the significance that the different historical trajectory of the Romaniotes and Sephardim may have had on Greek perceptions of the two communities. This is odd considering the crucial role that history has in the construction of the modern Greek identity and the idea of historical continuity developed by nineteenth-century historians like Paparrigopoulos, Zabelios, or Karolidis. Responding to the earlier challenge by Fallmerayer and the perceived threat of Panslavism, these historians expanded upon scattered earlier narratives to present a Hellenized version of Greek history that stretched continuously from antiquity to the present with the Byzantine Empire bridging the perceived gap of the middle ages.[130] Although the Greek state continued to promote a religious affiliation with Hellenism and forged ever-closer ties to the Patriarchate that controlled Orthodox education,[131] a fundamental tool for the nationalist indoctrination in the Greek *irredenta*, a more nuanced, historical identity was also talking hold, especially among the educated elites. To quote Neoklis Kazazis, a prominent scholar of the turn of the century:

> The Hellenic idea through Christianity, the Christian idea through Hellenism, working together as brothers imposed on the people the law of new historical truth, which was destined to lead them out of their fallacy, and to strengthen and civilize them.[132]

Jews of course could not participate fully in the above formulation but some could participate in part as later Jewish historians like Joseph Nehama would attempt to demonstrate.[133]

In this construct, the two Jewish communities, though never part of the Greek nation, appear in two very different historical moments. The Romaniotes become part of Greek history during the Hellenistic and Roman periods and therefore share a common historical trajectory with the Greek nation through the crucial Byzantine period. Sephardic Jews, on the other hand, arrive during the Ottoman period, invariably seen as a period of oppression, decline, and suffering for the Greek nation. If the link with the despised Ottoman period and authorities was emphasized by the Jewish historians of Salonica it would only serve to further alienate Jews from the historical destiny of the Greek nation, unlike their Romaniote compatriots who besides a common language shared with Greeks a common historical experience in times of "Greek" greatness (Hellenistic, Byzantine) as well as in times of subjugation (Roman, Ottoman). Furthermore, Romaniote Jews from Chalkis, with later additions from Kerkyra and Arta, also shared with Greeks the history of the "resurrected" modern Greek state while the first separate Sephardic communities to be incorporated in the Greek state were those of Thessaly in 1881, a mere decade before the eruption of the nationalist struggles in Macedonia and Epirus. If Romaniotes could not be members of the Greek state they had been co-travelers in the millennia of the constructed continuous Greek history while the Sephardim had been recent, by Greek standards, interlopers invited to Greek lands by a foreign occupier. The alienness of the Sephardim was therefore much more pronounced than the Romaniotes and their hostility toward the Greek nationalist cause expected.

A decade of conflict and destruction (1912–23)

The first decade of the twentieth century was a trying one for the Balkans. The simmering tensions in Macedonia, Crete, Thrace, and Epirus had already exploded in 1897 when Greece and the Ottoman Empire went to war over Greek support to the insurgents on Crete following several massacres of Christians.[134] The war was an unmitigated disaster for Greece. The Ottoman army easily routed the much smaller, less experienced, and inadequately equipped Greek forces, occupying Thessaly and marching toward Athens. The Ottomans had no interest in recovering substantial territories so the border remained more or less unchanged with some minor adjustments, but Greece was forced to pay a heavy indemnity to the Ottomans and abandon support for the Cretan rebels. Unable to pay the indemnity, since Greece had already defaulted on its debts in 1893, Greece had to accept foreign control over her finances. The disaster seriously damaged the Greek political class who had raised nationalist expectations without preparing the country for war as well as the monarchy since the Crown Prince had been the commander of the Greek army that was so easily defeated by the Ottomans.

The defeat of Greece was greeted with relief by its rivals in Macedonia as well as from the Jewish community of Salonica. It did not, however, restore order to Macedonia but rather led to an intensification of the clandestine conflict. In 1903, IMRO launched the ill-fated Illiden uprising which was easily suppressed by the Ottomans but Macedonia descended into a vicious conflict between the various nationalist groups with the occasional intervention of the Ottoman authorities. The near complete collapse of order in the region led to massive emigration from Macedonia and Epirus, including many Jews, and drew in the Great Powers of Europe who tried to force a program of reforms on the Ottoman government, the so-called Murstag reforms, only to see the government of Abdul Hamid II overthrown by a coup in 1908 which led to the rise to power of the nationalist Young Turks under the Committee for Union and Progress (CUP).[135] Bulgaria used the opportunity caused by the coup to declare its formal independence while Austria-Hungary annexed Bosnia-Herzegovina. Violence escalated as Albanian bands proliferated and were countered by Greek ones sponsored by the Greek foreign ministry.[136] The next year the Greek army imitated the Ottomans by staging its own coup which led to the rise of a new nationalist liberal politician, Eleftherios Venizelos, who would dominate Greek politics for the next quarter century. In 1911, the previously loyal Albanians rose in revolt against the Ottoman government in part due to the CUP policies demanding autonomy and in the same year Italy declared war on the Ottomans in order to seize Libya, Rhodes, and the other Dodecanese islands.[137] Alarmed by these developments Greece, Bulgaria, Serbia, and Montenegro momentarily put aside their differences in order to together confront the distracted Ottoman Empire by launching the first of two Balkan Wars in 1912, which would utterly transform the map of the region and lead to the eruption of the even deadlier First World War.

The Balkan Wars (1912–13) unleashed an orgy of violence by all those involved, not only on the battlefields, but also against the civilian populations, as a short story of the execution of Muslim villagers by Greek soldiers by Stratis Myrivilis candidly describes.[138] Armies and especially paramilitary units (*andartes, komitajis, cetniks*) that all combatants used extensively targeted ethnic groups that were thought to be a threat either to the advancing armies or toward the national aspirations of the corresponding states.[139] Muslims were by far the most targeted group since all Balkan states saw them as hostile minorities, but nearly every ethnicity suffered in this convoluted conflict. Montenegrin soldiers targeted Catholic as well as Muslim Albanians, Serbs, and Bulgarians massacred Albanians and other Muslims as well as Greeks, and Greeks did the same to Muslims and Bulgarians.[140] The damning report by a Carnegie Foundation sponsored committee, despite its deficiencies and prejudices, was indicative of the violence inflicted upon the population of Macedonia in what today we would characterize as ethnic cleansing, if not genocide. Hundreds of thousands of people fled their homes, most of them never to return, which of course was the point of much of the violence directed toward civilians.[141] Thousands more were forced to covert as was the case of perhaps 200,000 Muslim Pomaks in Thrace and Macedonia under pressure from Bulgarian authorities.[142]

In these circumstances of widespread violence, it is often interesting to examine where it did not take place, the cases where those in authority specifically directed their subordinates to eschew violence. For example, the Greek political authorities initially directed their military personnel in certain parts of Macedonia to be solicitous of Muslims and even Muslim refugees, in part as an attempt to undermine Bulgarian claims to regions of eastern Macedonia and to transfer the loyalty of Muslims from the Ottoman Empire to Greece, and it appears the Greek army responded with some restraint compared to the other combatants.[143] Thus, of the 140,000 Muslim refugees from Macedonia only 24,000 were from the areas occupied by Greece.[144] Similar efforts were later made by Greek authorities in Thrace with some success.[145] Similar concerns, however, were not present in areas where Bulgarians did not contest Greek claims such as Epirus and Albania where Albanian Muslims were the Greek enemy par excellence, or in areas of Western Macedonia where Greek claims were more secure especially after the conclusion of the first Balkan War.[146] There were also instances of cultural violence, as in the deliberate destruction by the Greek artillery of the city that was symbolic for Muslims, Gianitsa.[147]

Balkan states were acutely aware that whatever conquests they made were liable to be reversed on the negotiating table by the interests of the Great Powers who had been surprised by the outbreak of war. One example was Salonica where, while the French seemed to support Greek claims, Austria-Hungary would have preferred a Bulgarian occupation. Russia did not want either state to take control of such a strategic port. Greece also saw Britain as more supportive of its position as was Germany to a degree.[148] In Epirus and Albania, both Serbia and Greece confronted the hostility of Italy and Austria-Hungary to their presence on the Adriatic.[149] In such a fluid environment, any support or opposition could prove decisive in the allocation of territories regardless of military conquests.

In this context the Greek attitudes toward the Jewish communities of the region are informative. In Epirus there seems to have been no confrontation between the conquering Greek forces and the Jewish communities, quite the opposite. The Jews of Janina, soon to be renamed Ioannina, participated in the ceremonies following the capture of the city by the Greek army, and the Greek commander and Crown Prince visited the synagogue in a gesture of friendship that was appreciated by the Jewish authorities.[150] The Jews of Ioannina like their Christian neighbors immediately abandoned the fez and adopted European hats, in stark contrast to the Muslim population, expressing in a symbolic fashion where their loyalties lay.[151] There is no evidence of persecution of Jews in the region, nor any suspicion voiced by the Greek authorities regarding the loyalty of that community to their new state.

By contrast the Jews of Salonica, renamed Thessaloniki, openly supported the Ottoman cause as war clouds gathered and in the Balkan Wars.[152] In response the

Greek newspapers of Thessaloniki *Aletheia* and *Pharos* called for an economic boycott of Jewish businesses even before 1912, to the consternation of the Greek authorities, whose policy was more conciliatory, even the bishop of the city was displeased.[153] The entry of the Greek army into Thessaloniki was followed by looting and attacks on Jewish property and individuals in the city,[154] a situation that was only partially eased by the arrival of a force of Cretan gendarmerie to restore order.[155] Unlike Ioannina, the Greek occupying authorities were very concerned about the loyalty of the local Jewish community, their fears exacerbated by rumors that the Bulgarians, who also claimed the city and had barely failed to get there before the Greek army, were dispatching Bulgarian Jews to agitate in the city in favor of Bulgarian annexation. As a response, the Greek foreign ministry urgently recommended to the army headquarters the dispatch to the city of all Jews serving in the Greek armed forces to counter the Bulgarian propaganda.[156] Of course, the majority of Greek Jews serving in the army were Romaniotes whose loyalty to the Greek state the foreign ministry obviously trusted.

The contrast between the attitudes of the Greek authorities with regard to Thessaloniki and Ioannina is even more marked if one considers the fact that Ioannina surrendered to the Greek army only after a long, bitter, and costly siege while Thessaloniki surrendered without a fight and without causing any casualties to the Greek forces. On the other hand, the opposition of the Jews of Thessaloniki to the incorporation of the city to Greece and its requests to the Great Powers for the internationalization of the city according to an Austrian plan were well known, alongside circulated rumors of a willingness to accept even Bulgarian control, if Ottoman was impossible, over Greek rule.[157] The community also sought the intervention of the Central Zionist Committee, and continued to explore options of internationalization or its transformation to a free port for several years to come, entertaining propaganda of foreign states such as France, Italy, and Serbia.[158] The hostility of the local Jewish population toward Greek rule was known not only to Greek authorities but to European diplomats, whose influence on the eventual peace settlement was expected to be significant.[159] The Greek authorities therefore tried to appease the Jewish community by offering concessions and by hiring young Jews in the army and police to protect Jewish properties in the city.[160] Jewish civic leaders were convinced that these efforts were directly tied to the diplomatic efforts of Greece to gain the approval of the Great Powers rather than a sincere willingness to accommodate the Jews and some prominent members of the community even advanced the idea of a neutral Jewish state based around the city and unsuccessfully tried to garner Zionist support for the idea.[161] Nothing comparable existed in Ioannina where the Romaniote Jews appeared eager to exchange Ottoman or Bulgarian for Greek rule as was the case with other Jewish communities including some Sephardic ones like those of Xanthi.[162]

The Greek state's willingness to trust its own Jewish population to advance the cause of Greek nationalism in Thessaloniki, a mere two decades after the Kerkyra pogrom, was indicative of the attitude the state had toward what it considered Hellenized Jews. For the Greek state, Hellenized Jews were useful citizens even if not necessarily members of the Greek nation. Furthermore, in the context of the nationalist struggle in Macedonia, language had increasingly become a crucial element of assimilation and one that the Jews of Ioannina already enjoyed. Thus, both sides could find a quick and easy accommodation. This was not, however, the case with the Sephardic Jews of Thessaloniki who up to this point had had no need to adopt the Greek language but had persisted in the use of Ladino and later, through the *Alliance Israelite Universelle* schools, Hebrew and French. The question of language would gain new significance in the interwar period within the community with Jews advocating assimilation stressing the necessity to learn Greek, most traditionalists committed to the use of Ladino, while Zionists promoted Hebrew.[163]

The violence inflicted upon Jews with the entry of the Greek army in Thessaloniki, if moderate by the standards of the Balkan Wars, was an indication of the lack of trust that continued throughout the early occupation of the city by Greece. Rumors flourished that Jews had poisoned Greek soldiers and a blood libel accusation briefly gripped the Christian community in 1913.[164] In a meeting with the Greek king in 1913 the chief rabbi of the city frankly affirmed the preference of the community to have remained within Ottoman suzerainty further alarming Greek nationalists.[165] The Greek government sought to pacify the situation through the granting of a number of privileges including temporary exemption from military conscription without loss of voting rights, access to public administration, the right to keep accounts in Ladino, special dispensation for dietary laws, and allowances to Jewish communities and associations.[166] To a degree that policy worked and by 1919 Greek officials could claim at the Paris peace conference that the Greek government had addressed all justified demands of the Jewish community of Thessaloniki.[167] But this arrangement had set the Jews of Thessaloniki apart not only from Christian Greek society but also from the rest of the Jewish community and in particular from those of "Old" Greece. The latter had fought in the Greek army through the two Balkan Wars and would continue to do so in the ensuing First World War and Asia Minor War.[168]

The two Balkan Wars radically transformed the map of the Balkans by nearly expelling the Ottomans from Europe and adding large swathes of territory to Greece and Serbia, the two main beneficiaries of the wars, and less so to Bulgaria, Montenegro, and Romania. Greece was transformed by the addition of some 1,770,000 new inhabitants many of whom were non-Greeks including some 75,000 Jews.[169] However, the violence in the region was far from over but would continue for another decade. Although Greece was forced to abandon plans to annex southern Albania (or Northern Epirus as Greeks call it) due to Austrian and Italian pressure, it sponsored the declaration by the local Greek population of an autonomous state headed by Georgios Christaki Zographos, a former Greek foreign minister, whose forces, armed and supported by the Greek army, would frequently clash with Albanian regular and irregular units for a few years.[170] The declaration of war by Austria-Hungary on Serbia in 1914 launched the First World War that would drag in one by one all of the Balkan states, Bulgaria and the Ottoman Empire siding with the Central Powers while Romania and eventually in 1917 Greece sided with the Entente.

The years between 1914 and 1923 were quite dramatic for the Jews of Thessaloniki. Although the city had been finally and irrevocably allocated to Greece, the Jewish community through its temporary exemption from military service was set apart from the rest of Greek society and was particularly resented by the non-Jewish population, especially in the context of the near constant mobilization of Greek men from 1912 to 1923, a mobilization to which the Jews of the pre-1912 Greek provinces fully participated. Although exemptions from military service had a long history in the Ottoman Empire and both Jews and Christians had often benefited from it, Greece had rejected on its inception to grant such exemptions to its minorities and the CUP had abolished them in the Ottoman Empire just before the Balkan Wars. Although Ottoman subjects from the Christians of the Aegean islands to those of Albania strongly resisted conscription, thousands eventually served in the Ottoman army, despite suspicions regarding their reliability.[171] The attempts by the Thessaloniki community to evade conscription was not unique for Greece with other groups such as the Vlachs on the borders of the state with the Ottoman Empire also seeking to avoid military service,[172] but under the circumstances at the time, it seemed as the Jews of Thessaloniki were setting themselves apart from the Greek nation, even though it was only temporary since those born after 1902 would be liable for conscription in the future.[173] This evasion reinforced the existing suspicions regarding the commitment of the community to the Greek state. Still, Greece was not yet secure regarding its new conquests with their various minorities so it attempted to appeal to the Jewish community by being among the earliest proponents of a Jewish state in Palestine.[174]

Thessaloniki became a focal point of Entente operations following the debacle of the Gallipoli campaign and the subsequent opening of the Macedonian front. The presence of a large, multiethnic, and mostly inactive army in the city strained its resources and deteriorated the living conditions while the war itself isolated the city from its former hinterland. Trade, the lifeblood of the city, virtually disappeared while outburst of disease further strained the resources of the city. Added to the cost born by the city was the constant flood of refugees with perhaps half a million souls finding refuge in the city most on their way to some other final destination.[175] The economic woes of Thessaloniki were exacerbated by the 1917 great fire which devastated the city and in particular the Jewish neighborhoods leaving tens of thousands homeless. Some 3,900 shops and 14,200 homes were destroyed leaving 73,448 people without shelter of which 52,000 were Jews.[176] With the war still raging, and the Greek state in a very precarious financial situation, the rebuilding of the city would not begin until well after the conclusion of the war, although the government tried to come to the aid of the victims, and the Jewish community was the recipient of 500,000 drachmas in 1919 toward the rebuilding of its destroyed schools.[177] The Greek government also saw the fire as an opportunity to "modernize" and Hellenize the city. In 1918, it passed a law that essentially bypassed the existing property ownerships and land use to embark on an ambitious urban planning experiment. Naturally the previous owners of the properties, most of them Jews, protested and received the support from Jewish communities abroad notably France and Britain but did not change the government's plans. Nearly all the new neighborhoods created for the victims of the fire were not in the center of the town where their properties had originally been, thus relocating the Jewish neighborhoods from the center to the periphery of the new city.[178]

Thessaloniki also became the epicenter of a dramatic rift in Greek politics between King Constantine I, who had led the Greek army as commander in chief through the Balkan Wars and had assumed the throne following the assassination of his father in

Thessaloniki in 1913, and Prime Minister Eleftherios Venizelos. Venizelos wanted Greece to declare in favor of Entente from the onset of the First World War but the king had insisted on neutrality. The confrontation escalated with the resignation of Venizelos, new elections which Venizelos won, and a continuing impasse. During this time Greece was under constant foreign pressure, the Entente using Greek territory for their assault on Gallipoli, while the Central Powers and their ally Bulgaria violating and occupying Greek territory in Macedonia. In 1915, Venizelos staged what amounted to a coup against the king, establishing a rival regime based in Thessaloniki where he was protected by the Entente forces, while the king continued to exert authority over the southern, pre–Balkan Wars part of the country known as "Old" Greece. Both sides persecuted the supporters of the other and this National Rift (*ethnikos dichasmos*) persisted until 1917 when the Entente delivered an ultimatum to the king who was forced to abdicate. A nominally reunited country under Venizelos then entered the war just in time to reap the spoils of victory but not before Venizelos purged the state bureaucracy and army of the supporters of the king, with 570 judges, 6,500 public servants, 2,300 army officers, 3,000 gendarmes, and 500 naval officers losing their jobs and another 550 jailed or sent to internal exile.[179]

These convoluted politics inevitably drew in the Jewish communities of Greece. The choices were not easy for the Jews of Thessaloniki who had to deal with a nationalist politician or a conservative king, especially in view of the wartime conditions and the effects of the 1917 fire. Venizelos certainly tried to secure the loyalty of the Jewish community in a variety of ways including the support of Greece to the 1917 Balfour declaration for a Jewish homeland in Palestine, publicly reiterated in 1918 by the Greek foreign minister in parliamentary questions.[180] The Jewish community of Thessaloniki was not a monolithic block as has often been portrayed. There were significant fissures among the Thessaloniki Jews between those who favored a policy of assimilation, those who wanted to maintain a separate identity based on their traditions, and a growing Zionist faction that looked toward Palestine. To these, one must add the significant international socialist movement in the city that was spearheaded by the highly organized trade unions, to the degree that the Greek authorities during the Balkan Wars had been concerned about socialist provoked disorders specifically mentioning Jewish socialists.[181] The fact that Avraham Eliezer Benarogia the founder of the main workers organization *Federasion Sosialista Lavoradera de Saloniko* was a Bulgarian Jew from Vidin was an additional concern.[182]

This situation was made more complicated in the immediate postwar period. The treaties of Serves and Neuilly with the Ottoman Empire and Bulgaria, respectively, awarded Greece new territories in Thrace and Asia Minor. Venizelos had essentially fulfilled the *Megali Idea*, the nationalist dream first articulated in the nineteenth century. The signing of the treaties, however, did not mean the end of hostilities. In Anatolia Mustafa Kemal, later to be known as Ataturk, launched a Turkish nationalist movement aimed against the designs of France, Britain, Italy, and especially Greece on the remaining territories of the Ottoman Empire and Greek forces were dispatched to Smyrna. Venizelos returned from Paris and called new elections in 1920 certain that his achievements would ensure him victory only to see the electorate turn against him in favor of the Royalists.

The surprising electoral defeat of Venizelos in 1920 was mainly due to the continuing hostilities in Anatolia where the Greek army was engaged in a brutal campaign against the nationalists of Kemal, but a significant role was assigned to the vote of minorities that overwhelmingly supported the Royalists, including the Jews of Thessaloniki. The subsequent return of the king alienated Greece from its former allies and following an ill-conceived invasion of Anatolia the Greek army was eventually defeated in 1922 leading to a hasty retreat and evacuation of Asia Minor. The Greek forces had conducted a number of atrocities during the campaign in Asia Minor, both against Muslims and against Jews,[183] and the Turkish nationalists reciprocated with atrocities committed against the Christian population of Anatolia including the burning of Smyrna. King Constantine was once again deposed in 1922 and a Republic was proclaimed but the political situation remained combustible especially after the trial and execution of six prominent Royalists ministers and generals for treason over the conduct of the war in Anatolia.

In 1923, a new treaty negotiated in Lausanne between the victors of the First World War and the Republic of Turkey finally concluded the war as far as Greece was concerned. Among the clauses was the stipulation for the mandatory exchange of populations between Greece and Turkey based upon the religion of those concerned. Christians in Turkey with the exception of those in Istanbul and a couple small islands were forced to relocate to Greece while the Muslims of Greece followed the opposite paths. The Muslims of Thrace were excluded as were the Albanian Chams. This was the conclusion of a mass migration of populations that had commenced in 1912 with the Balkan Wars and had continued almost uninterrupted till 1923. In addition to the refugees from the Balkan Wars, the Ottoman Empire had begun a process of ethnic cleansing of Christians in 1914 with as many as 60,000 Christians left Thrace for Greece, and a further 130,000–240,000 Christians forcibly relocated to the interior of Anatolia, or converted to Islam, an exodus that had led to essentially an understanding to exchange populations with Greece that was interrupted by the eruption of the First World War.[184] Similarly, Bulgaria also displaced tens of thousands of Greeks from Thrace and Macedonia.[185] Greece was not exempt from such practices and it should be noted that frequently all that was needed from the state was to forward arriving refugees from other states to the villages of unwanted minorities where the behavior of the former often led to the flight of the latter.[186] In the ensuing conflict the ethnic cleansing of minorities resumed in the region, the Armenian genocide being the most horrific example, and even after the conclusion of the war in 1918 the process continued with a convention between Greece and Bulgaria making provisions for the voluntary exchange of populations. Although Lausanne covered the most extensive exchange, the movement of populations would continue in the interwar period though at reduced numbers. Some 1.5 million refugees eventually found their way to Greece representing almost 20 percent of the population of Greece while some 350,000 Muslims went to Turkey.

The influx of the refugees, however, was also an opportunity for Greece to solidify its hold over the territories of Macedonia and Thrace whose mixed population allowed neighboring states, especially Bulgaria, to dispute Greece's right to those territories. Such ideas had emerged as early as the late nineteenth century in Greece with plans to settle Pontic Greek to newly acquired Thessaly and even still-Ottoman Macedonia.[187]

In the aftermath of the Asia Minor War hundreds of thousands of refugees were settled in those regions, where the removal of Muslims had created the space to provide some with small parcels of land, radically transforming those regions and essentially Hellenizing them. This "demographic intervention" aimed to transform the "*xenophones*" into Greeks or at least reduce the impact of minorities in Macedonia and other contested regions.[188] Of course, many of these refugees were settled or drifted into the major towns of Greece including Thessaloniki where they soon became the clear ethnic majority changing the character of what had been a predominantly Jewish city.

Disloyal Jews and Good Jews: Interwar Politics and the Jewish Communities of Greece (1923–40)

After the disaster in Asia Minor Greece was a very different state from the one that went to war so exuberantly in 1912. On the one hand, Greece had dramatically grown incorporating rich agricultural lands in Macedonia and Thrace as well as important urban centers such as Thessaloniki, Kavala, Heraklion, and Ioannina. Thessaloniki in particular was a crucial port and railroad hub for the entire Balkan peninsula and had a substantial, by Balkan standards, industrial sector. Greece had doubled in population, essentially achieving in a decade the goal that had been set in the 1840s namely to bring into its fold those Greeks who lived under Ottoman rule. These gains, however, had come at a tremendous material, political, economic, and ideological cost.

Between 1912 and 1923 Greece had fought four wars and had experienced two internal revolts against the government. Tens of thousands of young men had been killed or maimed while the country had been torn asunder politically, socially, and economically. A Greek king had been assassinated, another twice deposed, the leadership of the Royalists had been put on trial for treason and executed, while the liberal government had launched a vicious campaign against communism and the labor movement. The *Megali Idea* had been shattered following the Asia Minor disaster, right at the moment of its apparent fulfillment, and hundreds of thousands of Christians had been expelled ancestral homes and sought shelter in Greece.

The most significant question facing the young republic was the settlement of displaced people. Greece had been a recipient of a steady flow of refugees from 1913 onwards. During the Balkan Wars, Greek speakers and *Grecomans* (Greek-maniacs), Slavic speakers associated with the Greek national cause, had fled the advancing Bulgarian and, to a lesser degree, Serbian armies, just as non-Greek minorities fled the other way. Following the conclusion of the Balkan Wars attitudes toward those of different ethnic or religious background hardened, especially in the Ottoman Empire, which had been more tolerant up to that point. A steady flow of refugees from Asia Minor and Eastern Thrace streamed into Greece while the Ottoman and Greek governments were in talks regarding their fate. More refugees arrived during the First World War as Ottoman policies turned genocidal against the Armenians and, to a lesser degree, against Greeks and other Christians.

There were some efforts at the conclusion of the First World War to regulate this movement and thus the 1919 Treaty of Neuilly that ended hostilities between Bulgaria and the Entente powers, and the subsequent Convention for Voluntary and Reciprocal Emigration of Minorities, included provisions for Greece and Bulgaria to voluntarily exchange populations.[1] The voluntary aspect was rather disregarded in Greece and 101,800 "Bulgarians" were exchanged with 52,891 Greeks.[2] Greece was therefore somewhat experienced in managing inflows of refugees but the numbers that came to the country from 1922 onwards were beyond the ability of the state to handle. The total number of refugees in Greece was nearly 1.5 million while 350,000 Muslims were forced to move to the new Republic of Turkey.[3] Such massive movements naturally disrupted the social and economic life of the region and put an enormous burden on the governments who had to settle and provide for these refugees.

The influx of almost 1.5 million refugees, however, gave Greece an opportunity to transform the composition of disputed regions like Macedonia.[4] Not only did hundreds of thousands of Muslims leave the area, "Greek" refugees could be settled in their place boosting the representation of "loyal" citizens as a counter to those who advocated an independent or Bulgarian Macedonia. As a result, of the 578,844 refugees that were settled in rural Greece 90 percent were concentrated in Macedonia and Thrace.[5] The slavophones (Slavic speakers) of the province were thus transformed overnight from a majority into a minority, still sizeable but no longer the threat it had posed between 1913 and 1923. The new settlers found themselves in precocious position facing hostility from the indigenous population, grecophone as well as slavophone,[6] and dependent for land, resources, economic assistance, and social services on the government and the Refugee Settlement Commission set up by the League of Nations. This predicament ensured their loyalty not only to the state but also the Liberal government.[7]

In addition to the "Hellenization" benefits of the influx of refugees from Anatolia and Bulgaria, the Liberal government saw political gains to be had since the refugees would dilute the pro-Royalist sentiments of the native population.[8] By contrast, the Royalists espoused, as we will see, the cause of the indigenous populations, Greek and non-Greek alike, often denying the very "Greekness" of the refugees.[9] The settlement of the refugees, which was accompanied by the sedentarization of the various pastoralist groups, naturally also transformed local economies, patterns of land tenure, and social structures.[10]

That is not to say of course that the Greek government, now a Republic, felt that the exchange of population with the republic of Turkey had solved the problem of minorities. Greece in 1923 still had significant minorities, especially in the border regions of Epirus, Macedonia, and Thrace, some of which could rely on support from neighboring states like Bulgaria, Albania, and Turkey. Combined with the continued presence of smaller Greek populations beyond the borders of Greece in Albania, the Italian-held Dodecanese islands, and British Cyprus, the question of minorities, minority rights, and their role in the Greek state was a more pressing question in the interwar years than at any time before, particularly since the state did not feel secure in its recent acquisitions. To examine it we need to consider the ways in which Greek nationalism and Greek identity politics changed as a result of the wars from 1912 to

1923, the international framework regarding minorities in Europe, and the structures the Greek state enacted in order to deal with its minorities.

Greece in the interwar period faced two particularly threatening situations with its minorities, the Muslim Cham Albanian minority in Epirus and the slavophone minority in Macedonia. The most politically dangerous was the first, even though the numbers of Albanians were considerably smaller than the slavophones. The independence of Albania had been proclaimed in 1913 but the state fully emerged only after the First World War. Greece and Serbia had strenuously opposed its creation, and then disputed its borders. Greece had sponsored a separatist movement in southern Albania composed predominantly of Greek speakers who proclaimed an autonomous Republic of Northern Epirus in 1914.[11] Greek forces had remained in Albanian territory until forced to withdraw by French and Italian troops and the border remained in dispute.[12] For Greece the situation was particularly threatening because Italy acted as a sponsor to the Albanian state.[13] Greek diplomats had noted the involvement of Italy in the region and its anti-Greek policies even before the Balkan Wars, and this involvement intensified after the rise of Mussolini. In 1923, following the murder of an Italian member of the commission charged to demarcate the Greek-Albanian border, Italy briefly occupied Kerkyra to exert pressure on the Greek government and Mussolini continued to agitate in favor of Albanian interests. The political disorder and unrest in Albania allowed Mussolini to exercise great influence over Albania and use Albanian irredentist claims against Greece and Yugoslavia. Gradually Albania became an Italian protectorate and then part of the Italian fascist kingdom. In this process the Cham minority in Greece was a useful tool for promoting Albanian irredentism and Italian imperialism. Although the Chams numbered only some 17,000–22,000 in 1928,[14] Greece found herself defending her policies regarding the minority in the League of Nations following complaints by Cham activists supported by Italy and Albania. Although there were many times more Christian Albanians in Greece, a group regularly ignored by official censuses, most were fully assimilated and those that were not, as in newly acquired Macedonia and Thrace, tended to form a pro-Greek component anyway.[15] Nevertheless, their presence was a concern as Italy became increasingly aggressive in the 1930s with the invasion of Ethiopia and the annexation of Albania.

The slavophone minority in Macedonia was an equally contentious issue especially since it often enjoyed the support of another neighboring state, Bulgaria. Unlike Italy and Albania, however, Bulgaria had been on the losing side of the Great War and thus had forfeited her military capabilities in the Treaty of Neuilly. In the immediate aftermath of the First World War, the new prime minister Aleksandar Stamboliyski of the Bulgarian Agrarian People's Union attempted to curb the terrorist activities of IMRO but faced intense resistance not only from nationalists but even from the Bulgarian Communist Party which supported the cause of Macedonian independence.[16] The resumption of a clandestine violent campaign by IMRO from bases in Bulgaria against Greek and Yugoslav Macedonia was a constant threat throughout the interwar years that provoked a brief invasion of Bulgaria by Greek troops in 1925 after a border incident.[17] That incursion, which took place during the buffoonish dictatorship of the "Liberal" nationalist Lieutenant-General Theodoros Pangalos, turned into a fiasco for

Greece. The final outcome was a protocol signed between a new Greek government and Bulgaria that was seen as a great success for Bulgaria and which alarmed Yugoslavia. The latter responded with a policy change and sought to appeal to Greek slavophones.[18] Greek politicians like Venizelos became particularly concerned believing the protocol as the first step of autonomy for Macedonia.[19]

To complicate matters further, the Third Communist International, following a campaign by the Bulgarian Communist Party, decided in 1924 to support the creation of a "United and Independent Macedonia" as part of a Balkan Soviet state.[20] Composed of parts of Bulgaria, Yugoslavia, and Greece the Comintern decision reverberated in the region, undermining the popularity of the Greek and Yugoslav communist parties, who were forced to acquiesce to this decision. This decision provided yet another weapon for nationalists to target the Slavic minority in Greece and intensified the perceived need for the Hellenization of the minorities of Greek Macedonia.[21] It was not a coincidence that the resettlement of minorities between Greece and Bulgaria agreed upon in the earlier convention, took place mostly from 1924 to 1925 with 101,800 Bulgarians and 52,891 Greeks exchanging places under the supervision of a Mixed Commission with another 40,000 doing so independently. By the end of the process the Bulgarian minority in Greece had been reduced to 140,000 people and the Greek minority in Bulgaria to a mere 12,000.[22]

Despite the similarities between the situation with the Albanian Chams and the slavophone Macedonians the Greek state had a very different policy toward the two groups, though undoubtedly hostile in both cases. The Chams, because of their religion, were seen as inherently unassimilable, and as a result, little effort was made to integrate them to Greek society or gain their loyalty unlike the efforts directed toward their Christian counterparts a century earlier.[23] The Greek state certainly monitored their activities, discriminated against them, and tried to deter them from embracing a nationalist Albanian identity that would cause potential problems for Greek rule over that part of Epirus, but beyond they were ignored.

Greek officials maintained that slavophones, however, were assimilable as long as the rival Bulgarian or Macedonian propaganda was countered.[24] Slavophones were predominantly Orthodox Christians so in the eyes of the Greek state their assimilation was simply a linguistic problem that could be addressed through a mixture of education and repression.[25] As early as 1913 the inspector general of Primary Education in Macedonia had published a manual for the role of kindergartens to imprint Greek sentiments in foreign speaking children.[26] Even before the annexation of Aegean Macedonia, many slavophones had espoused a Greek cultural identity and had supported the Greek nationalist cause.[27] Denounced as *Grecomans* by their rivals, this group was promoted by the Greek authorities as a model for emulation. At the same time repressive policies against the learning and use of Bulgarian in public were developed and rapidly implemented assisted by the effective introduction of a police presence in the region.[28] Such policies had a dual effect, both positive as far as the Greek governments were concerned. First, if successful, they would assimilate future generations into the Greek nation, and second they also drove those that resented it most to emigrate from Greece, thus removing themselves as a potential threat. These policies were primarily supported by the Venizelist Liberals, who dominated the political scene in the late 1920s and early 1930s, but slavophones found an unexpected source of support in the Royalist Populist Party (Laiko Komma). Its politicians gave assurances that they would protect slavophones from the abuses of government officials, leading even IMRO to urge them to vote for the conservative Populist Party.[29]

The ambivalence of Greece toward the slavophone minority was exemplified by the way Greek officials categorized them. Until 1925 Greece tended to identify slavophones, and especially those that adhered to the Exarchate, as a Bulgarian minority using terms such as Bulgarophones, Bulgarians, or Bulgarizing (*voulgarizonton*). After 1925 the same people become slavophones, or occasionally Macedonian Slavs (*makedonoslavoi*).[30] Their numbers were also in dispute partly because Greek officials tended to include only those with Exarchist affiliations to the Bulgarian/slavophone minority while the remaining slavophones who adhered to the patriarchate of Constantinople were simply added to the Greek population. Thus, officially a mere 81,984 Bulgarian (or slavophone) minority existed in Greece according to the 1928 census when the total number was at least twice that.[31]

Many of the policies mentioned above were of course counter to the Minority Treaties that Greece had signed after the First World War, and Greece found herself defending her policies to the League of Nations, as did most East European states.[32] Repeatedly, Greece was taken to task on the question of slavophone schools but despite repeated promises to the League of Nations Greece did not allow slavophone schools in the interwar period.[33] Greece, like many eastern European countries, strongly resented such accusations from Western countries who nonetheless had practised, and often continued to implement similar policies against their own minorities like the Basques, Bretons, Scotts, Irish, Catalans, and so on, but were exempt from the stipulations of the Minority Treaties.[34] Furthermore, nearly all Eastern and Central European states that had signed these treaties flouted them, including those that filed complaints against Greece on behalf of their minorities like Bulgaria, Albania, and Romania. For example, although Romania granted citizenship to all ethnic minorities, including Jews, with the 1923 constitution, such rights were challenged by various political forces such as the League of the National Christian Defense, later morphed into the National Christian Party, and the fascist Iron Guard. Such was the public pressure that in 1938 Romania issued several decrees establishing the "law of the blood" which "revised" the granting of citizenship to Jews.[35] In this context Greece felt justified to embark upon a forceful assimilation campaign against the Christian non-Greek speakers within its borders.

This policy targeted the Vlach population as much as the Slavic one though without necessarily the same intensity or violence.[36] Vlachs had held a marginal position in the region and despite efforts to organize them in the model of Greeks, Serbs, Bulgarians, or Albanians, their mobilization had been far less effective. In part this was due to the fact that they could not possibly hope to form their own state or join an existing one. Though they shared a linguistic affinity with Romanians multiple states intervened between them and Romania making their annexation impossible. Thus Vlachs, despite material support from Romania and to lesser extent France,[37] could only hope for some cultural recognition of their identity within the nation-states of others. Even that, however, was denied to them, not with the ferocity aimed at truly threatening minorities, but out of hand, as incompatible to the very notion of a nation-state. Vlachs, like Orthodox Slavs, were to be incorporated and assimilated to the Greek nation with equal, if less violent, persistence. These policies were quite successful managing to convince the majority of Vlachs to embrace a Greek national identity. As many as 30,000 Vlachs who resisted assimilation emigrated in the interwar period to Romania so that the official census by 1928 indicated a mere 19,703 Vlachs in Greece, although the numbers of those who had assimilated were much larger.[38]

There were three more minority groups to consider: Jews, Muslims exempted from the exchange of population with Turkey, and Roma. The latter, many of whom were Muslim, were more or less ignored. Their numbers were not significant, they were not politically organized, and they posed no national threat. Unlike many Balkan, and in fact European countries, and most notably Romania where Roma had been disenfranchised, persecuted, and the target of a eugenic discourse,[39] Greece had emancipated her Roma population from the very beginnings of its independent existence, admittedly simply by not explicitly excluding them. While in Romania Roma had been practically enslaved until well into the nineteenth century and were often included in Romanian dowry contracts as property.[40] Roma in Greece could participate in the political life of the country though our knowledge of the details is still greatly lacking. Greeks of all political and ideological stripes seem to have paid little attention to their Roma minority except as a useful statistical unit that could be used to manipulate minority data.

Jews and the Muslims of Thrace share a lot of similarities that have not been explored. Both were religious minorities divided into different linguistic subgroups. The Muslim minority was composed of a Turkish-speaking group, the Slavic-speaking Pomaks, and the Roma who were occasionally but not always grouped with one of the other two groups. The numbers of Pomaks and Roma show remarkable fluctuation from the interwar period to the present, depending upon the political needs of the Greek state which occasionally groups them with Muslims and at other times does not.[41] Jews were also divided among the Ladino-speaking Sephardim and the Greek-speaking Romaniotes, with some additional miniscule numbers of Italian Jews or Yiddish-speaking Ashkenazi. Both main groups were excluded in the public imaginary from the Greek nation due to their religious affiliations but Greek authorities had multiple options in how to handle these groups and in what manner to consider their presence in the Greek state.

There were certainly differences between the Muslims of Thrace and Jews, the most important being the existence of Turkey, a state that bordered the region where these Muslims lived, and a possible threat to Greek nationalist policies. Jews of course aspired to a state of their own but even if Israel had existed it would have been too distant to be a threat like Turkey had the potential to be. One would think that this threat, and the recent devastating defeat at the hands of nationalist Turkey, would have compromised the standing of the Muslim minority in Greece. However, that conflict had been resolved through the Treaty of Lausanne, which stipulated in quite specific detail the treatment of Greek and Turkish minorities. Neither republic had an immediate interest in conflict as both had hundreds of thousands of refugees to settle, new polities and institutions to establish, political opponents who supported the former monarchical regimes to marginalize, and other external threats to confront. Both states therefore were willing to cultivate better ties with each other and accept each other's policies of discrimination toward their minorities. The interwar period proved to be the most peaceful and amicable period in Greek-Turkish relations since Greek independence, especially after the expulsion of the anti-Kemalist refugees from Greece in 1931.[42]

This amicable entente was not reflected in the treatment of minorities in Turkey and Greece. Turkey embarked upon a deliberate program to supplant what was perceived as an inordinate influence of non-Muslims in the professions and economic sphere in general with a series of discriminatory policies. Greece was more concerned about the political influence of the Muslim minority and thus established a separate electoral college that guaranteed the election of a small number of Muslim members of parliament but which limited the impact of the Muslim vote in the general election. The interwar division between Venizelists and Royalists also found an expression in the relations of the state with the Muslim minority, in a rather counterintuitive way. The Liberals, because of their overwhelming support among the Asia Minor refugees, were determined to marginalize the political power of the Muslims in Thrace. By contrast the Royalists under the Laiko Koma (Populist Party) of Panagis Tsaldaris became the defenders of the minority to the extent that in party gatherings cries of "Long live Turkey, long live Kemal" (*zeto e Tourkia, zeto o Kemal*) were frequently heard![43]

This partial exclusion of the Muslims from political influence was made palatable by allowing Muslims to enjoy considerable educational autonomy, especially in matters of language and religion, and by not applying the assimilationist policies that the Greek state pursued with regard to other minorities. Education was a controversial issue among Greek Muslims since the Republic of Turkey had just abandoned the Arabic script for a Latin one, sparking a fierce debated between "old-Turks" (*Palaiotourkoi*), who tended to be anti-Kemalists, and modernizers. The Greek state tended to favor the "old-Turks," many of whom were refugees from the new Republic of Turkey,[44] and was willing to accept Turkish dominance in those fields in order to weaken the Slavic identity of the Muslim Pomaks which was seen as far more threatening.[45] In effect the Greek state was willing to see the assimilation of two Muslim minorities into a single broader Muslim group that was expected to be more loyal or at least less threatening. As we shall see below-this was very similar to the Greek state's policies toward the Sephardic community but not necessarily toward the Romaniote.

Before examining the case of the Jews of Thessaloniki, I should briefly mention the rather confused expectations the Greek state had with respect to minorities, and the uncertainty regarding citizenship and its duties that Fleming also noted.[46] In some cases the expectations were clear, as in the case of the Orthodox Christian minorities (slavophones, Vlachs, Albanians) who were supposed to assimilate fully and become indistinguishable from other Greeks. In the case of religious minorities, however, the question of assimilation was more complex, despite the assimilationist rhetoric of the state. Because of the nature of Greek nationalism and its strong religious component, non-Orthodox Christians could never hope to accepted as members of the nation. In many respects, conversion remained the only sure avenue for full assimilation in the Greek nation. Devin Naar briefly raised this issue in his work which correctly noted that the state did not seem particularly interested in the assimilation of the Jewish community as understood in other parts of Europe, maintaining barriers to the integration of Jews with the rest of society. For example, the state did not recognize civil marriages but only religious ones which negated the possibility of "mixed marriages" between Jews and Christians unless one of them converted. Thus intermarriage between Jews and Christians remained marginal in Greek society unlike much of Europe.[47] The Greek state was willing to accept the full autonomy of both Jewish rabbinical courts and Islamic courts in terms of family law, especially for marital disputes, which naturally acted as a barrier to integration.[48] Furthermore, Greece was quite willing to give her Jewish communities the standing of legal persons of public law, a unique case at the time.[49] Though beneficial in some instances, this legal classification set Jews, as well as certain Muslim groups, outside of the nation. Venizelos and others frequently used the example of the Romaniote Jews as an exemplar of successful assimilation but what they meant was that the Romaniote Jews were a loyal, and unthreatening, minority, that was acceptable to the Greek state, but they did not imply that Romaniote Jews were part of the Greek nation. These Liberal politicians extolled the Jews of Thessaloniki to become good Greek citizens not good Greeks, and it was indicative that in all such exaltations the word "citizen" (*polites*) was rarely absent as a qualifier.

Thessaloniki as an exceptional case

As seen in the last chapter, Thessaloniki was the city with the largest Jewish community in Greece by far. Two thirds of the entire Jewish population in Greece lived there and until its incorporation into the Greek state, Jews composed a plurality of the population of the city. Thessaloniki had been contested by Bulgaria during the Balkan Wars and again in the First World War and plans for its internationalization had been floated, with local Jewish support, before it was assigned to Greece. Its recent history, therefore, made Thessaloniki a city that the Greek state paid particular attention to, determined, as Mazower has put it, to "make the city Greek,"[50] especially since the conditions in the city had markedly deteriorated following its incorporation to the Greek state.

To begin with a remarkable percentage of the population was homeless, destitute, or living in makeshift accommodations. In part this was due to the arrival of thousands of refugees but many of the city's longtime residents had been rendered homeless by the 1917 fire. A significant part of the city remained a burnt-out husk, necessitating radical solutions. This critical situation allowed the state to undertake an ambitious project to rebuild the city and accommodate the thousands of people that needed housing while utterly transforming its urban environment. The plan raised a storm of controversy since it appropriated much of the destroyed property of the inhabitants of the city, the majority Jewish, for the purpose of rebuilding the city in a completely different plan.[51] The former owners would be compensated with new properties but the plan deliberately aimed to break up the old pattern of ethnic and sectarian neighborhoods and to establish the control of the Greek authorities over the city. It also aimed to transform the city visually and culturally by modernizing and Hellenizing its infrastructure and creating new institutions such as a modern university.[52] Thessaloniki was not the only city in Macedonia in need of rebuilding, but whereas the process in other areas like Serres, destroyed in the Balkan Wars, met with little opposition, if not by widespread acceptance of the urban modernization implicit in the new planning.[53] In Thessaloniki, however, the government action was clearly aimed at wrestling control of the city from the Jewish community, despite the modernizing rhetoric which is still echoed in scholarship to this day.[54] Greek officials ignored and even avoided meeting with Jewish representatives which was widely seen as Venizelos' abandonment of his earlier pro-Jewish policies and probably contributed significantly to the community turning toward the Royalists in the ensuing election.[55]

The ambitious urban plans for the rebuilding of Thessaloniki and the revisualization of its urban structure were bound to have a grave impact on the Jewish community. Through the appropriation of properties and reconstruction of the city, the sectarian neighborhood nature of city would have been undermined if not entirely dissolved. A more direct attack on the community, however, was the attempt by the municipality of Thessaloniki to expropriate the ancient Jewish cemetery, the largest Jewish cemetery in Europe, in order to construct a park, expand the new university, and settle refugees from Asia Minor.[56] The fate of the cemetery became emblematic of the struggle over the identity of the city. The Jewish community focused on the cemetery, the roots and antiquity of the community, and religious freedom, while the authorities focused on the university, modernization, and enlightenment, led by the philosophy professor and later rector Avrotelis Eleftheropoulos who accused the Jewish community of stifling the "evolution of the city and university."[57] The community defended its rights in the Greek courts and eventually succeeded in stopping the municipal authorities from destroying the cemetery, although certain parts were appropriated. In 1937, a compromise was reached that relinquished part of the cemetery to the university while the rest would be turned into a park with the tombs untouched, but the park never materialized and burials continued.[58] This affair is indicative of the animosity of the new local, and to some degree national, Greek authorities toward the Jewish community of Thessaloniki and the supposed Jewish stranglehold over the commercial, cultural, and political life of the city. The Greek municipal authorities would not abandon their plans despite the decisions of the Greek courts. As we will see in the next chapter, immediately after the occupation of Thessaloniki by the Axis powers the city council would successfully petition the new German authorities for the expropriation of the cemetery.[59]

The animosity of the Greek authorities had roots back to the attitude of the Sephardic community to the prospect of Greek rule, a suspicion that persisted among nationalist circles throughout the interwar period. Even minor incidents, such as the proposal for the turning of the port of Thessaloniki into a free trade area, could be seen or portrayed as indicative of the lack of loyalty of the Thessaloniki Jews toward Greece since it would give access to the port to neighboring states.[60] In 1921, another blood libel accusation on Easter Sunday was followed by riots and a dangerous tension diffused only when the authorities conclusively proved the accusation false.[61] Remarkably it appears that the community itself was not always aware of the suspicions of Greek nationalists regarding their loyalty, as for instance when it sought to entice the chief rabbi of Sofia Marcus Ehrenpreis, a man the Greek Ministry of Foreign Affairs believed to have supported the Bulgarian irredentist claims during the Balkan Wars, to accept the post of chief rabbi of Thessaloniki.[62] This hypersensitivity toward the potential threat posed by the Jewish community, however, was limited to the most rabidly nationalistic elements of Greece who were significant in local society but less so outside of the city or Macedonia in general. For the Greek government the primary concern was political and had to do with the continuing divide between Royalists and Republicans. The Jews of Thessaloniki, like the Muslims of Thrace and the slavophones in Macedonia, found themselves firmly attached, or perceived to be attached, to the Royalist faction while the recent refugees from Anatolia were just as firmly on the opposite side. As each side tried to gain political and economic advantages, the Jews of Thessaloniki were subjected to a series of regulations meant to diminish their electoral and economic power to the benefit of the newly arrived refugees.[63]

The most blatant of these stipulations was the change in the electoral law in 1923 that removed the Thessaloniki Jews from the body politic and placed them into a separate electoral college. This guaranteed them participation with their own members in the Greek parliament but removed their influence from the general vote, not to mention the message such a separation gave to the rest of Greek society. The Jewish vote in the city had become controversial from 1915 but especially since the 1920 elections that restored King Constantine in which the Thessaloniki Jews had voted massively in favor of the ex-king.[64] The pro-Liberal newspaper *Makedonia* announced the results with the title "Turks and Jews against Venizelos."[65] Liberals like Petros Levantis, the leader of the Liberal ballot in 1928, denounced the supposedly undue influence of Jews as he explicitly stated in an article in the newspaper:

> The Jews of Thessaloniki, living separately, unassimilated, and maintaining all the elements of an ethnic minority, appear as deciding regulators of Greek life with their 7,000 votes, which they apply in a conspirational manner, they can govern the fate of the entire party and, with the forty seats that are won or lost in our district, influence the composition of parliament.[66]

Separating the Thessaloniki Jews from the general electorate was also supported by Venizelos, who was convinced that the Jews of the city were set against his party and Greece in general.[67] Since the Liberal Party of Venizelos saw itself as the Republican bulwark against the restoration of the Monarchy, in its eyes the Thessaloniki Jews were a threat to the very existence of the Republic. As Venizelos told the *Jewish Post*:

> The Greeks do not want the Jews to influence Greek politics. That is why conflict has erupted in Thessaloniki between Christian and Jewish elements . . . the Jews of Thessaloniki follow a nationalist policy. They are not Greeks and do not feel so. They should not, as a consequence, immerse themselves in Greek affairs . . . . The Jews of Thessaloniki are not Greek patriots but Jewish patriots. They are closer to the Turks than us. In the other Greek cities, the Jews are very good citizens and do not manifest any separatist desire or any Jewish nationalism. They are fully assimilated with the Greeks.[68]

It is significant to note the distinction Venizelos made between the Jews of Thessaloniki and those of "other Greek cities," a distinction he reiterated in a letter to the Greek newspaper *Nea Alethia*:

Our opposition to the Israelites of Thessaloniki in this matter [the electoral college] cannot be attributed to my so-called anti-Semitic feelings. The Israelites of Old Greece[69] know how friendly are my feelings for them. I never ceased to recognize and proclaim the virtues of Israel . . . . They [the Jews of Thessaloniki] offer the worst service to the country, to which they are citizens and to themselves, but they are also in danger of poisoning the relations of the Israelites of the other [parts of] Greece with the rest of the elements of the population, while these relations have been harmonious for an entire century, and while those Israelites of the other [parts of] Greece we see them as we see the Catholics of the islands, as equally true Greeks with us the Orthodox, differing only in the dogma and the religion, in which nobody has the right to question the conscience of the other.[70]

The message of this separation of the Jews from the rest of the citizenry was reinforced if one considers the only other group that was similarly set apart. Of all the minorities in Greece, only the Jews of Thessaloniki and the Muslims of Thrace were given separate electoral colleges. The latter were of course clearly identified with a foreign state, the Republic of Turkey, with whom Greece had fought and lost a war. Their continued presence in Greece had been guaranteed by the Treaty of Lausanne in return for the exemption given to the Greek Orthodox of Istanbul from the mandatory population exchange. The Muslims of Thrace were not seen as simply another minority in 1923 but as a hostile group associated with a recent enemy that had shattered the dream of the *Megali Idea*. By placing the Jews of Thessaloniki to the same level, the Greek government identified them as an equal threat and comprehensively alienated them from the Greek nation.

The Liberals thought that their suspicions were confirmed by the ensuing voting pattern of the Jews of Thessaloniki, whose electoral college regularly elected members of the Royalist Populist Party and occasionally the equally reviled communists.[71] More surprising was the response of the conservative right-wing Royalist parties. As was the case with the Muslims of Thrace, the separate college was denounced by the leader of the Populist Party Panagis Tsaldaris and after the electoral victory of the Royalists in 1933 the college was declared unconstitutional and abolished.[72] The simplistic electoral analysis of the time masks the fact that in the 1920s the Jewish community of Thessaloniki was not a monolithic entity and that besides anti-Liberal members of parliament it also supported pro-Venizelist politicians like Senator Mallah, Deputy Bessantchi, and the mayor of Thessaloniki Vamvakas. It was the perceived anti-Semitism of the Liberals, and the virulent anti-Semitism of the main Venizelist newspaper of Thessaloniki, *Makedonia*, that led Jews to the Populist Party which eagerly accepted them and publicly defended them.[73]

One of the unique features of this blatant discrimination of the Greek state toward the Thessaloniki Jews was the fact that it did not extent to all Jews in Greece. The efforts to diminish the electoral power of Jews was aimed solely at the Jews of Thessaloniki. Neither the Jews of Ioannina, nor those of Athens or of other communities voted in separate electoral colleges. Jews in those cities, and even newly acquired ones like Xanthi, continued to vote in the general elections without any restrictions and there was no indication that their voting patterns differed substantially from the rest of the population.[74] Romaniote Jews could be found in the Greek civil service and in the armed forces just like the rest of Greeks and some rose to prominent ranks. At the time of Greece's entry into the Second World War, over 300 Jewish officers served in the Greek armed forces, many with combat experience from the Balkan Wars, the First World War, and the Asia Minor War.[75] Similarly the heated debates over education, participation in the economy, and the rise of a new type of anti-Semitism were much less disrupting in those cities than in Thessaloniki. It is evident, in part from the silence of the sources, that relations between Romaniote communities and the Greek state were less fraught with controversy and, as the quotes above by Venizeos indicate, the Romaniotes were often singled out as models that the Sephardic Jews should emulate.

The two areas where the Greek state pursued its most discriminatory practices against Jews in the interwar period were those of the economy and education. In the first case, Greece exited the long period of war in 1923 with an utterly devastated economy. Greece had entered the Balkan Wars in 1912 with an already weak economy having defaulted in 1893, been placed under international financial supervision in 1898, and having endured a particularly unstable political life until 1910. The near continuous mobilization and warfare between 1912 and 1923 alongside the political infighting of those years had further weakened the Greek economy despite the acquisition of significant new territories and population, while the continuation of the war past 1918 delayed the return to normalcy and the beginning of economic recovery. To make matters worse, the arrival of hundreds of thousands of refugees placed an enormous responsibility and cost on the Greek government that exceeded the substantial material aid provided by the League of Nations. Of these 100,000 to 120,000 settled in Thessaloniki.[76] The vast majority of the refugees arrived with little, if any, wealth. Talks with the Republic of Turkey regarding their abandoned properties would drag on and would finally be resolved with a mutual abandonment of claims in the treaty of Ankara, a pragmatic but economically disadvantageous solution for Greece.

The Greek state hoped to settle most of these refugees in Macedonia to replace the departing Muslim peasants of the region. Macedonia was a fertile region that produced significant export crops, notably tobacco, but many of the refugees came from urban environments and had little to no familiarity with farming. Naturally many refugees failed as farmers and drifted toward the main Greek urban centers where they joined other refugees who had already been settled there to create a labor pool that allowed a hesitant industrialization to make some progress in Greece.

The settlement of the refugees was of particular political importance to the interwar Liberal governments because they represented a solidly antimonarchical group that guaranteed a decade of electoral victories for the Liberals. Because the Asia Minor disaster had taken place under a Royalist government, the refugees blamed the king for their plight and fiercely supported the liberal, nationalist, and republican Venizelos, unlike "Old" Greece that tended to be conservative and monarchical. Venizelos recognized the significance of the refugees to his political success and embraced their cause while fending off other claimants to their loyalty such as the communist party.

Venizelos and the Liberal Party pursued several positive policies toward the refugees providing them with housing, land, education, technical advice on farming, loans, and so on. The Liberals also tried to give them advantages to allow them to integrate in Greek society and become successful members of the Greek economy often by replacing less desirable groups in certain areas including the Thessaloniki Jews. One example was the issue of Sunday as a mandatory holiday. There had been prior efforts dating from 1872 and 1890 to establish Sunday as a mandatory day of rest but it was only in 1909 that a law was passed to be applied only to the cities of Athens, Piraeus, and Volos. In 1914, the law was strengthened, but it was in 1924 that the Greek government attempted to extend the provision to the entire country, despite opposition in Greece and abroad.[77] Seemingly innocuous, this provision would have radical effects in Thessaloniki where Saturday had been the traditional day of rest for all inhabitants.[78] With the new regulations Jewish shop owners would be forced to either break the Sabbath or remain closed for two days during the week. The measure was promoted as a request of the Christian refugees of Thessaloniki who would have gained a significant economic advantage over their Jewish competitors who had continued to dominate the commercial life of the city, as they had for centuries.[79] Although meant to target the Jews of Thessaloniki, the law would also have had an impact on all Jews in Greece, including the very religious Romaniotes of Ioannina.[80] Attempts to establish Sunday as a mandatory day of rest were repeated in 1929 and throughout the 1930s to the vociferous opposition of Jewish authorities and organizations who appealed all the way to the League of Nations.[81]

It has been argued by Mazower and others that commercial rivalry between Christians and Jews in Thessaloniki was a prime cause for the rise of anti-Semitism in the interwar period.[82] State efforts to favor Christian business interests certainly led to the diminution of Jewish dominance in the commercial and banking sectors in this period. This decline is particularly evident in the banking sector where in 1920 more than half of the sixty-six banks and related institutions were Jewish but by 1930 out of the surviving thirty-one only three were in Jewish hands.[83] Nevertheless, by the eruption of the Second World War Jews still owned over 2,000 commercial stores in the city, 31 percent of import and sale of machinery and building materials, 26 percent of industrial companies, 29 percent of clothing stores, 30 percent of commercial and industrial representation companies, and 15 percent of food product companies. At the same time 7,300 Jews survived through food provided by the community.[84] Recent scholarship has also noted the proliferation of anti-profiteering laws in 1914–25 targeting "shameful profit."[85] Although scholars have not explored links to anti-Semitic rhetoric, the language and the timing seem indicative especially in cities like Thessaloniki.

The second area that the Greek state targeted, with great impact, the Jewish communities was the educational establishment especially in the new territories. Education had been a battlefield between the competing Balkan nationalist movements from the nineteenth century. Greece, Bulgaria, Serbia, and even Romania had sponsored schools in Macedonia, Thrace, and Epirus to cultivate national sentiments favorable to their agendas, and to shore up the numbers of those who spoke their national languages as an argument aimed at the European powers for the annexation of these areas. For Jews education in the late nineteenth and early twentieth centuries had also become a contested area but for very different reasons. On the one hand stood the proponents of tradition who wanted to preserve their unique cultural elements including language. Increasing numbers of Ottoman Jews, however, especially in Thessaloniki, had become proponents of modernization and wanted to introduce new schools based upon European models that would provide an education in tune with the modern world. Although some, as in other parts of Europe, saw this as a step toward the assimilation of Jews, a more radical element became enamored with the ideas of Zionism and the dream of an autonomous Jewish state. These modernizers often favored the use of other languages in the schools (French, Hebrew, Turkish), to the dismay of traditionalists.

At the time of the incorporation of the region to the Greek state most Jewish children in Salonica, Janina, and even Thrace were being educated in the *Alliance Israelite Universelle* schools which had been set up in the last decades of Ottoman rule to provide European-style education to the Jews of the Orient. Most of the classwork was done in French with some emphasis on the instruction of Hebrew. Greece inherited six such schools which in 1933 educated 1,862 pupils.[86] The Greek state however, following the experience of Macedonia prior to the Balkan Wars, was quite suspicious of schools with links to foreign entities especially if it thought that they did not give sufficient emphasis to the teaching of Greek language, history, and literature, seen as the primary vehicles of Hellenization of the minorities in the state. The *Alliance* schools were thus perceived as impediments to the nationalist policies of the Greek state, as did the preference many middle-class Jews in Thessaloniki showed for French.[87] In 1920, Greece instituted Law 2456 which though allowing the Jewish communities some autonomy, mandated the teaching of Greek and the teaching of history, geography, and science in Greek.[88]

Greece ideally would have liked minority students to attend its public education system but the government also provided funding to Jewish schools for the teaching of Greek.[89] The Greek language was the main instrument with which minorities in general, and non-Greek-speaking Jews in particular, would be incorporated in Greek society.[90] Law 2456 of 1920 aimed at precisely that while allowing Jews to be taught their religion in other languages.[91] Despite difficulties in procuring instructors, and problems with Christian instructors who often proselytized in the classroom, the efforts of the Greek state, assisted by a significant segment of the community leadership that embraced assimilation, bore fruit though primarily because increasing numbers of Jews sent their children to Greek public schools.[92] By the 1930s a quarter of Jewish students in Thessaloniki attended Greek public schools, in part as a result of scholarships,[93] a phenomenon witnessed in other parts of Greece as well where public schools made significant inroads to the Jewish communities including in Kerkyra where Gatenio Nata was switched to a Greek public school operating in the Jewish quarter from one run by Catholic Nuns because she was "picking up Christian habits" from the nuns.[94]

It was inevitable that there would be friction between the *Alliance* schools and the Greek Ministry of Education. Problems appeared as early as 1920 with the law mandating the use of Greek for several subjects.[95] A more insidious effort by the Greek state to undermine the *Alliance* schools was its introduction of teachers of Hebrew in all public schools with more than twenty Jewish pupils, making the Greek public education system more attractive especially to those who favored assimilation, who also happened to be the main supporters of the *Alliance*. Greece eventually banned the operation of schools run by foreign organizations, although Venizelos claimed that the Greek state was fully compliant with the obligations imposed through the signing of the Minority Treaties after the First World War since it continued to allow the teaching of minority languages through local and public schools.[96] Though the *Alliance* schools were probably not the main targets of the ban, the combined effect of the above policies was to undermine the communal educational system of the Jewish community.

From all indications it seems that Thessaloniki was again the crucible of the educational policies of Greece as well as the center of opposition by segments of the Jewish population. Questions of education became tied to questions of assimilation, as was the case elsewhere in Europe, where assimilationists, traditionalists, Zionists, and socialists expressed radically different positions some in support of the policies of the Greek state and some in vehement opposition. In Greece, nationalists frequently attacked Jews, especially those of Thessaloniki, for their supposed unwillingness to learn Greek, while anti-Venizelist newspaper occasionally came to the support of Jews stressing the community's efforts to embrace the Greek language.[97] Nationalists also pointed out there were few Jewish students at the University of Thessaloniki, an outcome perhaps of poor linguistic skills in Greek among young Jews, but for nationalists an indication of an unwillingness by Jews to embrace Hellenic civilization.[98]

It should be noted, however, that such issues impacted the Sephardim a lot more than the Romaniotes who were Greek speakers and thus had few objections in attending public schools especially after the introduction of Hebrew in areas with sufficient Jewish students as was the case in Ioannina. Young Jews in Thessaloniki appear cognizant of the fact that Greek education would be to their benefit under the new political circumstances, especially with the visible example of several successful Romaniotes who were assigned to mediate between the state and the Jewish community in Thessaloniki, foregoing the attachment to French of their elders.[99] A similar intercommunal conflict is visible in other Jewish communities as in the case of Didymoteicho where the *Alliance* was forced to cease operations after 1924.[100] These policies by the Greek state seem to be disproportionally aimed at the Sephardic community whose language, Ladino, was deliberately excluded from instruction in favor of Hebrew, to the point that the University of Thessaloniki refused a grant by the Spanish Embassy to create a chair for Spanish language and literature in 1930 on the grounds that it would obstruct the Hellenization of the Jews of the city, even though neither the Ministry of Education, nor the Ministry of Foreign Affairs objected.[101] The promotion of Hebrew over Ladino was not opposed by the entire Jewish community, however, and many Zionist and religious factions supported it.[102]

These policies should also be considered in the context of other, more threatening, minorities like the Slav Macedonians or Albanian Muslims whose demands for separate schools were seen as an attempt to undermine Greek authority in the newly conquered areas of Macedonia and Epirus and to allow nationalist agitation from Bulgaria and Albania. Similar educational policies were first implemented there,[103] and such groups were submitted to more authoritarian and even repressive measures with frequent use of force. Unlike the Sephardim who could use Ladino publicly, slavophones were subjected to police violence, and legislation was enacted to constrain the use of their language, names, and Slavic place names especially under the dictatorship of Ioannis

Metaxas.[104] Metaxas focused quite intently on the Hellenization of minorities and thus gave added emphasis to their education by instituting the inspectors of foreign and minority schools and producing textbooks for the teaching of Greek specifically for minority schools.[105]

The new anti-semitism

The interwar period in Europe saw the rise of several violent anti-Semitic movements from the National Socialists in Germany, to the Iron Guard in Romania, the *Action Française* in France, the *Ustasa* in Yugoslavia, and the Arrow Cross in Hungary. Their influence even in regions such as the United States and Turkey should not be underestimated, nor the appeal of their message in the conditions of the Great Depression. Anti-Semitic ideas that had emerged prior to the First World War in Austria-Hungary, France, Russia, and Germany proliferated and had a significant impact throughout Europe, and Greece was not an exception. The interwar period therefore sees the emergence of a new type of anti-Semitic rhetoric in Greece removed from the religious connotations of the previous century or the nationalist association of Jews with the now defunct Ottoman Empire. The emphasis on the association of Jews with money, banking, and capitalism, had existed earlier, but now it became the main focus of the rhetoric. Tied to these accusations were related condemnations with regard to Jewish cosmopolitanism, statelessness, and rootlessness. Illogically such accusations were often coupled with Jewish associations with communism and revolution in general and especially in the post-Bolshevik period with the USSR.[106] France whose liberal policies with respect to immigration saw some 120,000 Jews come to the country from eastern Europe experienced strong anti-Semitic movements most prominently the *Action Française* whose leader Charles Mauras insisted that Jews could never become "real" French while Louis-Ferdinand Celine essentially called for a genocide in his 1937 *Bagatelles Pour Un Massacre*.[107] Hungary had 10,000 anti-Semitic associations by the mid-1920s and quotas were placed on the percentage of Jews educational institutions could accept.[108] Poland renounced the Minority Treaties it had signed in 1934 and anti-Semitic violence erupted.[109] Even in America Jews faced restrictions in professions, residences, clubs, and quotas in universities while one impetus for the 1924 restrictions on immigration was to limit the number of Jews coming into the United States from Europe.[110]

Balkans anti-Semitism also had a revival led by the already strongly anti-Semitic Romanian society where older forms of anti-Jewish rhetoric were reinforced by a modern, eugenic discourse and new organizations like the Iron Guard were founded based upon fascist principles. Hundreds of priests and other members of the Romanian Church joined the Iron Guard, 218 Orthodox Priests going on trial in 1941 when the organization was suppressed.[111] Although Mazower considers Romania an outlier in the Balkans and the only Balkan government that condoned pogroms and boycotts against Jews in the interwar period,[112] several other Balkan states also experienced violent anti-Semitic incidents, often with the acquiescence of local or state authorities. In Turkey, for example, legislation to "Turkify" the economy and reduce the prominence of minorities like Jews, Greeks, and Armenians, certainly facilitated the eruption of pogroms in 1934 in Edirne, Kirklareli, Çanakale, and elsewhere, where synagogues and houses were attacked by mobs sparking a flight of Jews from the country.[113] Anti-Semitic rhetoric proliferated in Turkey, and although the roots date from the Ottoman period, it intensified after 1923 taking an anti-Zionist hue and targeting even the Dönme, the seventeenth-century Jewish converts to Islam, who had been expelled from Thessaloniki alongside other Muslims.[114]

Unsurprisingly the greatest penetration of these new anti-Semitic ideas in Greece can be found in Thessaloniki where a combination of a large Jewish community and an influx of thousands of refugees created a unique and highly combustible environment that did not have its equal elsewhere in interwar Greece. Despite the efforts of the Greek state many of the refugees became an impoverished underclass in the city and proved particularly susceptible to anti-Semitic rhetoric often promoted by local Liberal politicians and newspapers. The "otherness" of the Sephardic community who did not share a language or religion with the now majority Orthodox Greek speakers coupled with the ultranationalist sentiments of the recent arrivals and the continuing perceived threats to Greek rule in the region contributed to the antagonism between Jews and the Christian refugees. The economic hardship of many refugees contributed to the antagonism since Jews also formed the earlier proletariat of the city and thus competed for many of the lower-level jobs of the city. In 1927, George Kosmidis, a refugee from Asia Minor, founded the *Ethnike Enoses Ellas* (EEE) organization (National Union Greece) better known as EEE, the first truly anti-Semitic organization in the country, originally as a self-help organization.[115] Many poor refugees joined to improve their living conditions and economic prospects but the organizations' charter also included clauses for the protection of the Orthodox faith, the combating of foreign propaganda and threats to Greece's territorial integrity, the restoration of the army's morale following the defeat of 1923.[116] EEE saw Jews and communists as the primary obstacles to its goals and often received tacit support from local authorities.[117] Unlike similar contemporary movements in Europe like the National Socialists or Iron Guard, however, EEE failed to attract a mass following outside of Thessaloniki. In some ways the organization was a curious amalgamation of an attempt to imitate the structure of modern European extremist organizations while espousing an older form of anti-Semitism that involved burning effigies of Judas and spreading accusations of blood libel.[118] It did strike a chord in Thessaloniki where it found support in the nationalist newspaper *Makedonia*, the most prominent anti-Semitic publication in Greece. *Makedonia,* which was one of the very few major newspapers published outside Athens and controlled an early radio station,[119] would have a prominent and particularly nefarious role in the rabid anti-Semitic campaign of the late 1920s and early 1930s.[120] In 1928, on the occasion of the Greek edition of the *Protocols of the Elders of Zion* published by Aristidis Andronikos to wide circulation, *Makedonia* would discuss the supposedly Jewish worldwide conspiracy on its first page, and even state that it would serialize the *Protocols*, as did another newspaper in Thessaloniki *To Fos* (the Light).[121]

The confused ideology of EEE and other anti-Semites like Sitsa Karaiskaki, often portrayed Jews as allied with the regional enemies of Greece (Turkey, Bulgaria) as well as with international capitalism, socialism and communism. The latter claim resonated more plausibly in Thessaloniki, which had been at the forefront of the labor movement even before its incorporation to Greece under the guidance of Abraham Benaroya. Benaroya first founded the Socialist Club and in 1909 the more influential *Federacion Socialista Laboradeva* (Socialist Federation of Workers) and was later involved with the Second International.[122] These were the first significant socialist organizations as far as Greek territories were concerned and from them emerged both the mass labor movement as well as the Communist Party of Greece (KKE). The rapid gains of KKE in the 1920s coupled with its stance on the Macedonian question alarmed both the local and state authorities and Venizelos' government responded with the passage of a law in 1929, the famed *idionymo*, which gave wide powers to the authorities to prosecute as a criminal act any action considered to be against the existing social structure.[123] It is hardly surprising that the labor movement in Greece would emerge in arguably the most industrialized city of Greece but its association with the Jewish population provided ammunition to the anti-Semites. Furthermore, in the Greek case the frequent accusation voiced against communism with regard to anti-national policies was made plausible when the Communist International adopted in 1934 a declaration calling for the establishment of an independent Macedonian state from the Greek, Yugoslav, and Bulgarian territories. In anti-Semitic literature, therefore, the Jews of Thessaloniki were doubly tied to anti-Greek policies through their earlier stance on the annexation of the city and perceived pro-Bulgarian sentiments as well as through communism.

Similar confusion existed with regard to the Zionist movement. Zionists had been among the most fervent supporters of Venizelos and the Liberal Party among the Jewish community, in part due to Venizelos' early and continuing support for a Jewish state in Palestine.[124] Zionist publications were widely distributed, not only in Hebrew and Ladino, but also in Greek in the city.[125] Sympathy toward the Zionist cause was not rare in Greece and even in Thessaloniki where the most anti-Semitic newspaper, *Makedonia*, and its editor Nikolaos Fardis, who would be instrumental in several anti-Semitic events in the interwar period and the Second World War, published pro-Zionist articles on the occasion of anti-Jewish riots in Palestine. Frequently Zionism was compared to the Greek War of Independence and the Philike Etaireia.[126] At the same time, however, Zionism was seen with deep skepticism by nationalists, including in *Makedonia*, as an obstacle toward the assimilation of the Jews of Thessaloniki, a message unwittingly reinforced by the accusations leveled against Zionists by Jewish communists regarding their unpatriotic attitudes, which were often reproduced in Makedonia.[127] Ironically both Zionists and the left would become identified as anti-Venizelist.[128] As Papamichos Chronakis perceptively identified, the very fact that reports about Zionists were sent to the Ministry of Foreign Affairs indicate that for the Greek state Zionists, and by extension the entire Jewish community of Thessaloniki, were not essentially a domestic issue but a foreign threat rather like communism or foreign propaganda.[129]

To confuse the situation further, one of the greatest threats to Greece in the 1920s and 1930s was fascist Italy which had visions of dominating the Mediterranean, the Adriatic, and the Balkans.[130] Although the fascist regime in Italy had developed an ideology that saw the Italian race as superior to the Slavs often targeting its own Slav minorities,[131] in the Greek context Italy attempted to approach the Sephardic element of

Thessaloniki particularly through the sponsoring of Italian schools in the city which in the 1920s had more students than any other foreign schools save the French. Although changes in legislation restricting the operation of foreign schools in 1931 constrained Italian propaganda on that front, Italy also cultivated and sponsored several small fascist organizations in Thessaloniki which may have influenced the organizational outlook of EEE.[132]

In 1931, the propaganda of EEE culminated in the most famous anti-Semitic action in interwar Greece, the Campbell pogrom. A mob of 2,000 people attacked the Jewish neighborhood of Campbell, destroying twenty-six buildings and leaving 220 Jewish families homeless, allegedly because of an incident involving the participation of the Thessaloniki Jewish sport club Maccabi in a congress of Maccabi societies in Sofia where anti-Greek sentiments over the question of Macedonia were expressed.[133] The supposed incident had been widely covered in the press of Thessaloniki with various levels of condemnation ranging from moderate to vitriolic denunciations in *Makedonia*. The violence which was probably organized by the EEE and was supported by the articles of *Makedonia* caught the authorities by surprise. The local authorities and the gendarmerie were slow to react, but the Athenian government, in an action that has echoes of the Kerkyra pogrom, dispatched reinforcements to restore order. The Minister of Justice rushed to Thessaloniki, the office of Prime Minister Venizelos issued a statement expressing sympathy toward the Jewish community denouncing such acts as "anti-Hellenic," and the police urged Jews to return to their homes.[134] Confronted with this violence all newspapers agreed to refrain from inflammatory rhetoric except for *Makedonia* which continued her anti-Semitic rhetoric.

The Greek authorities saw EEE as the prime instigator of the riot and filed charges against the secretary of the organization Charitopoulos. *Makedonia's* refusal to abandon its anti-Semitic propaganda also resulted in the prosecution of its editor Nikos Fardis for complicity in the violence, who would later continue his anti-Semitic propaganda during the Nazi occupation of Thessaloniki.[135] The trial was moved from Thessaloniki because of the tensions to a nearby town where a jury acquitted both men. The acquittal, as much as the riots themselves, caused significant uproar in Greece. Several state officials, especially at the local level, were heavily criticized either for their inaction in the face of violence or for inflammatory statements as in the case of the Ministry of the Interior, which had issued a statement accusing the Thessaloniki Maccabi of anti-Greek activities.[136] Despite these statements and the general tendency of modern historiography to see the Campbell pogrom as a result of the resistance of the Sephardic community to assimilation, Devin Naar has recently suggested that one could see the pogrom as exactly the opposite, as a fearful reaction to increasingly successful assimilation, with youth movements on both sides playing crucial roles.[137] Similar outcomes have been visible in other parts of Europe, as in Germany where the deep immersion of German Jews in German *Kultur* often led to anger among non-Jewish Germans.[138] Similarly Donald Horowitz has shown how changes, or perceived changes, in the official or unofficial ethnic status can become the stimulus for a riot.[139] Maria Kavala on the other hand has pointed out the class dimension with both victims and perpetrators coming from poor, working-class environments.[140]

In the politically charged atmosphere of the time with yet another default in 1932, government instability, failed coups, and the restoration of the monarchy in 1935, it is not surprising that the Campbell riots were not given greater prominence outside of the Jewish press and community. The latter responded with a massive wave of emigration from Thessaloniki that a contemporary Salonican called "the new expulsion" in *El Luzero Sefaradi*, a New York Ladino publication, evoking memories of the Spanish expulsion of 1492.[141] This wave of emigration came on the heels of an earlier exodus due to military conscription, the 1917 fire, and "the antipathy that has always existed between the Israelite element and the Greek element" according to the French consul at the time.[142] A mass emigration to France after 1927 resulted in a 20,000 strong Parisian Jewish community from Thessaloniki by 1930 as reported by the Jewish press.[143] Between 1932 and 1934 a further 10,000 to 15,000 Jews emigrated from Thessaloniki, mostly toward Palestine, reducing the Jewish population of Thessaloniki to some 50,000 by the Second World War from the 80–90,000 at the turn of the century in a process resembling the migration from Kerkyra following the 1891 pogrom.[144] Furthermore, this emigration would be permanent since a 1927 decree allowed the state to withdraw Greek nationality from Greeks who had gained it, as all those living in "New" Greece had, if they left Greece with no intention to return.[145]

Despite the political uncertainty and the acquittal of its secretary, EEE was not able to capitalize on these events. Although EEE's lawyer boasted that prior to the Campbell pogrom the organization had a mere twelve chapters and 3,000 members while afterward it had grown to twenty-seven chapters and 7,000 members, EEE remained marginal outside of Thessaloniki.[146] It never exceeded 8,000 members nationally and despite the occasional demonstration in Thessaloniki and other Greek cities, including Athens, it could not generate mass support even in cities with significant Jewish minorities like Ioannina. EEE's lack of success can be ascribed to its failure to find a charismatic leader like Adolf Hitler or Corneliu Codreanu, but I believe it had more to do with the circumstances of Greece. Thessaloniki was the only place where the social, political, national, and economic fabric was conducive to the emergence of a true anti-Semitic organization and EEE's growth was partly due to the tolerance exhibited by the Liberal local authorities toward it and their hostility toward the Jews of the city. *Makedonia*, after all, was not an instrument of EEE but a nationalist newspaper that supported the Liberal Party. The anti-Semitic attitude of the Liberal Party in Thessaloniki, however, did not translate to a national context where Liberals did not promote anti-Semitic actions. The hostility of even the Liberal government in Athens toward such violent outbursts was evident and the conservative royalist opposition was even more hostile and actively courted the Jewish vote. The decline of the Liberal vote in the early 1930s and the resurgence of the monarchists eventually doomed EEE.

In 1936, Greece became a dictatorship through a parliamentary coup orchestrated by Ioannis Metaxas, a conservative, royalist, leader of a tiny party with somewhat fascist aspirations. Metaxas justified his authoritarian rule as a necessity in the face of the chaos of the previous period that threatened, in his view, to open the door to a communist takeover. He moved quickly to suppress labor and communist organizations and send its members to internal exile on desolate Greek islands. The powers of the police were expanded dramatically during his rule and were often used against suspect minorities.[147]

but he also disbanded and suppressed EEE which he rightly saw as a disruptive force in Greek society and one that could embarrass Greece internationally.[148]

Metaxas's regime (1936–41) tried desperately to negotiate the increasingly dangerous international situation while trying to construct his so-called Third Hellenic Civilization. His regime copied much of the imagery and vocabulary from its contemporary fascist movements in Italy and Germany but with little of their radical, transformational, ideology. Rather, Metaxas evoked a rather conservative, reactionary narrative that glorified Greece's ancient past, Orthodox Christianity, and family values as demonstrated by the regime's motto *Patris, Threskeia, Oikogeneia* (Fatherland, Religion, Family). Unlike the modernist fascist regimes with their industrial policies, Metaxas promoted agricultural development, while the past, always a powerful feature in the Greek imaginary, was venerated in ludicrous forms, including reenactments of ancient games and ceremonies replete with costumes, and in more serious scientific ones with a renewed emphasis on archaeology elevated to a sort of secular religion and given a new direction that would suit the regime's ideological imperatives.[149] Metaxas did copy certain elements of the fascist regimes such as a youth organization, but was unable to produce the mass movements that had propelled Hitler and Mussolini to power. His supposedly voluntary youth organization EON (National Youth Organization) was able to become a true mass organization reaching 1,200,000 members by 1940 but this was achieved only by becoming practically mandatory.[150] Although there is a widely held belief that EON excluded non-Christian children from membership,[151] Jewish children, and other non-Christian minorities, were not explicitly barred from membership despite the Christian character of the organization, which was certainly a deterrent. The dictator himself stated that Jews could be members though their membership required approval by the authorities and, as the picture of the young Jewish boy in an EON uniform indicates, some Jewish children did become members (see Figure 5.1).[152] Fleming has argued that during Metaxas' rule the Jews of Thessaloniki finally begun to develop a Greek Jewish identity interrupted, but also facilitated, by the Second World War.[153]

Before concluding our investigation with the horror of the Second World War, it is useful to reconsider the Greek Jewish experience during the first century of the Greek state's existence. At no point throughout this period were Jews considered full members of the Greek nation. Yet, as I tried to describe, over the course of the century the Greek state modified its stance on the Jewish communities, in part to confront the changing realities of the Balkans and the rise of competing Balkan nationalisms, and in part to address changes in Greek-society itself. The Greek state had to manage increasing numbers of Jews within its borders as new territories were added in 1863, 1881, and 1912–20. In such circumstances, some Jewish communities, and more specifically those that were already Greek speaking were seen as acceptable, even valuable citizens, if not by the wider public, certainly by the Greek state. Others however who were seen as unwilling to embrace the Greek national cause were viewed with suspicion and targeted through a variety of legal, political, and economic handicaps. Such discriminatory practices were often implemented with political goals in mind, such as to attract the votes of the 1923 refugees, rather than as a matter of state anti-Semitic policy even if the effects were not dissimilar. As a rule, the state authorities objected to

Figure 5.1 Isaak Cohen in EON uniform © Collection of the Jewish Museum of Greece.

blatant anti-Semitic acts, especially violent ones, and took measures to suppress them, partly as a matter of rule of law and partly to avoid the negative publicity such acts generated abroad. In a rather interesting contrast to the European political trends of the time, in the interwar period it was the Royalists and the political Right that acted in defense of Jewish rights, including the semi-fascist dictator Metaxas, while the Liberal republicans justifiably stood accused of anti-Semitism. Both, however, acted thus for internal political reasons and not out of any ideological imperative.

The Holocaust and the Destruction of Greek Jewry

Despite his semi-fascist ideology the Dictator Metaxas tried desperately to keep Greece out of the war that erupted with Germany's invasion of Poland in 1939. The main threat to Greek sovereignty were Hitler's allies, revisionist Bulgaria and especially Italy under Mussolini who had supported Albanian irredentism before absorbing Albania to its fascist empire. At the same time Greece was utterly dependent upon Germany for exports.[1]

Metaxas therefore tried to maintain a neutral attitude to the expanding war hoping that the commercial value of the Balkans would induce Germany to reign in the ambitions of Italy. The successes of the German armies against Poland, France, and Britain, however, had emboldened Mussolini and he entered the war on June 10, 1940, hoping to gain complete control over the Mediterranean and the Balkans. After a series of provocations Mussolini delivered an ultimatum to Metaxas on the night of October 28, 1940, and a few hours later Italian troops crossed the Albanian border and invaded Greece.

To the surprise of everyone, Greece was not only able to repulse the Italian invasion but went on the offensive invading Albania and occupying most of the area inhabited by the Greek minority. Even after the death of Metaxas on January 29, 1941, Greek forces (with the support of the British navy and air force) were able to withstand a new Italian offensive but the strain on Greek resources convinced the new prime minister Koryzis to accept an offer of troops from Britain in a support role that would allow the transfer of Greek forces from non-combat zones to the Albanian front. The presence of British forces in southern Europe on the eve of Germany's invasion of the Soviet Union was not something Hitler could accept and Germany attacked Greece and Yugoslavia on April 6, 1941. Koryzis committed suicide but the king and the rest of the government refused to surrender evacuating first to Crete and then to Egypt followed by several political figures, the Greek navy, and some other armed forces and continued to fight for the duration of the war as part of the Allied effort. Occupied Greece was divided into three zones. By far the largest was the Italian which included most of mainland Greece and the Ionian islands. Germany retained the most strategic parts of Greece including Athens, Thessaloniki, most of Crete, several islands adjacent to Turkey, and the border between Greece and Turkey. Bulgaria was compensated for allowing the free passage of German troops to invade Greece with the annexation of Thrace and Yugoslav Macedonia.

Minorities in war and occupation

The participation of minorities in the 1940 and 1941 campaigns has not been explored in detail. Minorities had been enlisted in the Greek armed forces since the nineteenth century and many, including Jews, had participated in the Balkan campaigns, the First World War, and the Asia Minor campaign. Some had risen through the ranks and by 1940 held senior positions. The mobilization of 1940 enlisted all minorities, including the Muslims of Thrace, Sephardic and Romaniote Jews, Vlachs, and Albanians, many of whom were among the 90,000 Greek casualties of the campaign.[2] The first high-ranking Greek officer to be killed in the Greek-Italian War was Colonel Mordohaios Frizis of Romaniote origin from the town of Chalkis. Frizis was a veteran of the wars of the early twentieth century and had risen through the ranks. His death was given widespread publicity by the Greek government and press, and Metaxas commented that he was an "Israelite by religion, but deeply Greek in his soul and spirit."[3] From October 28, 1940, to the fall of Greece 12,898 Jews had served in the Greek army, among them 343 officers including two lieutenant colonels and a colonel. In the fighting 613 Jewish soldiers had been killed and 3,743 wounded.[4] One regiment from Thessaloniki, the fiftieth, was nicknamed the Koen Battalion because it was predominantly Jewish.[5] These contributions were positively remarked upon by Greek officials in the newspapers of the time and many senior officers made references to the sacrifices of the Greek Jews, both at the time of and after the war. The overall commander of the Greek army general, later field marshall, Alexandros Papagos commented that Greek Jews "fulfilled their duty to their country in full measure."[6]

The fall of Greece dramatically changed the situation of the various minorities, though not all minorities were affected in identical ways. The occupiers, in their efforts to solidify their control over their zones of occupation, reduce the military requirements to garrison these areas, and in the case of Bulgaria and Italy to advance their designs of incorporating some of these territories to their own states, sought to recruit minorities into their own forces and sever whatever ties the latter may have had to the Greek state, as they did elsewhere most notably in Bosnia whose Muslims provided the core of the thirteenth SS division.[7] Thus, minorities like the slavophone Macedonians, Albanians, and Vlachs, were courted while others, especially Jews and Roma who ran afoul of the Nazi racial laws, saw their circumstances deteriorate even before the full implementation of the Final Solution.

The Bulgarian occupation was the most threatening to Greece because Bulgaria had been forced to cede those areas to Greece at the conclusion of the First World War. Thus their renewed occupation was seen as a prelude to full annexation. However, the Thrace that Bulgaria occupied in 1941 was very different from the Thrace it had abandoned in 1918. Although many slavophones embraced Bulgarian nationality with the arrival of Bulgarian troops,[8] the slavophone element of the region had been dramatically reduced through the population exchanges with Greece throughout the interwar period to 1941,[9] while the non-Slavic component had been enhanced by the arrival of the refugees from Asia Minor.

The Bulgarian authorities attempted to suppress Greek language and education. They took measures, including the widespread use of violence and terror, that would

Figure 6.1 Colonel Mordohaios Frizis © Collection of the Jewish Museum of Greece.

ensure the flight of those who identified themselves as Greek, a flight that begun even before the full occupation was effected.[10] The Bulgarian authorities also tried to entice the return of Bulgarians to Thrace who had emigrated to Bulgaria as part of the exchange of populations or who had fled Greek efforts to Hellenize them. They also attempted to build bridges with the non-Greek, non-Bulgarian minorities of the region like the Pomak Muslims and Jews whose numbers could be used to bolster Bulgarian claims in the region.[11] The terror was quite effective in provoking a mass flight of 100,000 Greek civilians toward the Nazi zone of occupation, by itself an indictment of the conditions in Thrace, while thousands of Muslims fled to Turkey.[12] Some Bulgarian refugees did return to Thrace but the violence and the emergence of a Greek resistance movement dissuaded many from remaining.

Italy was more successful in its efforts to build bridges with minorities partly because the Italian occupation was by far the least violent. Italy was seen as a patron of Albanian interests since the late nineteenth century, and in 1939 the Albanian crown had been "offered" to the king of Italy.[13] On the outset of the war Greek authorities had disarmed the Cham Albanians living on the border region adjacent to Albania, enlisting many in labor battalions and sending others to internal exile.[14] Unsurprisingly many Chams welcomed the Italian occupation.[15] Italian authorities convinced many Greek Albanians to enlist in pro-Axis units like the *Bal Komitare* that were used as counterinsurgency and occupation units, a fact used against them by Greek nationalist authors to this day.[16]

The second minority that Italians attempted to co-opt were the Vlachs whose Romance language supposedly showed a racial affinity with Italy and Rome and whose "fatherland," Romania, was an Axis ally. Vlachs were offered educational and cultural advantages as well as a promise of an autonomous province of their own in western Greece.[17] The extent to which Vlachs were open to these enticements remains unclear, in part because the total number of Greek Vlachs is uncertain. In prewar censuses Vlachs were often counted among Greeks since most were bilingual and had few reasons to deliberately stand out unless they were the "Roumanizontes" (Romanian-minded) who rejected integration. Evangelos Averoff, a Vlach and prominent politician in the postwar period, claimed that Vlachs numbered nearly a quarter of a million at the time, which would make Italian efforts a failure.[18] However, a small number of Vlachs led by Alkiviadis Diamantis did collaborate with the Italian authorities and even formed a Vlach legion.[19]

The final group that both Italians and Germans tried to sway were the group most repressed by the Greeks, the slavophone Macedonians, who had cause to despise Greek rule. Many slavophone Macedonians in Greece and Yugoslavia supported the Axis, although their early enthusiasm was curbed by the corruption, brutality, and inefficiency of Bulgarian rule and the rise of resistance movements. Nevertheless, thousands of slavophone Macedonians joined pro-Axis units and supported the occupation in both Greece and Yugoslavia.[20]

This attempt by Bulgaria, Italy, and Germany to use disaffected minorities amplified the preexisting fears of Greek nationalists with respect to the loyalty of minorities. Although the collaborationist governments of 1941–44 could not openly target minorities that had the support of the Axis, the widespread resistance movement that emerged in Greece could and did do so. The Greek resistance movement was one of the largest in Europe especially in the Italian zone of occupation where the combination of high mountain ranges, sparse communities, and Italian indifference to control the area beyond the major urban centers, allowed several effective resistance organizations to emerge. Although the largest resistance movement, the communist-led *National Liberation Front* (EAM) and its military wing the *Greek Popular Liberation Army* (ELAS) generally did not target minorities, the nationalist organizations like the *National Republican Greek League* (EDES) actively pursued minorities that it perceived as disloyal to Greece. To make matters worse, the operational range of EDES coincided with the areas inhabited by Albanians and Vlachs. The rising levels of violence, especially following the Italian capitulation, saw a free for all where nationalists, communists, Albanian and Vlach militias, and German troops fought each other and committed numerous atrocities in Paramythia, Kydonia, Distomo, Klisoura, Komeno, and many other places.[21]

The Holocaust in Greece

The chaotic circumstances of Greece from 1941 onwards made life unbearable for Greeks and minorities alike but their experiences did not compare with those of Jews. Both Romaniote and Sephardic communities were nearly wiped out during the Holocaust, an outcome that may prompt some to speculate that this decimation was a result of preexisting anti-Semitic sentiments among the Christian population.

The circumstances, however, were more complex. Despite Hannah Arendt's general assertion that the Greek population was indifferent to the fate of Jews,[22] there were no attacks on Jews by the local population in Greece like the massacre at Jedwabne in Poland or the 1941 pogroms in Iasi, Bukovina, and Bessarabia.[23] Even institutions with strong anti-Semitic tendencies like the Greek Orthodox Church conducted themselves rather admirably. Many bishops took an active role in saving Jews, including the metropolitan Joachim of Volos, the metropolitan of Zakynthos Chrysostomos, the metropolitan of Chalkis Gregorios, and the archbishop of Athens Damaskinos. Metropolitan Gregorios of Chalkis even protected the Talmud and other religious items entrusted to him by the local rabbi, while Archbishop Damaskinos directed Greek Orthodox priests to urge their congregations to offer assistance to Jews.[24] As Yomtov Yakoel noted in his diary:

> It was later known that the Church pointed out through appropriate sermons from the pulpit to its flock the humane duty of Christians towards their fellow citizens who were being tested, as did the teachers of the Greek schools who instructed the young regarding their proper conduct towards their Jewish brothers. The more touching attitude, as far as the Jews were concerned, was that of the organizations of the disabled, wounded, and victims of war. Those petitioned even the German SS and demanded that their Jewish companions who had suffered in the war, be excluded from the measures [against the Jews] in view of their patriotic behavior.[25]

Not all Jewish communities were under Nazi rule at first. Although the largest, that of Thessaloniki, was under German control from the moment of the capture of the city until the deportation of the community to the death camps, the communities of other cities like Ioannina, Kerkyra, or Patras, were under Italian occupation and thus not subject to the same persecution. Thessaloniki has rightly become the image of Jewish suffering in Greece due to the size of its community, the abuses heaped on it from 1941 onwards, and the fact that the Jews of Thessaloniki were among the first to be deported. The near total destruction of the Thessaloniki community has skewed the statistics of the Greek Holocaust which when broken down indicate that the experience of Jews and their chances of survival in Greece varied dramatically from place to place. Such statistics are controversial because of the uncertainty regarding the prewar numbers of Jews as well as those of survivors. Mazower gives the total number of Greek Jews to have been between 70,000 and 80,000 with 50,000 living in Thessaloniki. Ampatzopoulou also mentions 56,000 Jews in Thessaloniki, and Spengler-Axiopoulou gives 70,000 as the overall Jewish population of Greece. All agree that approximately 10,000 Greek Jews survived.[26]

Regardless of the exact numbers the variation in the survival rates of Jewish communities is so great as to indicate a significant difference between the communities of "Old" Greece whose casualties generally were between 25 and 50 percent of the prewar population (Athens, Chalkis, Larissa, Patras, Trikkala, Volos, Agrinio, Zakinthos) and those of "New" Greece whose victims exceeded 90 percent of the prewar population (Didimoticho, Hania, Langada, Nea Orestias, Thessaloniki, Alexandroupoli, Drama, Kavalla, Komotini, Serres, Xanthi, Karditsa, Kastoria, Ioannina, Preveza) with only a handful of exceptions such as Kerkyra or Katerini.[27] Although "Old" Greece communities were for the most part Grecophone Romaniote, Romaniotes in "New" Greece did not always have better survival records than the Sephardim as the cases of Ioannina and Preveza indicate.

Scholars have tried to explain the great variation in the survival rates of the Greek Jewish communities through several factors. For example, some have suggested that the proximity of mountains where the resistance organizations were active made it easier for Jews to escape, whereas those who did not have mountains nearby would find it harder to hide.[28] An important element was the warning that the communities had regarding the deportations, and what deportations meant. Much of "Old" Greece was under Italian occupation while much of "New" Greece was under German or Bulgarian rule where deportation started earlier.[29] Another factor was the degree of assimilation of the community into Greek society and the existence, or lack, of separate Jewish quarters, and the status of Greek Jewish relations prior to the war.[30] Others have pointed to local Jewish leadership, and whether it urged flight or acquiescence to Nazi authorities. In this context the destruction of the Thessaloniki community can be seen as inevitable because the city is relatively far from mountains, the leadership of the community proved particularly inept, the majority of the Jews in Thessaloniki lived rather segregated and had been further isolated following the occupation of the city, were Ladino speakers, who were not well integrated with the local Greek population, and were the first to be rounded up by the Nazis. The Athenian community, on the other hand, had effective leadership, the Greek resistance was quite active in the city and the surrounding areas, Athenian Jews were predominantly Greek speakers, and Jews lived in all neighborhoods alongside the rest of the population. Although on the surface these arguments appear convincing, and undoubtedly most, if not all, are valid to a degree, a closer examination of the history of each community allows a different element to emerge as well.

Mavrogordatos has claimed that the disparity of the survival rates can be explained by the degree of assimilation of Jews in Greek society. He makes a clear distinction between the "assimilated" Jews of "Old" Greece and the "unassimilated" Jews of "New" Greece, 83 percent of the latter having been deported to the death camps compared to 47 percent of the former (35 percent if Kerkyra is excluded).[31] Fleming also noted that "Hellenized Jews" had a better chance to survive the Holocaust.[32] It was true that the communities with the greatest losses, excluding the island communities which were cut off from all possible escape due to geography, also happen to be those that were added to the Greek state the latest and often experienced the highest instance of anti-Semitic behavior in the past. The second component does not necessarily imply that the Christian inhabitants of those cities actively denounced Jews to the Nazis, although a few did so, but it might indicate apathy toward the fate of Jews. While most Christians would not assist the Nazis, whose policies they considered barbaric and inhumane, they would not risk their own lives to shelter Jews. In the cases where Jewish communities suffered the least casualties, it is well documented that Christians provided valuable assistance in warning Jewish friends to flee, arranging routes of escape, and hiding Jews from the authorities. It is unclear however how Mavrogordatos perceives assimilation, because at no point were Jews seen as belonging to the Greek nation. But he was right to stress the role and differing responses of Greek authorities regarding the two groups of Jews.[33] An examination of the cases of Thessaloniki, Ioannina, Kerkyra, and Athens reveals the complex attitudes, not only of the public, but also of the Greek local and state authorities.

Thessaloniki was the site of the most recent major anti-Semitic outburst in Greece, the Campbell riot of 1931, and the city where tensions between Jews and Christians, especially those who had arrived from Asia Minor, were most acute. Although the anti-Semitic organization EEE had been disbanded by Metaxas, it reappeared with the arrival of the Nazis and resumed its anti-Semitic actions though it remained marginal till 1944 when it was reformed in a militarized capacity.[34] The Italian consul-general Zamboni, in his letters to the Italian Diplomatic Mission in Athens, captured the feelings of the population toward Jews and he frequently mentioned the "hatred" of Christians toward Jews.[35] The Nazi authorities quickly took measures to further isolate Jews from the rest of the population, both physically by forcing Jews into separate neighborhoods and mentally by subjecting them to all sorts of humiliations from the wearing of the yellow star, to a public registration in Thessaloniki's main square where Jews were forced to perform calisthenics under the apparently indifferent eyes of the local Christians, an act reminiscent of the public humiliation of the Jews in Vienna in 1938.[36] When the Germans begun to use forced Jewish labor for various projects Zamboni thought that the local Christians saw this conscription with satisfaction.[37] In those early days of Nazi anti-Semitic actions, Jews found little support among the Christian population,[38] a notable exception being the demobilized officers of the Greek army who protested their treatment as Yakoel mentioned.[39] This provoked a quick response by the German authorities who threatened the former officers with executions if they held any public pro-Jewish demonstrations.[40] During the occupation trade and professional associations in Thessaloniki failed to support their Jewish members, often expelling them before being directed to do so by the Nazis.[41] The only significant effort to save Jewish lives in the city was by a recently discovered network of illegal Christian adoptions of Jewish children.[42]

Christian Greeks, according to Zamboni, were alarmed when the Jewish community somehow gathered the required 2 billion *drachmas* demanded by the Germans to free their conscript laborers because they feared that the Germans would simply replace them with Christians and that "Greek workers will be enslaved with Jewish money."[43] Anti-Semitism and suspicion toward Jews, however, does not imply support for the violent actions of the Nazis. Some collaborators like the infamous anti-Semite Laskaris Papanaoum certainly exploited the circumstances to terrorize Jews and profit from their wealth but the increasing violence inflicted upon the Jews of Thessaloniki transformed the attitude of ordinary Christians in the city as the Italian consul reported.[44] Zamboni more and more referred to Greek dissatisfaction with Nazi activities as "too far-reaching and unjustified" reaching its peak with the deportations.[45] As the Nazi campaign reached its climax, Zamboni's letters indicate a rising indignation among the Greek population and mentioned Greek "rebels" sending messages into the newly created ghetto urging Jews to join them.[46] The communist-led resistance organization EAM informed the chief rabbi of Thessaloniki Koretz that it was ready to assist the Jews of that city to escape, but the rabbi refused to disobey the German authorities, or perhaps put trust in the non-Jewish population of the city.[47] What Zamboni's letters show was that many Christians in Thessaloniki viewed the initial Nazi measures almost with approval, but once humiliation turned to violence Christian attitudes changed from apathy to compassion.[48] By that time, however, Jews were already confined in a ghetto and between March and May of 1943 43,300 people were deported to Auschwitz-Birkenau and the Nazi authorities expressed satisfaction that the deportations had been accepted calmly by the population of Thessaloniki.[49]

The municipal authorities of Thessaloniki also saw the occupation as an opportunity to achieve goals that had eluded them in the interwar period, especially with regard to the Jewish cemetery that they had repeatedly tried to expropriate. That project had been blocked through the Greek courts but the arrival of the Nazis gave the municipality the opportunity to reopen the issue. The German authorities were not about to defend the rights of the Jewish community of course, yet they did negotiate a settlement between the community and the municipal authorities to allow families to remove the remains of their dead from the cemetery before its demolition.[50] The municipality, however, ignored the agreement and immediately begun the destruction of the ancient cemetery. Surprised Jews frantically tried to save the remains of their dead while municipal workers leveled the ground and destroyed the tombs, the headstones subsequently used in various building projects in the city including roads, latrines, patios, pathways, and even churches.[51] The destruction of the Jewish cemetery is of particular significance because it was not initiated or conducted by the Nazis, although later historiography, and even some Jewish accounts, have tried to portray it as such.[52] Throughout Europe the Nazis did not bother to destroy Jewish cemeteries, most of which survived the war.[53] This was a Greek project which involved numerous Greek actors whose callousness reflects the deep-seated animosity that Zamboni alluded to.[54]

A similar attitude was evident in the representatives of the Greek government in Thessaloniki.[55] The governor general of Macedonia Vasilis Symeonidis wanted to use the funds gathered from the properties of displaced Jews for the benefit of the Greek refugees from Bulgarian-occupied Thrace rather than for the safe internment of Jews in a Greek island as an unimplemented plan envisioned.[56] It has been suggested that the inspector general in Macedonia Athanasios Chrysochoou may have been the first to suggest the conscription of Jews for labor.[57] The same authorities attempted to exploit the deportation of Jews and the appropriation of their properties to settle the Greek refugees and to create a more homogenous city, although their efforts were partly derailed by the German authorities who preferred to reward their collaborators with Jewish wealth.[58] Thessaloniki, however, was unique in being the most anti-Semitic city in Greece, inhabited by Sephardic Jews many of whom did not have fluency in Greek and whose loyalty to the Greek state had historically been suspect.[59]

Athenians adopted a very different posture regarding the fate of their Jewish neighbors. When the Germans demanded that Chief Rabbi Barzalai provide lists with the names of all Jews living in the city, Barzalai, unlike Rabbi Koretz in Thessaloniki, chose to burn the community records and accept an offer by the resistance and Archbishop Damaskinos to flee Athens. He was spirited by EAM to the mountains where he was kept safe until the end of the war.[60] The disappearance of the chief rabbi was a blow to the German authorities and a clear message to the rest of the

Jews in Athens to go into hiding. Within days, almost the entire Jewish community of the city disappeared like their rabbi. With the aid of the resistance thousands of Jews were hidden in Christian homes and many were eventually spirited out of the country. EAM issued a general proclamation making it a capital crime to denounce Jews to the German authorities and enforced this decree with several assassinations of informants. Athenian Jews were also the most "Hellenized" and could thus easily hide among their Christian compatriots.[61]

It was not simply the resistance or the common people of Athens that assisted Jews. In a reversal from the situation in Thessaloniki the local authorities acted to defend their Jewish citizens, precisely because they conceived them as such. In a unique effort of collaboration between the communist-dominated resistance movement, the Greek Orthodox Church, and the Greek Police, thousands of Jews were hidden and hundreds were sent to the Middle East where some joined the Greek or British forces. As I mentioned above, Archbishop Damaskinos instructed the Greek clergy to urge their flock to give assistance to Jews, arranging for 560 to receive baptismal certificates in Athens alone, while Angelos Ebert, the chief of police in Athens, arranged or allowed the issuing of some 6,000 fake identification cards to Jews describing them as Orthodox Christians (see Figures 6.2 and 6.3).[62]

Athenian Jews also saw prominent Athenians and organizations appeal to the collaborationist government to intervene. Many prominent Athenians signed letters of protest and sent them to the German authorities, as did several organizations including the church. Among them were the president of the Academy of Athens,

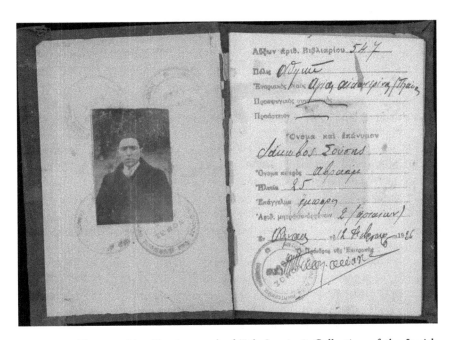

Figure 6.2 The true identification card of Zak Sousis © Collection of the Jewish Museum of Greece.

Figure 6.3 Zak Sousis's false identification card, with the name Demetrios Georgopoulos © Photographic Archive of the Jewish Museum of Greece.

along with several other academics, the chairmen of the Medical, lawyers, journalists, writers, commerce, pharmacists, dentists, and chemists associations, the chairman of the Commercial and Industrial Chamber of Athens, and Archbishop Damaskinos.[63] Even the collaborationist government tried to intervene on behalf of "Old" Greece Jews, whom they described as patriotic and fully citizens of the Greek state asking that they should be exempted from deportation.

The contrast with Thessaloniki whose commercial and trade associations easily expelled their Jewish members is stark.[64] The fact that Athens and Thessaloniki were different was not only demonstrated by the reactions of the Greek public, intellectuals, and authorities,[65] or by the different survival rates, but also by the fact that fleeing Jews from other parts of the country sought refuge in Athens but not in Thessaloniki. Athens had the distinction of coming out of the war with more Jews than she entered it. It was not a coincidence that even after the war many Jews who remained in Greece chose to move to Athens to the point that most Jews in Greece today live there.

In Kerkyra, the German commander Emil Jaeger initially opposed Jewish deportations because he feared that they would cause unrest among the population. Yet, when the deportations of the Jews begun, little help was given to the Corfiote Jews from their Christian neighbors.[66] In fact, the municipal authorities, led by the mayor of the town Kollas, published an open letter essentially thanking the German authorities for removing the Jews from their midst (see Figure 6.4).[67]

The local Greek attitude in Kerkyra stood in marked contrast to that of other Greeks who encountered the Corfiote Jews on their journey to Athens and the death camps.

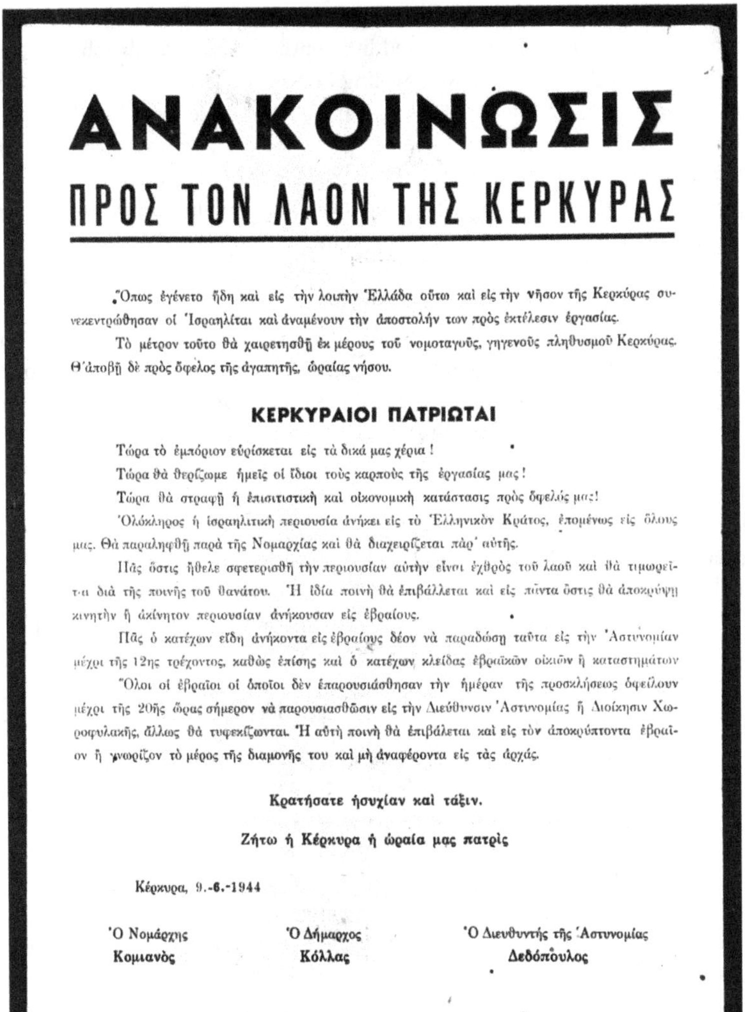

ΑΝΑΚΟΙΝΩΣΙΣ

ΠΡΟΣ ΤΟΝ ΛΑΟΝ ΤΗΣ ΚΕΡΚΥΡΑΣ

.Ὅπως ἐγένετο ἤδη καὶ εἰς τὴν λοιπὴν Ἑλλάδα οὕτω καὶ εἰς τὴν νῆσον τῆς Κερκύρας συνεκεντρώθησαν οἱ Ἰσραηλίται καὶ ἀναμένουν τὴν ἀποστολήν των πρὸς ἐκτέλεσιν ἐργασίας.

Τὸ μέτρον τοῦτο θὰ χαιρετισθῇ ἐκ μέρους τοῦ νομοταγοῦς, γηγενοῦς πληθυσμοῦ Κερκύρας. Θ'ἀποβῇ δὲ πρὸς ὄφελος τῆς ἀγαπητῆς, ὡραίας νήσου.

ΚΕΡΚΥΡΑΙΟΙ ΠΑΤΡΙΩΤΑΙ

Τώρα τὸ ἐμπόριον εὑρίσκεται εἰς τὰ δικά μας χέρια !

Τώρα θὰ θερίζωμε ἡμεῖς οἱ ἴδιοι τοὺς καρποὺς τῆς ἐργασίας μας !

Τώρα θὰ στραφῇ ἡ ἐπισιτιστικὴ καὶ οἰκονομικὴ κατάστασις πρὸς ὄφελός μας !

Ὁλόκληρος ἡ ἰσραηλιτικὴ περιουσία ἀνήκει εἰς τὸ Ἑλληνικὸν Κράτος, ἑπομένως εἰς ὅλους μας. Θὰ παραληφθῇ παρὰ τῆς Νομαρχίας καὶ θὰ διαχειρίζεται πὰρ' αὐτῆς.

Πᾶς ὅστις ἤθελε σφετερισθῇ τὴν περιουσίαν αὐτὴν εἶναι ἐχθρὸς τοῦ λαοῦ καὶ θὰ τιμωρεῖ-ται διὰ τῆς ποινῆς τοῦ θανάτου. Ἡ ἰδία ποινὴ θὰ ἐπιβάλλεται καὶ εἰς πάντα ὅστις θὰ ἀποκρύψῃ κινητὴν ἢ ἀκίνητον περιουσίαν ἀνήκουσαν εἰς ἑβραίους.

Πᾶς ὁ κατέχων εἴδη ἀνήκοντα εἰς ἑβραίους δέον νὰ παραδώσῃ ταῦτα εἰς τὴν Ἀστυνομίαν μέχρι τῆς 12ης τρέχοντος, καθὼς ἐπίσης καὶ ὁ κατέχων κλείδας ἑβραϊκῶν οἰκιῶν ἢ καταστημάτων

Ὅλοι οἱ ἑβραῖοι οἱ ὁποῖοι δὲν ἐπαρουσιάσθησαν τὴν ἡμέραν τῆς προσκλήσεως ὀφείλουν μέχρι τῆς 20ῆς ὥρας σήμερον νὰ παρουσιασθῶσιν εἰς τὴν Διεύθυνσιν Ἀστυνομίας ἢ Διοίκησιν Χωροφυλακῆς, ἄλλως θὰ τυφεκίζωνται. Ἡ αὐτὴ ποινὴ θὰ ἐπιβάλλεται καὶ εἰς τὸν ἀποκρύπτοντα ἑβραῖ-ον ἢ γνωρίζον τὸ μέρος τῆς διαμονῆς του καὶ μὴ ἀναφέροντα εἰς τὰς ἀρχάς.

Κρατήσατε ἡσυχίαν καὶ τάξιν.

Ζήτω ἡ Κέρκυρα ἡ ὡραία μας πατρὶς

Κέρκυρα, 9.-6.-1944

Ὁ Νομάρχης
Κομιανὸς

Ὁ Δήμαρχος
Κόλλας

Ὁ Διευθυντὴς τῆς Ἀστυνομίας
Δεδόπουλος

Figure 6.4 Announcement by the local authorities of Corfu, right after the deportation of the island's Jews, indicative of the then prevailing feelings of the population © Collection of the Jewish Museum of Greece.

While the Jews of Kerkyra were briefly incarcerated on the island of Lefkada, the local Christians showed considerably more empathy and tried to provide them with food through the barbed wire that separated them. Several Corfiote Jews were also offered help by the Christian population in the port city of Patras, another stop on their way to Athens. Armandos Aaron, for example, managed to escape there with the assistance of a complete stranger. On another occasion one of the Greek collaborators of the militia who were guarding the Jews told Perla Soussi to run while he looked away. She declined his offer not willing to leave her family behind, but according to her account the Greek collaborators in Patras showed little enthusiasm for their job.[68] There is a paradox in the fact that strangers were willing to help the Jews of Kerkyra while their own neighbors seemed indifferent. One explanation is that Kerkyra, like Thessaloniki, had strong anti-Semitic traditions, including the violent pogrom at the end of the nineteenth century, while the other areas of "Old" Greece from which the Jews passed on their way to Athens did not, their tiny local Jewish communities being Greek-speaking Romaniotes. Furthermore, Kerkyra had two distinct Jewish communities, one Greek-speaking, but also a larger Italian one; the two "never united but only in the concentration death camps."[69]

Beyond the behavior of the Christian population, however, it is also important to consider the options available to Jews in each case. In areas where Jews and Christians lived separately with little interaction, Jews would not have known where to turn for help. It would be next to impossible for a Jew to try and find refuge with people with whom she had no previous contact, or with whom she had differences, as may have been the case in Thessaloniki or Kerkyra,[70] especially when one considers that to help a Jew was a capital crime under Nazi rule. In Athens, on the other hand, Jews would have had social interactions with other Greeks to whom they could turn for aid and shelter. Only in rare cases would the same be true in Thessaloniki, like that of Sam Broudo and Moissis Bourla, two young Jewish men who were involved with Christian women.[71]

The final case I want to examine is that of the Jews of Ioannina. This case is significant because, although the community was Romaniote, it was one of those that had been incorporated to Greece in the Balkan Wars. It was also the second largest Jewish community in Greece after Thessaloniki. It too suffered great losses in the Holocaust even though it was originally under Italian occupation, and had some knowledge of what could happen once the Germans took over. Ioannina is also surrounded by mountains offering possible avenues of escape and where guerilla organizations, both communist and nationalist, were active. The case of the Romaniote Jews of Ioannina would therefore seem to counter the preceding argument.

Reports from survivors like Michael Matsas and Eftychia Nahman are often contradictory,[72] some stressing the inaction of the local Christians while others point to friendly relations between Jews and Christians in the city before and after the occupation. It was certainly the case that several Ioannina Christians assisted the Nazis in rounding up the Jews, and many more participated in the looting of the abandoned Jewish houses after their deportation. A German report noted with satisfaction that hardly any Christians moved to bid Jews farewell and that there was "secret joy" over the removal of Jews indicating the hostility of Greeks toward "this race."[73] Accounts collected decades later seem to indicate hostility toward Jews in part due to commercial competition.[74] There were also, however, many accounts of individuals helping Jews escape as the Germans rounded them up for deportation. The mayor of the city, Demetrios Vlahlidis, even managed to save the *Sefer Torah* from the Germans, allegedly to add it to the city museum, and he returned it to the synagogue after the war.[75]

It appears that the Ioannina Jewish community had ample opportunities to escape but failed to exploit them primarily due to a remarkable failure of the local Jewish leadership.[76] In Ioannina, the extremely influential Sabatai Kabeli played inadvertently a sinister role by insisting on full cooperation with the German authorities. He even convinced many families to ask their young men who had already fled to the resistance to return to the city. Some did indeed return after being told that their community was in danger because of their actions, only to be deported to the concentration camps. Kabeli even ignored a message warning him about the planned deportations sent by another prominent member of the Jewish community of the city, Dr. Koffinas, from his jail cell. When Koffinas joined the rest of the community as it was being deported, he is reported to have been incensed that his warnings had been ignored and accused Kabeli of personal responsibility for the destruction of their community.[77] It should also be noted that on August 9, 1943, the German Lt. Colonel Carl Vilhelm Tilo threatened the city of Ioannina and the surrounding villages with mass executions of hostages if the occupation authorities were not supported in their efforts, particularly in the fight against the guerillas.[78] By this time the German army had already destroyed several Greek villages throughout Greece in reprisal for guerilla activity, and such warnings would not have been easily dismissed.

The attitude of Greek authorities during the occupation demonstrates the evolution that took place in nationalist ideology over the previous decades, as well as the significant differences in municipal and state authorities. Despite the absence of the king and many of the political class who fled to Egypt and constituted a government in exile, when the measures for the Final Solution in Greece begun to be implemented, nearly all state level Greek figures of authority, from Archbishop Damaskinos to academics and professional bodies, even the collaborationist ministers, protested, insisting that the Jews were equal citizens to the rest of the population.[79] They did not protest in the same manner, however, over the fate of the Jews of Thessaloniki as they did over those of "Old" Greece. When Rabbi Koretz sought in April 1943 the intervention of the collaborationist Prime Minister Rallis, the latter was evasive.[80] The previous prime minister Logothetopoulos had been pressured by various segments of Greek society to send two memos to the German authorities requesting the recall of measures of "extermination abnormally taken against certain Greek citizens" insisting on the equal treatment of all Greek citizens but Rallis was less forceful with respect to the Jews of Thessaloniki.[81] Five months later, however, Rallis made impassioned pleas in support of the Jews of "Old" Greece:

> The Israelites of Old Greece have been linguistically and historically completely absorbed with the indigenous [population] producing poets who are distinguished for their Hellenic ideals . . . they fought on every occasion on behalf of Greece and many of them were distinguished in the fields of battle . . . . The implementation of the known measures against the Greek Israelites in Old Greece as well would wound the sentiment of the people.[82]

He added that "Old" Greece Jews held positions as civil servants, judges, and in the army, and that the Orthodox Church has always tolerated such a "negligible" minority. He concluded by stating that he wished for the exclusion of the Jews of "Old" Greece from deportation in the model of the Hungarian Jews.[83] Other members of the collaborationist governments like Nikolaos Louvaris, the minister of education, also sent appeals to the Germans to stop the persecutions of "the Jews of Old Greece."[84]

The clear distinction between the Jews of Thessaloniki and those of "Old" Greece does not necessarily reflect anti- or philo-Semitic attitudes by these individuals but rather a different understanding of the two communities. Greek authorities often intervened in favor of Jews, but usually when Greek-speaking Romaniotes especially those of "Old" Greece were concerned. In Arta, the local metropolitan Spyridon Gkinakas protested the order forcing Jews to wear the star of David and urged them to flee to the mountains, and the same took place in Volos.[85] In Chalkis, the communist-led guerillas of EAM worked closely with the local gendarmerie and the metropolitan of the town Grigorios to hide the community in the surrounding mountain villages and preserve the *Sefer Torah* of the synagogue which was entrusted to the metropolitan.[86] For the state and religious authorities, the "Old" Greece Jews were Greek citizens who had a long historical coexistence with the modern Greek state and in the process, had proven their loyalty particularly in the wars of the early twentieth century. The Jews of Thessaloniki, on the other hand, may have gained Greek citizenship; they may even have fought in the most recent war, but they had only been part of the Greek state for less than a generation. Previously they had been ambivalent about their inclusion to the Greek state and throughout the interwar period their political loyalties had been suspect. Jewish survivor accounts from southern and northern Greece differ substantially, the former often stressing the absence of anti-Semitism in Greece,[87] while the latter referring to its long history and the role of the church in fomenting it.[88]

The attitude of the Greek state authorities was not unique and in many ways resembles that of other neighboring states. The Bulgarian government for example, though allied with Germany, refused to deport its Jewish population to the death camps. However, the Bulgarian government implemented racial and anti-Semitic laws under pressure from Germany and was quite willing to deport Jews from the Greek and Yugoslav regions it occupied in 1941.[89] Although at first the Bulgarian authorities offered Jews in Macedonia the option of switching to a Bulgarian nationality and assisting in the Bulgarian plans to annex those regions, most seem to have refused and thus thousands of Greek and Yugoslav Jews from Thrace and Macedonia were deported to their deaths.[90]

Romania is often contrasted with Bulgaria regarding its treatment of Jews,[91] but even the notoriously anti-Semitic and brutal government of Romania, whose leader according to Hitler pursued more radical policies than Nazi Germany on the "Jewish question,"[92] did not deport its own "Old Romanian" Jews to the death camps. Although the massacre of Jews under Romanian authority began in 1940 and intensified over the next years, Romania decided to subject them, and the substantial Romanian Roma and Sinti population, to their own brutal pogroms and extermination policies rather than deliver them to the Nazis.[93] Romanian units assigned to the task pursued it with eagerness and even the Romanian Orthodox Church was heavily involved.[94] However, even in Romania not all Jews suffered the same. Those of what in Greek parlance could be termed "Old" Romania, that is Moldavia, Walachia, and Southern Transylvania, suffered less than those of the newly acquired territories of Bessarabia, Bukovina, and Transnistria, though some claim that policies there were a prelude for what was planned for the entire country.[95] Numerous explanations are offered for the differences between Bulgaria and Romania, including the different economic position of Jews in each state,[96] but in both cases the governments acted in defense of their sovereign rights, especially where Jews had been a part of the social fabric, drawing a clear distinction between "national" Jews and others. The same distinction was evident in Greece despite the vastly different circumstances since Greek collaborationist governments operated under a state of occupation.

This difference in the measure of response that can be seen from one city to another is, I believe, indicative of the ambivalence that existed regarding the identity of the Sephardim of Thessaloniki as opposed to that of the mostly Romaniote Jews of southern Greece. In the case of the Sephardim, individuals may have tried to help some Jews as a humanitarian act or due to personal ties. In the case of the Romaniotes, however, it was a nationalistic response, to protect some of the country's citizens who were under threat. The Sephardim never managed to be seen as loyal Greek nationals and thus the Greek reaction to their plight was half-hearted. The Romaniotes, on the other hand, were generally accepted as loyal Greek citizens and thus received effective assistance. This was particularly true in the Jewish communities of "Old Greece" where language and historical experience combined to reinforce their identity as Greek and help explain their higher survival rate. It was no accident that in those areas that nationalism was ideologically transformed from religiously based to a more nuanced construct, that such ideas were most developed and absorbed by the wider public. The escalation of resistance seen in Greece from the deportations of the Jews of Thessaloniki to those of Athens and southern Greece was not different from the experience of France or Holland where the reliability of local police participating in the deportations of Jews declined once the deportations shifted from foreign refugees to local Jews.[97] Similarly, the famed Italian tolerance toward Jews, including the Jews of the Italian occupation zone in Greece, had more to do with resistance to Nazi interference over what Italians perceived to be their sovereign rights. In areas of German occupation the Italians did not intervene to protect Jews in general but only to defend those that held Italian passports.[98]

As in many parts of Europe, the most active supporters of Jews was not the Greek government, who were after all collaborating with the Nazis, but the resistance organizations and especially the communist-led EAM and its military wing ELAS. EAM organized the hiding and transfer of Jews to safe locations and arranged with the *Haganah* the transportation of hundreds of Jews to neutral Turkey and the Middle East saving as many as 3,000 people.[99] Its publications like the newspaper of the Communist Party of Greece (KKE) *Rizospastis* published several articles in support of the Jews of Greece, as for example the following on October 10, 1943:

The Greek language Nazi press has published a shameful order of Stroop [Jurgen Stroop, the destroyer of the Warsaw Ghetto and SS *und Polizeifuhrer* in Greece] for the extermination of the Jews. The Greek people will riddle the measures of these human-beasts. The Greek people will give asylum to the Jews. They will protect them. With committees, with protests, it will force the cancellation of the order of the wild beasts. No Greek policeman will enforce the order of Stroop.[100]

Four days later another EAM publication, *Eleftheri Ellada* (Free Greece) printed the following announcement, which must have been particularly infuriating to the German authorities:

> The Chief Rabbi of Athens Elias Barzalai [who had already fled Athens and was in hiding with the resistance] sends a message to the Greek people in which he begs them to imitate the example of the EAM for the saving of the Greek Israelites against whom the Hitlerite beasts have unleashed their monstrous persecution.[101]

As early as January 1943, EAM condemned the policies of the Germans regarding the Jews, asking the Greek population to oppose them, and threatened the death penalty on those who denounced Jews.[102] EAM/ELAS conducted a series of attacks on anti-Semitic organizations, the most successful being the blowing up of the offices of the *Ethnike Socialistike Patriotike Organoses* (ESPO—Patriotic National Socialist Organization), that periodically attacked Jews and synagogues in Athens during the occupation, killing its leader Dr. Speros Sterodimos.[103] Fleeing Jews often found shelter in the guerilla-held mountains and on at least one occasion a guerilla band attacked a German battalion that had recaptured a group of Jews who had fled Larissa, freeing the prisoners before they could be deported.[104] Naturally many Jews joined the resistance to fight the Nazis. The numbers are debated but between 400 and 1,000 Jews may have joined the ranks of EAM and ELAS and several men and women rose to leadership positions including Colonel Mordoch, *Kapetan* Kitsos (born Yitzhak Moshe), and *Kapetanissa* Sarika (born Sarah Yehoshua).[105]

There was one final actor in the drama, the Greek government in exile around King George II. Governments in exile like the Polish and Czechoslovak ones played a crucial role in the dissemination of information about Nazi plans and actions, provided the first reports of the Final Solution, and passed on detailed information about the details of the Holocaust, including the "Auschwitz Protocols" in 1944.[106] The Greek government in exile also tried to help Greek Jews, especially those who crossed the Aegean to Turkey, in collaboration with Zionist organizations. Many Greek Jews who escaped were subsequently helped to settle in Palestine but quite a few joined the Greek armed forces in Egypt and continued fighting against the Axis powers.[107] The means of the Greek government in exile, however, were limited and rising tensions with the communist-led resistance in Greece quickly escalated to a direct confrontation in April 1944 in the form of a series of mutinies in the Greek Royal Navy in favor of a government of national unity that would include the representatives of the resistance movement. With the clouds of the civil war that was to ensue already gathering, the Greek government in exile did not consider the fate of the Greek Jews a priority, and even if it did, its influence within Greece until 1944 was minimal.

Returning to Greece

Few of the Greek Jews who were deported survived to the end of the war. In part this was due to the early dates of Greek deportations which meant that even those who were not immediately gassed upon arrival would have had to survive two years in the death camps. Greek Jews had a negative reputation in the camps both with the Nazis and with other Jews as suggested by Primo Levi.[108] Many Greek Jews had military experience and could prove troublesome, exemplified by the famed revolt on September 6, 1944, in Auschwitz when 135 Greek Jews from Thessaloniki, led by Lt. Colonel Joseph Baruch and Lieutenants Jose Levy and Maurice Aron, along with two French and one Hungarian commando groups, succeeded in destroying two of the four crematoria in the camp before the guards killed them.[109] On another occasion 400 Thessaloniki and 100 Athenian Jews refused to work as *Sonderkommandos* and were executed.[110]

Even the Jews who survived the camps or were able to evade capture often discovered that they had no place in postwar Greek society or, like Bernardo Melo, were advised by those that liberated them from the camps not to return.[111] Greece was devastated by the war in terms of both material and loss of life. Nazi Germany had little concern for the Balkans beyond their ability to provide materials for the war and as a result it pursued a harsh policy of expropriation of agricultural products in Greece that led to a devastating famine in the first year of occupation where as many as a quarter million civilians, primarily in the urban centers, died of hunger and hunger-related illnesses.[112] The emergence of a widespread resistance movement prompted the German authorities to employ a brutal policy of retaliation for guerilla attacks. This policy was initiated as early as the German invasion of Crete and led to the destruction of hundreds of Greek villages and towns and often the mass execution of their inhabitants. Allied bombings and guerilla attacks further undermined the infrastructure and productive capacity of the country, compounded by thousands of refugees who fled their homes, especially from the Bulgarian zone of occupation.

Greece was also soon engulfed in a long civil war (1944–45, 1946–49) between the Royal government in exile and the communist-led EAM/ELAS. The war was brutal and embroiled Britain and subsequently the United States. The desperate need of the nationalist government for troops, especially in the early phases of the civil war, allowed many Nazi collaborators, including the members of militias like the infamous security battalions, to escape retribution and in fact achieve prominent positions in the Greek army and society.[113]

The Germans had authorized such units to combat the rapidly expanding resistance movement which harsh reprisals, including the execution of hostages among them two Jewish former communist members of parliament, had failed to stem.[114] Although many joined these units from economic desperation, to avoid reprisals or persecution, for revenge, or simply for the opportunity to profit, rather than ideology[115] their continuing presence in positions of authority created an atmosphere of impunity.[116] Few Nazi collaborators were put on trial, and even in prominent cases like those of the collaborationist prime ministers the penalties handed down were remarkably mild. Only Tsolakoglou was condemned to death his sentence subsequently commuted on the recommendation of the court. Logothetopoulos and Rallis received life sentences, and some ministers received short prison terms.[117] Even German commanders like Maximilian Merten, the Commandant of Thessaloniki who was involved in the marginalization, persecution, and deportations of the Jews of Thessaloniki, served only a fraction of a prison term imposed for the persecution of Jews and destruction of the Jewish cemetery before being sent to Germany, possibly due to the ties he had developed in wartime with subsequently important Greek political figures.[118]

Besides the relative immunity that former collaborators enjoyed, the few that were brought to trial were often members of ethnic minorities. Most of those accused of collaboration in Northern Greece were accused of collaborating with the Bulgarian occupation forces and of exhibiting pro-Bulgarian sentiments. Many were also accused of being *Okhranists*, that is, members of Bulgarian sponsored units, many of whom subsequently joined the Slav-Macedonian National Liberation Front (SNOF) that fought alongside the communists in the Greek Civil War thus blurring the categories of collaborator with that of the communist insurgent. Unlike Nazi collaborators many of those who worked with the Bulgarian authorities were convicted, receiving particularly harsh sentences.[119] Of those accused for collaboration with the Germans the majority were accused of being informers, often of denouncing Jews and profiting with the gifts of confiscated Jewish properties.[120] Those accused of collaborating with the Italians were predominantly Vlachs, who had set up armed units under Italian guidance.[121] The effect of such accusations on public opinion was to reinforce suspicions regarding the loyalty to the state of minorities.[122]

The presence and influence of unprosecuted Greek collaborationists alongside other conservative elements in the nationalist coalition allowed the resurfacing of a strong anti-Semitic current.[123] Some military circles continued to see the Jews of Thessaloniki with a particularly suspicious eye and wanted measures taken against the "unpatriotic activities and attitude" of the Thessaloniki Jews who held "anarchist and anti-Greek beliefs."[124] The Liberal Club (*Lesche Phileleftheron*) alongside various political and professional interests created a coalition in Thessaloniki that stood in opposition to the Jewish community.[125] In striking similarity to the interwar years, in the first elections of March 31, 1946, the surviving Jews of Thessaloniki were placed in a single electoral center, leading to a complaint by the community that the Ministry of the Interior was abolishing the secrecy of the ballot box as far as Jews were concerned.[126] Nationalists voiced openly anti-Semitic statements a horrifying example being a speech by the journalist Pavlis, given in 1947 in Kerkyra, a town whose Jewish community had been decimated by the Holocaust, in which he warned Jews that if they did not cease being tools of what he called anarcho-communism "we would be the ones to continue and complete the works of Hitler."[127]

This was the political environment Jews encountered emerging out of hiding or from the horror of the death camps. Furthermore, Greek Jews, even those returning from the concentration camps, were not exempt from conscription to fight the communist insurgency.[128] Many Jews, however, had found refuge with the resistance movement and were often persecuted after the war as communist subversives, a trope carried over from the interwar years when Jews had been associated with socialism. Five Jews who had been members of EAM/ELAS were executed by firing squad during the civil war and at least thirty-one received long prison sentences or were sent to internal exile.[129]

One of the most difficult problems facing Jews returning from the death camps, exile, or hiding was the restitution of their properties that the Nazis and local authorities had confiscated. The Germans had ostensibly allowed Greek officials to administer the reallocation the Jewish properties of those who were sent to the death camps. In Thessaloniki, the Governor General Vasilis Simeonidis appointed Elias Douros, the director of the local branch of the National Mortgage Bank to oversee the process. Despite the efforts of Douros the process disintegrated into chaos. During the first nights following the deportations, looters stripped the properties of anything of value with the connivance of the police. Instead of distributing the properties to those in need, especially the refugees from the Bulgarian zone of occupation as was the original intent, the process was plagued by corruption allowing those well connected to the German authorities to profit handsomely. Douros was disgusted and often threatened and even attempted to resign but his resignation was not accepted.[130]

Although the collaborationist government of Rallis tried to legitimize the looting of Jewish properties just days before the withdrawal of German forces following liberation, the new Greek government enacted on January 22, 1946, Law 846 to facilitate the return of Jewish property to their rightful owners or their heirs.[131] In cases where no heirs survived, the law excepted Jewish property from being taken over by the state, as was the regular practice, turning possession to the Jewish community as a whole under the leadership of the Central Jewish Board.[132] Reinforcing official policy both the deputy minister of finance and the governor general of Macedonia personally pledged the full restitution of the properties of Greek Jews,[133] and the latter ordered the "caretakers" of Jewish properties to return them to their rightful owners or their relatives.[134] Greek officials even expressed "their deep sorrow when they were informed that the ancient historic tombstones of the great Jewish cemetery of Thessaloniki, which had been seized had not yet been collected and placed in their rightful place," the governor general promising to issue orders for the confiscation and return of all the tombstones and religious artifacts wherever they may be found.[135] This statement was printed in *Makedonia*, the infamous anti-Semitic newspaper of Thessaloniki that in the postwar period retained its nationalist tendencies and anticommunism but abandoned its overt anti-Semitism.[136]

At the time Greece was widely praised by Jewish organizations in Greece and abroad for being the first country in Europe to pass such laws, but Law 846 was not fully implemented.[137] Those who had gained possession of the properties used their political clout to delay its implementation until 1949 and formed the Association of Tenants of Jewish Real Estate of Northern Greece to fight the restitution of properties to their rightful owners.[138] Even the government raised bureaucratic obstacles, the Ministry of Justice recommended to the courts of Thessaloniki that they adjourn and postpone the review of restitution cases and the government delayed transferring even the properties that had not been allocated to new owners to the Central Jewish Board as the law dictated.[139] Jews faced great obstacles in recovering their properties since in most cases they could not produce deeds or other paperwork to prove their claims while most of their friends and family members who could have acted as witnesses were dead. Furthermore, profiteers and collaborators often formed the very committees that managed Jewish properties,[140] and refugees had taken over many of the houses left behind by Jews. In a replay of the 1920s circumstances of Thessaloniki, these refugees had the support of local municipal authorities who themselves had often profited as in the case of the Jewish cemetery of Thessaloniki.[141]

In this environment, legal disputes regarding the ownership of thousands of properties proliferated and lasted for decades.[142] Jewish accounts constantly refer to the difficulty of even finding shelter in their former cities, let alone recovering their properties.[143] Rozina Asser-Pardo's family found their apartment occupied and stripped of its furniture and other furnishings and had to rent a house only to be evicted when the mayor of Thessaloniki Paterakis requisitioned it.[144] Pavlos Simcha had similar memories as his mother struggled to find accommodations while his father was fighting with the Greek army, although their ordeal was resolved through a sympathetic judge who ruled in their favor.[145] Bouena Sarfatty, who had escaped to Palestine, managed to reclaim some of her property simply by recognizing the clothes and artifacts that strangers were sporting and confronting them in the street. She even tried to reclaim her family's house but she was only given two empty rooms in it. Although some volunteered to return items that had been entrusted to them, Bouena's memories lingered on the hostility she encountered from the residents of Thessaloniki.[146] The Greek Jewish press reported in 1945 and 1946 that out of 2,000 Thessaloniki Jews that returned to their city a mere 250 had been permanently settled and the same situation was true in Ioannina.[147] A year after liberation 6,000 Jews were dependent on humanitarian aid.[148]

After liberation, the Jewish community was particularly sensitive to the cases of Jews who had betrayed their community and who often tried to escape justice by claiming to be Greek nationalists and patriots while their accusers were communist. One such case was the infamous Avraam or Vital Chason, who had terrorized his fellow Jews in Thessaloniki. There were fears among the Jewish community that Chason would be pardoned after a court sentenced him to death. This fear prompted the chief rabbi of Athens to demand the death of those Jews who had betrayed their people in a 1947 article. Chason was eventually executed in Kerkyra by firing squad alongside six men convicted of taking part in the communist insurgency. In the firing squad was a Jewish survivor from Birkenau.[149] Still, the Jewish community had reasons to be alarmed. In 1959, the Greek parliament enacted Law 3933 and the Legislative Decree 401 suspending the prosecution of German war criminals and remanding even those convicted, like Maximilian Merten, to the jurisdiction of the Federal Republic of Germany where Merten was eventually acquitted in 1961.[150] It is noteworthy that of all those involved in the destruction of the Jews of Greece, the only ones who received quick and severe punishment were the Jewish collaborators.[151]

The result of these postwar conditions, in part, was an emigration of 3,000 to 5,000 Greek Jews to Western Europe, the United States, Latin America, and Israel.[152] The Jewish communities of Greece were thereby further diminished, their remnants clustered in Athens, also a gathering point for many of the civil war refugees. The concentration in Athens of both the Romaniote and the Sephardic communities led to their effective merger and the loss of much of their distinctiveness. In the postwar years, the Ladino language virtually disappeared, along with Romaniote rites, giving rise to a new Jewish community in Greece.

Although by no means comparable to the suffering of Jews, other minorities of Greece were also victims of the wartime conditions, the civil war, and the postwar policies of the Greek state. Some 18,000 Cham Albanians, attacked in 1944 by the nationalist EDES resistance movement, chose to flee to Albania rather than face a vengeful Greek state that considered the wartime association of many Chams with the occupying Axis forces as having marked the entire Cham population with complicity to the crimes of the Nazis. Some returned in 1944–45 when EAM-ELAS gained control of their region but the return of nationalists to the area led to renewed persecution and the final flight to Albania.[153] Their properties were confiscated by the Greek state with a series of laws and regulations from 1952 to 1983.[154] Similarly thousands of slavophones who had either collaborated with the Germans and Bulgarians, or who had supported the communist insurgents in the civil war, fled to Yugoslavia in the midst of a nationalist press campaign that essentially demanded an ethnic cleansing.[155] Their properties were also expropriated by the Greek government in 1948.[156] The Greek state, through a series of laws enacted in the interwar period, had the right to strip Greek citizenship from those who acquired it, which technically included all who had lived in "New" Greece since those territories were added to the Greek state from 1913 to 1923. The laws was used against the Chams and slavophones who left Greece for Albania, Bulgaria, or Yugoslavia, but also in the case of Jews and Circassians who emigrated before and after the Second World War and Armenians who had left for the USSR in the 1920s.[157] A new 1955 law confirmed the loss of citizenship regulations, targeting the Chams but then expanded to include Jews, Italians, Muslims, and Vlachs that had left Greece in the 1940s. Of the 104,754

Figure 6.5 Archrabbi of Volos, Moisis Pesah © Photographic Archive of the Jewish Museum of Greece.

citizens who had left Greece between 1941 and 1949 (24,776 between 1941 and 1945 and the remaining 77,978 during the civil war) 75,978 lost their citizenship ensuring that their emigration was permanent.[158] This policy was probably not devised for Jews, although several Jewish communists who had been convicted by Greek courts were allowed to emigrate to Israel after renouncing their Greek citizenship.[159] Unlike other minorities Jews did not threaten the Greek state and many were given commendations for their patriotism like the chief rabbi of Volos Moisis Pesah (see Figure 6.5).

Modern Greece and Greek Jews

In the postwar period, Greek governments barely had to consider their Jewish community since its numbers were so small and the state was faced with significant issues like reconstruction, the an ongoing crisis with regard to Cyprus, deteriorating relations with Turkey, and renewed challenges in the Balkans. The experience of occupation and the Holocaust succeeded in creating a unified Greek Jewish identity in place of the previously fragmented Jewish communities in Greece, an identity partly forged in the death camps where Greek Jews were outsiders to the Ashkenazi majority, and where Ladino became a "Greek" language because it was spoken by "Greeks."[160] The concentration of the remaining Jewish population in Athens accelerated the process of forging a single identity while their small numbers made the community more or less invisible in the rapidly expanding city.[161] By 1994, the 2,803 Athenian Jews composed 60 percent of the entire Jewish population of Greece.[162]

In postwar Greece there was little concern or even discussion among state agents about the Jewish community as the focus of Greek concern shifted toward Israel. Greece was among the earliest supporters of the Balfour declaration regarding the establishment of a Jewish state and continued to support the Zionist project in the interwar period, in part because it thought that the emigration of Jews to Palestine would reduce its own problems with the Sephardic minority. Greece, however, was one of only three non-Muslim United Nations member countries to vote against the creation of Israel on November 29, 1947. Greek state officials did not take part in early commemorations by Greek Jewish communities of the founding of Israel and Greece continued to resist full recognition of Israel until 1990.[163]

Once again Greek policies had little to do with anti-Semitism and more to do with national interests as understood in Greece. At the time of the vote in 1947 Greece had significant Greek communities in Turkey and Egypt whose well-being might be threatened by Greek support for Israel. In the long-term, Greek support for the Palestinian cause did not benefit those Greek communities which were essentially expelled from Turkey and Egypt in the 1950s and 1960s. Greece persisted in its pro-Palestinian policies when the socialist government of PASOK was in power from 1981 to 1988 primarily because of the economic interests of Greek companies in shipping, oil, and construction in the Arab world. Even the military dictatorship (1967–74) did not budge from this stance. The resumption of diplomatic ties between Egypt and Israel in 1979 did not induce the Greek government to fully recognize Israel and it only did so on the aftermath of the First Gulf War (1990–91) and the start of the Madrid Peace Talks between Israel and the PLO.

Domestic political considerations undoubtedly played a role as well since Greek society remains far more anti-Semitic than most other western democracies.[164] Anti-Semitic rhetoric is not the sole purview of fringe parties but can be found among several mainstream political parties of the right as well as of the left. Even a decade ago right-wing politicians could publish articles referring to Jews as the "murderers of Christ" with little reaction from the rest of the political world,[165] while anti-Semitic publications and "histories" by Holocaust deniers proliferate in mainstream bookstores by both Greek authors such as Konstantinos Plevris,[166] and foreign ones like David Irving. Postwar anti-Semitic rhetoric draws from the development of a racialized form of nationalism that was not particularly prominent prior to the Second World War. This focus on race, and the belief that Greeks are racially distinct from all other groups, becomes visible in early anticommunist writings from the time of the civil war, and many of these nationalist writings targeted Jews for their ungratefulness toward Greece who had supported them, often focusing on Jewish opposition to Greek claims over Macedonia, and their supposed preference for Bulgarian rule.[167] Purely anti-Semitic publications frequently repeat accusations found in other anti-Semitic literature regarding the alleged role of Jews in fostering conflict, their links to the masonic movement, international conspiracies, and so on, on occasion even sprinkling some local conspiracy theories, for example, the belief that the Young Turk movement was orchestrated by Jews and Freemasons.[168] Even prominent members of the church like the bishop of Corinth Karanikolas, repeated such accusations adding that "Jews hate Hellenism" despite the fact that Greeks, unlike Catholics, were always friendly toward Jews.[169] This juxtaposition of "Judaism" and "Hellenism" seems to be a prominent theme among Greek anti-Semites as is the enduring fascination with the Rothschild family.[170] This is due to the continuing strong links between Orthodoxy and the nation as well as between the church and the state.[171] So strong are such associations that they continue to influence Greek understandings of foreign events, most notably during the Wars of Yugoslavia in the 1990s when Greeks unequivocally sided with the Serbs, identifying Bosniaks with their "hereditary enemy" Turkey solely on the basis of religion.[172] Nationalists saw the conflict of Serbs and Albanians in Kosovo in similar terms,[173] and denounce indigenous religious minorities like the Pomaks, alternatively as pro-Bulgarian or pro-Turkish depending on political circumstances.[174]

Jewish intellectuals and journalists made some response to these anti-Semitic attacks and attempted to defend Israel but they also stressed the long relationship between Jews and Greeks in the region. Interestingly, these authors often referred to the existence of different Jewish communities, whether to stress the disappearance of the Sephardic community, the main bête noir of Greek anti-Semites, or to excuse the anti-Greek sentiments expressed by the Salonica Jews in 1912 as a result of their expulsion from Spain which deterred them from holding philhellenic sentiments "as we, the Jews of Old Greece, wanted."[175] Kambeli stressed that the same Jews who resisted the incorporation of Thessaloniki to Greece in 1912, after twenty-five years of Greek education took part in the "epic of our country in 1940, performing their duty exactly as Mr. Iatridis (a critic to whom Kambeli was responding) wanted, and as we, the Jews of Old Greece, rightly wished for."[176]

Responding to the dominant anti-Semitic beliefs of the general public, the Greek state allowed the marginalization of the Holocaust in Greek consciousness and even history. In place of the uniqueness of the Holocaust, the public discourse in Greece frequently refers to the notion of "Greek holocausts," a term used for German reprisals. A list of ninety-two sites of "holocaust" was compiled and recent publications reinforce the idea.[177] One of these, produced in 2006 to demand reparations from Germany, lists all sites of German reprisals with emphasis on the massacres at Kalavryta, Kommeno, Distomo, and Crete. The deportations of Jews was simply listed as one more atrocity among many. In the summary of the dead during the occupation, those who died in the camps are included but with no reference to their religion.[178] Similarly Greek literature dealing with the Holocaust frequently emphasizes the "passivity" of Jews, the "unpatriotic" acts of certain Jews, or their ineffectual leadership. In such novels Greek Jews are the protagonists but also they are often othered, "strangers" to the dominant culture.[179] Only in 1997 did a novel dare assign blame to Greek officials and the blame was assigned in the context of the 1891 Kerkyra pogrom and resulted in the author being attacked by the local press.[180] Even in the context of the latest economic crisis parallels were drawn between the Holocaust and contemporary Greece with statements like "we are the 'Jews' of the twenty-first century!"[181] or making analogies between the Holocaust and the exchange of populations between Greece and Turkey in 1923 and the "expropriation" of the Holocaust by Jews.[182] A recent report on anti-Semitism in Greece today showed that the Greek public overwhelmingly believes that Jews have exploited the Holocaust, that Israel treats Palestinians just as the Nazis treated Jews, that Jews are too powerful in the business world, and that Greek Jews (and Muslims) place their religious above their national identity.[183] The report met with widespread criticism for its findings even among prominent figures of the left like Giannis Dragasakis and the communist union federation PAME.[184] Holocaust commemoration ceremonies in various towns including Ioannina attract criticism from the local press even from the left with titles like "In the name of the Holocaust," "We are not scared by the fascist Jewish mentality,"[185] "Why the obsession of the Jews that we . . . honor them all the time?,"[186] "With ink made of blood."[187]

Yet despite the widespread anti-Semitism of Greek society, the Greek state frequently acts, and is expected to act, in support of Jews when that is seen to be in the national interests of Greece. Pressured by the international awareness regarding the Holocaust, and recent attention to the open anti-Semitism of Greek society,[188] state and municipal authorities have been much more active in recognizing the suffering of Jews during the Second World War. Since the 1990s the Greek state and local authorities have begun to erect monuments commemorating the Holocaust or Jewish heroes like Mordechai Frizis (see Figure 6.6).[189] In 1997, Thessaloniki erected a monument for the victims of the Holocaust followed by other cities though such monuments are frequently vandalized.[190] The ordeal of the renamed Jewish Martyrs Square in Thessaloniki is indicative of the problems of commemorating the Holocaust, since the square continues to be unknown by this name even to taxi drivers and its signposts are frequently vandalized.[191]

Figure 6.6 Mordohaios Frizis's statue, Chalkis © Collection of the Jewish Museum of Greece.

Some concluding thoughts

Throughout modern Greek history the Greek nation has been defined in part by its religious affiliation to the Greek Orthodox Church, sometimes formally but always with regard to popular perceptions. Even as other Orthodox Christians created their own states that were often in competition with Greece, that association was retained and augmented with the addition of language and a historical narrative that emphasized the ties of Greece to antiquity. In this context, *allotheskoi* (of another religion) had no place in the nation, an idea that clearly persists to this day. The focus on membership to the nation, however, tends to obscure the ability of other groups to integrate to a lesser degree in society and become, and be recognized as, useful citizens of the state. Although the population at large may fail to make this distinction, the state often does because of the usefulness of such groups.

This is what took place over the nineteenth century in Greece with regard to the Jewish communities. Grecophone Jews went from being closely associated with the enemy of the state, the Ottoman Empire, to be seen as useful citizens who could buttress Greek national and irredentist claims. At the same time, Sephardic Jews remained associated with the enemies of the nation-state and thus though technically citizens continued to be viewed with suspicion. Undoubtedly given time Sephardic Jews would also have graduated to the status of useful citizen through participation in the Greek educational system as Korais first suggested but the Second World War and the Holocaust ended that possibility. In the discussion above I try to shift the discussion of nationalism from the interaction of elites and the masses that authors like Hobsbawm and Billig focus on, or from societal and economic transformations that Gellner, Breuilly, and Hroch, among others, discuss to an examination of the how the state and its elites view and interact with groups that cannot become part of the nation but which could conceivably serve useful roles in the national aspirations of the state. I believe that I have shown that the state, despite the virulent and hegemonic nationalistic rhetoric that pervaded Greek society at the time, was remarkably pragmatic and nuanced in its approach toward the Jewish communities. I also make an effort to examine Greek Jewish history within the context of Greek history and the history of the Greek state in particular and not as something separate. I would be most gratified if other scholars pursued similar investigations with other groups like the Pomaks, Roma, Armenians, and so on. There is a lot more work to be done in this field including more examination of the Jewish communities of "Old" Greece and I can only hope this contribution helps generate more interest and research in these areas.

Notes

Preface

1 Thomas W. Gallant, *Modern Greece, from the War of Independence to the Present* (New York: Bloomsbury, 2016).

2 K. E. Fleming, *Greece a Jewish History* (Princeton: Princeton University Press, 2008).

3 Ernest Gellner, *Nations and Nationalism* (Oxford: Blackwell, 1983), 1.

4 Gellner, *Nations and Nationalism*, 11, 18.

5 "The Coming of Nationalism and Its Interpretation: The Myths of Nation and Class," in *Mapping the Nation*, ed. Gopal Balakrishnan (London: Verso, 1996), 110.

6 Gellner, *Nations and Nationalism*, 47, 55, 61.

7 Nicos Mouzelis, "Nationalism: Restructuring Gellner's Theory," in *Ernest Gellner and Contemporary Social Thought*, eds. Sinisa Malesevic and Mark Haugaard (Cambridge: Cambridge University Press, 2007), 132–33.

8 John Breuilly, "Nationalism and the State," in *Nationality, Patriotism and Nationalism in Liberal Democratic Societies*, ed. Roger Michener (Minnesota: Professors World Peace Academy, 1993), 1.

9 John Breuilly, "Approaches to Nationalism," in *Mapping the Nation*, ed. Gopal Balakrishnan (London: Verso, 1996), 163–64.

10 Breuilly, "Approaches to Nationalism," 165.

11 Breuilly, "Nationalism and the State," 23–24; Breuilly, "Approaches to Nationalism," 166.

12 Paul R. Bass, *Ethnicity and Nationalism: Theory and Comparison* (Newbury Park: Sage, 1991), 63–64.

13 Brendan O'Leary, "Ernest Gellner's Diagnoses of Nationalism: A Critical Overview, or, What Is Living and What Is Dead in Ernest Gellner's Philosophy of Nationalism," in *The State of the Nation: Ernest Gellner and the Theory of Nationalism*, ed. John A. Hall (Cambridge: Cambridge University Press, 1998), 73.

14 Eric J. Hobsbawm, "Introduction: Inventing Traditions," in *The Invention of Tradition*, eds. Eric J. Hobsbawm and Terence Ranger (Cambridge: Cambridge University Press, 1983), 1; see also Antonis Liakos, "The Construction of National Time: The Making of the Modern Greek Historical Imagination," *Mediterranean Historical Review* 16, no. 1 (2010): 27–42.

15 Hobsbawm, "Introduction: Inventing Traditions," 12; Eric J. Hobsbawm, "Mass-Producing Traditions: Europe, 1870-1914," in *The Invention of Tradition*, eds. Eric J. Hobsbawm and Terence Ranger (Cambridge: Cambridge University Press, 1983), 263–308.

16 "Mass-Peoducing Traditions: Europe, 1870-1914," 270–71.

17 *Nations and Nationalism since 1780: Programme, Myth, Reality* (Cambridge: Cambridge University Press, 1990), 10.

18 *Nations and Nationalism since 1780: Programme, Myth, Reality*, 14–45.

19 Benedict Anderson, *Imagined Communities: Reflections on the Origin and Spread of Nationalism* (London: Verso, 1991), 4.

20   Anderson, *Imagined Communities: Reflections on the Origin and Spread of Nationalism*, 6–7.

21   Ibid., 12–19, 38–43.

22   Ibid., 42–44.

23   James G. Kellas, *The Politics of Nationalism and Ethnicity* (London: Macmillan, 1991), 48.

24   Miroslav Hroch, "Modernization and Communication as Factors of Nation Formation," in *The Sage Handbook of Nations and Nationalism*, eds. Gerard Delanty and Krishan Kumar (London: Sage, 2006), 30.

25   "National Self-Determination from a Historical Perspective," in *Notions of Nationalism*, ed. Sukumar Periwal (Budapest: Central European University Press, 1995), 66–67.

26   *Social Preconditions of National Revival in Europe: A Comparative Analysis of the Social Composition of Patriotic Groups among the Smaller European Nations* (Cambridge: Cambridge University Press, 1985), 25–30; "From National Movement to Fully-Formed Nation: The Nation-Building Process in Europe," *New Left Review* 198 (1993), 7–8.

27   Hroch, "Modernization and Communication as Factors of Nation Formation," 25.

28   John A. Hall, "Nationalisms: Classified and Explained," *Daedalus* 122, no. 3 (1993): 25.

29   Miroslav Hroch, "Real and Constructed: The Nature of the Nation," in *The State of the Nation: Ernest Gellner and the Theory of Nationalism*, ed. John A. Hall (Cambridge: Cambridge University Press, 1998), 99.

30   Anthony D. Smith, "When Is a Nation?" *Geopolitics* 7, no. 2 (2002): 14–15; *Myths and Memories of the Nation* (Oxford: Oxford University Press, 1999), 29–56; and "The Geneology of Nations: An Ethno-Symbolic Approach," in *When Is the Nation?* eds. Atsuko Ichijo and Gordana Uzelac (New York: Routledge, 2005), 98.

31   Anthony D. Smith, *The Ethnic Origins of Nations* (Oxford: Blackwell, 1986), 17.

32   Anthony D. Smith, *National Identity* (London: Penguin, 1991), 14.

33   Smith, *National Identity*, 35–36.

34   Ibid., 82–83.

35   Sinisa Malesevic, *Identity as Ideology* (New York: Palgrave Macmillan, 2006), 131.

36   Michael Billig, *Banal Nationalism* (London: Sage, 1995), 41.

37   Billig, *Banal Nationalism*, 93–94, 96, 119.

38   Partha Chatterjee, *The Nation and its Fragments: Colonial and Postcolonial Histories* (Princeton: Princeton University Press, 1993), 13.

39   Rogers Brubaker, "Ethnicity without Groups," *Archives Europeenes de Sociologie* XLIII, no. 2 (2002): 166–68. See also *Nationalism Reframed: Nationhood and the National Question in the New Europe* (Cambridge: Cambridge University Press, 1996).

40   Eugen Weber, *Peasants into Frenchmen: The Modernization of Rural France 1870-1914* (Stanford: Stanford University Press, 1976).

41   Henriette-Rika Benveniste, "The Idea of Exile: Jewish Accounts and the Historiography of Salonika Revisited," in *Evraikes Koinotetes Anamesa Se Anatole Kai Dyse, 15os – 20os Aionas: Oikonomia, Koinonia, Politike, Politismos*, eds. Anna Machaira and Leda Papastefanaki (Ioannina: Isnafi, 2016), 43.

42   Efi Avdela, "Towards a Greek History of the Jews of Salonica?" *Jewish History* 28 (2014): 410.

43   Henriette-Rika Benveniste, "The Coming out of Jewish History in Greece," http://usagespublicsdupasse.ehess.fr/wp-content/uploads/sites/7/2014/05/Benveniste_Rika._The_Coming_Out_of_Jewish_History_in_Greece.pdf. 4; Avdela.406, 408.

44   Benveniste, "The Coming out of Jewish History in Greece," 7.

45 K. E. Fleming, *Greece: A Jewish History* (Princeton: Princeton University Press, 2008).

46 Steven Runciman, *The Great Church in Captivity* (Cambridge: Cambridge University Press, 1968), 121, 122.

47 *Convention on the Prevention and Punishment of the Crime of Genocide Adopted by the General Assembly of the United Nations on December 9, 1948*, 1021, 280.

48 Vasilis Kremmydas, *E Ellenike Epanastase Tou 1821: Tekmeria, Anapselafeseis, Emeneies* (Athens: Gutenberg, 2016), 99.

49 George Finlay, *A History of Greece from Its Conquest by the Romans to the Present Time*, vol. VI Part I (Oxford: Clarendon Press, 1877), 183; François Charles Hughes Laurent Pouqueville, *Istoria Tis Ellinikis Epanastasis*, vol. I (Athens: Afoi. Tolidi, 1996), 43.

Chapter 1

1 Guy G. Stroumsa, "Jewish Survival in Late Antique Alexandria," in *Jews in Byzantium*, ed. Robert Bonfil, et al. (Boston: Brill, 2012), 260, 261.

2 Stroumsa, "Jewish Survival in Late Antique Alexandria," 263. Oded Irshai, "Confronting a Christian Empire: Jewish Life and Culture in the World of Early Byzantium," in *Jews in Byzantium*, ed. Robert Bonfil, et al. (Boston: Brill, 2012), 58.

3 Ra'anan S. Boustan, "Immolating Emperors: Spectacles of Imperial Suffering and the Making of a Jewish Minority Culture in Late Antiquity," *Biblical Interpretation* 17 (2009): 221; Irshai, "Confronting a Christian Empire: Jewish Life and Culture in the World of Early Byzantium," 41.

4 Averil V. Cameron, "Byzantines and Jews: Some Recent Work on Early Byzantium," *Byzantine and Modern Greek Studies* 26 (1996): 249; Gilbert Dagron and Vincent Déroche, "Juifs Et Chrétiens Dans L'orient Du Viie Siècle," *Travaux et Mémoires* 11 (1991): 17–273; Averil V. Cameron, "Disputations, Polemical Literature, and the Formation of Opinion in Early Byzantineliterature," in *Dispute Poems and Dialogues in the Ancient and Medieval near East*, eds. G. J. Reinink and H. J. L. Vanstiphout, Orientalia Lovaniensia Analecta (Leuven: Peeters, 1991), 91–108; and Vincent Déroche, "La Polémique Anti-Judaïque Au Vie Et Au Viie Siècle, Un Mémento Inédit, Les Kephalaia," *Travaux et Mémoires* 11 (1991): 275–311.

5 Boustan, "Immolating Emperors: Spectacles of Imperial Suffering and the Making of a Jewish Minority Culture in Late Antiquity," 225.

6 Irshai, "Confronting a Christian Empire: Jewish Life and Culture in the World of Early Byzantium," 53; see David Biale, "Counter-History and Jewish Polemics against Christianity: The Sefer Toldot Yeshu and the Sefer Zerubavel," *Jewish Social Studies* 6, no. 1 (1999): 130–45.

7 Boustan, "Immolating Emperors: Spectacles of Imperial Suffering and the Making of a Jewish Minority Culture in Late Antiquity," 227.

8 Irshai, "Confronting a Christian Empire: Jewish Life and Culture in the World of Early Byzantium," 23.

9 Ibid., 28.

10 Ibid., 60.

11 Hagith Sivan, "From Byzantine to Persian Jerusalem: Jewish Perspectives and Jewish/Christian Polemics," *Greek, Roman, and Byzantine Studies* 41 (2000): 286, 299, 300; Elliott Horowitz, "'The Vengence of the Jews Was Stronger Than Their Avarice':

Modern Historians and the Persian Conquest of Jerusalem in 614," *Jewish Social Studies, New Series* 4, no. 2 (1998): 8, 9.

12 Irshai, "Confronting a Christian Empire: Jewish Life and Culture in the World of Early Byzantium," 64.

13 Ibid., 60, 61.

14 See Shmuel Shepkaru, "The Preaching of the First Crusade and the Persecutions of the Jews," *Medieval Encounters* 18 (2012): 93–145; David Malkiel, "Destruction or Conversion: Intention and Reaction, Crusaders and Jews, in 1096," *Jewish History* 15, no. 3 (2001): 257–80.

15 See James Howard-Johnson, "Byzantium and Its Neighbours," in *The Oxford Handbook of Byzantine Studies*, eds. Elizabeth Jeffreys, John Haldon, and Robin Cormack (Oxford: Oxford University Press, 2008), 939–56.

16 For a discussion on Greek identity in Byzantium see Anthony Kaldellis, *Hellenism in Byzantium, the Transformations of Greek Identity and the Reception of the Classical Tradition* (Cambridge: Cambridge University Press, 2007) and Gil Page, *Being Byzantine: Greek Identity before the Ottomans* (New York: Cambridge University Press, 2008).

17 Karen Barkey and Ira Katznelson, "States, Regimes, and Decisions: Why Jews Were Expelled from Medieval England and France," *Theory and Society* 40 (2011): 481.

18 See Benjamin Ravid, "The Legal Status of the Jewish Merchants of Venice, 1541–638," *The Journal of Economic History* 35, no. 1 (1975): 274–79.

19 See Youval Rotman, "Converts in Byzantine Italy: Local Representations of Jewish-Christian Rivalry," in *Jews in Byzantium*, ed. Robert Bonfil, et al. (Boston: Brill, 2012).

20 See Robert Bonfil, "Continuity and Discontinuity (641-1204)," in *Jews in Byzantium*, eds. Robert Bonfil, Oded Irshai, Guy G. Stroumsa, and Rina Talgam (Boston: Brill, 2012): 65–100.

21 Amnon Linder, "The Legal Status of Jews in the Byzantine Empire," in *Jews in Byzantium*, ed. Robert Bonfil, et al. (Boston: Brill, 2012), 209; Anna Lampropoulou, "E Evraike Parousia Sten Peloponneso Kata Te Byzantine Periodo," in *Oi Evraioi Ston Elleniko Choro: Zetemata Istorias Ste Makra Diarkeia*, ed. Efi Avdela (Athens: Ekdoseis Gavrilidis, 1995), 47.

22 Ilias Anagnostakis, "E Solomonteia Amphithymia Ton Proton Makedonon Aytokratoron Kai Oi Apokalyptikes Katavoles Tes," in *E Evraike Parousia Ston Elladiko Choro (4os-19os Ai.)*, eds. Anna Lambropoulou and Kostas Tsiknakis (Athens: Ethniko Idryma Erevnon, 2008), 41; Linder, "The Legal Status of Jews in the Byzantine Empire," 209.

23 Linder, "The Legal Status of Jews in the Byzantine Empire," 175.

24 Rabbi Benjamin of Tudela, *The Itinerary of Rabbi Benjamin of Tudela*, trans. A. Asher, vol. I (London: A. Asher & Co, 1840), 47, 50, 56.

25 Linder, "The Legal Status of Jews in the Byzantine Empire," 155.

26 Ibid., 156, 161, 166–67.

27 Ibid., 168, 169.

28 Yossi Soffer, "The View of Byzantine Jews in Islamic and Eastern Christian Sources," in *Jews in Byzantium*, eds. Robert Bonfil, Oded Irshai, Guy G. Stroumsa, and Rina Talgam (Boston: Brill, 2012), 845–70.

29 Ibid., 868; see also Cameron, "Disputations, Polemical Literature, and the Formation of Opinion in Early Byzantineliterature," 773; and Averil Cameron, "Jews and Heretics—a Category Error?," in *The Ways That Never Parted: Jews and Christians in Late Antiquity and the Early Middle Ages*, eds. Adam H. Becker and Annette Yoshiko Reed (Tubingen: J. C. B. Mohr (Paul Siebeck), 2003); and James Weiss, "Fortress

Forever at the Ready: The Jewish Ethos in the Byzantine Mind and Its Ruthenian Translation," *Greek Orthodox Theological Review* 46, no. 3-4 (2001): 287–344.

30 See Gilbert Dagron, "Judaïser," *Travaux et Mémoirés* 11 (1991): 359–80; Linder, "The Legal Status of Jews in the Byzantine Empire," 195.

31 Steven B. Bowman, *The Jews of Byzantium 1204-1453* (Jacksonville: Bloch Pub Co, 2001), 25, 57, 116, 123.

32 Tudela, *The Itinerary of Rabbi Benjamin of Tudela*, 56.

33 Bowman, *The Jews of Byzantium 1204-1453*, 114.

34 Tia M. Kolbaba, "Byzantine Perceptions of Latin Religious 'Errors': Themes and Changes from 850 to 1350," in *The Crusades from the Perspective of Byzantium and the Muslim World*, eds. Angeliki E Laiou and Roy Parviz Mottahedeh (Washington: Dumbarton Oaks Research Library and Collection, 2001), 125.

35 David Jacoby, "The Jews and the Silk Industry of Constantinople," in *The Jewish Presence in the Greek Territory (4th-19th Centuries)*, eds. Anna Lambropoulou and Kostas Tsiknakis (Athens: National Hellenic Research Foundation, 2008), 19, 22.

36 Jacoby, "The Jews in the Byzantine Economy (Seventh to Mid-Fifteenth Century)," in *Jews in Byzantium*, ed. Robert Bonfil, et al. (Boston: Brill, 2012), 232–33; Lampropoulou, "E Evraike Parousia Sten Peloponneso Kata Te Byzantine Periodo," 50, 53.

37 Jacoby, "The Jews in the Byzantine Economy (Seventh to Mid-Fifteenth Century)," 223; A. M. Andreadis, *Oi Evraioi En to Byzantino Kratei: Dialexe Genomene En Te Etaireia Byzantinon Spoudon* (Athens: Estia, 1929), 8; Tudela, *The Itinerary of Rabbi Benjamin of Tudela*, 46.

38 Andreadis, *Oi Evraioi En to Byzantino Kratei: Dialexe Genomene En Te Etaireia Byzantinon Spoudon*, 11.

39 Jacoby, "The Jews in the Byzantine Economy (Seventh to Mid-Fifteenth Century)," 249.

40 Jacoby, "The Jews and the Silk Industry of Constantinople," 26; Tudela, *The Itinerary of Rabbi Benjamin of Tudela*, 55. Karaite Jews reject rabbinical traditions.

41 Cyril Aslanov, "Judeo-Greek or Greek Spoken by Jews?" in *Jews in Byzantium*, ed. Robert Bonfil, et al. (Boston: Brill, 2012), 387.

42 Aslanov, "Judeo-Greek or Greek Spoken by Jews?" 390, 395.

43 Bowman, *The Jews of Byzantium 1204-1453*, 165–66.

44 Lampropoulou, "E Evraike Parousia Sten Peloponneso Kata Te Byzantine Periodo," 45.

45 Zvi Ankori, "Some Aspects of Karaite-Rabbanite Relations in Byzantium in the Eve of the First Crusade: Part II," *Proceedings of the American Academy for Jewish Research* 25 (1956): 173, 174.

46 Bowman, *The Jews of Byzantium 1204-1453*, 93, 109; Steven Bowman, "Survival in Decline: Romaniote Jewry Post-1204," in *Jews in Byzantium*, ed. Robert Bonfil, et al. (Boston: Brill, 2012), 104.

47 Bowman, *The Jews of Byzantium 1204-1453*, 17–18.

48 Ibid., 25.

49 Vincent Déroche, "Forms and Functions of Anti-Jewish Polemics: Polymorphy, Polysemy," in *Jews in Byzantium*, ed. Robert Bonfil, et al. (Boston: Brill, 2012), 546, 548.

50 Bowman, "Survival in Decline: Romaniote Jewry Post-1204," 126.

51 Bowman, *The Jews of Byzantium 1204-1453*, 40; Bowman, "Survival in Decline: Romaniote Jewry Post-1204," 113–14.

52 K. E. Fleming, "Constantinople: From Christianity to Islam," *The Classical World* 97, no. 1 (2003): 74.

53 Fleming, "Constantinople: From Christianity to Islam," 75; Bowman, *The Jews of Byzantium 1204-1453*, 178.

54 L. S. Stavrianos, "The Jews of Greece," *Journal of Central European Affairs* 8, no. 3 (1948): 256.

55 Mark Alan Epstein, *The Ottoman Jewish Communities and Their Role in the Fifteenth and Sixteenth Centuries* (Freiburg: Klaus Schwarz Verlag, 1980), 45, 138; Esther Benbassa and Aron Rodrigue, *The Jews of the Balkans* (Cambridge: Blackwell, 1995), 6.

56 See Alexander D. Beihammer, "Defection across the Border of Islam and Christianity: Apostasy and Cross-Cultural Interaction in Byzantine-Seljuk Relations," *Speculum* 86, no. 597–650 (2011); Nicholas Morton, "The Saljuq Turks' Conversion to Islam: The Crusading Sources," *Al-Masaq* 27, no. 2 (2015): 117.

57 Muhammad Ibn Battuta, *Travels in Asia and Africa 1325-1354* (New York: Routledge, 2005), 183–213.

58 Christine Isom-Verhaaren, "Constructing Ottoman Identity in the Reigns of Mehmed II and Bayezid II," *Journal of Ottoman and Turkish Studies* 1, no. 1–2 (2014): 113, 114, 117.

59 Alan Mikhail and Christine M Philliou, "The Ottoman Empire and the Imperial Turn," *Comparative Studies in Society and History* 54, no. 4 (2012): 733.

60 Kritovoulos, *History of Mehmed the Conqueror* (Westport: Greenwood Press, 1970), 94.

61 G. Georgiades Arnakis, "The Greek Church of Constantinople and the Ottoman Empire," *The Journal of Modern History* 24, no. 3 (1952): 236.

62 Tom Papademetriou, *Render unto the Sultan: Power, Authority, and the Greek Church in the early Ottoman Centuries* (Oxford: Oxford University Press, 2015), 140.

63 Charles A. Frazee, *The Orthodox Church and Independent Greece 1821-1852* (Cambridge: Cambridge University Press, 1969), 2.

64 Arnakis, "The Greek Church of Constantinople and the Ottoman Empire," 241.

65 Paraskevas Konortas, *Othomanikes Theoreseis gia to Oikoumeniko Patriarcheio* (Athens: Ekdoseis Alexandreia, 1998), 219–20, 225.

66 Runciman, *The Great Church in Captivity*, 203, 283.

67 Benbassa and Rodrigue, *The Jews of the Balkans*, 6.

68 Josef Nehama, *Istoria Ton Israeliton Tes Salonikes*, vol. I (Thessaloniki: University Studio Press, 2000), 166.

69 Benbassa and Rodrigue, *The Jews of the Balkans*, 13.

70 Uriel Heyd, "The Jewish Communities of Istanbul in the Seventeenth Century," *Oriens* 6, no. 2 (1953): 307, 308. Benbassa and Rodrigue, *The Jews of the Balkans*, 11.

71 Maria Efthymiou, *Evraioi Kai Christianoi Sta Tourkokratoumena Nesia Tou Notioanatolikou Aigaiou: Oi Dyskoles Plevres Mias Gonimes Synyparxes* (Athens: Trochalia, 1992), 34.

72 Nehama, *Istoria Ton Israeliton Tes Salonikes*, 225.

73 Benbassa and Rodrigue, *The Jews of the Balkans*, 9.

74 Ibid., 43.

75 Nehama, *Istoria Ton Israeliton Tes Salonikes*, 454, 460, 461.

76 Brian Pullan, "'A Ship with Two Rudders': 'Righetto Marrano' and the Inquisition in Venice," *The Historical Journal* 20, no. 1 (1977): 26; Nehama, *Istoria Ton Israeliton Tes Salonikes*, 387.

77 Ruth Lamdan, "Communal Regulations as a Source for Jewish Women's Lives in the Ottoman Empire," *The Muslim World* 95 (2005): 254.

78 Jonathan Schorsch, "Blacks, Jews and the Racial Imagination in the Writings of Sephardim in the Long Seventeenth Century," *Jewish History* 19 (2005): 110.

79 Yaron Ben-Naeh, "Blond, Tall with Honey-Colored Eyes: Jewish Ownership of Slaves in the Ottoman Empire," *Jewish History* 20 (2006): 317, 330.

80 Benbassa and Rodrigue, *The Jews of the Balkans*, xvii.

81 Efthymiou, *Evraioi Kai Christianoi Sta Tourkokratoumena Nesia Tou Notioanatolikou Aigaiou: Oi Dyskoles Plevres Mias Gonimes Synyparxes*, 45.

82 Benbassa and Rodrigue, *The Jews of the Balkans*, 45, 48; Traian Stoianovich, "The Conquering Balkan Orthodox Merchant," *The Journal of Economic History* 20, no. 2 (1960): 234–313.

83 Christine Philliou, "Communities on the Verge: Unraveling the Phanariot Ascendancy in Ottoman Governance," *Comparative Studies in Society and History* 51, no. 1 (2009): 153.

84 Konortas, *Othomanikes Theoreseis gia to Oikoumeniko Patriarcheio*, 145.

85 Philliou, "Communities on the Verge: Unraveling the Phanariot Ascendancy in Ottoman Governance," 171.

86 Suraiya Faroqhi, "Empires before and after the Post-Colonial Turn: The Ottomans," *SAYI The Journal of Ottoman Studies* 36 (2010): 69.

87 Giannis Spyropoulos, *Othomanike Dioikese Kai Koinonia Sten Proepanastatike Dytike Krete* (Rethymno: Genika Archeia tou Kratous, Archeia N. Rethymnis, 2015), 38.

88 Robert W. Zens, "In the Name of the Sultan: Haci Mustafa Pasha of Belgrade and Ottoman Provincial Rule in the Late 18th Century," *International Journal of Middle East Studies* 44, no. 01 (2012): 132; Spyropoulos, *Othomanike Dioikese Kai Koinonia Sten Proepanastatike Dytike Krete*, 132.

89 Dean J. Kostantaras, "Christian Elites of the Peloponnese and the Ottoman State, 1715-1821," *European History Quarterly* 43, no. 4 (2013): 633, 637.

90 Karen Barkey, *Bandits and Bureaucrats, the Ottoman Route to State Centralization* (Ithaca: Cornell University Press, 1994), 85–140, 103, 232, 234.

91 See Speros Vryonis, *The Decline of Medieval Hellenism in Asia Minor and the Process of Islamization from the Eleventh through the Fifteenth Century* (Berkeley: University of California Press, 1971).

92 Phokion P. Kotzageorgis, "Conversion to Islam in Ottoman Rural Societies in the Balkans: The Cases of Vallahades and Pomaks," in *Ottoman Rural Societies and Economies*, ed. Elias Kolovos (Rethymno: Crete University Press, 2015), 143, 146.

93 Suphan Kirmizialtin, "Conversion in Ottoman Balkans: A Historiographical Survey," *History Compass* 5, no. 2 (2007): 650.

94 Anton Minkov, *Conversion to Islam in the Balkans: Kisve Bahasi Petitions and Ottoman Social Life, 1670-1730* (Leiden: Brill, 2004), 92, 100, 102, 104, 105; Dennis P Hupchick, *The Bulgarians in the Seventeenth Century: Slavic Orthodox Society and Culture under Ottoman Rule* (Jefferson: McFarland, 1993), 59; and Adem Handzic, *Population of Bosnia in the Ottoman Period – a Historical Overview* (Istanbul: Organization of the Islamic Conference Research Centre for Islamic History, Art and Culture (IRCICA), 1994), 6.

95 See Marc Baer, "Islamic Conversion Narratives of Women: Social Change and Gendered Religious Hierarchy in Early Modern Ottoman Istanbul," *Gender & History* 16, no. 2 (2004).

96 Josef Nehama, *Istoria Ton Israeliton Tes Salonikes*, vol. II (Thessaloniki: University Studio Press, 2000), 715, 716, 719.

97 For detailed discussion of the Dönme see Marc David Baer, *The Dönme: Jewish Converts, Muslim Revolutionaries, and Secular Turks* (Stanford: Stanford University Press, 2009).

98 "The Great Fire of 1660 and the Islamization of Christian and Jewish Space in Istanbul," *International Journal of Middle East Studies* 36 (2004): 162.

99   Eyal Ginio, "Jews and European Subjects in Eighteenth-Century Salonica: The Ottoman Perspective," *Jewish History* 28 (2014): 296.

100 Minkov, *Conversion to Islam in the Balkans: Kisve Bahasi Petitions and Ottoman Social Life, 1670-1730*, 83.

101 Hupchick, *The Bulgarians in the Seventeenth Century: Slavic Orthodox Society and Culture under Ottoman Rule*, 62.

102 Kirmizialtin, "Conversion in Ottoman Balkans: A Historiographical Survey," 651; Antonina Zhelyazkova, "Islamization in the Balkans as a Historiographical Problem: The Southeast-European Perspective," in *The Ottomans and the Balkans: A Discussion of Historiography*, eds. Fikret Adanir and Suraiya Faroqhi (Leiden: Brill, 2002), 262.

103 See Natalie E. Rothman, *Brokering Empire: Trans-Imperial Subjects between Venice and Istanbul*, vol. (Ithaca: Cornell University Press, 2014); Eric R. Dursteler, *Venetians in Constantinople: Nation, Identity, and Coexistence in the Early Modern Mediterranean* (Baltimore: John Hopkins University Press, 2006); and Molly Greene, *A Shared World: Christians and Muslims in the Early Modern Mediterranean* (Princeton: Princeton University Press, 2002).

104 Daphne Lappa, "Variations on a Religious Theme: Jews and Muslims From the Eastern Mediterranean Converting to Christianity, 17th & 18th Centuries," PhD dissertation, (Florence: European University Institute, Department of History and Civilization, 2015), 33.

105 Pullan, "'A Ship with Two Rudders': 'Righetto Marrano' and the Inquisition in Venice," 37, 45.

106 Ibid., 51, 52.

107 Isom-Verhaaren, "Constructing Ottoman Identity in the Reigns of Mehmed II and Bayezid II," 124.

108 E. Natalie Rothman, "Becoming Venetian: Conversion and Transformation in the Seventeenth-Century Mediterranean," *Mediterranean Historical Review* 21, no. 1 (2006): 43, 47, 54.

109 Virginia Aksan, "Who Was an Ottoman? Reflections on 'Wearing Hats' and 'Turning Turk'," in *Europe and Turkey in the 18th Century*, ed. Barbara Schmidt-Haberkamp (Göttingen: Bonn University Press, 2011), 307.

110 Ayse Baltacioglu-Brammer, "The Formation of Kizilbas Communities in Anatolia and Ottoman Responses, 1450s-1630s," *International Journal of Turkish Studies* 20, no. 1–2 (2014): 38, 39; Bernard Heyberger, "Les Chrétiens D'alep (Syrie) À Travers Les Récits Des Conversions Des Missionnaires Carmes Déchaux (1657-1681)," *Mélanges de l'Ecole française de Rome. Moyen-Age, Temps modernes* 100, no. 1 (1988): 462.

111 Eyal Ginio, "Neither Muslims nor Zimmis: The Gypsies (Roma) in the Ottoman State," *Romani Studies 5* 14, no. 2 (2004): 118, 135.

112 Stephane Yerasimos, "Les Grecs D'istanbul Apres La Conquete Ottomane. Le Repeuplement De La Ville Et De Ses Environs (1453-1550)," *Revue des mondes musulmans et de la Méditerranée* 107–110 (2005): 379–382.

113 Kirmizialtin, "Conversion in Ottoman Balkans: A Historiographical Survey," 653.

114 Andrew Robarts, "Imperial Confrontation or Regional Cooperation?: Bulgarian Migration and Ottoman-Russian Relations in the Black Sea Region, 1768-1830s," *Turkish Historical Review* 3 (2012): 151, 153.

115 Minkov, *Conversion to Islam in the Balkans: Kisve Bahasi Petitions and Ottoman Social Life, 1670-1730*, 49.

116 Hupchick, *The Bulgarians in the Seventeenth Century: Slavic Orthodox Society and Culture under Ottoman Rule*, 39.

117 Antonis Anastasopoulos, "Political Participation, Public Order, and Monetary Pledges (Nezir) in Ottoman Crete," in *Popular Protest and Political Participation in the Ottoman Empire*, eds. Eleni Gara, M. Erdem Kabadayi, and Christoph K. Neumann (Istanbul: Bilgi University Press, 2011), 129; Giorgos D. Kontogiorgis, *Koinonike Dynamike Kai Politike Autodioikise* (Athens: Livanis, 1982), 59, 101.

118 Kirmizialtin, "Conversion in Ottoman Balkans: A Historiographical Survey," 654; See also Petar Petrovic-Njegos, *The Mountain Wreath* (Aristeus Books, 2012).

119 David Chambers and Brian Pullan, eds., *Venice: A Documentary History, 1450-1630* (Toronto: Toronto University Press, 2001), 338–49.

120 Pullan, "'A Ship with Two Rudders': 'Righetto Marrano' and the Inquisition in Venice," 54.

121 As was often the case between Sephardim and Romaniotes. The ultimate cause of the disputes can be traced to the Sephardim's break of the accepted rule in the Jewish world of newcomers embracing the customs of the Jews already established in the place. (Benbassa and Rodrigue, *The Jews of the Balkans*, 11–13).

122 Salo W. Baron, "Jewish Immigration and Communal Conflicts in Seventeenth-Century Corfu," in *The Joshua Starr Memorial Volume, Conference on Jewish Relations* (New York: Jewish Social Studies Publications, 1953), 170–72.

123 Lappa, "Variations on a Religious Theme: Jews and Muslims From the Eastern Mediterranean Converting to Christianity," 71, 177.

124 Olga Katsiardi-Hering and Ikaros Madouvalos, "The Tolerant Policy of the Habsburg Authorities Towards the Orthodox People from South-Eastern Europe and the Formation of National Identities (18th-Early 19th Century)," *Balkan Studies* 49 (2014): 20, 24, 28, 31.

125 Marco Dogo, "'a Respectable Body of Nation': Religious Freedom and High-Risk Trade: The Greek Merchant in Trieste, 1770-1830," *The Historical Review/La Revue Historique* 7 (2010): 204.

Chapter 2

1 Deno J. Geanakoplos, "Religion and Nationalism in the Byzantine Empire and After: Conformity or Pluralism?" *Journal of Ecumenical Studies* XIII, no. 4 (Fall 1976): 108; Nikos G. Svoronos, *To Elleniko Ethnos: Genese Kai Diamorphose Tou Newou Ellenismou* (Athens: Polis, 2017), 33.

2 David Aberbach, *The European Jews, Patriotism and the Liberal State 1789-1939: A Study of Literature and Social Psychology*, Kindle edition ed., Routledge Jewish Studies (New York: Routledge, 2012), 66, 67.

3 Eli Nathans, *The Politics of Citizenship in Germany: Ethnicity, Utility and Nationalism* (Oxford: Berg, 2004), 28.

4 Jacques Godechot, "The New Concept of the Nation and Its Diffusion in Europe," in *Nationalism in the Age of French Revolution*, eds. Otto Dann and John Dinwiddy (London: The Hambledon Press, 1988), 16.

5 Godechot, "The New Concept of the Nation and Its Diffusion in Europe," 16, 19.

6 Segeberg, "Germany," 148.

7 Aberbach, *The European Jews, Patriotism and the Liberal State 1789-1939: A Study of Literature and Social Psychology*, 23.

8 Ibid., 48, 49.

9 Jacob Katz, *From Prejudice to Destruction: Antisemitism, 1700-1933* (Cambridge, MA: Harvard University Press, 1980).

10 Aberbach, *The European Jews, Patriotism and the Liberal State 1789-1939: A Study of Literature and Social Psychology*, 23.

11 Ibid., 68.

12 Michael G. Müller, "Poland," in *Nationalism in the Age of French Revolution*, eds. Otto Dann and John Dinwiddy (London: The Hambledon Press, 1988), 120.

13 Aberbach, *The European Jews, Patriotism and the Liberal State 1789-1939: A Study of Literature and Social Psychology*, 25.

14 Ibid., 135; Shmuel Almog, *Nationalism and Antisemitism in Modern Europe 1815-1945* (Oxford: Pergamon Press, 1990), 8.

15 Nathans, *The Politics of Citizenship in Germany: Ethnicity, Utility and Nationalism*, 29, 30.

16 Almog, *Nationalism and Antisemitism in Modern Europe 1815-1945*, 7-8.

17 Aberbach, *The European Jews, Patriotism and the Liberal State 1789-1939: A Study of Literature and Social Psychology*, 40; Almog, *Nationalism and Antisemitism in Modern Europe 1815-1945*, 8.

18 Katz, *From Prejudice to Destruction: Antisemitism, 1700-1933*, 97, 99–100.

19 Almog, *Nationalism and Antisemitism in Modern Europe 1815-1945*, 9, 17, 21, 23.

20 Ibid., 22–23.

21 Ibid., 15.

22 Nathans, *The Politics of Citizenship in Germany: Ethnicity, Utility and Nationalism*, 68.

23 Allan Arkush, "Voltaire on Judaism and Christianity," *Association for Jewish Studies Review* 18, no. 2 (1993): 225; Martin Luther, *The Jews and Their Lies* (Los Angeles: Christian Nationalist Crusade, 1948), 29, 37, 49; and Aberbach, *The European Jews, Patriotism and the Liberal State 1789-1939: A Study of Literature and Social Psychology*, 24.

24 Aberbach, *The European Jews, Patriotism and the Liberal State 1789-1939: A Study of Literature and Social Psychology*, 135.

25 Maurizio Isabella, "Citizens or Faithful? Religion and the Liberal Revolutions of the 1820s in Southern Europe," *Modern Intellectual History* 12, no. 3 (2015), 556.

26 Isabella, "Citizens or Faithful? Religion and the Liberal Revolutions of the 1820s in Southern Europe," 556, 560.

27 Virginia H. Aksan, "Mobilization of Warrior Populations in the Ottoman Context, 1750-1850," in *Fighting for a Living: A Comparative History of Military Labour 1500-2000*, ed. Erik Jan Zürcher (Amsterdam: Amsterdam University Press, 2013), 341.

28 Nikiforos Diamantouros, *Oi Aparches Tes Sygkroteses Sygchronou Kratous Sten Ellada 1821-1828* (Athens: Morphotiko Idryma Ethnikis Trapezis, 2006), 78; Dennis P. Hupchick, *The Bulgarians in the Seventeenth Century: Slavic Orthodox Society and Culture under Ottoman Rule* (Jefferson: McFarland, 1993), 30, 69–70.

29 Kontogiorgis, *Koinonike Dynamike Kai Politike Autodioikise*, 34, 41, 42, 49; François Charles Hughes Laurent Pouqueville, *Taxidi Sten Ellada - Epeiros* (Athens: Afoi Tolidi, 1994), 67.

30 Zens, "In the Name of the Sultan: Haci Mustafa Pasha of Belgrade and Ottoman Provincial Rule in the Late 18th Century," *International Journal of Middle East Studies* 44 (2012), 134, 136.

31 Ibid., 139, 140.

32 Theod E. Theodorou, *E Ellenike Topike Autodioikise*, vol. 1 (Afoi Tolidi, 1996), 194, 195; Kontogiorgis, *Koinonike Dynamike Kai Politike Autodioikise*, 80, 101;

Diamantouros, *Oi Aparches Tes Sygkroteses Sygchronou Kratous Sten Ellada 1821-1828,* 83.

33 Dean J. Kostantaras, "Christian Elites of the Peloponnese and the Ottoman State, 1715-1821," *European History Quarterly* 43, no. 4 (2013): 635, 637, 638; Anastasia Kyrkini-Koutoula, *E Othomanike Dioikese Sten Ellada: E Periptose Tes Peloponnesou (1715-1821)* (Athens: Ekdoseis Arsenidi, 1996), 142, 148,157; Theodorou, *E Ellenike Topike Autodioikese,* 1, 194–95.

34 Aksan "Mobilization of Warrior Populations in the Ottoman Context, 1750-1850," 347–48.

35 Diamantouros, *Oi Aparches Tes Sygkroteses Sygchronou Kratous Sten Ellada 1821-1828,* 98.

36 Grégoire Bron, "Learning Lessons From the Iberian Peninsula: Italian Exiles and the Making of a Risorgimento without People (1820-48)," in *Mediterranean Diasporas, Politics and Ideas in the Long 19th Century,* eds. Maurizio Isabella and Konstantina Zanou (New York: Bloomsbury, 2016), 60, 61.

37 Isabella, "Citizens or Faithful? Religion and the Liberal Revolutions of the 1820s in Southern Europe," 557, 556.

38 Gabriel Paquette, "An Itinerant Liberal: Almeida Garret's Exilic Itineraries and Political Ideas in the Age of Southern European Revolutions (1820-34)," in *Mediterranean Diasporas, Politics and Ideas in the Long 19th Century,* eds. Maurizio Isabella and Konstantina Zanou (New York: Bloomsbury, 2016), 51; Isabella, "Mediterranean Liberals? Italian Revolutionaries and the Making of a Colonial Sea, Ca. 1800-30," 79.

39 K. W. Arafat, "A Legacy of Islam in Greece: Ali Pasha and Ioannina," *Bulletin (British Society of Middle Eastern Studies)* 14, no. 2 (1987): 173.

40 See Ieromonachos Agathaggelos, "Prorresis Etoi Profeteia," ed. Aristotle University of Thessaloniki (1810), Such prophesies could serve multiple ends and Russia was among those who tried to exploit them (Konstantina Zanou, "Imperial Nationalism and Orthodox Enlightenment: A Diasporic Story between the Ionian Islands, Russia and Greece, Ca. 1800-30," in *Mediterranean Diasporas, Politics and Ideas in the Long 19th Century,* eds. Maurizio Isabella and Konstantina Zanou (New York: Bloomsbury, 2016), 119.

41 Svoronos, *To Elleniko Ethnos: Genese Kai Diamorphose Tou Newou Ellenismou,* 84.

42 Agios Kosmas o Aitolos, *Didachai Kai Profeteiai Ag. Kosma Tou Aitolou* (Athens: Ekdoseis Lydia), 39, 44.

43 A strong alcoholic drink.

44 Charalambos Vasilopoulos, *Kosmas Aitolos O Ellin Ierapostolos* (Athens: Panellinios Orthodoxos Enosis, 1961), 154.

45 François Charles Hughes Laurent Pouqueville, *Taxidi Stin Ellada - Sterea Ellada, Attiki, Korinthos* (Athens: Ekdoseis Afon. Tolidi, 1995), 33–34.

46 Vasilopoulos, *Kosmas Aitolos O Ellin Ierapostolos,* 152.

47 Panagiotis F. Christopoulos, "E Evraiki Koinotes Navpaktou," *Epeteris Etaireias Stereoelladikon Meleton* A (1968): 291.

48 Henry Holland, *Taxidia Sta Ionia Nesia, Epeiro, Alvania (1812-1813)* (Athens: Afoi Tolidi, 1989), 99, 174; Arafat, "A Legacy of Islam in Greece: Ali Pasha and Ioannina," 176. For more on Ali Pasha see K. E. Fleming, *The Muslim Bonaparte: Diplomacy and Orientalism in Ali Pasha's Greece* (Princeton: Princeton University Press, 1999).

49 Holland, *Taxidia Sta Ionia Nesia, Epeiro, Alvania (1812-1813),* 78.

50 D. P. Petrokokkinou, *Chioi, Evraioi Kai Genovezoi* (Athens: Estia, 1912), 6.

51 A. P. Koutsalexis, *Diaferonda Kai Perierga Tina Istorimata* (Athens: Ekdoseis Vergina, 1996), 126. It should be noted that Jews were not the only minorities used for such roles. Centuries later similar imagery can be found in accounts of the Ottoman past involving Roma as in Ivo Andric's famous novel Bridge on the Drina.

52 Theodoros Kolokotronis, *Apomnimonevmata*, ed. Georgios Tertsetis (Athens: Ekdoseis Vergina, 1996), 40; Paschalis Kitromilides, "Republican Aspirations in Southeastern Europe in the Age of the French Revolution," in *Consortium on Revolutionary Europe, 1750-1850: Proceedings* (Athens: Consortium on Revolutionary Europe, 1980), 280.

53 Patriarch of Jerusalem Anthimos, *Didaskalia Patrike* (Constantinople: Ioannis Pagos ex Armenion, 1798), 10, 14.

54 Richard Clogg, "The 'Dhidhaskalia Patriki' (1798): An Orthodox Reaction to French Revolutionary Propaganda," *Middle Eastern Studies* 5, no. 2 (1969): 91; Kitromilides, "Republican Aspirations in Southeastern Europe in the Age of the French Revolution," 279–80.

55 Kyrkini-Koutoula, *E Othomanike Dioikese Sten Ellada: E Periptose Tes Peloponnesou (1715-1821),* 100–101.

56 See K. Th Dimaras, *Neoellenikos Diaphotismos* (Athens: Ermis, 1977); Paschalis M. Kitromilides, *Enlightenment and Revolution: The Making of Modern Greece* (Cambridge: Harvard University Press, 2013).

57 Efthymiou, *Evraioi Kai Christianoi Sta Tourkokratoumena Nesia Tou Notioanatolikou Aigaiou: Oi Dyskoles Plevres Mias Gonimes Synyparxes*, 115; Ali Arslan, *O Ellenikos Typos Sto Othomaniko Kratos* (Athens: Eptalofos, 2004), 16.

58 Alexandros Mavrokordatos, *Istoria Iera Etoi Ta Ioudaika* (Bucarest 1716).

59 This is often translated as "Rights of Man" but Human is a more accurate translation of the word Rigas used (*anthropou*) as opposed to man (*andros*) not to mention the fact that unlike the French prototype Rigas explicitly referred to women on several occasions in the text.

60 I. I. Vranousis, *Rigas* (Athens: I Zacharopoulos, 1953), 372; Giannis Kordatos, *Rigas Pheraios Kai I Balkaniki Omospondia* (Athens: Ioan, & P. Zacharopoulos, 1945), 136; *Epilekta Nomika Keimena Tes Ethnikes Paliggenesias*, (Athens Tameio Nomikon, 1971), 14.

61 Vranousis, *Rigas,* 371, 372, 377; *Epilekta Nomika Keimena Tes Ethnikes Paliggenesias.* 12, 14, 19, 21.

62 *Epilekta Nomika Keimena Tes Ethnikes Paliggenesias,* 14.

63 Ibid., 20.

64 Elpida K. Vogli, *Ellenes to Genos: E Ithageneia Kai E Taytoteta Sto Ethniko Kratos Ton Ellenon (1821-1844)* (Irakleio: Panepistimiakes Ekdoseis Kritis, 2008), 38.

65 Kordatos, *Rigas Pheraios Kai I Balkaniki Omospondia,* 124.

66 Vranousis, *Rigas,* 393.

67 Ibid., 378.

68 Ibid., 388. In 1962 a manuscript was found in Bucharest that included Jews in Article 122 of the "Constitution" and Woodhouse has argued that there is no reason for Rigas to have excluded them in the original (C. M. Woodhouse, *Rigas Velestinlis: The Proto-Martyr of the Greek Revolution* (Limni, Evia: Denise Harvey, 1995), 75).

69 Anonymous, *Elliniki Nomarchia Itoi Logos Peri Eleftherias* (Athens: Ekdoseis Aimopas, n.d.), 108. His anticlericalism is common among liberal intellectuals of the Mediterranean who frequently condemned priests for their counterrevolutionary activities (Bron. 62).

70 Anonymous, *Elliniki Nomarchia Itoi Logos Peri Eleftherias*, 192.

71 Ibid., 192–97.

72 Diamantouros, *Oi Aparches Tes Sygkroteses Sygchronou Kratous Sten Ellada 1821-1828*, 38, 43.

73 Adamantios Koraes, "Report on the Present State of Civilization in Greece," in *Nationalism in Asia and Africa*, ed. Elie Kedourie (New York: World Publishing Company, 1970), 156, 186.

74 Diamantouros, *Oi Aparches Tes Sygkroteses Sygchronou Kratous Sten Ellada 1821-1828*, 76.

75 Fotakos, *Apomnimonevmata*, vol. A (Athens: Ekdoseis Vergina, 1996), 19.

76 Spyridon Trikoupis, *Istoria Tis Ellinikis Epanastaseos*, vol. A (Athens: Giovanis, 1978), 10; *Epilekta Nomika Keimena Tes Ethnikes Paliggenesias*, 37.

77 *Epilekta Nomika Keimena Tes Ethnikes Paliggenesias*, 40.

78 Ibid., 44.

79 Irvin Cemil Schick, "Christian Maids, Turkish Revishes: The Sexualization of National Conflict in the Late Ottoman Period," in *Women in the Ottoman Balkans: Gender, Culture and History*, eds. Amila Buturovic and Irvin Cemil Schick (New York: I. B. Tauris, 2007), 280, 282.

80 *Epilekta Nomika Keimena Tes Ethnikes Paliggenesias*, 42; Vogli, *Ellenes to Genos: E Ithageneia Kai E Taytoteta Sto Ethniko Kratos Ton Ellenon (1821-1844)*, 43. Much later the famed commander of the Greek forces during the insurrection Theodore Kolokotronis again reaffirmed that the Greek revolution was not like those of Europe because it was a national one (Kolokotronis, *Apomnimonevmata*, 175).

81 *Epilekta Nomika Keimena Tes Ethnikes Paliggenesias*, 47.

82 Michael Glencross, "Greece Restored: Greece and the Greek War of Independence in French Romantic Historiography 1821-1830," *Journal of European Studies* xxvii (1997): 33, 35.

83 François-René de Chateaubriand, *Odoiporikon Ek Parision Eis Ierosolyma Kai Ex Ierosolymon Eis Parisious*, vol. A (Athens: Afoi. Tolidi, 1979 (1860)), 55; Pavlos Karolidis, *O Germanikos Filellenismos* (Athens 1917), 8, 18.

84 Robert Walpole, *Memoirs Relating to European and Asiatic Turkey* (London: Longman, Hurst, Rees, Orme, and Brown, 1818), 19; Bernard Randolph, *The Present State of the Morea, Called Anciently Peloponnesus: Together with a Description of the City of Athens, Islands of Zant, Strafades, and Serigo* (London: Will. Notts, 1689), 17.

85 Christopoulos, "E Evraiki Koinotes Navpaktou," 289.

86 Dimitrios Gr Kampouroglou, *Istoriai Ton Athenaion*, vol. 2 (Athens: Palmos N Antonopoulos & Sia, 1968), 158, 161.

87 Finlay, *A History of Greece from Its Conquest by the Romans to the Present Time*, VI Part I, 30.

88 Andreas Z. Mamoukas, ed., *Ta Kata Ten Anagennesin Tes Ellados Etoi Sylloge Ton Peri Ten Anagennomenen Ellada Syntachthenton Politeumaton, Nomon, Kai Allon Episemon Praxeon, Apo Tou 1821 Mechri Telous Tou 1832*, vol. 9 (Pireaus Ilia Christophidou Typografia Agathi Tychi, 1839), 59–65; Georg Ludwig von Maurer, *O Ellenikos Laos* (Athens: Afoi Tolidi, 1976), 317.

89 Finlay, *A History of Greece from Its Conquest by the Romans to the Present Time*, VI Part I, 174; John L. Comstock, *History of the Greek Revolution; Compiled from the Official Documents of the Greek Government* (New York: William W Reed & Co., 1828), 152; Gustav Friedrich Hertzberg, *Istoria Tes Ellenikes Epanastaseos*, trans. Pavlos Karolidis, vol. I (Athens: Georgios D Fexis, 1916), 8, 55; W. St. Clair, *That Greece Might Still Be Free: The Philhellenes in the War of Independence* (London:

Oxford University Press, 1972), 1–2, 12; Henry Wheaton, *Elements of International Law* (Boston: Little, Brown and Company, 1866 (1836)), 115.

90 Thomas Gordon, *History of the Greek Revolution*, vol. I (Edinburgh: William Blackwood, 1844), 100; Comstock, *History of the Greek Revolution; Compiled from the Official Documents of the Greek Government*, 149; Sophia Laiou, "The Greek Revolution in the Morea According to the Description of an Ottoman Official," in *The Greek Revolution of 1821: A European Event*, ed. Petros Pizanias (Istanbul: The Isis Press, 2011), 246.

91 Virginia H. Aksan, "Expressions of Ottoman Rule in an Age of Transition: 1760 and 1830," in *Hoca, 'Allame, Ouits De Science: Essays in Honor of Kemal H Karpat*, eds. Kaan Durukan, Robert W Zens, and Akile Zorlu-Durukan (Istanbul: The Isis Press, 2010), 90, 91.

92 Finlay, *A History of Greece from Its Conquest by the Romans to the Present Time*, VI Part I, 119, 120, 121; Hertzberg, *Istoria Tes Ellenikes Epanastaseos*, I. 7, 26, 105, 120, 121, 124.

93 Finlay, *A History of Greece from Its Conquest by the Romans to the Present Time*, VI Part I, 148–49, 151, 161–65, 215, ibid., 218–20, 226–27, 283; Hertzberg, *Istoria Tes Ellenikes Epanastaseos*, II, 49, 60–61, 83, 97, 160, 177–79; Gordon, *History of the Greek Revolution*, I, 149, 244–45, 401, 414, *History of the Greek Revolution*, vol. II (Edinburgh: William Blackwood, 1832), 49–52; Comstock, *History of the Greek Revolution; Compiled from the Official Documents of the Greek Government*, 153, 177–78, 187; Fotakos, *Apomnimonevmata*, A, 73, 198, 201; François Charles Hughes Laurent Pouqueville, *Istoria Tis Ellinikis Epanastasis*, vol. 1 (Athens: Afoi. Tolidi, 1996), 135; Kolokotronis, *Apomnimonevmata*, 90; Antoniou Andrea Miaouli, *Synoptike Istoria Ton Yper Tes Elevtherias Tes Anagennetheises Ellados Genomenon Navmachion Dia Ton Ploion Ton Trion Neson Ydras, Spatson Kai Psaron* (Athens: Ekdoseis Vergina, 1996), 34; and Palaion Patron Germanos, *Apomnemonevmata* (Athens: Vergina, 1996), 68.

94 Finlay, *A History of Greece from Its Conquest by the Romans to the Present Time*, VI Part I, 92, 148, 149, 163, 192, 220; Kremmydas, *E Ellenike Epanastase Tou 1821: Tekmeria, Anapselafeseis, Emeneies*, 91; Germanos, *Apomnemonevmata*, 68; and Kolokotronis, *Apomnimonevmata*, 92.

95 Pouqueville, *Istoria Tis Ellinikis Epanastasis*, 1, 25.

96 Efthymiou, *Evraioi Kai Christianoi Sta Tourkokratoumena Nesia Tou Notioanatolikou Aigaiou: Oi Dyskoles Plevres Mias Gonimes Synyparxes*, 77.

97 Finlay, *A History of Greece from Its Conquest by the Romans to the Present Time*, VI Part I, 180 185, 189, 190–91; Hertzberg, *Istoria Tes Ellenikes Epanastaseos*, I. 26; Ibid., 19, 73, 105, 120–21, 124–25; F. C. H. Pouqueville, *Istoria Tes Ellenikes Epanastaseos Etoi E Anagennesis Tes Ellados*, trans. Ioannis Th. Zafeiropoulos, vol. III (Athens: A Georgiou, P Tzelatou, G Fexi, 1890), 4, 12, 14–15. 31; 32; Gordon, *History of the Greek Revolution*, I, 188, 190–91, 311, 328; *History of the Greek Revolution*, II, 16; Miaouli, *Synoptike Istoria Ton Yper Tes Elevtherias Tes Anagennetheises Ellados Genomenon Navmachion Dia Ton Ploion Ton Trion Neson Ydras, Spatson Kai Psaron*, 16; Trikoupis, *Istoria Tis Ellinikis Epanastaseos*, A, 78, 94, 248; and Petros Mengous, *Apo Te Smyrni Sten Ellada Tou 1821: E Afegese Tou Petrou Meggou* (Ioannina: Isnafi, 2009 (1830)), 120, 126.

98 Finlay, *A History of Greece from Its Conquest by the Romans to the Present Time*, VI Part I, 260–61, 363, 345, 371; Pouqueville, III. 287–304; Comstock, *History of the Greek Revolution; Compiled from the Official Documents of the Greek Government*, 221; and Gordon, *History of the Greek Revolution*, I, 158.

99 Finlay, *A History of Greece from Its Conquest by the Romans to the Present Time*, VI Part I, 181, 190–91, 345, 363; Gordon, *History of the Greek Revolution*, I, 287.

100 Fotakos, *Apomnimonevmata*, A, 132–33; Finlay, *A History of Greece from Its Conquest by the Romans to the Present Time*, VI Part I, 208; Hertzberg, *Istoria Tes Ellenikes Epanastaseos*, II. 20; and Trikoupis, *Istoria Tis Ellinikis Epanastaseos*, B, 174.

101 Finlay, *A History of Greece from Its Conquest by the Romans to the Present Time*, VI Part I, 183.

102 Ibid., 139, 152, 164, 217; Fotakos, *Vioi Pelopponision Andron* (Athens: Ekdoseis Vergina, 1996), 15.

103 Finlay, *A History of Greece from Its Conquest by the Romans to the Present Time*, VI Part I, 120, 198–99, 315; Hertzberg, *Istoria Tes Ellenikes Epanastaseos*, I, 11, 37, 134; and Ibid., II, 114, 148.

104 Antonios Andreas Kriezis, *Apomnimonevmata* (Athens: Ekdoseis Vergina, 1996), 143–46.

105 Miaouli, *Synoptike Istoria Ton Yper Tes Elevtherias Tes Anagennetheises Ellados Genomenon Navmachion Dia Ton Ploion Ton Trion Neson Ydras, Spatson Kai Psaron*, 11; Gordon, *History of the Greek Revolution*, I, 168; Pouqueville, *Istoria Tis Ellinikis Epanastasis*, 1, 108–109; and Hertzberg, *Istoria Tes Ellenikes Epanastaseos*, I, 77.

106 "that most atrocious massacre of the seven thousand Turks and one thousand Jews, which no other European nation could have perpetrated but of which there is no doubt." (William Gell, *Narrative of a Journey in the Morea* (London: Longman, Hurst, Rees, Orne, and Brown, 1832), 311).

107 Kolokotronis, *Apomnimonevmata*, 90.

108 William Martin Leake, *Historical Outline of the Greek Revolution* (London: John Murray, 1826), 55.

109 Konstantinos Koumas, *Oi Ellenes (Istoriai Ton Anthropinon Praxeon Apo Ton Archaiotaton Chronon Eos Ton Emeron Mas)* (Athens: Notis Karavias, 1966), 622.

110 Fotakos, *Apomnimonevmata*, A, 202.

111 Ibid., 223.

112 Fotakos, *Vioi Pelopponision Andron*, 78.

113 Trikoupis, *Istoria Tis Ellinikis Epanastaseos*, B, 93.

114 Mengous, *Apo Te Smyrni Sten Ellada Tou 1821: E Afegese Tou Petrou Meggou*, 99. Dionysios Skylosofos led a revolt against the Ottomans at Janina. When the revolt failed Dionysios was captured, being allegedly betrayed by Jews, and skinned alive. As a result of the revolt the Christians were expelled from the *Kastro*, the fortified part of the town which became exclusively Muslim and Jewish. (Rae Delven, *The Jews of Janina* (Philadelphia: Cadmus Press, 1990), 20 and Dimitrios St. Salamagas, *Peripatoi Sta Jiannina* (Ioanina: Ekdoseis Etaireias Epirotikon Meleton, 1993), 25, 40, 67) (MOVE to earlier mention).

115 Fleming, *Greece a Jewish History*, 16.

116 "and as a consummation of ignominy in the eyes of the Greeks, his body (Patriarch Gregory) was delivered to Jews to be dragged through the streets." Leake, *Historical Outline of the Greek Revolution*, 47).

117 Trikoupis, *Istoria Tis Ellinikis Epanastaseos*, A, 86.

118 Robert Walsh, *A Residence at Constantinople* (London 1836), 316–17; Pouqueville, *Istoria Tis Ellinikis Epanastasis*, 1, 76; Hertzberg, *Istoria Tes Ellenikes Epanastaseos*, I, 94; Finlay, *A History of Greece from Its Conquest by the Romans to the Present Time*, VI Part I, 187–88; Comstock, *History of the Greek Revolution; Compiled from the Official Documents of the Greek Government*, 442; and Trikoupis, *Istoria Tis Ellinikis Epanastaseos*, A, 86.

119 Fotakos, *Apomnimonevmata*, A, 202.

120 Trikoupis, *Istoria Tis Ellinikis Epanastaseos*, B, 199.

121 Pouqueville, *Istoria Tis Ellinikis Epanastasis*, 1, 216.

122 Pouqueville, III, 40, 117, 302; Comstock, *History of the Greek Revolution; Compiled from the Official Documents of the Greek Government*, 168, 441.

123 Pouqueville, III, 38, 39, 52, 331, 332.

124 Pouqueville, *Istoria Tis Ellinikis Epanastasis*, 1, 202–04.

125 Ibid., 511.

126 Ibid.

127 Trikoupis, *Istoria Tis Ellinikis Epanastaseos*, B, 174.

128 Ioannis K. Vasdravellis, *Oi Makedones Kata Ten Epanastase Tou 1821* (Thessaloniki 1967), 128, 129, 130, 182, 206; and Hertzberg, *Istoria Tes Ellenikes Epanastaseos*, II, 19.

129 Vasdravellis, *Oi Makedones Kata Ten Epanastase Tou 1821*, 134–35.

130 Unless they were particularly wealthy of course. Leake mentions regarding the capture of Tripoli that "several rich Turks and Jews purchased the promise of a safe conduct from Kolokotroni and Mavromichali; but these, though they received the price of their engagements, were never able to execute them." (Leake, *Historical Outline of the Greek Revolution*, 54) See also the Fotakos quote regarding Tripolitsa above.

131 Pouqueville, III. 123; Fleming, *Greece a Jewish History*, 17; and Comstock, *History of the Greek Revolution; Compiled from the Official Documents of the Greek Government*, 185.

132 Fotakos, *Apomnimonevmata*, A, 198, 201; Germanos, *Apomnemonevmata*, 66, 68; Dimitrios Ainianos, *Apomnemonevmata Gia Ten Epanastase Tou 1821* (Athens: Ekdoseis Vergina, 1996), 56–59; St. Clair, *That Greece Might Still Be Free: The Philhellenes in the War of Independence*, 45; Gordon, *History of the Greek Revolution*, I, 245.

133 Josef Nehama, *Istoria Ton Israeliton Tes Salonikes*, vol. II (Thessaloniki: University Studio Press, 2000), 1155.

134 Local stories suggested that the town had been founded by Jews expelled from Lepanto, Aggelokastro, and Akarnania (Pouqueville, *Taxidi Stin Ellada - Sterea Ellada, Attiki, Korinthos*), 294.

135 Trikoupis, *Istoria Tis Ellinikis Epanastaseos*, A, 266.

136 Nehama, *Istoria Ton Israeliton Tes Salonikes*, II, 868, 1154, 1156; Ibid., III, 1354, 1361.

137 Delven. 29; Nehama, *Istoria Ton Israeliton Tes Salonikes*, II, 1157.

138 Aser R. Moysis, *E Filia Ellenon Kai Israeliton Dia Mesou Ton Aionon* (Athens: Israilitiki Morfotiki Leschi Thessalonikis "I Adelphotis," 1953), 22; Moysi K. Konstantini, *E Symvole Ton Evraion Eis Ton Apeleftherotikon Agona Ton Ellenon* (Athens 1971), 7, 11, 13; and Karolidis, *O Germanikos Filellenismos*, 25, 26.

139 Almog, *Nationalism and Antisemitism in Modern Europe 1815-1945*, 18.

140 Pouqueville, III, 43; Comstock, *History of the Greek Revolution; Compiled from the Official Documents of the Greek Government*, 173.

141 Gordon, *History of the Greek Revolution*, I, 229; Laiou, "The Greek Revolution in the Morea According to the Description of an Ottoman Official," 247.

142 Fleming, *Greece a Jewish History*, 17.

143 Aksan, "Expressions of Ottoman Rule in an Age of Transition: 1760 and 1830," 90; Lucien J. Frary, "Russian Consuls and the Greek War of Independence (1821–31)," *Mediterranean Historical Review* 28, no. 1 (2013): 47.

144 Kostas Kostis, *Ta Kakomathemena Paidia Tes Istorias: E Diamorfose Tou Neoellenikou Kratous 18os-21os Aionas* (Athens: Polis, 2013), 160.

145 *Epilekta Nomika Keimena Tes Ethnikes Paliggenesias*, 93.

146 Vasilis Kremmydas, "E Diakyvernese Kapodistria: Koinonia, Politike, Ideologia," in *O Kyvernetes Ioannis Kapodistrias*, ed. Giorgos Georgis (Athens: Kastaniotis, 2015), 53.

147 1832 Convention, "Convention between Great Britain, France, and Russia, on the One Part, and Bavaria on the Other, Relative to the Sovereignty of Greece," *The American Journal of International Law* 12, no. 2 (1918): 72, 73.

148 Eleonora Naxidou, "National Identity in the 19th-Century Balkans: The Case of Hatzichristos," *Nationalism and Ethnic Politics* 17, no. 3 (2011): 322–23.

149 Naxidou, "National Identity in the 19th-Century Balkans: The Case of Hatzichristos," 324, 326, 327–28.

150 Dimitrios Ainianos, *Georgios Karaiskakis* (Athens: Ekdoseis Vergina, 1996), 66; Fotakos, *Apomnimonevmata*, A, 331403, 404; *Apomnemonevmata Tou 1821*, vol. B (Athens: Ekdoseis Vergina, 1996), 39, 186; Kolokotronis, *Apomnimonevmata*, 89, 189; and Gordon, *History of the Greek Revolution*, II, 174.

151 Naxidou, "National Identity in the 19th-Century Balkans: The Case of Hatzichristos," 330.

152 Finlay, *A History of Greece from Its Conquest by the Romans to the Present Time*, VI Part I, 28, 29.

153 Vogli, *Ellenes to Genos: E Ithageneia Kai E Taytoteta Sto Ethniko Kratos Ton Ellenon (1821-1844)*, 46, 48.

154 Alexandros Svolos, *Ta Ellinika Syntagmata 1822-1975/1986. I Syntagmatiki Istoria Tis Ellados* (Athens: Stochastis, 1998), 108, 121.

155 Svolos, *Ta Ellinika Syntagmata 1822-1975/1986. I Syntagmatiki Istoria Tis Ellados*, 122.

156 Ibid., 107–08.

157 Ibid., 135–38. The restriction did not extend to higher clergy which had held significant posts in the revolutionary governments.

158 Ibid., 150.

159 Charles Frazee, "Catholics," in *Minorities in Greece Aspects of a Plural Society*, ed. Richard Clogg (London: Hurst & Company, 2002), 34.

160 Charles A. Frazee, "The Greek Catholic Islanders and the Revolution of 1821," *East European Quarterly* 13, no. 3 (1979): 321, 322.

161 J. L. S. Bartholdy, *Taxidiotikes Entyposeis Apo Ten Ellada 1803-1804* (Athens: Ekati, 1993), 155; see also Eleni Koukkou, *Oi Koinotekoi Thesmoi Stis Kyklades Kata Ten Tourkokratia* (Athens: Istoriki kai Ethnologiki Etaireia tis Ellados, 1980), 84, 180, 207.

162 Maurer, *O Ellenikos Laos*, 325; Gordon, *History of the Greek Revolution*, I, 472–473; *History of the Greek Revolution*, II, 17; Hertzberg, *Istoria Tes Ellenikes Epanastaseos*, II, 101; Charles A. Frazee, *The Orthodox Church and Independent Greece 1821-1852* (Cambridge: Cambridge University Press, 1969), 43; Pouqueville, III. 250; Vogli, *Ellenes to Genos: E Ithageneia Kai E Taytoteta Sto Ethniko Kratos Ton Ellenon (1821-1844)*, 178.

163 *Le Courrier de Smyrne*, Vol. II, No. 57 (March 22, 1829), 1.

164 Vogli, *Ellenes to Genos: E Ithageneia Kai E Taytoteta Sto Ethniko Kratos Ton Ellenon (1821-1844)*, 79.

165 Finlay, *A History of Greece from Its Conquest by the Romans to the Present Time*, VII Part II, 130; Vogli, *Ellenes to Genos: E Ithageneia Kai E Taytoteta Sto Ethniko Kratos Ton Ellenon (1821-1844)*, 74.

166 Constanine Michailovitz Bazili, *Enas Rosos Sten Ellada Tou Kapodistria* (Athens: Kalentis, 2000), 37; Hertzberg, *Istoria Tes Ellenikes Epanastaseos*, II, 172.

167 Ainianos, *Apomnemonevmata Gia Ten Epanastase Tou 1821*, 7, 50; Comstock, *History of the Greek Revolution; Compiled from the Official Documents of the Greek Government*, 357.

168 Anastasios Polyzoidis, *Keimena Gia Te Demokratia 1824-1825*, eds. Filimon Paionidis and Elpida Vogli (Athens: Ekdoseis Okto, 2011), 73–75.

169 Vogli, *Ellenes to Genos: E Ithageneia Kai E Taytoteta Sto Ethniko Kratos Ton Ellenon (1821-1844)*, 59.

170 Adamantios Korais, *Semeioseis Eis to Prosorinon Politevma Tes Ellados Tou 1822 Etous* (Athens 1983), 9.

171 Korais, *Semeioseis Eis to Prosorinon Politevma Tes Ellados Tou 1822 Etous*, 10.

172 Ibid., 12–13.

173 Ibid., 14–17.

174 Isabella, "Citizens or Faithful? Religion and the Liberal Revolutions of the 1820s in Southern Europe," 575.

175 Pouqueville, III. 302. Vogli, *Ellenes to Genos: E Ithageneia Kai E Taytoteta Sto Ethniko Kratos Ton Ellenon (1821-1844)*, 69.

176 U. Ozkirimli and S. Sofos, *Tormented by History: Nationalism in Greece and Turkey* (London: Hurst and Company, 2008), 145–46.

177 Fotakos, *Apomnimonevmata*, A, 321.

178 Spyridon G. Ploumidis, "To Orama Tou Ioanni Kapodistria Gia to Elleniko Ethnos Kai Ten Koinonia," in *O Kyvernetes Ioannis Kapodistrias*, ed. Giorgos Georgis (Athens: Kastaniotis, 2015), 76.

179 Ploumidis, "To Orama Tou Ioanni Kapodistria Gia to Elleniko Ethnos Kai Ten Koinonia," 72, 73, 77–78; *Epilekta Nomika Keimena Tes Ethnikes Paliggenesias*, 98, 106.

180 Giorgos Georgis, "E Anatolike Politike Tou Kyvernete Ioanni Kapodistria," in *O Kyvernetes Ioannis Kapodistrias*, ed. Giorgos Georgis (Athens: Kastaniotis, 2015), 180, 186; Ploumidis, "To Orama Tou Ioanni Kapodistria Gia to Elleniko Ethnos Kai Ten Koinonia," 79.

181 Georgis, "E Anatolike Politike Tou Kyvernete Ioanni Kapodistria," 184, 192; Hertzberg, *Istoria Tes Ellenikes Epanastaseos*, IV, 29.

182 Pouqueville, III, 293–94, 302, 303.

183 Georgis, "E Anatolike Politike Tou Kyvernete Ioanni Kapodistria," 187–88.

184 Apostolos E. Vakalopoulos, *Aichmalotoi Ellenon Kata Ten Epanastase Tou 1821* (Athens: Irodotos, 2000), 10, 23; Hertzberg, *Istoria Tes Ellenikes Epanastaseos*, III, 11, 12.

185 Fotakos, *Apomnimonevmata*, A, 209.

186 Vakalopoulos, *Aichmalotoi Ellenon Kata Ten Epanastase Tou 1821*, 7, 24, 39, 46.

187 Ibid., 11, 21.

188 Ibid., 52–55; Trikoupis, *Istoria Tis Ellinikis Epanastaseos*, B, 239.

189 Georgis, "E Anatolike Politike Tou Kyvernete Ioanni Kapodistria," 189.

190 Michael Molho, "Le Judaisme Grec En General Et La Communaute Juive De Salonique En Particulier Entre Les Deux Guerres Mondiales," in *Homenaje a Millas-Villicrosa* (Barcelona: Consejo Superior de Investigaciones Cientificas, 1956), 75–76; Fleming, *Greece a Jewish History*, 17.

191 Politikon Syntagma Tes Ellados, Ch. B' Demosion e Koinon Dikaion Ton Ellenon, Par. 1 Peri Threskeias, Art. 6. Pg. 1, Navplio March 15, 1832.

192 Politikon Syntagma Tes Ellados, Ch. B' Demosion e Koinon Dikaion Ton Ellenon, Par. 3 Peri Patriografeseos kai Politografeseos, Art. 16. Pg. 5, Navplio March 15, 1832.

193 Politikon Syntagma Tes Ellados, Ch. B' Demosion e Koinon Dikaion Ton Ellenon, Par. 1 Peri Threskeias, Art. 6. Pg. 1, Navplio March 15, 1832.

194 Politikon Syntagma Tes Ellados, Ch. ST' Peri tou Nomotelestikou, Par. 1 Peri tes Exousias tou Egemonos, Art. 220. Pg. 31, Navplio March 15, 1832.

195 Politikon Syntagma Tes Ellados, Ch. B' Demosion e Koinon Dikaion Ton Ellenon, Par. 4 Koina Dikaia kai Chree ton Ellenon, Art. 27, 29, 30. Pg. 6–7, Navplio March 15, 1832.

196 A. Mansola, *Politeiografikai Pleroforiai Peri Ellados* (Athens: Ethniko Typografeio, 1867), 2, 19. Significantly even the non-Orthodox Christian population indicates a marked decline since prior to the Greek War of Independence just in the islands of Syros and Tinos the Catholic population numbered over 14,000 (Frazee, *The Orthodox Church and Independent Greece 1821-1852*, 32–33) and Thiersch estimated the number of Catholics in Greece at the end of the conflict at 30,000 (Friedrich Thiersch, *E Ellada Tou Kapodistria*, vol. B (Athens: Afoi Tolidi, 1972), Dalegre also estimates over 90,000 Muslims in the lands that become part of Greece in 1821 a third higher than official Greek statistics (Joelle Dalegre, *Grecs Et Ottoamns 1453-1923* (Paris: L' Harmattan, 2002), 109).

Chapter 3

1 Finlay, *A History of Greece from Its Conquest by the Romans to the Present Time*, VII Part II, 54.

2 Nikolaos I. Pantazopoulos, "Georg Ludwig Von Maurer, E Pros Evropaika Protypa Oloklerotike Strofe Tes Neoellenikes Nomothesias," *Epistimoniki Epetiris Scholis Nomikon kai Oikonomikon Epistimon* 13 (1968): 1346–1506; John Anthony Petropoulos and Aikaterini Koumarianou, *E Themeliose Tou Ellenikou Kratous 1833-1843* (Athens: Ekdoseis Papazisi, 1982), 16.20.

3 G. A. Rallis and M. Potlis, *Oi Ellenikoi Kodikes Meta Ton Tropopoiounton Autous Neoteron Nomon Kai Vasilikon Diatagmaton Eis Prosetethesan to Politiko Syntagma Tes Ellados*, vol. A (Athens: G Chartofylakas, 1844), 203.

4 B. K. Nikolopoulos and A. I. Kakoulidis, eds., *Sylloge Apanton Ton Nomon, Diatagmaton, Egkyklion, Odegion, Kai Eidopoieseon Ton Ypourgeion, Synthekon Tes Ellados Meta Ton Allon Ethnon*, vol. 1 (Athens: Typois Ch. Nikolaidoy Filadelfeos, 1859), 213.

5 Thomas Drikos, *E Porneia Sten Ermoupole to 19o Aiona (1820-1900)* (Athens: Ellinika Grammata, 2002); Kostis, *Ta Kakomathemena Paidia Tes Istorias: E Diamorfose Tou Neoellenikou Kratous 18os-21os Aionas,* 248.

6 Finlay, *A History of Greece from Its Conquest by the Romans to the Present Time*, VI Part I, 3, 7, 8.

7 Ibid., 11.

8 Marios Hatzopoulos, "From Resurrection to Insurrection: 'Sacred' Myths, Motifs, and Symbols in the Greek War of Independence," in *The Making of Modern Greece: Nationalism, Romanticism and the Uses of the Past (1797-1896)*, ed. Roderick Beaton and David Ricks (New York: Ashgate, 2009), 88, 90.

9 Diamantouros, *Oi Aparches Tes Sygkroteses Sygchronou Kratous Sten Ellada 1821-1828*, 241; Finlay, *A History of Greece from Its Conquest by the Romans to the Present Time*, VII Part II, 126.

10 Friedrich Thiersch, *E Ellada Tou Kapodistria*, vol. B (Athens: Afoi Tolidi, 1972), 160.

11 Pantazopoulos, "Georg Ludwig Von Maurer, E Pros Evropaika Protypa Oloklerotike Strofe Tes Neoellenikes Nomothesias," 1400; Finlay, *A History of Greece from Its Conquest by the Romans to the Present Time*, VII Part II, 128; Dimitris Stamatopoulos, "The Orthodox Church of Greece," in *Orthodox Christianity and Nationalism in Nineteenth-Century Southeastern Europe*, ed. Lucian N Leustean (New York: Fordham University Press, 2014), 36; Stephanos P. Papageorgiou, *Apo to Genos Sto Ethnos: E Themeliose Tpu Ellenikou Kratous 1821-1862* (Athens: Ekdoseis Papazisi, 2005), 346–47; and Thiersch, *E Ellada Tou Kapodistria*, B, 160.

12 Slobodan G. Markovich, "Patterns of National Identity Development among the Balkan Orthodox Christians During the Nineteenth Century," *Balcanica* XLIV (2013): 231; Christos Giannaras, *Orthodoxia Kai Dyse Ste Neotere Ellada* (Athens: Domos, 1999), 267; Chrysostomos Papadopoulos, *Istoria Tes Ekklesias Tes Ellados*, vol. A (Athens: P. A Patrakou, 1920), 104; and Vrasidas Karalis, "In Search of Neo-Hellenic Culture: Confronting the Ambiguities of Modernity in an Ancient Land," *Interactions: Studies in Communication & Culture* 3, no. 2 (2012): 134.

13 Vogli, *Ellenes to Genos: E Ithageneia Kai E Taytoteta Sto Ethniko Kratos Ton Ellenon (1821-1844)*, 189.

14 Vassiliki Georgiadou, "Greek Orthodoxy and the Politics of Nationalism," *International Journal of Politics, Culture, and Society* 9, no. 2 (1995): 303.

15 Lucien J. Frary, *Russia and the Making of Modern Greek Identity, 1821-1844* (Oxford: Oxford University Press, 2015), 126.

16 Georg Ludwig von Maurer, *O Ellenikos Laos* (Athens: Afoi Tolidi, 1976), 50; Petropoulos and Koumarianou, *E Themeliose Tou Ellenikou Kratous 1833-1843*, 106; Edmond About, *E Ellada Tou Othonos* (Athens Ekdoseis Afon Tolidi, 1992 (1855)), 178; Frary, *Russia and the Making of Modern Greek Identity, 1821-1844*, 115, 132; Stamatopoulos, The Orthodox Church of Greece, 39.

17 Petropoulos and Koumarianou, *E Themeliose Tou Ellenikou Kratous 1833-1843*, 113.

18 Finlay, *A History of Greece from Its Conquest by the Romans to the Present Time*, VII Part II, 131.

19 Pavlos Kalligas, *Systema Romaikou Dikaiou*, vol. B (Athens: Georgios Fexis kai Yios, 1930), 15.

20 Nikolopoulos and Kakoulidis, *Sylloge Apanton Ton Nomon, Diatagmaton, Egkyklion, Odegion, Kai Eidopoieseon Ton Ypourgeion, Synthekon Tes Ellados Meta Ton Allon Ethnon*, 206; Thiersch, *E Ellada Tou Kapodistria*, B, 105.

21 Finlay, *A History of Greece from Its Conquest by the Romans to the Present Time*, VII Part II, 129, 154.

22 John Anthony Petropoulos, *Politics and Statecraft in the Kingdom of Greece 1833-1843* (Princeton: Princeton University Press, 1968), 38; Finlay, *A History of Greece from Its Conquest by the Romans to the Present Time*, VII Part II, 145; Kostis, *Ta Kakomathemena Paidia Tes Istorias: E Diamorfose Tou Neoellenikou Kratous 18os-21os Aionas*, 185.

23 About, *E Ellada Tou Othonos*, 72, 198.

24 Historical Archive of the Ministry of Foreign Affairs of Greece (thereafter HAMFA), Kentrike Yperesia (Central Service thereafter KY), 1838/49:1, 2130, May 30, 1838; HAMFA, KY, 1838/49:1, 2170, May 21, 1838.

25 Thiersch, *E Ellada Tou Kapodistria*, A, 230, 231.

26 HAMFA, KY, 1834/49:1, 2727 (2452), February 5, 1834.

27 HAMFA, KY, 1834/49:1, 248, Navplio, March 31, 1834.

28 HAMFA, KY, 1834/49:1, 210, Navplio, March 19, 1834.

29 HAMFA, KY, 1853/32.2, 72/243, Ioannina, July 21, 1853.

30 About, *E Ellada Tou Othonos*, 198.

31 Diamantouros, *Oi Aparches Tes Sygkroteses Sygchronou Kratous Sten Ellada 1821-1828*, 127, 184, 189; Finlay, *A History of Greece from Its Conquest by the Romans to the Present Time*, VII Part II, 119.

32 Diamantouros, *Oi Aparches Tes Sygkroteses Sygchronou Kratous Sten Ellada 1821-1828*, 213.

33 Ibid., 253, 255.

34 Thiersch, *E Ellada Tou Kapodistria*, B, 105.

35 Pliny Fisk, "Appeal in Behalf of Greece," *The Wesleyan-Methodist Magazine* 1827, 309; Mengous, *Apo Te Smyrni Sten Ellada Tou 1821: E Afegese Tou Petrou Meggou*, 303; John O Iatrides, "Evangelicals," in *Minorities in Greece: Aspects of a Plural Society*, ed. Richard Clogg (London: Hurst & Company, 2002), 51.

36 "Missionary Intelligence.: Education in Greece," *Episcopal Recorder*, September 1, 1832, 86; "Greece.: Extracts from Letters of Mr. Arnold," *Baptist Missionary Magazine*, September 1845, 240.

37 "Missionary.: Board of Missions of the Protestant Episcopal Church," *Episcopal Recorder*, July 15, 1837, 61.

38 "Anderson's Observations in Greece," *The North American Review*, January 1, 1832, 2; Theodore Saloutos, "American Missionaries in Greece: 1820-1869," *Church History* 24, no. 2 (1955): 157.

39 "Missionary Intelligence.: Evangelism in Greece," *New York Evangelist*, September 30, 1869, 8; "Anderson's Observations in Greece," 3; "Greece.: Extracts from a Letter of Mr. Arnold," *Baptist Missionary Magazine*, November 1845, 282.

40 "Greece.: Extracts from the Journal of Rev. Eliuas Riggns," *The Missionary Herald*, September 1833, 309; "Greece.: Extracts from Letters of Mr. Arnold," 240; "Missionary Intelligence.: Education in Greece," 86.

41 "Greece.: Extracts from the Journal of Rev. Eliuas Riggns," 309.

42 Saloutos, American Missionaries in Greece: 1820-1869, 167.

43 Jack Fairey, "'Discord and Confusion . . . Under the Pretext of Religion': European Diplomacy and the Limits of Orthodox Ecclesiastical Authority in the Eastern Mediterranean," *The International History Review* 34, no. 1 (2012): 28; Polly Thanailaki, "American Schools in Greece in the Nineteenth Century: The Missionary Josiah Brewer and His School on the Island of Syros," *Greek Orthodox Theological Review* 51, no. 1–4 (2006): 98.

44 "Anderson's Observations in Greece," 4, 9.

45 Papageorgiou, *Apo to Genos Sto Ethnos: E Themeliose Tpu Ellenikou Kratous 1821-1862*, 460; About, *E Ellada Tou Othonos*, 230.

46 "Greece.: Extracts from a Letter of Mr. Arnold," 282.

47 Effi Gazi, "Revisiting Religion and Nationalism in Nineteenth-Century Greece," in *The Making of Modern Greece: Nationalism, Romanticism, and the Uses of the Past (1797-1896)*, ed. Rodeick Beaton and David Ricks (New York: Routledge, 2016), 98.

48 Petropoulos and Koumarianou, *E Themeliose Tou Ellenikou Kratous 1833-1843*, 215; Papageorgiou, *Apo to Genos Sto Ethnos: E Themeliose Tpu Ellenikou Kratous 1821-1862*, 460; and Aikaterini Koumarianou, *E Eleftherofrosyne Tou Theofilou Kairi* (Athens, 1967), 8–9, 13.

49 Giannis Makrygiannis, *Oramata Kai Thamata* (Athens: Morphotiko Idryma Ethnikis Trapezis, 2002), 59, 65, 169, 172, 178, 181, 183, 187. Interestingly Russian officials also condemned the writings of Kairis (Frary, *Russia and the Making of Modern Greek Identity, 1821-1844*, 162).

50 Papageorgiou, *Apo to Genos Sto Ethnos: E Themeliose Tpu Ellenikou Kratous 1821-1862*; Kostis, *Ta Kakomathemena Paidia Tes Istorias: E Diamorfose Tou Neoellenikou Kratous 18os-21os Aionas*, 329, 459.

51 Sparti Maragkou-Drygiannaki, "E Philorthodoxos Etaireia Kai E Metastrophe Tes Ellenikes Exoterikes Politikes Pros Te Rosia" (Athens: Panteio University, 1995), 106–07); Frary, *Russia and the Making of Modern Greek Identity, 1821-1844*, 175, 176.

52 Fairey, "'Discord and Confusion . . . Under the Pretext of Religion': European Diplomacy and the Limits of Orthodox Ecclesiastical Authority in the Eastern Mediterranean," 31; Maragkou-Drygiannaki, "E Philorthodoxos Etaireia Kai E Metastrophe Tes Ellenikes Exoterikes Politikes Pros Te Rosia," 156–57.

53 Frary, *Russia and the Making of Modern Greek Identity, 1821-1844*, 190–91.

54 Papageorgiou, *Apo to Genos Sto Ethnos: E Themeliose Tpu Ellenikou Kratous 1821-1862*, 384; Petropoulos and Koumarianou, *E Themeliose Tou Ellenikou Kratous 1833-1843*, 204.

55 Maragkou-Drygiannaki, "E Philorthodoxos Etaireia Kai E Metastrophe Tes Ellenikes Exoterikes Politikes Pros Te Rosia," 114, 197.

56 Marc Baer, "Islamic Conversion Narratives of Women: Social Change and Gendered Religious Hierarchy in Early Modern Ottoman Istanbul," *Gender & History* 16, no. 2 (2004): 434.

57 Elyse Semerdjian, "Armenian Women, Legal Bargaining, and Gendered Politics of Conversion in Seventeenth- and Eighteenth-Century Aleppo," *Journal of Middle East Women's Studies* 12, no. 1 (2016): 3, 13; Sebnem Koser Akcapar, "Conversion as a Migration Strategy in a Transit Country: Iranian Shiites Becoming Christians in Turkey," *The International Migration Review* 40, no. 4 (2006): 819.

58 Fahd Kasumovic, "Understanding Ottoman Heritage in Bosnia and Herzegovina: Conversions to Islam in the Records of the Sarajevo Sharia Court, 1800-1851," *Belleten Türk Tarih Kurumu, Atatürk kültür dil ve tarih yüksek kurumu* LXXX, no. 288 (2016): 507.

59 See Marc David Baer, "An Enemy Old and New: The Dönme, Anti-Semitism, and Conspiracy Theories in the Ottoman Empire and Turkish Republic," *Jewish Quarterly Review* 103, no. 4 (2013).

60 Selim Deringil, *Conversion and Apostasy in the Late Ottoman Empire* (Cambridge: Cambridge University Press, 2012), 22, 66.

61 Deringil, *Conversion and Apostasy in the Late Ottoman Empire*, 91, 98, 173–74.

62 Yvette Talhamy, "American Protestant Missionary Activity among the Nusayris (Alawis) in Syria in the Nineteenth Century," *Middle Eastern Studies* 47, no. 2 (2011): 216.

63 Lucien J. Frary, "Russian Consuls and the Greek War of Independence (1821–31)," *Mediterranean Historical Review* 28, no. 1 (2013): 56.

64 HAMFA, KY, 1843/76.1, 5086, January 11, 1843.

65 HAMFA, KY, 1837/76.1, Athens, August 22, 1836.

66 General State Archives (hereafter GAK) Civil Decisions of the Appeals Court of Athens (hereafter PA), vol. 119A, pg. 725, no.17974, March 25, 1860; GAK, PA, vol. 121, pg. 2281, no. 18419, October 8, 1860 among many.

67 HAMFA, KY, 1837/76.1, 1357, March 22, 1837 (23 de la lune Zilhetze l'an de l'hegire 1252).

68 HAMFA, KY, 1837/76.1, 20698, 22716, May 29, 1837.

69 HAMFA, KY, 1838/76.1, 1601, July 8, 1838.

70 HAMFA, KY, 1840/76.1, 2353, July 12, 1840; HAMFA, KY, 1840/76.1, 3350, September 30, 1840; HAMFA, KY, 1840/76.1, 3716, August 7, 1840; and HAMFA, KY, 1840/76.1, 2314, July 10/22, 1840.

71 HAMFA, KY, 1841/76.1, 4346, November 14/26, 1841; HAMFA, KY, 1841/76.1, 360, September 25/October 7, 1841; and HAMFA, KY, 1841/76.1, 3394, September 9/21, 1841.

72 HAMFA, KY, 1841/76.1, 3565, September 15/27, 1841.

73 HAMFA, KY, 1841/76.1, 4346, November 14/26, 1841; HAMFA, KY, 1841/76.1, 3172, August 31, 1841.

74 HAMFA, KY, 1841/76.1, 3083, August 21/September 2, 1841; HAMFA, KY, 1841/76.1 2925, August 12/24, 1841.

75 HAMFA, KY, 1841/76.1, 1817, Patras, May 23, 1841.

76 HAMFA, KY, 1841/76.1, 4477, Athens, November 24, 1841.

77 HAMFA, KY, 1841/76.1, 10144, August 25, 1841.

78 HAMFA, KY, 1841/76.1, 3665, Chalkis, August 29, 1841.

79 HAMFA, KY, 1841/76.1, 3253, Athens, September 7, 1841.

80 Kriezotis behaved as if Euboea was his fiefdom and in 1843 he was accused of a whole range of illegal act for which he was arrested in 1847 but was able to escape from prisonand raise a force of 2,000 men leading to a series of engagements which resulted in Kriezotis leaving permanently Greece for Smyrna (Izmir) (Papageorgiou, *Apo to Genos Sto Ethnos: E Themeliose Tpu Ellenikou Kratous 1821-1862*, 440–41).

81 HAMFA, KY, 1842/76.1, 289, Athens, January 24/February 5, 1842; HAMFA, KY, 1842/76.1, 4912, August 19, 1842; HAMFA, KY, 1842/76.1, 1380, August 13, 1842; HAMFA, KY, 1842/76.1, 1380/1675, May 5, 1842; HAMFA, KY, 1842/76.1, 1554, June 4, 1842; HAMFA, KY, 1842/76.1, 1244, November 17, 1841; HAMFA, KY, 1842/76.1, 2238/2335, June 15, 1842; HAMFA, KY, 1842/76.1, 4948, December 11, 1842; and HAMFA, KY, 1842/76.1, 4280, October 16/28, 1842.

82 HAMFA, KY, 1842/76.1, 1673, Athens, February 9, 1842; HAMFA, KY, 1843/76.1, 12918, October 7, 1843. It should be noted, however, that the Greek government did not always give way easily to Ottoman complaints as the case of the Ottoman ambassador Mousouris indicates. Mousouris was publicly insulted by Otto in 1847 leading the Ottoman government to close all Greek consulates, suspend Greek guilds in the Empire, and ban Greek shipping from its ports. The Greek government and King continued to refuse to apologize for almost a year despite the economic repercussions and foreign mediation (Papageorgiou, *Apo to Genos Sto Ethnos: E Themeliose Tpu Ellenikou Kratous 1821-1862*, 437–39).

83 HAMFA, KY, 1856/76.1, April 27, 1855; HAMFA, KY, 1856/76.1, 6757, Athens, May 9, 1855.

84 HAMFA, KY, 1856/76.1, 9167, Athens, April 16, 1855.

85 HAMFA, KY, 1856/76.1, May 9, 1855; HAMFA, KY, 1856/76.1, 3169, Chalkida, April 20, 1855.

86 HAMFA, KY, 1856/76.1, 3943, Chalkida, May 18, 1855; HAMFA, KY, 1856/76.1, 3169, Chalkida, April 20, 1855.

87 HAMFA, KY, 1856/76.1, 195, Chalkida, May 20, 1855.

88 HAMFA, KY, 1856/76.1, 13435, Athens, May 24, 1855; HAMFA, KY, 1856/76.1, January 13/25, 1856; HAMFA, KY, 1856/76.1, 68, Pera, January 19, 1856; and HAMFA, KY, 1856/76.1, 349, Pera, April 27, 1856.

89 HAMFA, KY, 1856/76.1, Athens, November 21, 1855; HAMFA, KY, 1856/76.1, Athens, June 20, 1856.

90 HAMFA, KY, 1845/75.1, 523, Athens, January 30/February 11, 1845.

91 HAMFA, KY, 1845/75.1, 248, February 5, 1845.

92 HAMFA, KY, 1845/75.1, 5943, March 6, 1845.

93 HAMFA, KY, 1845/75.1, 711, March 10/22, 1845.

94 HAMFA, KY, 1845/75.1, 1647, May 4/26, 1845.

95 HAMFA, KY, 1845/75.1, 30903, undated.

96 HAMFA, KY, 1845/75.1, 31562, August 25, 1845.

97 HAMFA, KY, 1845/75.1, 3172, September 3/15, 1845.

98 Vogli, *Ellenes to Genos: E Ithageneia Kai E Taytoteta Sto Ethniko Kratos Ton Ellenon (1821-1844)*, 198–99.

99 Frary, "Russian Consuls and the Greek War of Independence (1821–31)," 55.

100 Thiersch, *E Ellada Tou Kapodistria*, A, 235.

101 Petropoulos and Koumarianou, *E Themeliose Tou Ellenikou Kratous 1833-1843*, 248; Kostis , *Ta Kakomathemena Paidia Tes Istorias: E Diamorfose Tou Neoellenikou Kratous 18os-21os Aionas*, 196.

102 Petropoulos and Koumarianou, *E Themeliose Tou Ellenikou Kratous 1833-1843*, 223.

103 See Peter Mackridge, *Language and National Identity in Greece 1766-1976* (Oxford: Oxford University Press, 2009).

104 *Peri Ton Epistemonikon Kai Technologikon Syllogon, Peri Anakalypseos Kai Diatereseos Ton Archaioteton Kai Tes Chreseos Auton*, (June 16, 1834), 184.

105 Charis Athanasiadis, *Ta Aposyrthenta Vivlia: Ethnos Kai Scholike Istoria Sten Ellada 1858-2008* (Athens: Alexandreia, 2015), 254.

106 George Th Mavrogordatos, "Orthodoxy and Nationalism in the Greek Case," *West European Politics* 26, no. 1 (2003): 129; Alexandros Svolos, *Ta Ellinika Syntagmata 1822-1975/1986. I Syntagmatiki Istoria Tis Ellados* (Athens: Stochastis, 1998), 108, 121.

107 See Nicholas V. Riasanovsky, *Nicholas I and Official Nationality in Russia 1825-1855* (Berkeley: University of California Press, 1969).

108 Vogli, *Ellenes to Genos: E Ithageneia Kai E Taytoteta Sto Ethniko Kratos Ton Ellenon (1821-1844)*, 326; Stamatopoulos, The Orthodox Church of Greece, 44.

109 Elli Skopatea, *To "Protypo Vasileio" Kai E Megale Idea, Opseis Tou Ethnikou Provlematos Sten Ellada (1830-1880)* (Athens: Polytypo, 1988), 49.

110 About, *E Ellada Tou Othonos*, 68; Papageorgiou, *Apo to Genos Sto Ethnos: E Themeliose Tpu Ellenikou Kratous 1821-1862*, 416–19.

111 Skopatea, *To "Protypo Vasileio" Kai E Megale Idea, Opseis Tou Ethnikou Provlematos Sten Ellada (1830-1880)*, 50–57; Vogli, *Ellenes to Genos: E Ithageneia Kai E Taytoteta Sto Ethniko Kratos Ton Ellenon (1821-1844)*, 345.

112 Konstantinos Svolopoulos, "O Ioannis Kapodistrias Metaxy Apolytarchias Kai Fileleftherismou," in *O Kyvernetes Ioannis Kapodistrias*, ed. Giorgos Georgis (Athens: Kastaniotis, 2015), 44.

113 Vasilis Kremmydas, *E Megale Idea: Metamorphoseis Enos Ethnikou Ideologematos* (Athens: Ekdoseis Typotheto, 2010), 25, 35; Skopatea, *To "Protypo Vasileio" Kai E Megale Idea, Opseis Tou Ethnikou Provlematos Sten Ellada (1830-1880)*, 258.

114 Kremmydas, *E Megale Idea: Metamorphoseis Enos Ethnikou Ideologematos*, 29.

115 Ibid., 65.

116 Papageorgiou, *Apo to Genos Sto Ethnos: E Themeliose Tpu Ellenikou Kratous 1821-1862*, 386, 388.

117 See Anastasia Stouraiti and Alexander Kazamias, "The Imaginary Topographies of the Megali Idea: National Territory as Utopia," in *Spatial Conceptions of the Nation: Modernizing Geographies in Greece and Turkey*, ed. Nikiforos Diamandouros, Thalia Dragonas, and Caglar Keyder (London: I. B. Tauris, 2010): 11–34.

118 Athanasiadis, *Ta Aposyrthenta Vivlia: Ethnos Kai Scholike Istoria Sten Ellada 1858-2008*, 228.

119 Kremmydas, *E Megale Idea: Metamorphoseis Enos Ethnikou Ideologematos,* 47; Karalis, "In Search of Neo-Hellenic Culture: Confronting the Ambiguities of Modernity in an Ancient Land," 131.

120 Antoniou Andrea Miaouli, *Synoptike Istoria Ton Yper Tes Elevtherias Tes Anagennetheises Ellados Genomenon Navmachion Dia Ton Ploion Ton Trion Neson Ydras, Spatson Kai Psaron* (Athens: Ekdoseis Vergina, 1996), 31, 98.

121 Kremmydas, *E Megale Idea: Metamorphoseis Enos Ethnikou Ideologematos,* 19.

122 John S. Koliopoulos and Thanos M. Veremis, *Greece the Modern Sequel, from 1821 to the Present* (New York: New York University Press, 2002), 245; Karalis, "In Search of Neo-Hellenic Culture: Confronting the Ambiguities of Modernity in an Ancient Land," 131.

123 Gunnar De Boel, "Fallmerayer and Dragoumis on the Greek Nation and Its Mission," in *(Mis)Understanding the Balkans: Essays in Honour of Raymond Detrez,* ed. Michel De Dobbeleer and Stijn Vervaet (Gent: Academia Press, 2013), 97.

124 Jakob Philipp Fallmerayer, *Peri Tes Katagoges Ton Semerinon Ellenon,* trans. Konstantinos P. Romanos (Athens: Nefeli, 1984), 127.

125 Fallmerayer, *Peri Tes Katagoges Ton Semerinon Ellenon,* 64, 119, 128.

126 Ibid., 76; Stathis Gourgouris, *Dream Nation: Enlightenment, Colonization and the Institutions of Modern Greece* (Stanford: Stanford University Press, 1996), 142–43; Boel, "Fallmerayer and Dragoumis on the Greek Nation and Its Mission," 101.

127 Fallmerayer, *Peri Tes Katagoges Ton Semerinon Ellenon,* 73.

128 Gourgouris, *Dream Nation: Enlightenment, Colonization and the Institutions of Modern Greece,* 148; Michael Herzfeld, *Ours Once More: Folklore, Ideology and the Making of Modern Greece* (Austin: University of Texas Press, 1982), 8, 79; Petropoulos and Koumarianou, *E Themeliose Tou Ellenikou Kratous 1833-1843,* 52.

129 See Konstantinos Paparrigopoulos, *Istoria Tou Ellenikou Ethnous* (Athens: Eleftheroudakis, 1932).

130 Nikolae Iorga, *To Vyzantio Meta to Vyzantio* (Athens: Gutenberg, 1985), 128.

131 Effi Gazi, "Reading the Ancients: Remnants of Byzantine Controversies in the Greek National Narrative," *Historein* 6 (2006): 147.

132 Boel, "Fallmerayer and Dragoumis on the Greek Nation and Its Mission," 98.

133 Article A, Part A, Paragraph A of the Temporary Constitution of Greece of the First National Assembly of Epidaurus; Article A, Part A, Paragraph A of the Temporary Constitution of Greece of the Second National Assembly of Astros; Chapter A, Article 1 of the Political Constitution of Greece of the Third National Assembly in Troezina; Article 1 of the Constitution of Greece of March 18, 1844; Article 1 of the Constitution of Greece according to the 2nd National Assembly, in Svolos, 107, 121, 135, 153, 169.

134 Gazi, "Revisiting Religion and Nationalism in Nineteenth-Century Greece," 100.

135 Philip Carabott, "E Evraike Parousia Sten Athena Tou 19ou Aiona: Apo Ton Maximo Rotsild Sten Israelitike Adelfoteta," in *Evraikes Koinotetes Anamesa Se Anatole Kai Dyse, 15os-20os Aionas: Oikonomia, Koinonia, Politike, Politismos,* ed. Anna Machaira and Leda Papastefanaki (Ioannina: Isnafi, 2016), 183, 184.

136 George F. Peters, "'Jeder Reiche Ist Ein Judas Ischariot': Heinrich Heine and the Emancipation of the Jews," *Monatshefte* 104, no. 3 (2012): 217.

137 Julie Kalman, "The Unyielding Wall: Jews and Catholics in Restoration and July Monarchy France," *French Historical Studies* 26, no. 4 (2003): 663, 667.

138 Gary Kates, "Jews into Frenchmen: Nationality and Representation in Revolutionary France," *Social Research* 56, no. 1 (1989): 221.

139 See Christopher J. Tozzi, *Nationalizing France's Army: Foreign, Black, and Jewish Troops in the French Military, 1715-1831* (Charlottesville: University of Virginia Press, 2016), esp 199–216.

140 HAMFA, KY, 1840/76.1, 2353, July 12, 1840; 1841/76.1, 3565, September 15/27, 1841; HAMFA, KY, 1841/76.1, 3083, August 21/September 2, 1841; among many.

141 See Mark Mazower, *Salonica City of Ghosts* (New York: Vintage Books, 2006).

142 HAMFA, KY, 1858/36.2, 347, Thessaloniki, April 29, 1858.

143 HAMFA, KY, 1835/36.2, 34.22, Thessaloniki, February 15, 1835.

144 HAMFA, KY, 1858/36.2, 877, Thessaloniki, December 20, 1858.

145 HAMFA, KY, 1852/36.2a, 493/264, Thessaloniki, December 9, 1852.

146 HAMFA, KY, 1853/36.2, 525/287, Thessaloniki, December 30, 1852; HAMFA, KY, 1853/36.2, 6/2, Thessaloniki, January 6, 1853; HAMFA, KY, 1853/36.2, 28, Thessaloniki, January 29, 1853; and HAMFA, KY, 1853/36.2, 257/97, Thessaloniki, July 11, 1853.

147 HAMFA, KY, 1853/36.2, 525/287, Thessaloniki, December 30, 1852.

148 HAMFA, KY, 1853/36.2, 28, Thessaloniki, January 29, 1853.

149 HAMFA, KY, 1836/36.2, 2130, Thessaloniki, April 16/28, 1836.

150 HAMFA, KY, 1853/36.2, 318, Thessaloniki, August 20, 1853.

151 HAMFA, KY, 1862/36.2, 17, Dyrrachio, January 18, 1862.

152 HAMFA, KY, 1847/36.2, 444, Ioannina, October 24, 1847; HAMFA, KY, 1845/36.2, 17987, Ioannina, November 4, 1845; and HAMFA, KY, 1862/36.2, 200, Ioannina, July 19, 1862.

153 HAMFA, KY, 1854/4 IV γ, 413, Preveza, December 14, 1853; HAMFA, KY, 1854/4 IV γ, 69, Preveza, February 23, 1854; and HAMFA, KY, 1854/4 IV γ, 70, Preveza, February 24, 1854.

154 HAMFA, KY, 1846/36.2, 54, Ioannina, April 26, 1846; HAMFA, KY, 1849/36.2, 235, Ioannina, May 22, 1849.

155 HAMFA, KY, 1861/36.2, 287, Ioannina, June 2, 1861.

156 HAMFA, KY, 1851/36.2, 181/241, Ioannina, July 5, 1851.

157 Although not mentioned in the document this could have been a case of the parading of the Judas Iscariot effigy before its ceremonial burning as was customary around the region and as I will discuss further below.

158 HAMFA, KY, 1851/36.2, 43/141, Ioannina, April 24, 1851.

159 Kremmydas, *E Megale Idea: Metamorphoseis Enos Ethnikou Ideologematos*, 49, 55; Skopatea, *To "Protypo Vasileio" Kai E Megale Idea, Opseis Tou Ethnikou Provlematos Sten Ellada (1830-1880)*, 326.

160 Georgiadou, "Greek Orthodoxy and the Politics of Nationalism," 306.

161 HAMFA, KY, 1860/36.2, 816, Thessaloniki, December 7, 1859.

162 HAMFA, KY, 1861/36.2, Ioannina, June 1, 1861.

163 HAMFA, KY, 1861/36.2, 556, Ioannina, October 18, 1861; HAMFA, KY, 1862/36.2, 200, Ioannina, July 19, 1862.

164 HAMFA, KY, 1861/76.1, 35, Adrianople, February 28, 1861.

165 HAMFA, KY, 1861/76.1, 28, Pera, March 10, 1861; HAMFA, KY, 1861/76.1, 18, Pera, February 24, 1861.

166 HAMFA, KY, 1861/76.1, 204, St. Petersburg, August 22, 1861.

167 HAMFA, KY, 1861/36.2, Ioannina, June 1, 1861; HAMFA, KY, 1861/36.2, Ioannina, March 22, 1861; and HAMFA, KY, 1861/76.1, 35, Phillipoupoli, May 9, 1861.

168 Talhamy, "American Protestant Missionary Activity among the Nusayris (Alawis) in Syria in the Nineteenth Century," 219; Deringil, *Conversion and Apostasy in the Late Ottoman Empire*, 52, 68.

169 HAMFA, KY, 1835/36.2, 34.22, February 15, 1835; HAMFA, KY, 1845/76.1, 172, April 2, 1845.

170 HAMFA, KY, 1855/76.1, 107, Smyrna, June 29, 1855; HAMFA, KY, 1856/76.1, 222, Thessaloniki, May 29, 1856; and HAMFA, KY, 1861/76.1, Therapeiois, June 2, 1861.

171 HAMFA, KY, 1855/ 76.1, 91, Smyrna, June 22, 1855.

172 HAMFA, KY, 1856/76.1, Chios April, 2, 1856.

173 Deringil, *Conversion and Apostasy in the Late Ottoman Empire,* 13, 14, 21–22.

174 Ibid., 22–23, 33–34, 38, 57, 66.

175 HAMFA, KY, 1861/76.1, 717, Pera, March 31, 1861; HAMFA, KY, 1861/76.1, 341, March 25, 1861; HAMFA, KY, 1861/76.1, 872, April 12, 1861; and HAMFA, KY, 1861/76.1, 1087, May 3, 1861.

176 Deringil, *Conversion and Apostasy in the Late Ottoman Empire,* 85.

177 Ibid., 86, 88.

178 HAMFA, KY, 1856/76.1, 75, Chania, June 11/23, 1856.

179 HAMFA, KY, 1856/76.1, 79, Chania, July 4/16, 1856.

180 Deringil, *Conversion and Apostasy in the Late Ottoman Empire,* 87, 90–91, 97–98, 109.

181 Ibid., 90, 98, 111.

182 Yorgos Tzedopoulos, "Public Secrets: Crypto-Christianity in the Pontos," 16 (2009): 168; Deringil, *Conversion and Apostasy in the Late Ottoman Empire,* 93.

183 HAMFA, KY, 1859/36.2, 197, Thessaloniki, March 28, 1859.

184 HAMFA, KY, 1861/76.1, 511, Cairo, November 10/22, 1861.

185 HAMFA, KY, 1845/76.1, 172, Cairo, April 2, 1845.

186 HAMFA, KY, 1856/76.1, 10, Herakleio, July 12, 1856.

187 HAMFA, KY, 1843/76.1, 1865, August 13/25, 1843.

188 Vogli, *Ellenes to Genos: E Ithageneia Kai E Taytoteta Sto Ethniko Kratos Ton Ellenon (1821-1844),* 275.

189 See Fairey.

190 Lucien J. Frary, "Russian Missions to the Orthodox East: Antonin Kapustin (1817-1894) and His World," *Russian History* 30 (2013): 136.

191 Rafail A. Frezis, *Psefides Istorias Tou Ellenikou Evraismou* (Volos 2007), 362.

192 Fragiski Ampatzopoulou, *O Allos En Diogmo. E Eikona Tou Evraiou Ste Logotechnia, Zetemata Istorias Kai Mythoplasias* (Athens: Ekdoseis Themelio, 1998), 198.

193 Bernard Pierron, *Juifs Et Chretiens De La Grece Moderne, Histoire Des Relations Intercommunautaires De 1821 a 1945* (Paris: Editions L'Harmattan, 1996), 24; Makrygiannis, *Apomnemonevmata* (Athens: Ekdoseis A. Karavia, 1996), 531; Dolphus Whitten, "The Don Pacifico Affair," *The Historian* 48, no. 2 (1986): 255, 256; About.

194 Finlay, *A History of Greece from Its Conquest by the Romans to the Present Time,* VII Part II, 209; "The Greek Case," *The Economist,* March 16, 1850, 3; "The Greek Claims and the House of Lords,"*The Economist,* June 15, 1850, 1; Whitten, "The Don Pacifico Affair," 257.

195 Geoffrey Hicks, "Don Pacifico, Democracy, and Danger: The Protectionist Party Critique of British Foreign Policy, 1850-1852,"*The International History Review* 26, no. 3 (2004): 519.

196 HAMFA, KY, 1848/68.1 γ, July 16/28, 1848.

197 Saloutos, American Missionaries in Greece: 1820-1869, 169.

198 HAMFA, KY, 1848/68.1 γ, February 15/27, 1847.

199 HAMFA, KY, 1848/68.1 γ, 1152, January 24, 1848.

200 HAMFA, KY, 1848/68.1 γ, 21822, September 4, 1847; HAMFA, KY, 1848/68.1 γ, 3302/4092, September 12, 1847; HAMFA, KY, 1848/68.1 γ, 6927, October 1, 1847; and HAMFA, KY, 1848/68.1 γ, 788, March 24, 1847.

201 "The Greek Case." 3; Makrygiannis. 531.

202 Whitten, "The Don Pacifico Affair," 259. Papageorgiou, *Apo to Genos Sto Ethnos: E Themeliose Tpu Ellenikou Kratous 1821-1862*, 455.

203 Whitten, "The Don Pacifico Affair," 260, 263; Hicks, "Don Pacifico, Democracy, and Danger: The Protectionist Party Critique of British Foreign Policy, 1850-1852," 517–18, 520.

204 Hicks, "Don Pacifico, Democracy, and Danger: The Protectionist Party Critique of British Foreign Policy, 1850-1852," 524.

205 David Brown, *Palmerston and the Politics of Foreign Policy, 1846-55* (Manchester: Manchester University Press, 2003), 102, 108.

206 Whitten, "The Don Pacifico Affair," 265–66.

207 Ibid., 266.

208 Brown, *Palmerston and the Politics of Foreign Policy, 1846-55*, 128.

209 K. E. Fleming, *Greece, A Jewish History* (Princeton: Princeton University Press, 2008); Fleming, *Greece, A Jewish History*, 27.

210 "The Greek Case." 3.

211 Finlay, *A History of Greece from Its Conquest by the Romans to the Present Time*, VII Part II. 272.

212 "The Greek Claims and the House of Lords." 1.

213 HAMFA, KY, 1848 68.1.γ, 761, Athens, March 12, 1848.

214 Whitten, "The Don Pacifico Affair," 259, 263.

215 Even the name of the case in Greek historiography, the "Parkerika," refers to the commander of the British fleet rather than to Don Pacifico who is often not even mentioned (see Kostis, *Ta Kakomathemena Paidia Tes Istorias: E Diamorfose Tou Neoellenikou Kratous 18os-21os Aionas,* 264) (Papageorgiou, *Apo to Genos Sto Ethnos: E Themeliose Tpu Ellenikou Kratous 1821-1862,* 453).

216 Miranda Stavrinos, "Palmerston and the Cretan Question, 1839-1841," *Journal of Modern Greek Studies* 10, no. 2 (1992), 250, 252, 259.

217 David Hannell, "Lord Palmerston and the 'Don Pacifico Affair' of 1850: The Ionian Connection," 19 (1989): 495; Mirada Paximadopoulou-Stavrinou, "Oi Exegerseis Tes Kephallenias Kata Ta Ete 1848 Kai 1849" (Panteio University, 1980), 28, 78.

218 Finlay, *A History of Greece from Its Conquest by the Romans to the Present Time*, VII Part II. 209; Charles A. Frazee, *The Orthodox Church and Independent Greece 1821-1852* (Cambridge: Cambridge University Press, 1969), 173.

219 Electra Kostopoulou, "The Multiple Faces of Autonomy: Ottoman Reform and 19th Century Crete," *Cretica Chronica* 36 (2016): 42.

220 Giorgos Georgis, "E Anatolike Politike Tou Kyvernete Ioanni Kapodistria," in *O Kyvernetes Ioannis Kapodistrias,* ed. Giorgos Georgis (Athens: Kastaniotis, 2015), 193; Finlay, *A History of Greece from Its Conquest by the Romans to the Present Time*, VII Part II, 161, 206.

221 George Gavrilis, "The Greek-Ottoman Boundary as Institution, Locality, and Process, 1832-1882," *American Behavioral Scientist* 51, no. 10 (2008): 1517.

222 Gavrilis, "The Greek-Ottoman Boundary as Institution, Locality, and Process, 1832-1882," 1525; Lucien J. Frary, "Russian-Greek Relations During the Crimean War," *Slovo* 21, no. 1 (2009): 17, 21; Finlay, *A History of Greece from Its Conquest by the Romans to the Present Time*, VII Part II, 200–202, 222; Kremmydas, *E Megale Idea:*

Metamorphoseis Enos Ethnikou Ideologematos, 38; and Papageorgiou, *Apo to Genos Sto Ethnos: E Themeliose Tpu Ellenikou Kratous 1821-1862,* 469.

223 Antonis Liakos, *E Italike Enopoiese Kai E Megale Idea 1859-1862* (Athens: Themelio, 1985), 37.

224 Frary, "Russian-Greek Relations During the Crimean War," 25, 27; Kostis, *Ta Kakomathemena Paidia Tes Istorias: E Diamorfose Tou Neoellenikou Kratous 18os-21os Aionas,* 263.

225 Papageorgiou, *Apo to Genos Sto Ethnos: E Themeliose Tpu Ellenikou Kratous 1821-1862,* 456, 473.

226 Liakos, *E Italike Enopoiese Kai E Megale Idea 1859-1862,* 111, 137.

Chapter 4

1 Philip Carabott, "E Evraike Parousia Sten Athena Tou 19ou Aiona: Apo Ton Maximo Rotsild Sten Israelitike Adelfoteta," in *Evraikes Koinotetes Anamesa Se Anatole Kai Dyse, 15os-20os Aionas: Oikonomia, Koinonia, Politike, Politismos,* eds. Anna Machaira and Leda Papastefanaki (Ioannina: Isnafi, 2016), 187.

2 Carabott, "E Evraike Parousia Sten Athena Tou 19ou Aiona: Apo Ton Maximo Rotsild Sten Israelitike Adelfoteta," 189.

3 Steven Bowman, "Jews in Wartime Greece," *Jewish Social Studies* 48, no. 1 (1986): 46; Nikolaos I. Solomos, *Istoria Ton Evraion Apo Ton Archaiotaton Chronon Mechri Ton Emeron Mas* (Athens: Arg. Drakopoulos, 1893), 234–35.

4 Theodore George Tatsios, *The Megali Idea and the Greek-Turkish War of 1897: The Impact of the Cretan Problem on Greek Irredentism, 1866-1897* (Boulder: East European Monographs, 1984), 44; Edouard Driault, *E Megale Idea: E Anagennese Tou Ellenismou* (Athens: Istoritis, 1998 (1920)), 180.

5 Evaggelos Kofos, *O Ellenismos Sten Periodo 1869-1881* (Athens: Ekdotiki Athinon, 1981), 124.

6 See Robert Holland and Diana Makrides, *The British and the Hellenes: Struggles for Mastery in the Eastern Mediterranean 1850-1960* (Oxford: Oxford University Press, 2008); George J. Markopoulos, "King George I and the Expansion of Greece, 1875-1881," *Balkan Studies* 9 (1968): 21–39; and Tatsios, *The Megali Idea and the Greek-Turkish War of 1897: The Impact of the Cretan Problem on Greek Irredentism, 1866-1897,* 180.

7 "Preliminary Treaty of Peace between Russia and Turkey: Signed at San Stefano, February 9/March 3, 1878," *The American Journal of International Law* 2, no. 4 (1908): 391, 394.

8 "Treaty between Great Britain, Germany, Austria, France, Italy, Russia, and Turkey for the Settlement of Affairs in the East: Signed at Berlin, July 13, 1878," *The American Journal of International Law* 2, no. 4 (1908): 406, 413, 416, 419, 422, 423.

9 See Articles IV and XI in the Treaty of San Stefano ("Preliminary Treaty of Peace between Russia and Turkey: Signed at San Stefano, February 9/March 3, 1878," 391, 394) and Articles XII, XXX, and XXXIX in the Treaty of Berlin ("Treaty between Great Britain, Germany, Austria, France, Italy, Russia, and Turkey for the Settlement of Affairs in the East: Signed at Berlin, July 13, 1878," 408, 415, 418).

10 See Articles III, IV, VI, VIII, X, XI (George J. Goschen, "Despatch from Mr. Goschen Forwarding the Convention for the Settlement of the Frontier between Greece and Turkey," ed. House of Commons (London: Harrison and Sons, 1881), 2–3).

11 See Djordje Stefanovic, "Seeing the Albanians through Serbian Eyes: The Inventors of the Tradition of Intolerance and Their Critics, 1804-1939," *European History Quarterly* 35, no. 3 (2005): 465–92.

12 Constantin Iordachi, "The Unyielding Boundaries of Citizenship: The Emancipation of 'Non-Citizens' in Romania, 1866-1918," *European Review of History* 8, no. 2 (2001): 159; Radu Ioanid, *The Holocaust in Romania: The Destruction of Jews and Gypsies under the Antonescu Regime, 1940-1944* (Chicago: Ivan R Dee, 2000), 6, 7, 10; and see also Emanuela Costantini, "Neither Foreigners, nor Citizens: Romanian Jews' Long Road to Citizenship," in *The Jews and the Nation-States of Southeastern Europe from the 19th Century to the Great Depression*, eds. Tullia Catalan and Marco Dogo (Newcastle upon Tyne: Cambridge Scholars Publishing, 2016): 2–22.

13 Milan Ristovic, "The Jews of Serbia (1804-1918): From Princely Protection to Formal Emancipation," in *The Jews and the Nation-States of Southeastern Europe from the 19th Century to the Great Depression*, eds. Tullia Catalan and Marco Dogo (Newcastle upon Tyne: Cambridge Scholars Publishing, 2016), 28, 30, 32.

14 Mark Mazower, *The Balkans, a Short History* (New York: The Modern Library, 2002), 116; Mark Biondich, *The Balkans. Revolution, War and Political Violence since 1878* (Oxford: Oxford University Press, 2011), 49, 66; Slobodan Drakulic, "Anti-Turkish Obsession and the Exodus of Balkan Muslims," *Patterns of Prejudice* 43, no. 3–4 (2009): 243, 247; Justin McCarthy, *Death and Exile, the Ethnic Cleansing of Ottoman Muslims 1821-1922* (Princeton: The Darwin Press, 1995), 86; Ulf Brunnbauer, "The Perception of Muslims in Bulgaria and Greece: Between the 'Self' and the 'Other'" *Journal of Muslim Minority Affairs* 21, no. 1 (2001): 40; and Andreas Lyberatos, "Unstable Regimes, Strong Consciousness: Eastern Rymelia and Crete after the Berlin Congress (1878)," *Cretica Chronika* 36 (2016): 83.

15 McCarthy, *Death and Exile, the Ethnic Cleansing of Ottoman Muslims 1821-1922*, 121; Robarts, "Imperial Confrontation or Regional Cooperation?: Bulgarian Migration and Ottoman-Russian Relations in the Black Sea Region, 1768-1830s," 3 (2012): 151–53.

16 McCarthy, *Death and Exile, the Ethnic Cleansing of Ottoman Muslims 1821-1922*, 16, 17, 31, 34.

17 Mazower, *The Balkans, a Short History*, 116; McCarthy, *Death and Exile, the Ethnic Cleansing of Ottoman Muslims 1821-1922*, 113.

18 McCarthy, *Death and Exile, the Ethnic Cleansing of Ottoman Muslims 1821-1922*, 47, 60, 121.

19 Devin E. Naar, "The 'Mother of Israel' or the 'Sephardi Metropolis'?: Sephardim, Ashkenazim, and Romaniotes in Salonica," *Jewish Social Studies* 22, no. 181–29 (2016): 84; Soukrou Ilitzak, "O Evraikos Sosialismos Sten Othomanike Thessaloniki," in *Ellenes Kai Evraioi Ergates Ste Thessaloniki Ton Neotourkon* (Ioannina: Isnafi, 2004), 10.

20 HAMFA, KY, 1892, A12-1, 102208, December 9, 1892; HAMFA, KY, 1892, A12-1, 2888, October 11, 1891; HAMFA, KY, 1892, A12-1, 2754, September 27, 1891; HAMFA, KY, 1892, A12-1, 2457, September 7, 1891; and HAMFA, KY, 1892, A12-1, 11417, October 18, 1891.

21 Yitzchak Kerem, "The Influence of Anti-Semitism on the Jewish Immigration Pattern from Greece to the Ottoman Empire in the Nineteenth Century," in *Decision Making and Change in the Ottoman Empire*, ed. Cesar E. Farah (Kirksville: Thomas Jefferson University Press, 1993): 305–14; Thrasyvoulos Or Papastratis, *Oi Evraioi Tes Kavallas* (Athens: "Sylloges" Argyri Vourna, 2010), 11.

22 Konstantinos A. Tsiligiannis, *E Evraike Koinoteta Tes Artas* (Athens: Kentriko Israilitiko Symvoulio tes Ellados, 2004), 27, 30, 31; Esdras D. Moysis, *E Evraike Koinoteta Tes Larisas Prin Kai Meta to Olokaytoma* (Larisa: Melanos, 2000), 26–27; Giorgos Chaniotis, "E Evraike Koinoteta Tes Kerkyras (1860-1939) Entos Kai Ektos Tes, 'Ovriakes," in *Oi Evraioi Ston Elleniko Choro: Zetemata Istorias Ste Makra Diarkeia*, eds. Efi Avdela and Ontet Varon-Vasar (Athens: Ekdoseis Gavriilidis, 1995), 66.

23 Gatenio Osmo Nata, *Apo Ten Kerkyra Sto Birkenau Kai Ten Ierousalem - E Istoria Mias Kerkyraias* (Athens: Gavriilidis, 2005), 18; Tsiligiannis, *E Evraike Koinoteta Tes Artas*, 22; Aphroditi Agoropoulou-Birbili, "E Evraike Synoikia Tes Kerkyras," in *E Evraike Parousia Ston Elladiko Choro (4os-19os Ai.)*, eds. Anna Lambropoulou and Kostas Tsiknakis (Athens: Ethniko Idryma Erevnon, 2008), 126.

24 Lappa, "Variations on a Religious Theme: Jews and Muslims From the Eastern Mediterranean Converting to Christianity, 17th & 18th Centuries," 4.

25 N. G. Moschonas, "E Evraike Diaspora Sto Ionio (12os - 16os Aionas)," in *E Evraike Parousia Ston Elladiko Choro (4os-19os Ai.)*, eds. Anna Lambropoulou and Kostas Tsiknakis (Athens: Ethniko Idryma Erevnon, 2008), 108, 111–12, 114, 116; Nikos E. Karapidakis, "Gia Ten Evraike Koinoteta Kerkyras," in *E Evraike Parousia Ston Elladiko Choro (4os-19os Ai.)*, ed. Anna Lambropoulou and Kostas Tsiknakis (Athens: Ethniko Idryma Erevnon, 2008), 151, 153.

26 Maria Couroucli, *Erga Kai Emeres Sten Kerkyra: Istorike Anthropologia Mias Topikes Koinonias* (Les oliviers du lignage. Une Grece de tradition venitienne, G.-P. Maisonneuve et Larose, 1985), trans. Maria Gyparaki (Athens: Ekdoseis Alexandreia, 2008), 34, 35; Lappa, "Variations on a Religious Theme," 69; Sakis Gekas, *Xenocracy: State, Class, and Colonialism in the Ionian Islands, 1815-1864* (New York: Berghahn Books, 2016), 216.

27 See Thomas W. Gallant, *Experiencing Dominion. Culture, Identity, and Power in the British Mediterranean* (Notre Dame: University of Notre Dame Press, 2002); Thomas Gallant, "Peasant Ideology and Excommunication for Crime in a Colonial Context: The Ionian Islands (Greece), 1817-1864," *Journal of Social History* 23, no. 3 (1990): 485–512; Spyridon G. Malakis, *Apomnemonevmata Epi Tes Sygchronou Istorias, E Istorikon Epeisodion Epi Ton Energeion Drasanton Prosopon Pros Epitevxin Tes Megales Ideas* (Athens 1895), 21; and Gekas, *Xenocracy: State, Class, and Colonialism in the Ionian Islands, 1815-1864*, 216.

28 Malakis, *Apomnemonevmata Epi Tes Sygchronou Istorias, E Istorikon Epeisodion Epi Ton Energeion Drasanton Prosopon Pros Epitevxin Tes Megales Ideas*, 289.

29 Aggelo-Dionysi Demponou, "Evraika," *E Kephalonitiki Proodos* Z, no. 79–80 (1978): 133; Demponou, "Evraika," Z, 166.

30 Gekas, *Xenocracy: State, Class, and Colonialism in the Ionian Islands, 1815-1864*, 218.

31 Gaston Deschamps, *E Ellada Semera: Odoiporiko 1890* (Athens: Trochalia, 1992), 322.

32 Biondich, *The Balkans. Revolution, War and Political Violence since 1878*, 49.

33 A similar outcome has been observed in other parts of the Balkans like Eastern Rumelia (Lyberatos, "Unstable Regimes, Strong Consciousness: Eastern Rymelia and Crete after the Berlin Congress (1878)," 84).

34 Aberbach, *The European Jews, Patriotism and the Liberal State 1789-1939: A Study of Literature and Social Psychology*, 137.

35 Robert Weinberg, *Blood Libel in Late Imperial Russia: The Ritual Murder Trial of Mendel Beilis, Indiana-Michigan Series in Russian and East European Studies* (Indiana: Indiana University Press, 2013), 5.

36 Alain Corbin, *Women for Hire: Prostitution and Sexuality in France after 1850* (Cambridge: Harvard University Press, 1990), 292; Laura Engelstein, *The Keys to*

Happiness: Sex and the Search for Modernity in Fin-De-Siecle Russia (Ithaca: Cornell University Press, 1992), 299–300.

37 Engelstein, *The Keys to Happiness: Sex and the Search for Modernity in Fin-De-Siecle Russia*, 301, 307, 318, 320; Petros Kasimatis, *Aima, Evraioi, Talmoud, Etoi Apodeixeis Threskevtikai, Istorikai Kai Dikastikai Peri Tes Yparxeos Ton Anthropothysion Par' Ebraiois* (Athens 1891), 47; See also Otto Weininger, *Sex and Character: An Investigation of Fundamental Principles* (Bloomington: Indiana University Press, 2005), 272.

38 Naar, "The 'Mother of Israel' or the 'Sephardi Metropolis'?: Sephardim, Ashkenazim, and Romaniotes in Salonica," 106.

39 Bozo Skerlj, "Eugenics or Racial Hygiene?," in *The History of East-Central European Eugenics 1900-1945*, ed. Marius Tudra (New York: Bloomsbury, 2015), 388.

40 Iuliu Moldovan, "The Hygiene of the Nation: Eugenics," in *The History of East-Central European Eugenics 1900-1945*, ed. Marius Tudra (New York: Bloomsbury, 2015), 300; Sabin Manuila, "Romania's Racial Problem," *The History of East-Central European Eugenics 1900-1945*, ed. Marius Tudra (New York: Bloomsbury, 2015), 324–25.

41 Aberbach, *The European Jews, Patriotism and the Liberal State 1789-1939: A Study of Literature and Social Psychology*, 26, 27, 50; Deborah Dwork and Robert Jan van Pelt, *Holocaust a History* (New York: W. W. Norton & Company, 2003), 17.

42 16.

43 Weinberg, *Blood Libel in Late Imperial Russia: The Ritual Murder Trial of Mendel Beilis, Indiana-Michigan Series in Russian and East European Studies*, 142, 148, 159, 163.

44 Zvi Ankori, "Greek Orthodox - Jewish Relations in Historic Perspective - the Jewish View," *Journal of Ecumenical Studies* XIII, no. 4 (1976): 55, 56; Aberbach, *The European Jews, Patriotism and the Liberal State 1789-1939: A Study of Literature and Social Psychology*, 25.

45 Weinberg, *Blood Libel in Late Imperial Russia: The Ritual Murder Trial of Mendel Beilis, Indiana-Michigan Series in Russian and East European Studies* 11, 13–14 .

46 Ibid., 15.

47 Ibid., 46, 62.

48 Ibid., 65–66.

49 Aberbach, *The European Jews, Patriotism and the Liberal State 1789-1939: A Study of Literature and Social Psychology*, 11, 68, 76, 109, 110, 115, 116, 119; Donald L. Horowitz, *The Deadly Ethnic Riot* (Berkeley: California University Press, 2001), 82, 289–90; and Robin Okey, *Eastern Europe 1740-1985* (Minneapolis: University of Minnesota Press, 1986).

50 Efthymiou, *Evraioi Kai Christianoi Sta Tourkokratoumena Nesia Tou Notioanatolikou Aigaiou: Oi Dyskoles Plevres Mias Gonimes Synyparxes*, 75–77, 80, 186.

51 Panagiotis Moullas, *O Choros Tou Efemerou, Stoicheia Gia Te Paralogotechnia Tou 19ou Aiona* (Athens: Ekdoseis Sokoli, 2007), 191.

52 Neophytos Kavsokalybitis, *Ta Ioudaika Etoi Anatrope Tes Threskeias Ton Evraion Kai Ton Ethimon Avton Met' Apodeixeon Ek Tes Agias Grafes* (Zakynthos: Parnassos, 1861),

53 Kasimatis, *Aima, Evraioi, Talmoud, Etoi Apodeixeis Threskevtikai, Istorikai Kai Dikastikai Peri Tes Yparxeos Ton Anthropothysion Par' Ebraiois*, 47.

54 Fragiski Ampatzopoulou, "Evraioi, Olokavtoma Kai Logotechnike Anaparastase Stis Arches Tou 21ou Aiona," *Nea Estia* 169, no. 1842 (2011): 418.

55 Veis Osman, *E Katakteses Tou Kosmou Ypo Ton Ioudaion* (Odessa: Urlich and Sulche, 1874).

56 Osman, *E Katakteses Tou Kosmou Ypo Ton Ioudaion*, 27, 33, 38, 49.

57 Kavsokalybitis, *Ta Ioudaika Etoi Anatrope Tes Threskeias Ton Evraion Kai Ton Ethimon Avton Met' Apodeixeon Ek Tes Agias Grafes*, iv, xii, xv.

58 Spyridon Papageorgiou, *Sfazousin Oi Evraioi Christianopaidas Kai Pinousi to Aima Ton?* (Athens: Michail I. Saliveros, 1902); Aser R. Moysis, *E Filia Ellenon Kai Israeliton Dia Mesou Ton Aionon* (Athens: Israelitike Morphotike Lesche Thessalonikes "E Adelphotes," 1953), 23.

59 L. L. "Esquisse d'une Histoire des Juifs en Grèce," *L' Univers Israelite*, 53eme Anne, 44, 22 Juillet 1898, 563Alexandre Buchon, *Voyage Dans L'eubee Les Iles Ioniennes Et Les Cyclades En 1841* (Paris: Emile-Paul Editeur, 1911), 261.

60 Ibid. 94; "Les Juifs a Corfu." *L'Univers Israelite*, 2eme Anne (1845), 52–53; Andre Alexander Bonar and Robert Murray McCheyne, *Narrative of a Mission of Inquiry to the Jews from the Church of Scotland* (Philadelphia: Presbyterian Board of Publication, 1839), 527; Henri Belle, *Taxidi Sten Ellada 1861-1874*, vol. B (Athens: Istoretes, 1993), vol c, 54; and Maria Margaroni, "Antisemitic Rumours and Violence in Corfu at the End of the 19th Century," *Quest Issues in Contemporary Jewish History*, no. 3 (2012): 270.

61 Dimitrios Varvaritis, "'The Jews Have Got into Trouble Again': Responses to the Publication of 'Cronaca Insraelitica' and the Question of Jewish Emancipation in the Ionian Islands (1861-1863)," *Varvaritis Quest Issues in Contemporary Jewish History*, no. 7 (2014): 34.

62 Paximadopoulou-Stavrinou, "Oi Exegerseis Tes Kephallenias Kata Ta Ete 1848 Kai 1849," 28, 78.

63 Kostas G. Tsiknanis, "Metra Kata Tes Kykloforias Evraikon Vivlion Ton 16o Aiona," in *E Evraike Parousia Ston Elladiko Choro (4os-19os Ai.)*, eds. Anna Lambropoulou and Kostas Tsiknakis (Athens: Ethniko Idryma Erevnon, 2008), 168.

64 Sakis Gekas, "For Better or for Worse? A Counter-Narrative of Corfu Jewish History and the Transition from the Ionian State to the Greek Kingdom (1815-1890s)," in *Evraikes Koinotetes Anamesa Se Anatole Kai Dyse, 150s-200s Aionas: Oikonomia, Koinonia, Politike, Politismos*, eds. Anna Machaira and Leda Papastefanaki (Ioannina: Isnafi, 2016), 162.

65 Demponos, "Evraika," Z, no. 79–80 (1978): 133; Demponos, "Evraika," Z, no. 81–82 (1978): 166; Sakis Gekas, "The Port Jews of Corfu and the 'Blood Libel' of 1891: A Tale of Many Centuries and of One Event," *Jewish Culture and History* 7, no. 1–2 (2012): 172; and Varvaritis, "'The Jews Have Got into Trouble Again . . .': Responses to the Publication of 'Cronaca Insraelitica' and the Question of Jewish Emancipation in the Ionian Islands (1861-1863)," 35.

66 Margaroni, "Antisemitic Rumours and Violence in Corfu at the End of the 19th Century," 271.

67 Giorgos Margaritis, "Ellenikos Antisemitismos: Mia Periegese, 1821, 1891, 1931" (paper presented at the O Ellenikos Evraismos, Athens, 1998), 19.

68 Eytychia D. Liata, *E Kerkyra Kai E Zakynthos Ston Kyklona Tou Antisemitismou. E Sykofantia Gia to Aima Tou 1891* (Athens: Institouto Neoellinikon Erevnon Ethnikou Idrymatos Erevnon, 2006), 20.

69 Liata, *E Kerkyra Kai E Zakynthos Ston Kyklona Tou Antisemitismou. E Sykofantia Gia to Aima Tou 1891*, 21–23, 51.

70 Nata, *Apo Ten Kerkyra Sto Birkenau Kai Ten Ierousalem - E Istoria Mias Kerkyraias*, 20.

71 Liata, *E Kerkyra Kai E Zakynthos Ston Kyklona Tou Antisemitismou. E Sykofantia Gia to Aima Tou 1891*, 31; Josua Eli Plaut, *Greek Jewry in the Twentieth Century 1913-1983* (London: Farleigh Dickinson University Press, 1996), 30; Gekas, "For Better or for

Worse? A Counter-Narrative of Corfu Jewish History and the Transition from the Ionian State to the Greek Kingdom (1815-1890s)," 165.

72 Gekas "The Port Jews of Corfu and the 'Blood Libel' of 1891: A Tale of Many Centuries and of One Event." 172.

73 Ibid., 184–85. Many Catholics and Jews apparently did not choose to take Greek citizenship in 1864 though the reasons behind such a decision are debatable (Gregoris Psallidas, "Social Solidarity on the Periphery of the Greek Kingdom: The Case of the Workers' Fraternity of Corfu," in *Greek Society in the Making, 1863-1913*, ed. Philip Carabott (Aldershot: Ashgate, 1997), 24).

74 Gekas, "The Port Jews of Corfu and the 'Blood Libel' of 1891: A Tale of Many Centuries and of One Event," 172.

75 Ibid., 186.

76 Ibid., 187.

77 See Henri Desportes, *Le Mystere Du Sang Chez Les Juifs De Tous Les Temps* (Paris: Albert Savine Editeur, 1890).

78 Kasimatis, *Aima, Evraioi, Talmoud, Etoi Apodeixeis Threskevtikai, Istorikai Kai Dikastikai Peri Tes Yparxeos Ton Anthropothysion Par' Ebraiois*, 155–56, 185–89.

79 Liata, *E Kerkyra Kai E Zakynthos Ston Kyklona Tou Antisemitismou. E Sykofantia Gia to Aima Tou 1891*, 23.

80 Ibid., 39–40.

81 Ibid., 63.

82 Ampatzopoulou, *O Allos En Diogmo. E Eikona Tou Evraiou Ste Logotechnia, Zetemata Istorias Kai Mythoplasias*, 226; Georgios A. Zavitsianos, *Aktis Photos. Katadiogmos Ton Evraion En Te Istoria. Skepseis* (Kerkyra: N Petsali, 1891); and Christos Christovasilis, *Peri Evraion* (Athens: Ekdoseis Roes, 2007).

83 Demponou, "Evraika." 137.

84 Malakis, *Apomnemonevmata Epi Tes Sygchronou Istorias, E Istorikon Epeisodion Epi Ton Energeion Drasanton Prosopon Pros Epitevxin Tes Megales Ideas*, 24, 37.

85 HAMFA, KY, 1868, 99:1, 788 (8341), Galati, September 24, 1868.

86 HAMFA, KY, 1868, 99:1, 8941, Athens, October 15, 1868; HAMFA, KY, 1868, 99:1, 809, Galati, October 12, 1868.

87 HAMFA, KY, 1871, 49:2, 527 (7025), Bucharest, July 28, 1871.

88 HAMFA, KY, 1871, 49:2, 1059 (6258), Bucharest, August 3/15, 1871; HAMFA, KY, 1871, 49:2, 7025, Athens, August 17, 1871; HAMFA, KY, 1871, 49:2, 579 (8003), Galati, August 26, 1871; HAMFA, KY, 1871, 49:2, 1318, Bucharest, October 2, 1871; and HAMFA, KY, 1871, 49:2, 9673, Galati, October 15/27, 1871.

89 Margaroni, "Antisemitic Rumours and Violence in Corfu at the End of the 19th Century," 279–80; Eftychia Liata, "The Anti-Semitic Disturbances on Corfu and Zakynthos in 1891 and Their Socio-Political Consequences," *The Historical Review/ La Revue Historique* 4 (2007): 163; and Effi Gazi, "Revisiting Religion and Nationalism in Nineteenth-Century Greece," in *The Making of Modern Greece: Nationalism, Romanticism, and the Uses of the Past (1797-1896)*, eds. Rodeick Beaton and David Ricks (New York: Routledge, 2016), 103.

90 Solomos, *Istoria Ton Evraion Apo Ton Archaiotaton Chronon Mechri Ton Emeron Mas*, 235; Constantinos A. Caloyanni, *Histoire Des Hebreux* (Alexandrie: A Dracopoulos, 1895), 220; and Papageorgiou, *Sfazousin Oi Evraioi Christianopaidas Kai Pinousi to Aima Ton?* 6, 12.

91 Biondich, *The Balkans. Revolution, War and Political Violence since 1878*, 64; Basil C. Gounaris, "National Claims, Conflicts and Developments in Macedonia, 1870-1912," in *The History of Macedonia*, ed. Ioannis Koliopoulos (Thessaloniki: Museum of the Macedonian Struggle Foundation, 2007), 186.

92 Philip Carabott, "Aspects of the Hellenization of Greek Macedonia, Ca. 1912-Ca. 1959," *Kambos: Cambridge Papers in Modern Greek* 13 (2005): 27.

93 See Basil C. Gounaris, "Preachers of God and Martyrs of the Nation: The Politics of Murder in Ottoman Macedonia in the Early 20th Century," *Balkanologie* IX, no. 1–2 (2005): 31–43; Dimitris Livanios, "'Conquering the Souls': Nationalism and Greek Guerilla Warfare in Ottoman Macedonia, 1904-1908," *Byzantine and Modern Greek Studies* 23 (1999); and Tasos Kostopoulos, "'Land to the Tiller.' On the Neglected Agrarian Component of the Macedonian Revolutionary Movement, 1893-1912," *Turkish Historical Review* 7 (2016).

94 Evaggelos Kofos, "Ethnike Kleronomia Kai Ethnike Tautoteta Ste Makedonia Tou 19ou Kai Tou 20ou Aiona," in *Ethnike Tautoteta Kai Ethnikismos Ste Neotere Ellada*, ed. Thanos Veremis (Athens: Morfotiko Idryma Ethnikis Trapezis, 1997), 203.

95 HAMFA, KY, 1861, 76.1, 204, Petroupolis, August 22, 1861; HAMFA, KY, 1861, 76.1, 18, Pera, February 24, 1861; HAMFA, KY, 1861, 76.1, 35, Adrianople, February 28, 1861; HAMFA, KY, 1870, 36/2, 389, Thessaloniki, May 27, 1870; and Konstantinos Vakalopoulos, *To Makedoniko Zetema: Genese - Diamorphose - Exelixe - Lyse (1856-1912)* (Athens: Dimosiographikos Organismos Labraki, 2009), 23, 46, 50, 52, 90.

96 HAMFA, KY, 1895, A5-1, 717, Dyrrachio, June 23, 1895; Michael G. Tritos, *To Tagma Ton Lazariston Kai E Roumanike Propaganda* (Thessaloniki: Kyromanos, 2004), 12–14.

97 HAMFA, KY, 1877, 36/2, 55, Avlon, February 10, 1877; HAMFA, KY, 1861, 36.2, Ioannina, March 22, 1861; HAMFA, KY, 1862, 36.2, 200, Ioannina, July 19, 1862; and Anastasios Provatas, *Syntomos Politike Istoria Tou Voreioepeirotikou Zetematos* (Athens: Kentrike Epitrope Voreioepeirotikou Agonos, 1969), 7.

98 Mackridge, *Language and National Identity in Greece 1766-1976.*

99 Philip Carabott, "Politics, Orthodoxy and the Language Question in Greece: The Gospel Riots of November 1901," *Journal of Mediterranean Studies* 3, no. 1 (1993): 117–38.

100 HAMFA, KY, 1867, 76.1, 2018, Pera, July 7, 1867; HAMFA, KY, 1870, 36/2, Serres, January 2, 1870.

101 Anastasia Karakasidou, *Fields of Wheat, Hills of Blood: Passages to Nationhood in Greek Macedonia, 1870-1990* (Chicago: University of Chicago Press, 1997), 96.

102 HAMFA, KY, 1891, A5-1, Athens, June 18, 1891.

103 Tritos, *To Tagma Ton Lazariston Kai E Roumanike Propaganda*, 19, 35–36.

104 Stefanos I. Papadopoulos, "Education in Macedonia and Her Contribution in the Development of the Preconditions for the Success of the Macedonian Struggle," in *O Makedonikos Agonas* (Thessaloniki: Institute for Balkan Studies, 1987), 27.

105 Andrew Tosheff, *The Bulgarian-Serbian Debate* (Sofia: The Royal Printing Office, 1932), 67.

106 HAMFA KY, 1904 IΔ AAK 62.3, 309, June 5, 1904; HAMFA KY, 1904 IΔ AAK 62.3, 15, February 10, 1904; HAMFA KY, 1904 IΔ AAK 62.3, 39, February 16, 1904; HAMFA KY, 1910 K, 793, August 18, 1910; HAMFA KY, 1910 K, 476, April 9, 1910; HAMFA KY, 1910 K, September 12, 1910; and HAMFA KY, 1911 94.1, 348/17007, July 26, 1911 (January 15, 1911).

107 Ilias G. Skoulidas, "Ellenes Proxenoi Se 'Epeiro Kai Alvania' Sta Tele Tou 19ou Aiona: Ideologikoi Prosanatolismoi Kai Kratike Politike," in *To Ethnos Peran Ton Synoron*, eds. Lina Ventoura and Lampros Mpaltsiotis (Athens: Vivliorama, 2013), 83, 88; Haris Exertzoglou, "Shifting Boundaries: Language, Community and the Non-Greek-Speaking Greeks," *Historein* 1 (1999): 88; and Vladislav B. Sotirović, "Macedonia between Greek, Bulgarian, Albanian, and Serbian National Aspirations, 1870-1912,"

Serbian Studies: Journal of the North American Society for Serbian Studies 23, no. 1 (2009): 22.

108 Liakos, *E Italike Enopoiese Kai E Megale Idea 1859-1862*, 159–61, 186; Kostis, *"Ta Kakomathemena Paidia Tes Istorias" E Diamorfose Tou Neoellenikou Kratous, 18os-21os Aionas*, 366; and Lydia Tricha, *Charilaos Trikoupis, O Politikos Tou "Tis Ptaiei"; Kai Tou "Dystychos Eptochevsamen"* (Athens: Polis, 2016), 276.

109 Michalis Kokolakis, *To Ystero Gianniotiko Pasaliki: Choros, Dioikese Kai Plythysmos Sten Tourkokratoumene Epeiro (1820-1913)* (Athens: Kentro Neoellinikon Erevnon, Ethniko Idryma Erevnon, 2003), 48, 95.

110 HAMFA KY, 1913 9.2, 3848, February 4, 1913; HAMFA KY, 1913 9.2, 4401, February 10/23, 1913.

111 HAMFA KY, 1906 64.3, 348, August 16, 1906; HAMFA KY, 1911 62.2, July 23, 1911. Ironically Greek relations with Romania, the one state that did not border Macedonia, deteriorated the most in the period prior to 1912 leading to a suspension of diplomatic relations, and Romanian measures against schools and Greek citizens (Vakalopoulos, *To Makedoniko Zetema: Genese - Diamorphose - Exelixe - Lyse (1856-1912)*, 204).

112 Christovasilis, *Peri Evraion*, 57.

113 Meropi Anastassiadou, *Salonique 1830-1912* (New York: Brill, 1997), 110–15; Devin E. Naar, "From the 'Jerusalem of the Balkans' to the Goldene Medina: Jewish Immigration from Salonika to the United States," *American Jewish History* 93, no. 4 (2007): 439, 440.

114 HAMFA, KY, 1863, 36:2, 714 (5702), Thessaloniki, October 5, 1863.

115 HAMFA KY, 1852 36.2a, 498/264, December 9, 1852; HAMFA KY, 1853 36.2, 525/287, December 30, 1852; and HAMFA KY, 1853 36.2, 257/97, July 11, 1853.

116 See Dimitris Stamatopoulos, "Between Middle Classes and Grand Bourgeoisie: Greek-Bulgarian Confrontation and Political Hegemony in Thessaloniki from the Bulgarian Schism (1872) to the Slaughter of the Consuls (1876)," in *Balkan Nationalism(S) and the Ottoman Empire*, ed. Dimitris Stamatopoulos (Istanbul: The Isis Press, 2015), 101–41.

117 HAMFA, KY, 1874, 36/2, 1068, Thessaloniki, September 18, 1874.

118 Fleming, *Greece a Jewish History*, 56; Anastassiadou, *Salonique 1830-1912*, 407–08; Stanford Shaw, *The Jews of the Ottoman Empire and the Turkish Republic* (New York: New York University Press, 1991), 196; and "Antisémitisme et Sionisme en Turquie," *Revue du Monde Musulman*, 9 (1910): 175.

119 Fleming, *Greece a Jewish History*, 57.

120 Ibid., 45.

121 HAMFA, KY, 1879, 36/2, 12, Kavalla, January 14, 1879; HAMFA, KY, 1879, 36/2, 12, Kavalla, January 14, 1879; HAMFA, KY, 1879, 36/2, 26, Thessaloniki, January 9, 1879; HAMFA, KY, 1880, 36/2, 4, Kavalla, January 2, 1880; HAMFA, KY, 1880, 36/2, 28, Thessaloniki, January 8, 1880; HAMFA, KY, 1881, 36/2, Kavalla, March 30, 1881; and HAMFA, KY, 1881, 36/2, Thessaloniki, January 10, 1881.

122 HAMFA, KY, 1851 36.2, 43/141, April 24, 1851.

123 Tsiligiannis, *E Evraike Koinoteta Tes Artas*, 27, 30, 34, Fleming, *Greece a Jewish History*, 46.

124 Moysis, *E Filia Ellenon Kai Israeliton Dia Mesou Ton Aionon*, 26.

125 Ibid., 142.

126 Ilias G. Skoulidas, "Arta: Ena Antiparadeigma," in *Apo Ten Apeiro Chora Sten Megale Epeiro*, eds. Katerina Liampi, Nikolaos Katsikoudis, and Nikolaos Anastasopoulos (Ioannina: Kosmeteia Philosophikis Scholis, 2016), 174.

127 Skoulidas, "Arta: Ena Antiparadeigma," 179.

128 Dimitris Kamouzis, "Elites and the Formation of National Identity: The Case of the Greek Orthodox Millet (Mid-Nineteenth Century to 1922)," in *State-Nationalisms in the Ottoman Empire, Greece and Turkey: Orthodox and Muslims, 1830-1945*, ed. Benjamin C. Fortna, et al. (London: Routledge, 2013), 24.

129 Devin E. Naar, "Fashioning the 'Mother of Israel': The Ottoman Jewish Historical Narrative and the Image of Jewish Salonica," *Jewish History* 28 (2014): 341, 354.

130 Paschalis M. Kitromilides, "On the Intellectual Content of Greek Nationalism: Paparrigopoulos, Byzantium and the Great Idea," in *Byzantium and the Modern Greek Identity*, eds. David Ricks and Paul Magdalino (Aldershot: Ashgate, 1998), 28, 31; Stratos Myrogiannis, *The Emergence of a Greek Identity (1700-1821)* (Newcastle upon Tyne: Cambridge Scholars Publishing, 2012), 153, 158.

131 Arslan, *O Ellenikos Typos Sto Othomaniko Kratos*, 17.

132 Neoklis Kazazis, *To Panepistemion Kai E Ethnike Idea* (Athens: Typografeio tou Kratous, 1902), 13.

133 Devin E. Naar, *Jewish Salonica: Between the Ottoman Empire and Modern Greece* (Stanford: Stanford University Press, 2016), 217.

134 Tatsios, *The Megali Idea and the Greek-Turkish War of 1897: The Impact of the Cretan Problem on Greek Irredentism, 1866-1897*, 78, 86–87, 90, 92, 111.

135 See Basil C. Gounaris, "Emigration from Macedonia in the Early Twentieth Century," *Journal of Modern Greek Studies* 7, no. 1 (1989): 133–53; Adam J. Goldwyn, "Joseph Eliyia and the Jewish Question in Greece: Zionism, Hellenism, and the Struggle for Modernity," *Journal of Modern Greek Studies* 33, no. 2 (2015): 367; and see Julian Brooks, "A 'Tranquilizing' Influence? British 'Proto-Peacekeeping' in Ottoman Macedonia 1904-1905," *Peace & Change* 36, no. 2 (2011).

136 Spyros Tsoutsoumpis, "Land of the Kapedani: Brigandage, Paramilitarism and Nation-Building in 20th Century Greece," *Balkan Studies* 51 (2016): 44; Spyros Ploumidis, "Nuances of Irredentism: The Epirote Society of Athens (1906-1912)," *The Historical Review/La Revue Historique* 8 (2011): 149.

137 Richard C. Hall, *The Balkan Wars 1912-1913: Prelude to the First World War* (New York: Routledge, 2000), 9.

138 Stratis Myrivilis, "E Proelase Tes V Merarchias," in *To Kokkino Vivlio* (Athens: Estia, 2009).

139 McCarthy, *Death and Exile, the Ethnic Cleansing of Ottoman Muslims 1821-1922*, 139, 141; Tasos Kostopoulos, *Polemos Kai Ethnokatharse - E Xechasmene Plevra Mias Dekaetous Ethnikes Exormeses (1912-1922)* (Athens: Vivliorama, 2007), 40.

140 McCarthy, *Death and Exile, the Ethnic Cleansing of Ottoman Muslims 1821-1922*, 143, 149, 152.

141 Josef Redlich et al., *Report of the International Commission to Inquire into the Causes and Conduct of the Balkan Wars* (Washington DC: Carnegie Endowment for International Peace, 1914). *The Other Balkan Wars* (Washington DC: Carnegie Endowment for International Peace, 1993), 154; Hall, *The Balkan Wars 1912-1913: Prelude to the First World War*, 137; and Emilia Salvanou, "The First World War and the Refugee Crisis: Historiography and Memory in the Greek Context," *Historein* 16, no. 1–2 (2017): 122.

142 Mary Neuburger, "Pomak Borderlands: Muslims on the Edge of Nations," *Nationalities Papers: The Journal of Nationalism and Ethnicity* 28, no. 1 (2010): 185.

143 HAMFA KY, 1913 16.3, 705, February 6, 1913; HAMFA KY, 1913 16.3, 220, January 31, 1913. McCarthy, *Death and Exile, the Ethnic Cleansing of Ottoman Muslims 1821-1922*, 148.

144 Loukianos I. Hassiotis, "Macedonia, 1912-1923: From the Multinational Empire to Nation State," in *The History of Macedonia*, ed. Ioannis Koliopoulos (Thessaloniki: Museum of the Macedonian Struggle Foundation, 2007), 251.

145 Lena Divani, *Ellada Kai Meionotetes. To Sytema Diethnous Prostasias Tes Koinonias Ton Ethnon* (Athens: Kastaniotis, 1999), 60.

146 Redlich et al. Carnegie, *The Other Balkan Wars*, 201–07; McCarthy, *Death and Exile, the Ethnic Cleansing of Ottoman Muslims 1821-1922*, 149.

147 Kostopoulos, *Polemos Kai Ethnokatharse - E Xechasmene Plevra Mias Dekaetous Ethnikes Exormeses (1912-1922)*, 38.

148 Pavlos B. Petridis, *Xenike Exartisi Kai Ethniki Politike 1910-1918* (Athens: Parateretes, 1981), 131, 132, 135, 138, 140, 141.

149 Jacob Gould Schurman, *The Balkan Wars 1912-1913* (Princeton NJ: Princeton University Press, 1914), 70.

150 Dimitrios Salamanka, *Kathos Charaze E Levteria* (Ioannina: Ipeirotiki Estia, 1963), 200.

151 Guy Chantepleure and (Jeanne Violet Dussap), *La Ville Assiegee - Janina Octobre 1912 - Mars 1913* (Paris: Calmann-Levy, 1913), 235.

152 Rena Molcho, *Oi Evraioi Tes Thessalonikis 1856-1919* (Athens: Ekdoseis Pataki, 2014), 243.

153 Maria Kavala, "E Thessalonike Ste Germanike Katoche (1941-1944): Koinonia, Oikonomia, Diogmos Evraion" (University of Crete, 2009), 47, 52; Ilitzak, "O Evraikos Sosialismos Sten Othomanike Thessaloniki," 49, 52.

154 Molcho, *Oi Evraioi Tes Thessalonikis 1856-1919*, 244; Rena Molho, "Popular Antisemitism and State Policy in Salonika During the City's Annexation to Greece," *Jewish Social Studies* 50, no. 3/4 (1988): 257; and Shaw, *The Jews of the Ottoman Empire and the Turkish Republic*, 195.

155 Leon Sciaky, *Farewell to Salonica* (New York: Current Books, 1946), 213.

156 HAMFA KY, 1913 22.4, 4635, February 13, 1913; HAMFA KY, 1913 22.4, 5594, February 23, 1913; and HAMFA KY, 1913 22.4, 5594, March 8, 1913; Molcho, *Oi Evraioi Tes Thessalonikis 1856-1919*, 258.

157 Fleming, *Greece a Jewish History*, 68–69; Bernard Lory, "1912 Les Hellenes Entrent Dans La Ville" in *Salonique 1850-1918, La 'Ville Des Juifs' Et Le Reveil Des Balkans*, ed. Gilles Veinstein (Paris: Lory: Editions Autrement, 1992), 250–51; Molcho, *Oi Evraioi Tes Thessalonikis 1856-1919*, 254; N. M. Gelber, "An Attempt to Internationilize Salonika," *Jewish Social Studies* 17 (1955); Rena Molho, *Oi Evraioi Tes Thessalonikis 1856-1919* (Athens: Themelio, 2001), 254.

158 Molho "Popular Antisemitism and State Policy in Salonika During the City's Annexation to Greece," 261; Hassiotis, "Macedonia, 1912-1923: From the Multinational Empire to Nation State," 255–56; Paris Papamichos Chronakis, "De-Judaizing a Class, Hellenizing a City: Jewish Merchants and the Future of Salonica in Greek Public Discourse, 1913-1914," *Jewish History* 28 (2014): 384; and Maria Kavala, *E Katastrophe Ton Evraion Tes Elladas (1941-1944)* (Athens: Syndesmos Ellinikon Akadimaikon Vivliothikon, 2015), 21.

159 Benbassa and Rodrigue, *The Jews of the Balkans*, 96; Rena Molcho, "E Avevaioteta Tes Ellenikes Kyriarchias Ste Thessalonike Meta to 1912," *Sygchrona Themata* B 17, no. 52–54 (1994): 25–26.

160 Mocho, *Oi Evraioi Tes Thessalonikis 1856-1919*, 271, 274.

161 Ibid., 251, 266.

162 Thomas P. Exarchou, *Oi Evraioi Sten Xanthi* (Xanthi: Politistiko Anaptyxiako Kentro Thrakis, 2001), 71.

163 Mazower, *Salonica City of Ghosts*, 377.

164 Molho, "Popular Antisemitism and State Policy in Salonika During the City's Annexation to Greece." 256, 259.

165 Naar, "From the 'Jerusalem of the Balkans' to the Goldene Medina: Jewish Immigration from Salonika to the United States," 451.

166 Molho, "Popular Antisemitism and State Policy in Salonika During the City's Annexation to Greece." 260.

167 Ioannis Saias, *La Grece Et Les Israelites De Salonique* (Paris: Impremerie de la conference de la Paix, 1919), 76.

168 Steven B. Bowman, *The Agony of Greek Jews 1940-1945* (Stanford: Stanford University Press, 2009), 19.

169 Biondich, *The Balkans. Revolution, War and Political Violence since 1878*, 78.

170 Kostopoulos, *Polemos Kai Ethnokatharse - E Xechasmene Plevra Mias Dekaetous Ethnikes Exormeses (1912-1922)*, 77; Athina Kakouri, *Ta Dyo Veta* (Athens: Ekdoseis Kapon, 2016), 107.

171 Fikret Adanir, "Non-Muslims in the Ottoman Army and the Ottoman Defeat in the Balkan War of 1912-1913," in *A Question of Genocide, Armenians and Turks at the End of the Ottoman Empire*, eds. Ronald Grigor Suny, Fatma Müge Göçek, and Norman M Naimark (Oxford: Oxford University Press, 2011), 117–18.

172 HAMFA, KY, 1892, A:12-1, June 2, 1308 (1892).

173 "Grèce – Les obligations militaires des Juifs," *Paix et Droit*, 7 no. 4 (1927): 11.

174 Moysis, *E Filia Ellenon Kai Israeliton Dia Mesou Ton Aionon*, 23.

175 Rouben Paul Adalian, "Comparative Policy and Differential Practice in the Treatment of Minorities in Wartime: The United States Archival Evidence on the Armenians and Greeks in the Ottoman Empire," *Journal of Genocide Research* 3, no. 1 (2001): 39.

176 Kavala, *E Katastrophe Ton Evraion Tes Elladas (1941-1944)*, 24.

177 Albertos Nar, *Keimene Epi Aktes Thalasses... Meletes Kai Arthra Gia Ten Evraike Koinoteta Tes Thessalonikis* (Thessaloniki: University Studio Press/Ekfrasi, 1997), 161.

178 Kavala, *E Katastrophe Ton Evraion Tes Elladas (1941-1944)*, 25.

179 Kakouri, *Ta Dyo Veta*, 17.

180 Photini Constantopoulou and Thanos Veremis, eds., *Documents on the History of the Greek Jews* (Athens: Kastanidis, 1999), 31; Rafail Frezis, *E Israelitike Koinoteta Volou* (Volos: Epikoinonia, 2002), 78; and Molcho, *Oi Evraioi Tes Thessalonikis 1856-1919*, 278.

181 HAMFA KY, 1913 22.4, 4689, February 12, 1913.

182 Ilitzak, "O Evraikos Sosialismos Sten Othomanike Thessaloniki," 26.

183 McCarthy, *Death and Exile, the Ethnic Cleansing of Ottoman Muslims 1821-1922*, 279, 284; Kostopoulos, *Polemos Kai Ethnokatharse - E Xechasmene Plevra Mias Dekaetous Ethnikes Exormeses (1912-1922)*, 98, 99, 125.

184 Adalian, "Comparative Policy and Differential Practice in the Treatment of Minorities in Wartime: The United States Archival Evidence on the Armenians and Greeks in the Ottoman Empire," 34; Kostopoulos, *Polemos Kai Ethnokatharse - E Xechasmene Plevra Mias Dekaetous Ethnikes Exormeses (1912-1922)*, 71; Kakouri, *Ta Dyo Veta*, 109; McCarthy, *Death and Exile, the Ethnic Cleansing of Ottoman Muslims 1821-1922*, 155; and Matthias Bjørnlund, "The 1914 Cleansing of Aegean Greeks as a Case of Violent Turkification," *Journal of Genocide Research* 10, no. 1 (2008): 42, 44.

185 Divani, *Ellada Kai Meionotetes. To Sytema Diethnous Prostasias Tes Koinonias Ton Ethnon*, 55.

186 Spyros Marketos, "E Ensomatose Tes Sepharadikes Thessalonikes Sten Ellada: To Plaisio, 1912-1914" (paper presented at the O Ellenikos Evraismos, Athens, 1998), 74.

187 Giannis Papadopoulos, "Schedia Epoikismou Prin Apo Ten Ellenotourkike Antallage Plethysmon," *Mnemon* 32 (2012): 159, 164.
188 Tassos Kostopoulos, "How the North Was Won: Épuration Ethnique, Échange Des Populations Et Politique De Colonisation Dans La Macédoine Grecque.," *European Journal of Turkish Studies* 12 (2011): 2.

Chapter 5

1 Theodora Dragostinova, "Navigating Nationality in the Emigration of Minorities between Bulgaria and Greece, 1919-1941," *East European Politics and Societies* 23, no. 2 (2009): 185.
2 Dragostinova, "Navigating Nationality in the Emigration of Minorities between Bulgaria and Greece," 186.
3 Renee Hirschon, *Heirs to the Greek Catastrophe: The Social Life of Asia Minor Refugees in Pireaus* (Oxford: Clarendon Press, 1989), 8.
4 Mark Mazower, "Minorities and the League of Nations in Interwar Europe," *Daedalus* 126, no. 2 (1997): 48.
5 George Mavrogordatos, *Stillborn Republic: Social Coalitions and Party Strategies in Greece, 1922-1936* (Berkeley: University of California Press, 1983), 185–86.
6 Karakasidou, *Fields of Wheat, Hills of Blood: Passages to Nationhood in Greek Macedonia, 1870-1990*, 147.
7 Ibid., 147, 152.
8 Mavrogordatos, *Stillborn Republic: Social Coalitions and Party Strategies in Greece, 1922-1936*.
9 George Th Mavrogordatos, "The Holocaust in Greece: A Vindication of Assimilation," *Etudes Balkaniques* XLVIII, no. 4 (2012): 6.
10 Karakasidou, *Fields of Wheat, Hills of Blood: Passages to Nationhood in Greek Macedonia, 1870-1990*, 143.
11 Provatas, *Syntomos Politike Istoria Tou Voreioepeirotikou Zetematos*, 8.
12 Ibid., 9.
13 Divani, *Ellada Kai Meionotetes. To Sytema Diethnous Prostasias Tes Koinonias Ton Ethnon*, 83.
14 Tasos Kostopoulos, "Counting the 'Other': Official Census and Classified Statistics in Greece (1830–2001)," *Jahrbücher für Geschichte und Kultur Südosteuropas* 5 (2003): 63.
15 Kostopoulos, "Counting the 'Other': Official Census and Classified Statistics in Greece (1830-2001)," 64, 65.
16 Vlasis Vlasidis, "The 'Macedonian Question' on the Bulgarian Political Scene (1919-23)," *Balkan Studies* 32, no. 1 (1991): 73, 77, 81.
17 Areti Tounta-Fergadi, *Elleno-Voulgarikes Meionotetes. Protokollo Politi-Kalfof 1924-1925* (Thessaloniki: Institute for Balkan Studies, 1986), 47.
18 Tounta-Fergadi, *Elleno-Voulgarikes Meionotetes. Protokollo Politi-Kalfof 1924-1925*, 87, 90; Divani, *Ellada Kai Meionotetes. To Sytema Diethnous Prostasias Tes Koinonias Ton Ethnon*, 142–43.
19 Tounta-Fergadi, *Elleno-Voulgarikes Meionotetes. Protokollo Politi-Kalfof 1924-1925*, 118.
20 Spyros Sfetas, "Birth of Macedonianism in the Interwar Period," in *The History of Macedonia*, ed. Ioannis Koliopoulos (Thessaloniki: Museum of the Macedonian Struggle Foundation, 2007), 285.

21 Sfetas, "Birth of Macedonianism in the Interwar Period," 292.

22 Dragostinova, "Navigating Nationality in the Emigration of Minorities between Bulgaria and Greece, 1919-1941," 186.

23 Divani, *Ellada Kai Meionotetes. To Sytema Diethnous Prostasias Tes Koinonias Ton Ethnon*, 262; Lambros Mpaltsiotis, "E Ithageneia Ston Psychro Polemo," in *Ta Dikaiomata Sten Ellada 1953-2003. Apo to Telos Tou Emfyliou Sto Telos Tes Metapolitevses*, eds. Michalis Tsapogas and Dimitris Christopoulos (Athens: Ekdoseis Kastanioti, 2004), 84.

24 Theodora Dragostinova, "Speaking National: Nationalizing the Greeks of Bulgaria. 1900-1939," *Slavic Review* 67, no. 1 (2008): 163; Mpaltsiotis, "E Ithageneia Ston Psychro Polemo," 84.

25 Dragostinova, "Speaking National: Nationalizing the Greeks of Bulgaria. 1900-1939," 164.

26 Carabott, "Aspects of the Hellenization of Greek Macedonia, Ca. 1912-Ca. 1959," 39.

27 Dragostinova, "Speaking National: Nationalizing the Greeks of Bulgaria. 1900-1939," 172.

28 Karakasidou, *Fields of Wheat, Hills of Blood: Passages to Nationhood in Greek Macedonia, 1870-1990*, 176, 187.

29 Ibid., 170.

30 Divani, *Ellada Kai Meionotetes. To Sytema Diethnous Prostasias Tes Koinonias Ton Ethnon*, 323; Kostopoulos, "Counting the 'Other': Official Census and Classified Statistics in Greece (1830-2001)," 66. After the Second World War a third category was instituted the *refstosyneidetoi* – literally "those with fluid consciousness" (ibid. 67).

31 Iakovos D Michailidis, "The Statistical Battle for the Population of Greek Macedonia," in *The History of Macedonia*, ed. Ioannis Koliopoulos (Thessaloniki: Museum of the Macedonian Struggle Foundation, 2007), 277; Kostopoulos, "Counting the 'Other': Official Census and Classified Statistics in Greece (1830-2001)," 66.

32 Mazower, "Minorities and the League of Nations in Interwar Europe," 49, 52; Carabott, "Aspects of the Hellenization of Greek Macedonia, Ca. 1912-Ca. 1959," 47.

33 Divani, *Ellada Kai Meionotetes. To Sytema Diethnous Prostasias Tes Koinonias Ton Ethnon*, 324.

34 Mazower, "Minorities and the League of Nations in Interwar Europe," 52, 53.

35 Radu Ioanid, "The Holocaust in Romania: The Iasi Pogrom of June 1941," *Contemporary European History* 2, no. 2 (1993): 119.

36 Carabott, "Aspects of the Hellenization of Greek Macedonia, Ca. 1912-Ca. 1959," 51.

37 Kostis A Tsioumis, *Meionotetes Sten Ellada: Ellenikes Meionotetes Sta Valkania* (Thessaloniki: Ekdotikos Oikos Ant. Stamouli, 2008), 22.

38 Tsioumis, *Meionotetes Sten Ellada: Ellenikes Meionotetes Sta Valkania*, 23, 27; Evangelos Averoff, *E Politike Plevra Tou Koutsovlachikou Zetematos* (Trikala, 1987), 19–20; Kostopoulos, "Counting the 'Other': Official Census and Classified Statistics in Greece (1830-2001)," 63.

39 See M. Benjamin Thorne, "Assimilation, Invisibility, and the Eugenic Turn in the 'Gypsy Question' in Romanian Society, 1938–1942," *Romani Studies* 21, no. 2 (2011).

40 Angela Jianu, "Women, Dowries, and Patrimonial Law in Old Regime Romania (C. 1750-1830)," *Journal of Family History* 34, no. 2 (2009): 196.

41 Kostopoulos, "Counting the 'Other': Official Census and Classified Statistics in Greece (1830-2001)," 61, 63.

42 Divani, *Ellada Kai Meionotetes. To Sytema Diethnous Prostasias Tes Koinonias Ton Ethnon*, 191.

43 Zafeirios K. Mekos, *Mousoulmanoi, Armenioi Kai Evraioi Sympolites Mou Komotenaioi* (Thessaloniki: Ant. Stamoulis Publishing, 2007), 64–65.

44 Mekos, *Mousoulmanoi, rmenioi Kai Evraioi Sympolites Mou Komotenaioi*, 64; Christina Borou, "The Muslim Minority of Western Thrace in Greece: An Internal Positive or an Internal Negative 'Other'?," *Journal of Muslim Minority Affairs* 29, no. 1 (2009): 9.

45 Brunnbauer, "The Perception of Muslims in Bulgaria and Greece: Between the 'Self' and the 'Other'," 48.

46 Fleming, *Greece a Jewish History*, 97.

47 Naar, *Jewish Salonica: Between the Ottoman Empire and Modern Greece*, 63.

48 Aser R. Moysis, *Eisagoge Eis to Oikogeneiakon Dikaion Ton En Elladi Israeliton* (Thessaloniki: Triantafyllos M, 1934), 24, 28, 29.

49 Konstantinos D. Kerameos, *Nomike Prosopikotes Kai Kratike Epopteia Israelitikon Idrymaton En Elladi: Dyo Gnomodoteseis* (Thessaloniki1976; repr., Reprint from Journal Armenopoulos, volume 30, issue 10).; Rena Molho, "The Zionist Movement in Thessaloniki 1899-1919," in *The Jewish Communities in Southeastern Europe: From the Fifteenth Century to the End of World War II*, ed. I. K. Hassiotis (Thessaloniki: Institute of Balkan Studies, 1997), 348; Naar, *Jewish Salonica: Between the Ottoman Empire and Modern Greece*, 39.

50 Mazower, *Salonica City of Ghosts*, 275.

51 Alexandra Yerolympos, "Thessaloniki (Salonika) before and after 1917. Twentieth Century Planning Versus 20 Centuries of Urban Evolution," *Planning Perspectives* 3 (1988): 158, 159.

52 Yerolympos, "Thessaloniki (Salonika) before and after 1917," 147, 148. Rena Molho, "The Close Ties between Nationalism and Antisemitism," in *Jahrbuch Für Antisemitismisforschung 24*, eds. Werner Bergmann, Marcus Funck, and Dilek Güven (Berlin: Metropol Verlag, 2015), 218; Naar, *Jewish Salonica: Between the Ottoman Empire and Modern Greece*, 158.

53 Alexandra Yerolympos, "A New City for a New State. City Planning and the Formation of National Identity in the Balkans (1820s-1920s)," *Planning Perspectives* 8 (1993): 242.

54 Mazower, *Salonica City of Ghosts*. 306; "Travellers and the Oriental City C 1840-1920," *Transactions of the Royal Historical Society* 12, no. Sixth Series (2002); Vilma Hastaoglou-Martinidis, "A Mediterranean City in Transition: Thessaloniki between the Two World Wars," *Facta Univeritatis Archaeology and Civil Engineering* 1, no. 4 (1997): 495, 497.

55 Molho, "The Close Ties between Nationalism and Antisemitism," 218.

56 Giomtov Giakoel, *Apomnemonevmata 1941-1943* (Thessaloniki: Parateretes, 1993), 86; Aristotle A Kallis, "The Jewish Community of Salonica under Siege: The Antisemitic Violence of the Summer of 1931," *Holocaust and Genocide Studies* 20, no. 1 (2006): 42, 43; Leon Saltiel, "Dehumanizing the Dead the Destruction of Thessaloniki's Jewish Cemetery in the Light of New Sources," *Yad Vashem Studies* 42, no. 1 (2014): 2; Naar, *Jewish Salonica: Between the Ottoman Empire and Modern Greece*, 246.

57 Devin E. Naar *Jewish Salonica: Between the Ottoman Empire and Modern Greece* (Stanford: Stanford University Press, 2016), 250, 259, 261, 266.

58 Saltiel, "Dehumanizing the Dead the Destruction," 2; Naar, *Jewish Salonica: Between the Ottoman Empire and Modern Greece*, 270.

59 Mazower, *Salonica City of Ghosts*, 397; Nicholas Stavroulakis, *Salonika: Jews and Dervishes* (Athens: Talos Press, 1993), 17. Giakoel, *Apomnemonevmata 1941-1943*, 87; Mark Mazower, *Inside Hitler's Greece, the Experience of Occupation 1941-1944* (New

Haven: Yale University Press, 1993), 240; Michael Matsas, *The Illusion of Safety: The Story of Greek Jews During the Second World War* (New York: Pella, 1997), 38.

60 See Chronakis, "De-Judaizing a Class, Hellenizing a City," 373–403.

61 Molho, "The Close Ties between Nationalism and Antisemitism," 219.

62 Naar, *Jewish Salonica: Between the Ottoman Empire and Modern Greece*, 113–14.

63 Fleming, *Greece a Jewish History*, 87.

64 Michael Molho, "Le Judaisme Grec En General Et La Communaute Juive De Salonique En Particulier Entre Les Deux Guerres Mondiales," 91; Dimosthenis Ch Dodos, *Oi Evraioi Tes Thessalonikis Stis Ekloges Tou Ellenikou Kratous 1915-1936* (Athens: Savvalas, 2005), 102; Leon A Nar, *Oi Israelites Vouleutes Sto Elleniko Koinovoulio (1915-1936)* (Athens: Idryma tis Voulis ton Ellinon, 2011), 32.

65 Dodos, *Oi Evraioi Tes Thessalonikis Stis Ekloges Tou Ellenikou Kratous 1915-1936*, 142.

66 Manolis Kandylakis, *Efemeridografia Tes Thessalonikis, vol. C 1923-1941* (Thessaloniki: University Studio Press, 2008), 65–66.

67 Jules Crepin, "En Grèce – M. Venizelos Et Les Juifs," *Paix et Droit* 14, no. 8 (1934): 11.

68 Crepin, "En Grèce – M. Venizelos Et Les Juifs," 12.

69 He refers here to the provinces that composed Greece before the Balkan Wars.

70 S. I. Stefanou, ed. *Eleftheriou Venizelou. Ta Keimena. 1909-1935*, vol. D (Athens: Lesche Filileftheron, 1981), 695–96.

71 Kallis, "The Jewish Community of Salonica under Siege: The Antisemitic Violence of the Summer of 1931," 36.

72 "Les élections législatives à salonique," *Paix et Droit* 12, no. 8 (1932): 2; "Grèce—Les Élections législatives," *Paix et Droit* 13, no. 2 (1933): 7–8; "Grèce—Les Élections législatives," *Paix et Droit* 13, no. 5 (1933): 16; Mazower, *Salonica City of Ghosts*, 382.

73 Crepin, "En Grèce – M. Venizelos Et Les Juifs," 11.

74 Exarchou, *Oi Evraioi Sten Xanthi*, 78.

75 Plaut, *Greek Jewry in the Twentieth Century 1913-1983*, 55.

76 Maria Kavala, "E Thessalonike Ste Germanike Katoche (1941-1944)," 64. E. A. Hekimoglou, "Topoi Egkatastaseos Kai Katoikias Ton Prosphygon Ste Thessalonike 1922-1927" (paper presented at the B' Panellenio Synedrio gia ton Ellenismo tes Mikras Asias, Thessaloniki, 1994), 152.

77 Nikos Potamianos, "Regulation and the Retailing Community: The Struggle over the Establishment of the Holiday of Sunday in Greece, 1872-1926," *History of Retailing and Consumption* 0, no. 0 (2017): 4, 6–7; Kavala, "E Thessalonike Ste Germanike Katoche (1941-1944)," 67.; Molho, "The Close Ties between Nationalism and Antisemitism," 220.

78 Christovasilis, *Peri Evraion*, 107.

79 Israel Cohen, "Letters from Abroad—Whose Glory Is Departed," *The Menorah Journal* XII, no. 5 (1926): 524; Photini Constantopoulou and Thanos Veremis, eds., *Documents on the History of the Greek Jews* (Athens: Kastanidis, 1999), 145.

80 Delven, *The Jews of Ioannina*, 36; Mekos, *Mousoulmanoi, Armenioi Kai Evraioi Sympolites Mou Komotenaioi*, 131.

81 Kallis, "The Jewish Community of Salonica under Siege: The Antisemitic Violence of the Summer of 1931," 41; Kavala, "E Thessalonike Ste Germanike Katoche (1941-1944)," 67. The origins of the law date to 1909 for Athens, Pireaus, Patra, and Volos but numerous exemptions were subsequently added though local municipal authorities could ask to be included (Antonis Liakos, *Ergasia Kai Politike Sten Ellada Tou Mesopolemou. To Diethnes Grafeio Ergasias Kai E Anadyse Ton Koinonikon Thesmon* (Athens: Idryma Erevnas kai Paideias tes Emporikis Trapezas tis Ellados, 1993), 255–56); Naar, *Jewish Salonica: Between the Ottoman Empire and Modern Greece*, 30.

82 Mark Mazower, *Greece and the Inter-War Economic Crisis* (New York and Oxford [England]: Clarendon Press, 1991), 136; Plaut, *Greek Jewry in the Twentieth Century 1913-1983*, 59.

83 Evaggelos A. Chekimoglou, *Trapezes Kai Thessaloniki 1900-1936. Opseis Leitourgias Kai to Provlema Tes Chorotheteses* (Thessaloniki, 1987), 124.

84 Maria Kavala, "Epibiose Viologike Kai Pnevmatike," in *O Foros Tou Aimatos Sten Katochike Thessaloniki: Xene Kyriarchia, Antistase Kai Epibiose*, eds. Vasilis K Gounaris and Petros Papapolyviou (Thessaloniki: Paratiritis, 2001), 17, 30.

85 Nikos Potamianos, "Moral Economy?: Popular Demands and State Intervention in the Struggle of Anti-Profiteering Laws in Greece," *Journal of Social History* 48, no. 4 (2015): 804.

86 "Tableaux Des Écoles De L' Alliance," *Paix et Droit* 13, no. 1 (1933): 8.

87 Esther Benbassa, "Questioning Historical Narratives: The Case of Balkan Sephardi Jewry," in *Simon Dubnow Institute Yearbook*, ed. Dan Diner (Stuttgart: Deutsche Verlagsanstalt, 2003); Rena Molho, "Popular Antisemitism and State Policy in Salonika During the City's Annexation to Greece," 254; Aron Rodrigue, "From Millet to Minority: Turkish Jewry in the 19th and 20th Centuries," in *Paths of Emancipation: Jews within States and Capitalism*, eds. Pierre Birnbaum and Ira Katznelson (Princeton: Princeton University Press, 1995), 261; Sarah Abrevaya Stein, *Making Jews Modern: The Yiddish and Ladino Press in the Russian and Ottoman Empires* (Bloomington: Indiana University Press, 2006), 56.

88 Devin E. Naar, "Ta Oria Tou Ellenismou: Glossa Kai Afosiose Metaxy Salonikion Evraion, 1917-1933," in *Thessaloniki: Mia Pole Se Metavase, 1912-2012*, ed. Dimitris Kairidis (Thessaloniki: Epikentro, 2015), 208.

89 Maria Vasilikou, "E Ekpaidevse Ton Evraion Tes Thessalonikes Sto Mesopolemo," in *O Ellenikos Evraismos*, ed. Maria Stephanopoulou (Athens: Idryma Moraiti, 1999), 129.

90 Naar, *Jewish Salonica: Between the Ottoman Empire and Modern Greece*, 140.

91 Ibid., 157.

92 Ibid., 162, 167, 177; Maria Vasilikou, "E Ekpaideuse Ton Evraion Tes Thessalonikis Sto Mesopolemo" (paper presented at the O Ellenikos Evraismos, Athens, 1998), 139.

93 Naar, "Ta Oria Tou Ellenismou: Glossa Kai Afosiose Metaxy Salonikion Evraion, 1917-1933," 211, 214.

94 Nata, *Apo Ten Kerkyra Sto Birkenau Kai Ten Ierousalem—E Istoria Mias Kerkyraias*, 27.

95 Constantopoulou and Veremis, eds., *Documents on the History of the Greek Jews*, 104.

96 Molho, "Popular Antisemitism and State Policy in Salonika During the City's Annexation to Greece," 86; see also Plaut, *Greek Jewry in the Twentieth Century 1913-1983*, 37, 46; Stefanou, ed., *Eleftheriou Venizelou. Ta Keimena. 1909-1935*, vol. C, 382.

97 Naar, *Jewish Salonica: Between the Ottoman Empire and Modern Greece*, 169.

98 Devin Naar also points to the hostility displayed toward Jews by the faculty and student organizations of the University, the latter playing a prominent role in the anti-Semitic pogrom of 1931 discussed below, as a possible deterrent to Jewish students (ibid., 261).

99 Naar, "The 'Mother of Israel' or the 'Sephardi Metropolis'?: Sephardim, Ashkenazim, and Romaniotes in Salonica," 98, 102; Sciaky, *Farewell to Salonica*, 261.

100 Thrasyvoulos Or Papastratis, *Oi Evraioi Tou Didymoteichou* (Athens: Ekdoseis Tsoukatou, 2001), 37.

101 Dimitris Philippis, *Profasimos, Ekfasismos, Psevdofasismos. Ellada, Italia, Kai Ispania Ston Mesopolemo* (Thessaloniki: University Studio Press, 2010), 199–201; Naar, *Jewish Salonica: Between the Ottoman Empire and Modern Greece*, 172.

102 Naar, "Ta Oria Tou Ellenismou: Glossa Kai Afosiose Metaxy Salonikion Evraion, 1917-1933," 214.

103 That did not stop the Greek state from supporting a complaint by the Greek minority in Albania to the League of Nations over educational restrictions instituted in Albania in 1933 (Tsioumis, *Meionotetes Sten Ellada: Ellenikes Meionotetes Sta Valkania*, 10, 15); Naar, *Jewish Salonica: Between the Ottoman Empire and Modern Greece*, 169.

104 See G. Th Mavrogordatos, "Oi Ethnikes Meionotetes," in *Istoria Tes Ellados Tou 20ou Aiona*, ed. Ch. Chatzeiosef (Athens: Vivliorama, 2003), 9–35; Karakasidou. Philip Carabott, "The Politics of Integration and Assimilation Vis-a-Vis the Slavo-Macedonian Minority of Inter-War Greece: From Parliamentary Inertia to Metaxist Repression," in *Ourselves and Others: The Development of a Greek Macedonian Cultural Identity since 1912*, eds. Peter Mackridge and Eleni Yannakakis (Oxford: Berg, 1997), 66.

105 Tsioumis, *Meionotetes Sten Ellada: Ellenikes Meionotetes Sta Valkania*, 42, 43; Naar, *Jewish Salonica: Between the Ottoman Empire and Modern Greece*, 182.

106 See Herman Fest and Sitsa Karaiskaki, *Evraioi Kai Kommounismos, Ta Aitia Kai Oi Skopoi Tes Synergasias Ton* (Athens: Nea Genia, 1934), 4, 6, 10, 13, 17, 24, 45, 50–51, 73.

107 Aberbach, *The European Jews, Patriotism and the Liberal State 1789-1939: A Study of Literature and Social Psychology*, 30; Louis -Ferdinand Celine, *Bagatelles Pour Un Massacre* (Paris: Editions Denoel, 1937).

108 Randolph L. Braham, *The Politics of Genocide, the Holocaust in Hungary*, 2 vols., vol. 1 (New York: Columbia University Press, 1981), 21; Aberbach, *The European Jews, Patriotism and the Liberal State 1789-1939: A Study of Literature and Social Psychology*, 82.

109 Aberbach, *The European Jews, Patriotism and the Liberal State 1789-1939: A Study of Literature and Social Psychology*, 91, 92; Dwork and van Pelt, *Holocaust a History*, 119.

110 Aberbach, *The European Jews, Patriotism and the Liberal State 1789-1939: A Study of Literature and Social Psychology*, 147.

111 William O. Oldson, "Alibi for Prejudice: Eastern Orthodoxy, the Holocaust, and Romanian Nationalism," *East European Quarterly* XXXVI, no. 3 (2002): 306, 307.

112 Mark Mazower, *The Balkans, a Short History*, 122.

113 Papastratis, *Oi Evraioi Tou Didymoteichou*, 43–45.

114 Baer, "An Enemy Old and New: The Dönme, Anti-Semitism, and Conspiracy Theories in the Ottoman Empire and Turkish Republic," 528.

115 Molho, "Popular Antisemitism and State Policy in Salonika During the City's Annexation to Greece," 99; Kavala, *E Katastrophe Ton Evraion Tes Elladas (1941-1944)*, 36; Maria Vasilikou, "Ethnotikes Antitheseis Sten Ellada Tou Mesopolemou. E Periptose Tou Empresmou Tou Kampel," *Istor* 7 (1994): 157.

116 Theodosis Tsironis, "E Organose Ethnike Enosis 'E Ellas' (E.E.E.) Ste Thessaloniki Tou Mesopolemou (1927-1936). Ta Katastatika Kai E Drase Tes," *Epistemoniki Epeterida tou Kentrou Istorias Thessalonikis tou Demou Thessalonikis* 6 (2002): 294, 296.

117 Tsironis, "E Organose Ethnike Enosis 'E Ellas' (E.E.E.) Ste Thessaloniki Tou Mesopolemou (1927-1936). Ta Katastatika Kai E Drase Tes," 294, 296; Kavala, *E Katastrophe Ton Evraion Tes Elladas (1941-1944)*, 36.

118 "Lettre De Salonique – La Situation Économique Et La Population Juive 17 Mai 1932," *Paix et Droit* 12, no. 5 (1932): 8.

119 Minos-Athanasios Karyotakis, "E Apeikonise Ton Evraion Sten Efemerida
     'Makedonia' Ten Periodo 1945-1948" (Thessaloniki: Aristotle University of
     Thessaloniki, 2016); 39.

120 Dimitris Psarras, *To Best Seler Tou Misous* (Athens: Ekdoseis Polis, 2013), 114.

121 Psarras, *To Best Seler Tou Misous*, 114–19; Fleming, *Greece a Jewish History*, 95.
     Naar, *Jewish Salonica: Between the Ottoman Empire and Modern Greece*, 26; For
     a history of the Protocols see Norman Cohn, *Warrant for Genocide: The Myth of
     the Jewish World Conspiracy and the Protocols of the Elders of Zion* (London: Serif,
     1996).

122 Joshua Starr, "The Socialist Federation of Salonika," *Jewish Social Studies* VII (1945):
     324–25, 328–29; Fest and Karaiskaki, *Evraioi Kai Kommounismos, Ta Aitia Kai Oi
     Skopoi Tes Synergasias Ton*, 4, 17.

123 Kavala, *E Katastrophe Ton Evraion Tes Elladas (1941-1944)*, 35

124 Naar, *Jewish Salonica: Between the Ottoman Empire and Modern Greece*, 122; Moysis,
     E Filia Ellenon Kai Israeliton Dia Mesou Ton Aionon, 23.

125 See for example Chaim Weizmann, *O Evraikos Laos Kai E Palaistine* (Thessaloniki:
     Keren Kagiemet kai Keren Agiesod, 1937).

126 Paris Papamichos Chronakis, "'Vipers' and 'Snakes', 'Komitadjis' and 'Pseudo-
     Nationalists': Anti-Zionist Discourses in Interwar Greece," in *Antisemitism in Greece:
     Past and Present Trajectories* (Berlin: The Center for Research on Antisemitism,
     Berlin Technical University, 2014), 2; see Georgios A. Tsormpatzis, *Eos Tes Evraikes
     Paliggenesias Apo Ellenikes Skopias* (Athens: Eleftheroudakis, 1925).

127 Chronakis, "'Vipers' and 'Snakes', 'Komitadjis' and 'Pseudo-Nationalists': Anti-Zionist
     Discourses in Interwar Greece," 4,5.

128 Leon A. Nar, *Oi Israelites Vouleutes sto Elleniko Koinovoulio (1915-1936)* (Athens:
     Idryma tis Voulis ton Ellinon, 2011), 66.

129 Chronakis, "'Vipers' and 'Snakes', 'Komitadjis' and 'Pseudo-Nationalists': Anti-Zionist
     Discourses in Interwar Greece," 6. A similar attitude persists to this day with scholars
     associating the Zionist (and communist) movements with resistance to assimila-
     tion (Mavrogordatos, "Oi Ethnikes Meionotetes," 9) while specialists provide a more
     nuanced picture (Naar, *Jewish Salonica: Between the Ottoman Empire and Modern
     Greece*, 45–47). Similar arguments persist over the numbers of Thessaloniki Jews with
     foreign nationality which range from over 5,000 individuals (Mavrogordatos, "Oi
     Ethnikes Meionotetes," 10) to 477 families (Maria Kavala, "Aspects of Anti-Semitism
     in Salonika, During the Nazi Occupation (1941-1944): The Authorities, the Press
     and the People. An Example of Differentiation and Exclusion" (paper presented at
     the Croatian Serbian Relations; Minority Rights, fight against discrimination, 6th
     International Scientific Conference, Novi Sad, 2013), 195).

130 Aristotle A Kallis, "To Expand or Not to Expand? Territory, Generic Fascism
     and the Quest for an 'Ideal Fatherland'," *Journal of Contemporary History* 38, no. 2
     (2003): 246.

131 Davide Rodogno, "Italiani Brava Gente? Fascist Italy's Policy Toward the Jews in the
     Balkans, April 1941–July 1943," *European History Quarterly* 35, no. 2 (2005): 216.

132 Kavala, *E Katastrophe Ton Evraion Tes Elladas (1941-1944)*, 28.

133 Molho, "Popular Antisemitism and State Policy in Salonika During the City's
     Annexation to Greece," 100; Constantopoulou and Veremis, eds., *Documents on the
     History of the Greek Jews*, 175–92; "Les Désordres Antijuifs De Salonique," *Paix et
     Droit* 11, no. 6 (1931): 5–6; "L' épilogue des désordres De 1931," *Paix et Droit* 12, no. 4
     (1932): 8.

134 Giorgos Margaritis, "Ellenikos Antisemitismos: Mia Periegese, 1821, 1891, 1931" (paper presented at the O Ellenikos Evraismos, Athens, 1998), 24; Kavala, *E Katastrophe Ton Evraion Tes Elladas (1941-1944)*, 38. Nevertheless, the communist newspaper Rizospastis held both the government and the local authorities in Thessaloniki responsible for the pogrom and for the crimes of the "fascists" (Takis Fitsos, "Apokalypseis Gia Ta Pogrom Kata Ton Evraion," Rizospastis, July 2, 1931, 1931.); Dodos, *Oi Evraioi Tes Thessalonikis Stis Ekloges Tou Ellenikou Kratous 1915-1936*, 182.

135 Kavala, "Aspects of Anti-Semitism in Salonika, During the Nazi Occupation (1941-1944): The Authorities, the Press and the People. An Example of Differentiation and Exclusion," 200.

136 Giorgos Margaritis, *Anepithymetoi Sympatriotes* (Athens: Vivliorama, 2005), 63, 64; Kallis, "The Jewish Community of Salonica under Siege: The Antisemitic Violence of the Summer of 1931," 49.

137 Naar, "Ta Oria Tou Ellenismou: Glossa Kai Afosiose Metaxy Salonikion Evraion, 1917-1933," 217–18.

138 Aberbach, *The European Jews, Patriotism and the Liberal State 1789-1939: A Study of Literature and Social Psychology*, 43.

139 Horowitz, *The Deadly Ethnic Riot*, 308.

140 Kavala, *E Katastrophe Ton Evraion Tes Elladas (1941-1944)*, 38.

141 Devin E. Naar, "From the 'Jerusalem of the Balkans' to the Goldene Medina: Jewish Immigration from Salonika to the United States," 448.

142 Naar, "From the 'Jerusalem of the Balkans' to the Goldene Medina: Jewish Immigration from Salonika to the United States," 353, 355. It should be noted that this concern with conscription is not a widely shared phenomenon in Jewish communities either in Europe or even in Greece. Only the Alsacian Jews exhibited a similar opposition to conscription (Aberbach, *The European Jews, Patriotism and the Liberal State 1789-1939: A Study of Literature and Social Psychology*, 151).

143 Kavala, "E Thessalonike Ste Germanike Katoche (1941-1944): Koinonia, Oikonomia, Diogmos Evraion," 69.

144 "Les Désordres Antijuifs De Salonique," 6; Molho, "Popular Antisemitism and State Policy in Salonika During the City's Annexation to Greece," 101; Naar, "From the 'Jerusalem of the Balkans' to the Goldene Medina: Jewish Immigration from Salonika to the United States," 448, 457; Molho, "The Close Ties between Nationalism and Antisemitism," 221; Exarchou, *Oi Evraioi Sten Xanthi*, 136–37.

145 Mpaltsiotis, "E Ithageneia Ston Psychro Polemo," 83; Tasos Kostopoulos, "Aphaireseis Ithageneias: E Skoteine Pleura Tes Neoellenikes Istorias (1926-2003)," *Sygchrona Themata*, no. 83 (2003): 54; see also Eutychia Evaggelou, "E Apoleia Tes Ellenikes Ithageneias Ton Ellenon Evraion Apo Te Dekaetia Tou 1920 Eos to 1965" (Panteion Panepistimio Koinonikon & Politikon Epistimon, 2015).

146 Kavala, *E Katastrophe Ton Evraion Tes Elladas (1941-1944)*, 39.

147 Karakasidou, *Fields of Wheat, Hills of Blood: Passages to Nationhood in Greek Macedonia, 1870-1990*, 176.

148 Benbassa and Rodrigue, *The Jews of the Balkans*, 161; Molho, "The Close Ties between Nationalism and Antisemitism," 102.

149 See Yannis Hamilakis, *The Nation and Its Ruins: Antiquity, Archaeology, and National Imagination in Greece* (Oxford: Oxford University Press, 2007). especially chapter 5.

150 Vaggelis Aggelis, "Metaxike Propaganda Kai Neolaia 1936-1940" (Athens: Panteio University, 2004), 72.

151 Andrew Apostolou, "'The Exception of Salonika': Bystanders and Collaborators in Northern Greece," *Holocaust and Genocide Studies* 14, no. 2 (2000): 173; Bowman, *The Agony of Greek Jews 1940-1945*, 187.

152 Aggelis, "Metaxike Propaganda Kai Neolaia 1936-1940" 170.

153 K. E. Fleming, "The Stereotyped 'Greek Jew' from Auschwitz-Birkenau to Israeli Pop Culture," *Journal of Modern Greek Studies* 25, no. 1 (2007).

Chapter 6

1 Allan G. B. Fisher, "The German Trade Drive in Southeastern Europe," *International Affairs* 18, no. 2 (1939): 161.

2 Mekos, *Mousoulmanoi, Armenioi Kai Evraioi Sympolites Mou Komotenaioi*, 25.

3 Georgios K. Zographakis, ed., *Mordochaios I Frizis: O Protos Anoteros Ellenas Axiomatikos Pou Epese Machomenos Ston Ellenoitaliko Polemo* (Athens: Kentriko Israilitikon Symvoulion, 1977), 15, 37, 41.

4 Zographakis, ed., *Mordochaios I Frizis: O Protos Anoteros Ellenas Axiomatikos Pou Epese Machomenos Ston Ellenoitaliko Polemo*, 10. Moissis gives the numbers as 513 killed and 3,743 wounded as does Bowman (Esdra D. Moissis, *E Evraiki Koinoteta Tes Larisas Prin Kai Meta to Olokautoma* (Larisa: Melanos, 2000), 176; Bowman, "Jews in Wartime Greece," 48).

5 Fleming, *Greece a Jewish History*, 106.

6 Isaac Kabeli, *The Resistance of Greek Jews*, vol. VIII, Yivo Annual of Jewish Social Science (New York: Yiddish Scientific Institute—Yivo, 1953), 281. According to Constantopoulou and Veremis, there were 513 dead, 3,743 wounded and 1,412 disabled Greek Jewish soldiers out of 12,898 soldiers and officers (Constantopoulou and Veremis, eds., *Documents on the History of the Greek Jews*, 34).

7 Biondich, *The Balkans. Revolution, War and Political Violence since 1878*, 142.

8 Dragostinova, "Navigating Nationality in the Emigration of Minorities between Bulgaria and Greece, 1919-1941," 201.

9 Ibid., 201.

10 Fragiski Ampatzopoulou, *To Olokautoma Stis Martyries Ton Ellenon Evraion* (Athens: Epikentro, 1993), 86; Bowman, *The Agony of Greek Jews 1940-1945*, 47. See also Christos Kardaras, *E Voulgarike Propaganda Ste Germanokratoumene Makedonia: Voulgarike Lesche Thessalonikis, 1941-1944* (Athens: Ekdoseis Epikairotita, 1997). Some of these Jewish families escaped to Palestine but many returned to Greece only to be later deported to the death camps (Thrasyvoulos Or Papastratis, *Oi Evraioi Tou Didymoteichou*, 56).

11 Papastratis, *Oi Evraioi Tes Kavallas*, 13.

12 Mazower, *Inside Hitler's Greece, the Experience of Occupation 1941-1944*, 20; Mekos, *Mousoulmanoi, Armenioi Kai Evraioi Sympolites Mou Komotenaioi*, 70.

13 Provatas, *Syntomos Politike Istoria Tou Voreioepeirotikou Zetematos*, 13.

14 Mark Mazower, "Three Forms of Political Justice: Greece, 1944-1945," in *After the War Was Over. Reconstructing the Family, Nation, and State in Greece, 1943-1960*, ed. Mark Mazower (Princeton: Princeton University Press, 2000), 25.

15 Divani, *Ellada Kai Meionotetes. To Sytema Diethnous Prostasias Tes Koinonias Ton Ethnon*, 257.

16 Mazower, "Three Forms of Political Justice: Greece, 1944-1945," 25; Vasilis Krapsitis, *E Istorike Aletheia Gia Tous Mousoulmanous Tsamedes* (Athens, 1992), 83, 109, 245.

17 Elene Haidia, "Ellenes Evraioi Tes Thessalonikis: Apo Ta Stratopeda Sygkentroses Stis Aithouses Dikasterion," in *Oi Evraioi Tes Elladas Sten Katoche*, ed. Rika Mpenveniste (Thessaloniki: Ekdoseis Vanias, 1998), 44.

18 Averoff, *E Politike Plevra Tou Koutsovlachikou Zetematos*, 19–20.

19 Tsioumis, *Meionotetes Sten Ellada: Ellenikes Meionotetes Sta Valkania*, 32.

20 John S. Koliopoulos, "The War over the Identity and Numbers of Greece's Slav Macedonians," in *Ourselves and Others: The Development of a Greek Macedonian Cultural Identity since 1912*, eds. Peter Mackridge and Eleni Yannakakis (Oxford: Berg, 1997), 51.

21 Mazower, *Inside Hitler's Greece, the Experience of Occupation 1941-1944*, 167, Martin Seckendorf, *E Ellada kato apo ton Agkyloto Stavro* (Athens: Sygchroni Epochi, 1991), 102; Krapsitis, *E Istorike Aletheia Gia Tous Mousoulmanous Tsamedes*, 145, 181, 195.

22 Hannah Arendt, *Eichmann in Jerusalem. A Report on the Banality of Evil* (New York: The Viking Press, 1963), 187.

23 See Jan T. Gross, *Neighbors: The Destruction of the Jewish Community in Jedwabne, Poland* (New York: Penguin, 2002); Vladimir Solonari, "Patterns of Violence: The Local Population and the Mass Murder of Jews in Bessarabia and Northern Bukovina, July – August 1941," *Kritika: Explorations in Russian and Eurasian History* 8, no. 4 (2007): 762, 768; Ioanid, "The Holocaust in Romania: The Iasi Pogrom of June 1941," 130.

24 Philip Friedman, *Their Brother's Keepers* (New York: Crown Publishers, 1957), 110; Matsas, *The Illusion of Safety: The Story of Greek Jews During the Second World War*, 55, 122; 318; Mazower, *Inside Hitler's Greece, the Experience of Occupation 1941-1944*, 259.

25 Yomtov Yakoel, *Apomnemonevmata 1941-1943* (Thessaloniki: Paratiritis, 1993), 111.

26 Mazower, *Inside Hitler's Greece, the Experience of Occupation 1941-1944*, 256; Ampatzopoulou, *To Olokautoma Stis Martyries Ton Ellenon Evraion*, 30; Barbara Spengler-Axiopoulou, "Alleleggye Kai Voetheia Pros Tous Evraious Tes Elladas Kata Te Diarkeia Tes Katoches: 1941-1944," in *Oi Evraioi Tes Elladas Sten Katoche*, ed. Rika Benveniste (Thessaloniki: Ekdoseis Vanias, 1998), 16; Hagen Fleischer, "Greek Jewry and Nazi Germany: The Holocaust and Its Antecedents" (paper presented at the Oi Evraioi ston Elleniko Choro: Zetemata Istorias ste Makra Diarkeia, Thessaloniki, 1991), 194.

27 Matsas, *The Illusion of Safety: The Story of Greek Jews During the Second World War*, 29, 75, 83.

28 Ibid., 98; Moissis, *E Evraiki Koinoteta Tes Larisas Prin Kai Meta to Olokautoma*, 179.

29 Michael Matsas considers this as the main cause for the destruction of Greek Jewry, and accuses primarily the allied news sources, like the BBC for keeping quiet about the issue (Matsas, *The Illusion of Safety: The Story of Greek Jews During the Second World War*, 25, 26).

30 Alexander Kitroeff, *War-Time Jews. The Case of Athens* (Athens: ELIAMEP, 1995), 50; Matsas, *The Illusion of Safety: The Story of Greek Jews During the Second World War*, 96; Spengler-Axiopoulou, "Alleleggye Kai Voetheia Pros Tous Evraious Tes Elladas Kata Te Diarkeia Tes Katoches: 1941-1944," 26.

31 Mavrogordatos, "The Holocaust in Greece: A Vindication of Assimilation," 6, 10.

32 Fleming, *Greece a Jewish History*, 113.

33 Mavrogordatos, "The Holocaust in Greece: A Vindication of Assimilation," 15.

34 Seckendorf, *E Ellada kato apo ton Agkyloto Stavro*, 38, Stavros Asteriou Papagiannis, *Ethnikos Agrotikos Syndesmos Antikomounistikes Drases* (Athens: Ekdoseis Sokoli, 2007), 29.

35 Daniel Capri, ed., *Italian Diplomatic Documents on the History of the Holocaust in Greece* (Tel Aviv: Tel Aviv University, 1999), 81, 83, 125.

36 Apostolou, "'The Exception of Salonika': Bystanders and Collaborators in Northern Greece," 178; Dwork and van Pelt, *Holocaust a History*, 96.

37 Capri, ed., *Italian Diplomatic Documents on the History of the Holocaust in Greece*, 83.

38 Kavala, *E Katastrophe Ton Evraion Tes Elladas (1941-1944)*, 74–76.

39 Yakoel, *Apomnemonevmata 1941-1943*, 97.

40 Ibid., 112.

41 See Leon Saltiel, "Professional Solidarity and the Holocaust: The Case of Thessaloniki," in *Jahrbuch FüR Antisemitismusforschung 24*, eds. Werner Bergmann, Marcus Funck, and Dilek Güven (Berlin: Metropol Verlag, 2015).

42 "Prospatheies Diasoses Evraiopaidon Thessalonikis Kata Ten Katoche: Ena Agnosto Kykloma Paranomon Yiothesion," *Sygchrona Themata 36*, no. 127 (2014).

43 Capri, ed., *Italian Diplomatic Documents on the History of the Holocaust in Greece*, 115.

44 Kavala, *E Katastrophe Ton Evraion Tes Elladas (1941-1944)*, 61; "Epibiose Viologike Kai Pnevmatike," 31; Capri, ed., *Italian Diplomatic Documents on the History of the Holocaust in Greece*, 83.

45 Daniel Capri, *Italian Diplomatic Documents on the History of the Holocaust in Greece* (Tel Aviv: Tel Aviv University 1999), 125, 129, 148.

46 Capri, *Italian Diplomatic Documents on the History of the Holocaust in Greece*, 139, 151.

47 Kitroeff, *War-Time Jews. The Case of Athens*, 49.

48 Yakoel, *Apomnemonevmata 1941-1943*, 59–60.

49 Kavala, *E Katastrophe Ton Evraion Tes Elladas (1941-1944)*, 72; "Aspects of Anti-Semitism in Salonika, During the Nazi Occupation (1941-1944): The Authorities, the Press and the People. An Example of Differentiation and Exclusion" (paper presented at the Croatian Serbian Relations; Minority Rights, fight against discrimination, 6th International Scientific Conference, Novi Sad, 2013), 201.

50 Leon Saltiel, "Dehumanizing the Dead the Destruction of Thessaloniki's Jewish Cemetery in the Light of New Sources," *Yad Vashem Studies 42*, no. 1 (2014): 11.

51 Devin E. Naar, *Jewish Salonica: Between the Ottoman Empire and Modern Greece*, 275–76; Kavala, *E Katastrophe Ton Evraion Tes Elladas (1941-1944)*, 67–69.

52 Polychronis K Enepekidis, *Oi Diogmoi Ton Evraion En Elladi 1941-1944* (Athens: Ekdotikos Oikos Viktoros A Papazisi, 1969), 21; Rozina Asser-Pardo, *548 Emeres Me Allo Onoma* (Athens: Ekdoseis Gavriilidis, 1999), 8; Fleming, *Greece a Jewish History*, 119; Naar, *Jewish Salonica: Between the Ottoman Empire and Modern Greece*, 240.

53 Carla Hesse and Thomas W. Laqueur, "Orata Kai Aorata Somata: E Exaleipse Tou Evraikou Nekrotafeiou Apo Te Zoe Tes Sygchrones Thessalonikis," in *E Paragoge Tou Koinonikou Somatos*, eds. Martha Mihailidou and Alexandra Halkia (Athens: Katarti, 2006), 45.

54 Saltiel, "Dehumanizing the Dead the Destruction of Thessaloniki's Jewish Cemetery in the Light of New Sources," 20–21.

55 Apostolou, "'The Exception of Salonika': Bystanders and Collaborators in Northern Greece," 176.

56 Enepekidis, *Oi Diogmoi Ton Evraion En Elladi 1941-1944*, 35.

57 Hagen Fleischer, *Stemma Kai Svastika: E Ellada Tes Katoches Kai Tes Antistases 1941-1944* (Athens: Papazisi, 1995), 303–04; Evangelos Kofos, *Nationalism and Communism in Macedonia* (Thessaloniki: Institute of Balkan Studies and Society for Macedonian Studies, 1964), 102.

58 Mavrogordatos, "The Holocaust in Greece: A Vindication of Assimilation," 15; Maria Kavala, "Oi Oikonomikes Drasteriotetes Ton Epicheireseon Tes Thessalonikes Sta Chronia Tes Katoches," in *E Epoche Ton Rexeon. E Ellenike Koinonia Ste Dekaetia Tou 1940*, ed. Polymeris Voglis, et al. (Athens: Epikentro, 2012), 84.

59 Paul Hagouel, "The History of the Jews of Salonika and the Holocaust," *Sephardic Horizons* 3, no. 3 (2013): 5.

60 Spengler-Axiopoulou, "Alleleggye Kai Voetheia Pros Tous Evraious Tes Elladas Kata Te Diarkeia Tes Katoches: 1941-1944," 22; Mazower, *Inside Hitler's Greece, the Experience of Occupation 1941-1944*, 250.

61 Hagouel, "The History of the Jews of Salonika and the Holocaust," 18.

62 Friedman, *Their Brother's Keepers*, 107–08; Aser R. Moysis, *E Filia Ellenon Kai Israeliton Dia Mesou Ton Aionon*, 23–24; Asser-Pardo, *548 Emeres Me Allo Onoma*, 11; Spengler-Axiopoulou, "Alleleggye Kai Voetheia Pros Tous Evraious Tes Elladas Kata Te Diarkeia Tes Katoches: 1941-1944," 23; Mavrogordatos, "The Holocaust in Greece: A Vindication of Assimilation," 15, 16. Kitroeff gives a much higher number of fake identity cards, 18.500 in total (Kitroeff, *War-Time Jews. The Case of Athens*, 67).

63 Constantopoulou and Veremis, eds., *Documents on the History of the Greek Jews*, 249–53.

64 Saltiel, "Professional Solidarity and the Holocaust: The Case of Thessaloniki," 236, 246.

65 Spengler-Axiopoulou, "Alleleggye Kai Voetheia Pros Tous Evraious Tes Elladas Kata Te Diarkeia Tes Katoches: 1941-1944," 19.

66 Matsas, *The Illusion of Safety: The Story of Greek Jews During the Second World War*, 292.

67 Fleming, *Greece a Jewish History*, 112–13; Bowman, *The Agony of Greek Jews 1940-1945*, 74.

68 Mazower, *Inside Hitler's Greece, the Experience of Occupation 1941-1944*, 254–55; Matsas, *The Illusion of Safety: The Story of Greek Jews During the Second World War*, 293–94.

69 Gatenio Osmo Nata, *Apo Ten Kerkyra Sto Birkenau Kai Ten Ierousalem - E Istoria Mias Kerkyraias*, 24.

70 Hans Kohn, "Letters from Abroad - New Regime in Greece," *The Menorah Journal* XVI, no. 5 (1929): 444.

71 Matsas, *The Illusion of Safety: The Story of Greek Jews During the Second World War*, 48.

72 Evtychia Nahman, *Giannena - Taxidi Sto Parelthon* (Athens: Talos Press, 1966). 35, 95.

73 Enepekidis, *Oi Diogmoi Ton Evraion En Elladi 1941-1944*, 156–57.

74 Christoph U. Schminck-Gustavus, *Mnemes Katoches II. Italoi Kai Germanoi Sta Giannena Kai E Katastrophe Tes Evraikes Koinotetas* (Ioannina: Isnafi, 2008), 192, 193.

75 Matsas, *The Illusion of Safety: The Story of Greek Jews During the Second World War*, 202

76 Bowman, *The Agony of Greek Jews 1940-1945*, 70.

77 Matsas, *The Illusion of Safety: The Story of Greek Jews During the Second World War*, 198, see also Delven, *The Jews of Ioannina*, 43–45; Schminck-Gustavus, *Mnemes Katoches II. Italoi Kai Germanoi Sta Giannena Kai E Katastrophe Tes Evraikes Koinotetas*, 60

78 Martin Zekendorf, *E Ellada Kato Apo Ton Agyloto Stavro* (Athens: Sychroni Epochi, 1991), 188

79 Kitroeff, *War-Time Jews. The Case of Athens*, 82, 112.

80 Enepekidis, *Oi Diogmoi Ton Evraion En Elladi 1941-1944*, 27–28.

81 Ibid. 38, 36, 38; Apostolou. 181; Seckendorf. 213.

82 Enepekidis, *Oi Diogmoi Ton Evraion En Elladi 1941-1944*, 43.

83 Ibid. 43–44. See also Mazower, *Inside Hitler's Greece, the Experience of Occupation 1941-1944*, 251.

84 Mazower, *Inside Hitler's Greece, the Experience of Occupation 1941-1944*, 259.

85 Ibid. 251; Konstantinos A. Tsiligiannis, *E Evraike Koinoteta Tes Artas* (Athens: Kentriko Israilitiko Symvoulio tes Ellados, 2004). 47; Kavala, *E Katastrophe Ton Evraion Tes Elladas (1941-1944)*, 128.

86 Alexis Menexiadis, "Oi Evraioi Tes Chalkidas Den Xegelastekan Apo Tous Germanous," *Chronika*, no. 201 (2006): 39; Sotiris Papastratis, "Oi Evraioi Tes Chalkidas Sten Katoche," *Chronika*, no. 44 (1981): 9–12.

87 Ampatzopoulou, *To Olokautoma Stis Martyries Ton Ellenon Evraion*, 130.

88 Ibid., 166.

89 E. J. Hollander, "The Final Solution in Bulgaria and Romania: A Comparative Perspective," *East European Politics & Societies* 22, no. 2 (2008): 217, 220.

90 Papastratis, *Oi Evraioi Tes Kavallas*, 12; Ampatzopoulou, *To Olokautoma Stis Martyries Ton Ellenon Evraion*, 183, 186; Spengler-Axiopoulou, "Alleleggye Kai Voetheia Pros Tous Evraious Tes Elladas Kata Te Diarkeia Tes Katoches: 1941-1944," 18

91 William I. Brustein and Ryan D. King, "Balkan Anti-Semitism: The Cases of Bulgaria and Romania before the Holocaust," *East European Politics and Societies* 18, no. 3 (2004): 692.

92 William O. Oldson, "Alibi for Prejudice: Eastern Orthodoxy, the Holocaust, and Romanian Nationalism," *East European Quarterly* XXXVI, no. 3 (2002): 301.

93 Hollander, "The Final Solution in Bulgaria and Romania: A Comparative Perspective," 231, 232; Radu Ioanid, *The Holocaust in Romania: The Destruction of Jews and Gypsies under the Antonescu Regime, 1940-1944* (Chicago: Ivan R Dee, 2000), 38; Solonari, "Patterns of Violence: The Local Population and the Mass Murder of Jews in Bessarabia and Northern Bukovina, July – August 1941," 755.

94 Oldson, "Alibi for Prejudice: Eastern Orthodoxy, the Holocaust, and Romanian Nationalism," 302, 303; For German units see Christopher R. Browning, *Ordinary Men. Reserve Police Battalion 101 and the Final Solution in Poland* (New York: HarperPerennial, 1992).

95 Vladimir Solonari, *Purifying the Nation: Population Exchange and Ethnic Cleansing in Nazi-Allied Romania* (Baltimore: John Hopkins University Press, 2010), 152. Ioanid, *The Holocaust in Romania: The Destruction of Jews and Gypsies under the Antonescu Regime, 1940-1944*, 111; "The Holocaust in Romania: The Iasi Pogrom of June 1941," 120.

96 Brustein and King, "Balkan Anti-Semitism: The Cases of Bulgaria and Romania before the Holocaust," 698.

97 Michael R. Marrus and Robert O. Paxton, "The Nazis and the Jews in Occupied Western Europe, 1940-1944," *Journal of Modern History* 54, no. 4 (1982): 707.

98 Rodogno, "Italiani Brava Gente? Fascist Italy's Policy toward the Jews in the Balkans, April 1941–July 1943," 219, 233.

99 Spengler-Axiopoulou, "Alleleggye Kai Voetheia Pros Tous Evraious Tes Elladas Kata Te Diarkeia Tes Katoches: 1941-1944," 22, 24; Bowman, *The Agony of Greek Jews 1940-1945*, 153.

100 L. S. Stavrianos, "The Jews of Greece," 263.

101 Kitroeff, *War-Time Jews. The Case of Athens*, 63.

102 Matsas, *The Illusion of Safety: The Story of Greek Jews During the Second World War*, 127, 279; Exarchou, *Oi Evraioi Sten Xanthi*, 111.

103 Benbassa and Rodrigue, *The Jews of the Balkans*, 170; Seckendorf, *E Ellada kato apo ton Agkyloto Stavro*, 152.

104 Ampatzopoulou, *To Olokautoma Stis Martyries Ton Ellenon Evraion*, 114; Matsas, *The Illusion of Safety: The Story of Greek Jews During the Second World War*, 274–80; Bowman, *The Agony of Greek Jews 1940-1945*, 154, 163–64.

105 Kitroeff, *War-Time Jews. The Case of Athens*, 61; Papastratis, *Oi Evraioi Tes Kavallas*, 14; Moissis, *E Evraiki Koinoteta Tes Larisas Prin Kai Meta to Olokautoma*, 180; Tsiligiannis, *E Evraike Koinoteta Tes Artas*, 40, 42, 70; Katerina Kralova, "The 'Holocausts' in Greece: Victim Competition in the Context of Postwar Compensation for Nazi Persecution," *Holocaust Studies* 23, no. 1–2 (2017): 152.

106 Jan Lanicek, "Governments-in-Exile and the Jews During and After the Second World War," *Holocaust Studies*, 18, no. 2–3 (2012).

107 Bowman, *The Agony of Greek Jews 1940-1945*, 176.

108 Primo Levi, *Survival in Auschwitz* (New York: Simon & Schuster, 1986), 71.

109 Kabeli, *The Resistance of Greek Jews*, VIII. 287. Although this incident and Greek participation is widely recounted among the memoirs of Greek Jews who survived Polish Jewish accounts do not mention the Greeks (Bowman, *The Agony of Greek Jews 1940-1945*, 96–98, 53).

110 Matsas, *The Illusion of Safety: The Story of Greek Jews During the Second World War*, 241; Bowman, *The Agony of Greek Jews 1940-1945*, 95.

111 Vernardos Melo, *Ta Pathe Kai E Exontose Ton Ellenoevraion* (Thessaloniki: Paratiritis, 1998), 35.

112 Mazower, *Inside Hitler's Greece, the Experience of Occupation 1941-1944*, 41.

113 Bowman, *The Agony of Greek Jews 1940-1945*, 218.

114 Maria Kavala, "Oi Ekteleseis Evraion Ste Thessaloniki Sta Chronia Tes Katoches. Politike Antipoinon Kai Fyletismos," in *Evraikes Koinotetes Anamesa Se Anatole Kai Dyse, 15os-20os Aionas: Oikonomia, Koinonia, Politike, Politismos*, eds. Anna Machaira and Leda Papastefanaki (Ioannina: Isnafi, 2015), 260; Zekendorf, *E Ellada Kato Apo Ton Agyloto Stavro*, 39.

115 Papagiannis, *Ethnikos Agrotikos Syndesmos Antikomounistikes Drases*, 23.

116 Schminck-Gustavus, *Mnemes Katoches II. Italoi Kai Germanoi Sta Giannena Kai E Katastrophe Tes Evraikes Koinotetas*, 256.

117 Mazower, "Three Forms of Political Justice: Greece, 1944-1945," 34.

118 Susan-Sophia Spilioti, "'Mia Ypothese Tes Politikes Kai Ochi Tes Dikaiosynes'. E Dike Tou Merten (1957-1959) Kai Oi Elleno-Germanikes Scheseis," ed. Rika Mpennveniste (Thessaloniki: Ekdoseis Vanias, 1998), 31, 38.

119 Eleni Haidia, "The Punishment of Collaborators in Northern Greece, 1945-1946," in *After the War Was Over. Reconstructing the Family, Nation, and State in Greece, 1943-1960*, ed. Mark Mazower (Princeton: Princeton University Press, 2000), 48–50.

120 Haidia, "The Punishment of Collaborators in Northern Greece, 1945-1946," 51.

121 Ibid., 53.

122 Ibid., 56.

123 Bowman, *The Agony of Greek Jews 1940-1945*, 218.

124 Phillip Carabott, "'Na Exafanisthoun Oi Katadotes Apo to Prosopon Tes Ges': Evraioi 'Dosilogoi' Kai E Skia Tes Prodosias (1944-1963)," in *Ten Epavrion Tou Olokavtomatos*, eds. Evanghelos Chekimoglou and Anna Maria Droumbouki (Thessaloniki: Jewish Museum of Thessaloniki, 2017), 110.

125 Mark Mazower, "Oi Synepeies Tou Diogmou Ton Evraion Gia Ten Pole Tes Thessalonikes," in *Oi Evraioi Tes Elladas Sten Katoche*, ed. Rika Benveniste (Thessaloniki: Ekdoseis Vanias, 1998), 59.

126 Nar, *Keimene Epi Aktes Thalasses . . . Meletes Kai Arthra Gia Ten Evraike Koinoteta Tes Thessalonikis*, 271.

127 Carabott, "'Na Exafanisthoun Oi Katadotes Apo to Prosopon Tes Ges': Evraioi 'Dosilogoi' Kai E Skia Tes Prodosias (1944-1963)," 110–11.

128 Ampatzopoulou, *To Olokautoma Stis Martyries Ton Ellenon Evraion*, 163.

129 Matsas, *The Illusion of Safety: The Story of Greek Jews During the Second World War*, 324–25; Moissis, *E Evraiki Koinoteta Tes Larisas Prin Kai Meta to Olokautoma*,188; Kralova, "The 'Holocausts' in Greece: Victim Competition in the Context of Postwar Compensation for Nazi Persecution," 152.

130 Mazower, *Inside Hitler's Greece, the Experience of Occupation 1941-1944*, 246–47.

131 Kavala, *E Katastrophe Ton Evraion Tes Elladas (1941-1944)*, 104; Bowman, *The Agony of Greek Jews 1940-1945*, 214; Hagouel, "The History of the Jews of Salonika and the Holocaust," 32.

132 Constantopoulou and Veremis, eds., *Documents on the History of the Greek Jews*, 331.

133 Iakov Simpi and Karina Lampsa, *E Zoe Ap' Ten Arche: E Metanastevsh Ton Ellenon Evraion Sten Palaistini (1945-1948)* (Athens: Ekdoseis Alexandreia, 2010), 133.

134 Stratos N. Dordanas, "Exontose Kai Leelasia: E Yperesia Diacheiriseos Israelitikon Periousion," in *To Olokavtoma Sta Valkania*, eds. Giorgos Antoniou, Stratos N. Dordanas, and Nikos Maratzidis (Athens: Epikentro, 2011), 346.

135 Minos-Athanasios Karyotakis, "E Apeikonise Ton Evraion Sten Efemerida 'Makedonia' Ten Periodo 1945-1948" (Aristotle University of Thessaloniki, 2016), 57.

136 Karyotakis, "E Apeikonise Ton Evraion Sten Efemerida 'Makedonia' Ten Periodo 1945-1948" 53, 70.

137 Fleming, *Greece a Jewish History*, 175, 176; Maria Kavala and Kostis Kornetis, "O Ellenikos Kratikos Mechanismos Kai E Diacheirise Ton Evraikon Perousion Tes Thessalonikes," in *Ten Epaurion Tou Olokautomatos*, eds. Evaggelos Hekimoglou and Anna Maria Droumpouki (Thessaloniki: Jewish Museum of Thessaloniki, 2017), 135–36.

138 Kralova, "The 'Holocausts' in Greece: Victim Competition in the Context of Postwar Compensation for Nazi Persecution," 153.

139 Bowman, *The Agony of Greek Jews 1940-1945*, 214. Hagouel, "The History of the Jews of Salonika and the Holocaust," 32; Kavala, *E Katastrophe Ton Evraion Tes Elladas (1941-1944)*. 104–05; Kralova, "The 'Holocausts' in Greece: Victim Competition in the Context of Postwar Compensation for Nazi Persecution," 153.

140 Ampatzopoulou, *To Olokautoma Stis Martyries Ton Ellenon Evraion*, 233.

141 Kralova, "The 'Holocausts' in Greece: Victim Competition in the Context of Postwar Compensation for Nazi Persecution," 152.

142 Constantopoulou and Veremis, eds., *Documents on the History of the Greek Jews*, 330; Moisis Asche, *Les Juifs En Europe (1939-1945)*, vol. 8, Etudes Et Monographies (Paris: Editions du Centre de Documentation Juive Contemporaire, 1949), 49. See also Photini Constantopoulou and Thanos Veremis, eds., *Documents on the History of the Greek Jews* (Athens: Kastanidis, 1999), 354.

143 Bea Lewkowicz, "'After the War We Were All Together': Jewish Memories of Postwar Thessaloniki," in *After the War Was Over. Reconstructing the Family, Nation, and State in Greece, 1943-1960*, ed. Mark Mazower (Princeton: Princeton University

Press, 2000), 259; Kavala and Kornetis, "O Ellenikos Kratikos Mechanismos Kai E Diacheirise Ton Evraikon Perouson Tes Thessalonikes," 133.

144 Asser-Pardo, *548 Emeres Me Allo Onoma*, 71.

145 Ampatzopoulou, *To Olokautoma Stis Martyries Ton Ellenon Evraion*, 173–74.

146 Renee Levine Melammed, "The Memoirs of a Partisan from Salonika," *Nashim: A Journal of Jewish Women's Studies & Gender Issues* 7, no. 1 (2004): 164.

147 Ampatzopoulou, *To Olokautoma Stis Martyries Ton Ellenon Evraion*, 230, 232.

148 Kralova, "The 'Holocausts' in Greece: Victim Competition in the Context of Postwar Compensation for Nazi Persecution," 152.

149 Carabott, "'Na Exafanisthoun Oi Katadotes Apo to Prosopon Tes Ges': Evraioi 'Dosilogoi' Kai E Skia Tes Prodosias (1944-1963)," 102, 104, 108–09.

150 Hagouel, "The History of the Jews of Salonika and the Holocaust," 33.

151 Kavala and Kornetis, "O Ellenikos Kratikos Mechanismos Kai E Diacheirise Ton Evraikon Perouson Tes Thessalonikes," 132.

152 Benbassa and Rodrigue, *The Jews of the Balkans*, 189; Bowman, *The Agony of Greek Jews 1940-1945*, 57; 226; Kralova, "The 'Holocausts' in Greece: Victim Competition in the Context of Postwar Compensation for Nazi Persecution," 152; Lewkowicz "'After the War We Were All Together': Jewish Memories of Postwar Thessaloniki," 248.

153 Krapsitis, *E Istorike Aletheia Gia Tous Mousoulmanous Tsamedes*, 256–57; Mazower, "Three Forms of Political Justice: Greece, 1944-1945," 25–26.

154 Krapsitis, *E Istorike Aletheia Gia Tous Mousoulmanous Tsamedes*, 258.

155 Christina Alexopoulos, "La Question Macédonienne Pendant La Guerre Civile Grecque," *Cahiers balkaniques* 38–39 (2011): 4.

156 Georgi Stardelov, Cvetan Grozdanov, and Blaze Ristovski, eds., *Macedonia and Its Relations with Greece* (Skopje: Macedonian Academy of Sciences and Arts, 1993), 81–83.

157 Mpaltsiotis, "E Ithageneia Ston Psychro Polemo," 84.

158 Ibid., 86.

159 Lewkowicz, "'After the War We Were All Together': Jewish Memories of Postwar Thessaloniki," 249.

160 K. E. Fleming, "The Stereotyped 'Greek Jew' from Auschwitz-Birkenau to Israeli Pop Culture," *Journal of Modern Greek Studies* 25, no. 1 (2007): 21, 23–24.

161 Bowman, *The Agony of Greek Jews 1940-1945*, 228.

162 Esdras D. Moysis, *E Evraike Koinoteta Tes Larisas Prin Kai Meta to Olokaytoma*, 191.

163 Ibid., 244.

164 See Anti-Defamation League, "Adl Global 100: An Index of Anti-Semitism" (2015).

165 Giorgos Karatzaferis, "Einai 'Evr(Ai)Os' Gnosto . . ." *AlfAena*, January 3-4, 2009 (2009): 9.

166 Konstantinos A. Plevris, *Oi Evraioi. Ole E Aletheia* (Athens: Ilektron, 2006).

167 Dimitrios S. Soutsos, *O Dodekalogos Tou Ethnikiste*, Ethnikistikos Syndesmos (Athens: Nik. Sakkoulas, 1946), 5, 10; D. K. Vogazlis, *Fyletikes Kai Ethnikes Meionotetes Sten Ellada Kai Te Voulgaria* (Athens: Etaireia Thrakikon Meleton, 1954), 6, 14, 16.

168 Nikolaos V. Patrinelis, "Evraioi Kai Ellenes—O Theskevtikos Kai Ylistikos Dogmatismos Choris Maska," (1972), 99, 120, 121, 137.

169 Panteleimonas K. Karanikolas, *Evraioi Kai Christianoi* (Corinth: Pnoi, 1980), 8, 9, 10, 14, 19, 38.

170 Grigoris D. Kontraros, *Ellenismos-Evraismos (Drase)-(Antidrase) Ellenes Kai Evraioi (Kai Mazi Kai Choria)* (Athens, 2003), 11, 16, 41; Patrinelis, "Evraioi Kai Ellenes—O Theskevtikos Kai Ylistikos Dogmatismos Choris Maska," 90.

171 Basilius J. Groen, "Nationalism and Reconciliation: Orthodoxy in the Balkans," *Religion, State and Society* 26, no. 2 (1998): 116–17.

172 Groen, "Nationalism and Reconciliation," 119.

173 Stephanos N. Sotiriou, *Meionotetes Kai Alytrotismos* (Athens: Elliniki Evroekdotiki, 1991), 39,40.

174 Brunnbauer, "The Perception of Muslims in Bulgaria and Greece: Between the 'Self' and the 'Other,'" 48, 55. Lately some nationalists have argued for an inherent Greek origin of the Pomaks but they are in the minority (See Giannis Magkriotis, *Pomakoi E Rodopaioi, Oi Ellenes Mousoulmanoi* (Athens: Ekdoseis Risos, 1990).

175 Aser R. Moysis, *Elleno-Ioudaikai Meletai* (Athens, 1958), 58; Isak I. Kambeli, *Eis Tas Epalxeis Tou Evraismou* (Athens, 1950), 46.

176 Isak I. Kambeli Eis, tas Epalxeis tou Evraismou Athens 1950.

177 Kralova, "The 'Holocausts' in Greece: Victim Competition in the Context of Postwar Compensation for Nazi Persecution," 163.

178 Petros Antaios et al., eds., *Mavre Vivlos Tes Katoches* (Athens: Ethniko Symvoulio gia te Diekdikese ton Ofeilon tes Germanias pros ten Ellada, 2006), 60, 68, 99, 105, 109, 111, 126.

179 Ampatzopoulou, "Evraioi, Olokavtoma Kai Logotechnike Anaparastase Stis Arches Tou 21ou Aiona," 417; *O Allos En Diogmo. E Eikona Tou Evraiou Ste Logotechnia, Zetemata Istorias Kai Mythoplasias* (Athens: Ekdoseis Themelio, 1998). 113. 114, 128, 289.

180 Ampatzopoulou, "Evraioi, Olokavtoma Kai Logotechnike Anaparastase Stis Arches Tou 21ou Aiona," 418–19.

181 Sia Anagnostopoulou, "E Tapeinose Ton Ellenon Einai Tapeinose Tes Evropes," *Epochi* (2012), http://www.koinonia-demo.gr/2012/02/%CE%B7-%CF%84% CE%B1%CF%80%CE%B5%CE%AF%CE%BD%CF%89%CF%83%CE%B7- %CF%84%CF%89%CE….

182 "15-09-16 O Theodosis Pelegrinis Gia Ten 'Emera Ethnikes Mnemes Gia Ten Katastroge Tou Mikrasiatikou Ellenismou," news release, 2016; Protagon Team, "Gia Antisemitika Stereotypa Kategorei Ton Pelegrini to Kentriko Israelitiko Symvoulio," *Protagon.gr*, September 21, 2016, 2016; "Pelegrinis: Epicheirei Na Anaskevasei Meta Ten Katakravge," *E Kathimerini*, September 19, 2016.

183 Giorgos Antoniou et al., eds., *Anti-Semitismos Sten Ellada Semera. Emfanseis, Aitia Kai Antimetopise Tou Phainomenou* (Thessaloniki: Heinrich Böll Stiftung Ellada, 2017), 21, 23, 31.

184 Dimitris Psarras, "O Antisemitismos Sten Ellada Kai E Aristera," *Efimerida ton Syntakton*, May 29, 2017.

185 Kostas D Kaltsis, "Den Mas Phovizei E Fasizousa Evraike Nootropia!" *stotapsi.gr*, August 9, 2016.

186 "Pros Ti E Epimone Ton Evraion Na Tous . . . Timoume Synechos?" *Proinos Logos*, August 4, 2016, 2016.

187 Stathis, "Me Melane Apo Aima," *enikos.gr*, May 10, 2017.

188 Andrew Apostolou, "The Crudest Hatred: Antisemitism and Apologia for Terrorism in Contemporary Greece," *Antisemitism and Xenophobia Today* (2005).

189 Kavala, "Aspects of Anti-Semitism in Salonika, During the Nazi Occupation (1941-1944): The Authorities, the Press and the People. An Example of Differentiation and Exclusion," 203–04.

190 Protagon Team, "Apotropiasmos Gia Tous Vandalismous Sto Mnemeio Tou Olokavtomantos Sten Kavala," http://www.protagon.gr/epikairoti-ta/44341383275-44341383275; Hagouel, "The History of the Jews of Salonika and the Holocaust," 33.

191 Lewkowicz, "'After the War We Were All Together': Jewish Memories of Postwar Thessaloniki," 250.

Bibliography

Unpublished Sources

Historical Archive of the Ministry of Foreign Affairs of Greece (HAMFA), Kentrike Yperesia (KY), 1834, subfolder 49.1, Peri Ellenikes Ithageneias
HAMFA, KY, 1835, 36.2, Proxeneia Ellados, Proxeneia eis Makedonian (Thessaloniki)
HAMFA, KY, 1837, 76.1, Peri Neofotiston
HAMFA, KY, 1838, 49.1, Apoktesis Ellenikes Ithageneias
HAMFA, KY, 1838, 76.1, Neofotistoi
HAMFA, KY, 1840, 76.1, Threskeia (neofotistoi)
HAMFA, KY, 1841, 76.1, Threskeia (neof.)
HAMFA, KY, 1842, 76.1, Threskeia (peri neof.)
HAMFA, KY, 1843, 76.1, Threskeia (neofot.)
HAMFA, KY, 1845, 36.2, Proxeneia Ellados (Ioannina, Thessaloniki)
HAMFA, KY, 1845, 76.1, Threskeia - neofotistoi
HAMFA, KY, 1846, 36.2, Proxeneia Ellados (Ioannina, Thessaloniki)
HAMFA, KY, 1847, 36.2, Proxeneia kai Ypoproxeneia (Thessaloniki, Ioannina)
HAMFA, KY, 1848, 68.1 γ, Ypothesis Patsifikou
HAMFA, KY, 1849, 36.2, Proxeneia Ellados (Epeiros, Alvania, Thessaloniki)
HAMFA, KY, 1851, 36.2, Proxeneia Ellados (Epeiro kai Alvania)
HAMFA, KY, 1852, 36.2a, Proxeneio Thessalonikis
HAMFA, KY, 1853, 36.2, Proxeneio Epeirou, Proxeneio Thessalonikis
HAMFA, KY, 1854, 4 IV γ, Proxeneio Ioanninon
HAMFA, KY, 1855, 76.1, Ekklesiastika
HAMFA, KY, 1856, 76.1, Threskeia, Ekklesiastika
HAMFA, KY, 1858, 36.2, Proxeneia Ioanninon, Thessalonikis
HAMFA, KY, 1859, 36.2, Proxeneio Thessalonikis
HAMFA, KY, 1860, 36.2, Proxeneia Thessalonikis, Ioanninon
HAMFA, KY, 1861, 36.2, Proxeneia Ioanninon kai Thessalonikis
HAMFA, KY, 1861, 76.1, Peri Threskeias, Panslavismos
HAMFA, KY, 1862, 36.2, Proxeneia Thessalonikis, Ioanninon
HAMFA, KY, 1863, 36:2, Proxeneia Thessalonikis, Ioanninon
HAMFA, KY, 1867, 76.1, Threskeia – exislamismos Ioudaion eis Artan
HAMFA, KY, 1868, 99:1, Peri ton en Galazio epeisodion metaxy Moldavon kai Ioudaion
HAMFA, KY, 1870, 36.2, Proxenikai Archai Ioanninon, Thessalonikis
HAMFA, KY, 1871, 49.2, Zetema ethnikotetas en Roumania Israeliton
HAMFA, KY, 1874, 36.2, Allelografia Ellenikon proxeneion Epeirou kai Makedonias
HAMFA, KY, 1877, 36.2, Proxeneia Thessalonikis
HAMFA, KY, 1879, 36.2, Proxenika Thessalonikis

HAMFA, KY, 1880, 36.2, Prox. Thessalonikis

HAMFA, KY, 1881, 36.2, Proxenika Thessalonikis

HAMFA, KY, 1891, A5-1, Ektheseis Pres. Kai Prox.

HAMFA, KY, 1892, A12-1, Metanastai (egkat. Ebraion Rossias)

HAMFA, KY, 1895, A5-1, Ektheseis Pres. Kai Prox.

HAMFA, KY, 1904, IΔ AAK 62.3, Alvanika

HAMFA, KY, 1906, 64.3, Epeiro, Alvania

HAMFA, KY, 1910, K, Diaphora

HAMFA, KY, 1911, 94.1, Politikes Ektheseis

HAMFA, KY, 1911, 62.2, Proxeneia Thessalonikis

HAMFA, KY, 1913, 9.2, Edafikes Diekdikeseis

HAMFA, KY, 1913, 16.3, Esoterike Politike

HAMFA, KY, 1913, 22.4, Propaganda Voulgaron

General State Archives (GAK), Civil Decisions of the Athens Appeals Court (PA), 1837, Vol. 1

GAK, PA, 1837, 2

GAK, PA, 1838, 4

GAK, PA, 1860, 119A

GAK, PA, 1860, 120

GAK, PA, 1860, 121

Published Sources

Aberbach, David. *The European Jews, Patriotism and the Liberal State 1789-1939: A Study of Literature and Social Psycholeogy.* Routledge Jewish Studies. Kindle ed. New York: Routledge, 2012.

About, Edmond. *E Ellada Tou Othonos.* Athens: Ekdoseis Afon Tolidi, 1992 (1855).

Adalian, Rouben Paul. "Comparative Policy and Differential Practice in the Treatment of Minorities in Wartime: The United States Archival Evidence on the Armenians and Greeks in the Ottoman Empire." *Journal of Genocide Research* 3, no. 1 (2001): 31–48.

Adanir, Fikret. "Non-Muslims in the Ottoman Army and the Ottoman Defeat in the Balkan War of 1912-1913." *In A Question of Genocide, Armenians and Turks at the End of the Ottoman Empire,* edited by Ronald Grigor Suny, Fatma Müge Göçek, and Norman M. Naimark, 113–25. Oxford: Oxford University Press, 2011.

Agathaggelos, Ieromonachos. "Prorresis Etoi Profeteia." edited by Aristotle University of Thessaloniki, 1810.

Aggelis, Vaggelis. "Metaxike Propaganda Kai Neolaia 1936-1940." Panteio University, 2004.

Agoropoulou-Birbili, Aphroditi. "E Evraike Synoikia Tes Kerkyras." In *E Evraike Parousia Ston Elladiko Choro (4os-19os Ai.),* edited by Anna Lambropoulou and Kostas Tsiknakis, 123–48. Athens: Ethniko Idryma Erevnon, 2008.

Ainianos, Dimitrios. *Apomnemonevmata Gia Ten Epanastase Tou 1821.* Athens: Ekdoseis Vergina, 1996.

Ainianos, Dimitrios. *Georgios Karaiskakis.* Athens: Ekdoseis Vergina, 1996.

Aitolos, Agios Kosmas o. *Didachai Kai Profeteiai Ag. Kosma Tou Aitolou.* Athens: Ekdoseis Lydia.

Akcapar, Sebnem Koser. "Conversion as a Migration Strategy in a Transit Country: Iranian Shiites Becoming Christians in Turkey." *The International Migration Review* 40, no. 4 (Winter 2006): 817–53.

Aksan, Virginia H. "Expressions of Ottoman Rule in an Age of Transition: 1760 and 1830." In *Hoca, 'Allame, Ouits De Science: Essays in Honor of Kemal H Karpat*, edited by Kaan Durukan, Robert W. Zens, and Akile Zorlu-Durukan, 81–95. Istanbul: The Isis Press, 2010.

Aksan, Virginia H. "Who Was an Ottoman? Reflections on 'Wearing Hats' and 'Turning Turk." In *Europe and Turkey in the 18th Century*, edited by Barbara Schmidt-Haberkamp, 305–24. Göttingen: Bonn University Press, 2011.

Aksan, Virginia H. "Mobilization of Warrior Populations in the Ottoman Context, 1750-1850." In *Fighting for a Living: A Comparative History of Military Labour 1500-2000*, edited by Erik Jan Zürcher, 331–51. Amsterdam: Amsterdam University Press, 2013.

Alexopoulos, Christina. "La Question Macédonienne Pendant La Guerre Civile Grecque." *Cahiers Balkaniques* 38–39 (2011): 1–35.

Almog, Shmuel. *Nationalism and Antisemitism in Modern Europe 1815-1945*. Oxford: Pergamon Press, 1990.

Ampatzopoulou, Fragiski. "Evraioi, Olokavtoma Kai Logotechnike Anaparastase Stis Arches Tou 21ou Aiona." *Nea Estia* 169, no. 1842 (March 2011 2011): 408–30.

Ampatzopoulou, Fragiski. *O Allos En Diogmo. E Eikona Tou Evraiou Ste Logotechnia, Zetemata Istorias Kai Mythoplasias*. Athens: Ekdoseis Themelio, 1998.

Ampatzopoulou, Fragiski. *To Olokautoma Stis Martyries Ton Ellenon Evraion*. Athens: Epikentro, 1993.

Anagnostakis, Ilias. "E Solomonteia Amphithymia Ton Proton Makedonon Aytokratoron Kai Oi Apokalyptikes Katavoles Tes." In *E Evraike Parousia Ston Elladiko Choro (4os-19os Ai.)*, edited by Anna Lambropoulou and Kostas Tsiknakis, 39–60. Athens: Ethniko Idryma Erevnon, 2008.

Anagnostopoulou, Sia. "E Tapeinose Ton Ellenon Einai Tapeinose Tes Evropes." *Epochi* (2012). Published electronically February 20, 2012. http://www.koinonia-demo. gr/2012/02/%CE%B7-%CF%84%CE%B1%CF%80%CE%B5%CE%AF%CE%BD%CF% 89%CF%83%CE%B7-%CF%84%CF%89%CE... (since removed).

Anastasopoulos, Antonis. "Political Participation, Public Order, and Monetary Pledges (Nezir) in Ottoman Crete." In *Popular Protest and Political Participation in the Ottoman Empire*, edited by Eleni Gara, M. Erdem Kabadayi, and Christoph K. Neumann, 127–42. Istanbul: Bilgi University Press, 2011.

Anastassiadou, Meropi. *Salonique 1830-1912*. New York: Brill, 1997.

"Anderson's Observations in Greece." *The North American Review*, January 1, 1832: 1–23.

Anderson, Benedict. *Imagined Communities: Reflections on the Origin and Spread of Nationalism*. London: Verso, 1991.

Andreadis, A. M. *Oi Evraioi En to Byzantino Kratei: Dialexe Genomene En Te Etaireia Byzantinon Spoudon*. Athens: Estia, 1929.

Ankori, Zvi. "Some Aspects of Karaite-Rabbanite Relations in Byzantium in the Eve of the First Crusade: Part II." *Proceedings of the American Academy for Jewish Research* 25 (1956): 157–76.

Ankori, Zvi. "Greek Orthodox–Jewish Relations in Historic Perspective–the Jewish View." *Journal of Ecumenical Studies* XIII, no. 4 (Fall 1976): 17–57.

Anonymous. *Elliniki Nomarchia Itoi Logos Peri Eleftherias*. Athens: Ekdoseis Aimopas, n.d.

Antaios, Petros, Panagiotis Aronis, Manolis Glezos, Athina Kakolyri, Petros Kouloufakos, Giannis Kyriakakos, Fragiskos Konstantarakis, et al., eds. *Mavre Vivlos Tes Katoches*.

Athens: Ethniko Symvoulio gia te Diekdikese ton Ofeilon tes Germanias pros ten Ellada, 2006.

Anthimos, Patriarch of Jerusalem. *Didaskalia Patrike*. Constantinople: Ioannis Pagos ex Armenion, 1798.

Antoniou, Giorgos, Spyros Kosmidis, Ilias Dinas, and Leon Saltiel, eds. *Anti-Semitismos Sten Ellada Semera. Emfanseis, Aitia Kai Antimetopise Tou Phainomenou*. Thessaloniki: Heinrich Böll Stiftung Ellada, 2017.

Apostolou, Andrew. "The Crudest Hatred: Antisemitism and Apologia for Terrorism in Contemporary Greece." *Antisemitism and Xenophobia Today* (2005): 1–9. Published electronically 30 August 30, 2005.

Apostolou, Andrew. "'The Exception of Salonika': Bystanders and Collaborators in Northern Greece." *Holocaust and Genocide Studies* 14, no. 2 (Fall 2000): 165–96.

Arafat, K. W. "A Legacy of Islam in Greece: Ali Pasha and Ioannina." *Bulletin (British Society of Middle Eastern Studies)* 14, no. 2 (1987): 172–82.

Arendt, Hannah. *Eichmann in Jerusalem. A Report on the Banality of Evil*. New York: The Viking Press, 1963.

Arkush, Allan. "Voltaire on Judaism and Christianity." *Association for Jewish Studies Review* 18, no. 2 (1993): 223–43.

Arnakis, G. Georgiades. "The Greek Church of Constantinople and the Ottoman Empire." *The Journal of Modern History* 24, no. 3 (September 1952): 235–50.

Arslan, Ali. *O Ellenikos Typos Sto Othomaniko Kratos*. Athens: Eptalofos, 2004.

Asche, Moisis. *Les Juifs En Europe (1939-1945)*. Etudes Et Monographies. Volume 8, Paris: Editions du Centre de Documentation Juive Contemporaire, 1949.

Aslanov, Cyril. "Judeo–Greek or Greek Spoken by Jews?." In *Jews in Byzantium*, edited by Robert Bonfil, Oded Irshai, Guy G Stroumsa, and Rina Talgam, 385–98. Boston: Brill, 2012.

Asser-Pardo, Rozina. *548 Emeres Me Allo Onoma*. Athens: Ekdoseis Gavriilidis, 1999.

Athanasiadis, Charis. *Ta Aposyrthenta Vivlia: Ethnos Kai Scholike Istoria Sten Ellada 1858-2008*. Athens: Alexandreia, 2015.

Avdela, Efi. "Towards a Greek History of the Jews of Salonica?." *Jewish History* 28 (2014): 405–10.

Averoff, Evangelos. *E Politike Plevra Tou Koutsovlachikou Zetematos*. Trikala: F.I.L.O.S., 1987. 1948.

Baer, Marc. "An Enemy Old and New: The Dönme, Anti-Semitism, and Conspiracy Theories in the Ottoman Empire and Turkish Republic." *Jewish Quarterly Review* 103, no. 4 (2013): 523–55.

Baer, Marc. "The Great Fire of 1660 and the Islamization of Christian and Jewish Space in Istanbul." *International Journal of Middle East Studies* 36 (2004): 159–81.

Baer, Marc. "Islamic Conversion Narratives of Women: Social Change and Gendered Religious Hierarchy in Early Modern Ottoman Istanbul." *Gender & History* 16, no. 2 (August 2004): 425–58.

Baer, Marc. *The Dönme: Jewish Converts, Muslim Revolutionaries, and Secular Turks*. Stanford: Stanford University Press, 2009.

Baltacioglu-Brammer, Ayse. "The Formation of Kizilbas Communities in Anatolia and Ottoman Responses, 1450s-1630s." *International Journal of Turkish Studies* 20, no. 1–2 (2014): 21–47.

Barkey, Karen. *Bandits and Bureaucrats, the Ottoman Route to State Centralization*. Ithaca: Cornell University Press, 1994.

Barkey, Karen, and Ira Katznelson. "States, Regimes, and Decisions: Why Jews Were Expelled from Medieval England and France." *Theory and Society* 40 (2011): 475–503.

Baron, Salo W. "Jewish Immigration and Communal Conflicts in Seventeenth-Century Corfu." In *The Joshua Starr Memorial Volume, Conference on Jewish Relations*. New York: Jewish Social Studies Publications, 1953.

Bartholdy, J. L. S. *Taxidiotikes Entyposeis Apo Ten Ellada 1803-1804*. Athens: Ekati, 1993.

Bass, Paul R. *Ethnicity and Nationalism: Theory and Comparison*. Newbury Park: Sage, 1991.

Bazili, Constanine Michailovitz. *Enas Rosos Sten Ellada Tou Kapodistria*. Athens: Kalentis, 2000.

Beihammer, Alexander D. "Defection across the Border of Islam and Christianity: Apostasy and Cross-Cultural Interaction in Byzantine-Seljuk Relations." *Speculum* 86: 597–650 (2011).

Belle, Henri. *Taxidi Sten Ellada 1861-1874*. Volume B, Athens: Istoretes, 1993.

Benbassa, Esther. "Questioning Historical Narratives: The Case of Balkan Sephardi Jewry." In *Simon Dubnow Institute Yearbook*, edited by Dan Diner, 15–22. Stuttgart: Deutsche Verlagsanstalt, 2003.

Benbassa, Esther, and Aron Rodrigue. *The Jews of the Balkans*. Cambridge: Blackwell, 1995.

Ben-Naeh, Yaron. "Blond, Tall with Honey-Colored Eyes: Jewish Ownership of Slaves in the Ottoman Empire." *Jewish History* 20 (2006): 315–32.

Benveniste, Henriette-Rika. "The Coming out of Jewish History in Greece." Published electronically 2008. http://usagespublicsdupasse.ehess.fr/wp-content/uploads/sites/7/2014/05/Benveniste_Rika._The_Coming_Out_of_Jewish_History_in_Greece.pdf.

Benveniste, Henriette-Rika. "The Idea of Exile: Jewish Accounts and the Historiography of Salonika Revisited." In *Evraikes Koinotetes Anamesa Se Anatole Kai Dyse, 15os—20os Aionas: Oikonomia, Koinonia, Politike, Politismos*, edited by Anna Machaira and Leda Papastefanaki, 31–53. Ioannina: Isnafi, 2016.

Biale, David. "Counter-History and Jewish Polemics against Christianity: The Sefer Toldot Yeshu and the Sefer Zerubavel." *Jewish Social Studies* 6, no. 1 (1999): 130–45.

Biondich, Mark. *The Balkans. Revolution, War and Political Violence since 1878*. Oxford: Oxford University Press, 2011.

Billig, Michael. *Banal Nationalism*. London: Sage, 1995.

Bjørnlund, Matthias. ""The 1914 Cleansing of Aegean Greeks as a Case of Violent Turkification."". *Journal of Genocide Research* 10, no. 1 (2008): 41--58.

Boel, Gunnar De. "Fallmerayer and Dragoumis on the Greek Nation and Its Mission." In *(Mis)Understanding the Balkans: Essays in Honour of Raymond Detrez*, edited by Michel De Dobbeleer and Stijn Vervaet, 97–108. Gent: Academia Press, 2013.

Bonar, Andre Alexander, and Robert Murray McCheyne. *Narrative of a Mission of Inquiry to the Jews from the Church of Scotland*. Philadelphia: Presbyterian Board of Publication, 1839.

Bonfil, Robert. "Continuity and Discontinuity (641-1204)." In *Jews in Byzantium*, edited by Robert Bonfil, Oded Irshai, Guy G Stroumsa, and Rina Talgam, 65–100. Boston: Brill, 2012.

Borou, Christina. "The Muslim Minority of Western Thrace in Greece: An Internal Positive or an Internal Negative 'Other'?." *Journal of Muslim Minority Affairs* 29, no. 1 (2009): 5–26.

Boustan, Ra'anan S. "Immolating Emperors: Spectacles of Imperial Suffering and the Making of a Jewish Minority Culture in Late Antiquity." *Biblical Interpretation* 17 (2009): 207–38.

Bowman, Steven. "Jews in Wartime Greece." *Jewish Social Studies* 48, no. 1 (Winter 1986): 45–62.

Bowman, Steven. "Survival in Decline: Romaniote Jewry Post-1204.." In *Jews in Byzantium*, edited by Robert Bonfil, Oded Irshai, Guy G Stroumsa, and Rina Talgam, 101–32. Boston: Brill, 2012.

Bowman, Steven. *The Agony of Greek Jews 1940-1945*. Stanford: Stanford University Press, 2009.

Bowman, Steven. *The Jews of Byzantium 1204 - 1453*. Jacksonville: Bloch Pub Co, 2001.

Braham, Randolph L. *The Politics of Genocide, the Holocaust in Hungary*. 2 vols, Volume 1, New York: Columbia University Press, 1981.

Breuilly, John. "Approaches to Nationalism." In *Mapping the Nation*, edited by Gopal Balakrishnan, 146–74. London: Verso, 1996.

Breuilly, John. "Nationalism and the State." In *Nationality, Patriotism and Nationalism in Liberal Democratic Societies*, edited by Roger Michener, 19–48. Minnesota: Professors World Peace Academy, 1993.

Bron, Grégoire. "Learning Lessons From the Iberian Peninsula: Italian Exiles and the Making of a Risorgimento without People (1820-48)." In *Mediterranean Diasporas, Politics and Ideas in the Long 19th Century*, edited by Maurizio Isabella and Konstantina Zanou, 59–76. New York: Bloomsbury, 2016.

Brooks, Julian. "A 'Tranquilizing' Influence? British 'Proto-Peacekeeping' in Ottoman Macedonia 1904-1905." *Peace & Change* 36, no. 2 (2011): 172–90.

Brown, David. *Palmerston and the Politics of Foreign Policy, 1846-55*. Manchester: Manchester University Press, 2003.

Browning, Christopher R. *Ordinary Men. Reserve Police Battalion 101 and the Final Solution in Poland*. New York: HarperPerennial, 1992.

Brubaker, Rogers. "Ethnicity Without Groups." *Archives Europeenes de Sociologie* XLIII, no. 2 (2002): 163–89.

Brubaker, Rogers. *Nationalism Reframed: Nationhood and the National Question in the New Europe*. Cambridge: Cambridge University Press, 1996.

Brunnbauer, Ulf. "The Perception of Muslims in Bulgaria and Greece: Between the 'Self' and the 'Other'." *Journal of Muslim Minority Affairs* 21, no. 1 (2001): 39–61.

Brustein, William I., and Ryan D. King. "Balkan Anti-Semitism: The Cases of Bulgaria and Romania before the Holocaust." *East European Politics and Societies* 18, no. 3 (2004): 430–54.

Buchon, Alexandre. *Voyage Dans L'eubee Les Iles Ioniennes Et Les Cyclades En 1841*. Paris: Emile-Paul Editeur, 1911.

Caloyanni, Constantinos A. *Histoire Des Hebreux*. Alexandrie: A Dracopoulos, 1895.

Cameron, Averil V. "Byzantines and Jews: Some Recent Work on Early Byzantium." *Byzantine and Modern Greek Studies* 26 (1996): 249–74.

Cameron, Averil V. "Disputations, Polemical Literature, and the Formation of Opinion in Early Byzantineliterature." In *Dispute Poems and Dialogues in the Ancient and Medieval near East*, edited by G. J. Reinink, H. J. L. Vanstiphout, and Orientalia Lovaniensia Analecta, 91–108. Leuven: Peeters, 1991.

Cameron, Averil V. "Jews and Heretics—a Category Error?" In *The Ways That Never Parted: Jews and Christians in Late Antiquity and the Early Middle Ages*, edited by Adam H. Becker and Annette Yoshiko Reed, 345–60. Tubingen: J. C. B. Mohr (Paul Siebeck), 2003.

Capri, Daniel, ed. *Italian Diplomatic Documents on the History of the Holocaust in Greece*. Tel Aviv: Tel Aviv University, 1999.

Carabott, Phillip. "Aspects of the Hellenization of Greek Macedonia, Ca. 1912-Ca. 1959." *Kambos: Cambridge Papers in Modern Greek* 13 (2005): 21–61.

Carabott, Phillip. "E Evraike Parousia Sten Athena Tou 19ou Aiona: Apo Ton Maximo Rotsild Sten Israelitike Adelfoteta." In *Evraikes Koinotetes Anamesa Se Anatole Kai Dyse, 15os-20os Aionas: Oikonomia, Koinonia, Politike, Politismos*, edited by Anna Machaira and Leda Papastefanaki, 182–95. Ioannina: Isnafi, 2016.

Carabott, Phillip. "'Na Exafanisthoun Oi Katadotes Apo to Prosopon Tes Ges': Evraioi 'Dosilogoi' Kai E Skia Tes Prodosias (1944-1963)." In *Ten Epavrion Tou Olokavtomatos*, edited by Evanghelos Chekimoglou and Anna Maria Droumbouki, 102–22. Thessaloniki: Jewish Museum of Thessaloniki, 2017.

Carabott, Phillip. "The Politics of Integration and Assimilation Vis-a-Vis the Slavo-Macedonian Minority of Inter-War Greece: From Parliamentary Inertia to Metaxist Repression." In *Ourselves and Others: The Development of a Greek Macedonian Cultural Identity since 1912*, edited by Peter Mackridge and Eleni Yannakakis, 59–78. Oxford: Berg, 1997.

Carabott, Phillip. "Politics, Orthodoxy and the Language Question in Greece: The Gospel Riots of November 1901." *Journal of Mediterranean Studies* 3, no. 1 (1993): 117–38.

Celine, Louis-Ferdinand. *Bagatelles Pour Un Massacre*. Paris: Editions Denoel, 1937.

Chambers, David, and Brian Pullan, eds. *Venice: A Documentary History, 1450-1630*. Toronto: Toronto University Press, 2001.

Chaniotis, Giorgos. "E Evraike Koinoteta Tes Kerkyras (1860-1939) Entos Kai Ektos Tes 'Ovriakes.'" In *Oi Evraioi Ston Elleniko Choro: Zetemata Istorias Ste Makra Diarkeia*, edited by Efi Avdela and Ontet Varon-Vasar, 63–74. Athens: Ekdoseis Gavriilidis, 1995.

Chantepleure, Guy, and (Jeanne Violet Dussap). *La Ville Assiegee—Janina Octobre 1912—Mars 1913*. Paris: Calmann-Levy, 1913.

Chateaubriand, François-René de. *Odoiporikon Ek Parision Eis Ierosolyma Kai Ex Ierosolymon Eis Parisious*. Volume A, Athens: Afoi Tolidi, 1979 (1860).

Chatterjee, Partha. *The Nation and Its Fragments: Colonial and Postcolonial Histories*. Princeton: Princeton University Press, 1993.

Chekimoglou, Evaggelos A. *Trapezes Kai Thessaloniki 1900-1936. Opseis Leitourgias Kai to Provlema Tes Chorotheteses*. Thessaloniki, 1987.

Christopoulos, Panagiotis F. "E Evraiki Koinotes Navpaktou." *Epeteris Etaireias Stereoelladikon Meleton* A (1968): 277–300.

Christovasilis, Christos. *Peri Evraion*. Athens: Ekdoseis Roes, 2007.

Chronakis, Paris Papamichos. "De-Judaizing a Class, Hellenizing a City: Jewish Merchants and the Future of Salonica in Greek Public Discourse, 1913-1914." *Jewish History* 28 (2014): 373–403.

Chronakis, Paris Papamichos. "'Vipers' and 'Snakes', 'Komitadjis' and 'Pseudo-Nationalists': Anti-Zionist Discourses in Interwar Greece." In *Antisemitism in Greece: Past and Present Trajectories*. Berlin: The Center for Research on Antisemitism, Berlin Technical University, 2014.

Clogg, Richard. "The 'Dhidhaskalia Patriki' (1798): An Orthodox Reaction to French Revolutionary Propaganda." *Middle Eastern Studies* 5, no. 2 (May 1969): 87–115.

Cohen, Israel. "Letters from Abroad—Whose Glory Is Departed." *The Menorah Journal* XII, no. 5 (October–November 1926): 522–27.

Cohn, Norman. *Warrant for Genocide: The Myth of the Jewish World Conspiracy and the Protocols of the Elders of Zion*. London: Serif, 1996.

Comstock, John L. *History of the Greek Revolution; Compiled from the Official Documents of the Greek Government*. New York: William W Reed & Co., 1828.

Constantopoulou, Photini, and Thanos Veremis, eds. *Documents on the History of the Greek Jews*. Athens: Kastanidis, 1999.

Convention. 1832. "Convention between Great Britain, France, and Russia, on the One Part, and Bavaria on the Other, Relative to the Sovereignty of Greece." *The American Journal of International Law* 12, no. 2 (1918): 68–74.

Corbin, Alain. *Women for Hire: Prostitution and Sexuality in France after 1850.* Cambridge: Harvard University Press, 1990.

Costantini, Emanuela. "Neither Foreigners, nor Citizens: Romanian Jews' Long Road to Citizenship." In *The Jews and the Nation-States of Southeastern Europe from the 19th Century to the Great Depression*, edited by Tullia Catalan and Marco Dogo, 2–22. Newcastle upon Tyne: Cambridge Scholars Publishing, 2016.

Couroucli, Maria. *Erga Kai Emeres Sten Kerkyra: Istorike Anthropologia Mias Topikes Koinonias* [Les oliviers du lignage. Une Grece de tradition venitienne, G.-P. Maisonneuve et Larose, 1985]. Translated by Maria Gyparaki. Athens: Ekdoseis Alexandreia, 2008.

Crepin, Jules. "En Grèce—M. Venizelos Et Les Juifs." *Paix et Droit* 14, no. 8 (October 1934): 11–12.

Dagron, Gilbert. "Judaïser." *Travaux et Mémoirés* 11 (1991): 359–80.

Dagron, Gilbert, and Déroche, Vincent. "Juifs Et Chrétiens Dans L'orient Du Viie Siècle." *Travaux et Mémoires* 11 (1991): 17–273.

Dalegre, Joelle. *Grecs Et Ottomans 1453-1923*. Paris: L' Harmattan, 2002.

Delven, Rae. *The Jews of Janina.* Philadelphia: Cadmus Press, 1990.

Demponos, Aggelo-Dionysis. "Evraika." *E Kefalonetike Proodos Z*, no. 79–80 (1978): 133–39.

Demponos, Aggelo-Dionysis. "Evraika." *E Kefalonetike Proodos Z*, no. 81–82 (1978): 165–70.

Deringil, Selim. *Conversion and Apostasy in the Late Ottoman Empire.* Cambridge: Cambridge University Press, 2012.

Déroche, Vincent. "La Polémique Anti-Judaïque Au Vie Et Au Viie Siècle, Un Mémento Inédit, Les Kephalaia." *Travaux et Mémoires* 11 (1991): 275–311.

Deroche, Vincent. "Forms and Functions of Anti-Jewish Polemics: Polymorphy, Polysemy." In *Jews in Byzantium*, edited by Robert Bonfil, Oded Irshai, Guy G Stroumsa, and Rina Talgam, 535–48. Boston: Brill, 2012.

Deschamps, Gaston. *E Ellada Semera: Odoiporiko 1890.* Athens: Trochalia, 1992. 1892.

Desportes, Henri. *Le Mystere Du Sang Chez Les Juifs De Tous Les Temps.* Paris: Albert Savine Editeur, 1890.

Diamantouros, Nikiforos. *Oi Aparches Tes Sygkroteses Sygchronou Kratous Sten Ellada 1821-1828.* Athens: Morphotiko Idryma Ethnikis Trapezis, 2006.

Dimaras, K. Th. *Neoellenikos Diaphotismos.* Athens: Ermis, 1977.

Divani, Lena. *Ellada Kai Meionotetes. To Sytema Diethnous Prostasias Tes Koinonias Ton Ethnon.* Athens: Kastaniotis, 1999.

Dodos, Dimosthenis Ch. *Oi Evraioi Tes Thessalonikis Stis Ekloges Tou Ellenikou Kratous 1915-1936.* Athens: Savvalas, 2005.

Dogo, Marco. "'A Respectable Body of Nation': Religious Freedom and High-Risk Trade: The Greek Merchant in Trieste, 1770-1830." *The Historical Review/La Revue Historique* 7 (2010): 199–211.

Dordanas, Stratos N. "Exontose Kai Leelasia: E Yperesia Diacheiriseos Israelitikon Periousion." In *To Olokavtoma Sta Valkania*, edited by Giorgos Antoniou, Stratos N. Dordanas, and Nikos Maratzidis. Athens: Epikentro, 2011.

Dragostinova, Theodora. "Navigating Nationality in the Emigration of Minorities between Bulgaria and Greece, 1919-1941." *East European Politics and Societies* 23, no. 2 (2009): 185–212.

Dragostinova, Theodora. "Speaking National: Nationalizing the Greeks of Bulgaria. 1900-1939." *Slavic Review* 67, no. 1 (Spring 2008): 154–81.

Drakulic, Slobodan. "Anti-Turkish Obsession and the Exodus of Balkan Muslims." *Patterns of Prejudice* 43, no. 3–4 (2009): 233–49.

Driault, Edouard. *E Megale Idea: E Anagennese Tou Ellenismou*. Athens: Istoritis, 1998 (1920).

Drikos, Thomas. *E Porneia Sten Ermoupole to 19o Aiona (1820-1900)*. Athens: Ellinika Grammata, 2002.

Dursteler, Eric R. *Venetians in Constantinople: Nation, Identity, and Coexistence in the Early Modern Mediterranean*. Baltimore: John Hopkins University Press, 2006.

Dwork, Deborah, and Robert Jan van Pelt. *Holocaust a History*. New York: W. W. Norton & Company, 2003.

Efthymiou, Maria. *Evraioi Kai Christianoi Sta Tourkokratoumena Nesia Tou Notioanatolikou Aigaiou: Oi Dyskoles Plevres Mias Gonimes Synyparxes*. Athens: Trochalia, 1992.

Enepekidis, Polychronis K. *Oi Diogmoi Ton Evraion En Elladi 1941-1944*. Athens: Ekdotikos Oikos Viktoros A Papazisi, 1969.

Engelstein, Laura. *The Keys to Happiness: Sex and the Search for Modernity in Fin-De-Siecle Russia*. Ithaca: Cornell University Press, 1992.

Epilekta Nomika Keimena Tes Ethnikes Paliggenesias. Athens: Tameio Nomikon, 1971.

Epstein, Mark Alan. *The Ottoman Jewish Communities and Their Role in the Fifteenth and Sixteenth Centuries*. Freiburg: Klaus Schwarz Verlag, 1980.

Evaggelou, Eutychia. "E Apoleia Tes Ellenikes Ithageneias Ton Ellenon Evraion Apo Te Dekaetia Tou 1920 Eos to 1965." Panteion Panepistimio Koinonikon & Politikon Epistimon, 2015.

Exarchou, Thomas P. *Oi Evraioi Sten Xanthi*. Xanthi: Politistiko Anaptyxiako Kentro Thrakis, 2001.

Exertzoglou, Haris. "Shifting Boundaries: Language, Community and the Non-Greek-Speaking Greeks." *Historein* 1 (1999): 75–92.

Fairey, Jack. "'Discord and Confusion.. Under the Pretext of Religion': European Diplomacy and the Limits of Orthodox Ecclesiastical Authority in the Eastern Mediterranean." *The International History Review* 34, no. 1 (2012): 19–44.

Fallmerayer, Jakob Philipp. *Peri Tes Katagoges Ton Semerinon Ellenon*. Translated by Konstantinos P. Romanos. Athens: Nefeli, 1984.

Faroqhi, Suraiya. "Empires before and after the Post-Colonial Turn: The Ottomans." *SAYI The Journal of Ottoman Studies* 36 (2010): 57–76.

Fest, Herman, and Sitsa Karaiskaki. *Evraioi Kai Kommounismos, Ta Aitia Kai Oi Skopoi Tes Synergasias Ton*. Athens: Nea Genia, 1934.

Finlay, George. *A History of Greece from Its Conquest by the Romans to the Present Time*. Volume VI, Part I, Oxford: Clarendon Press, 1877.

Finlay, George. *A History of Greece from Its Conquest by the Romans to the Present Time*. Volume VII, Part II, Oxford: Clarendon Press, 1877.

Fisher, Allan G. B. "The German Trade Drive in Southeastern Europe." *International Affairs* 18, no. 2 (March–April 1939): 143–70.

Fisk, Pliny. "Appeal in Behalf of Greece." *The Wesleyan-Methodist Magazine*, 1827, 339–10.

Fitsos, Takis. "Apokalypseis Gia Ta Pogrom Kata Ton Evraion." *Rizospastis*, July 2, 1931.

Fleischer, Hagen. "Greek Jewry and Nazi Germany: The Holocaust and Its Antecedents." Paper presented at the Oi Evraioi ston Elleniko Choro: Zetemata Istorias ste Makra Diarkeia, Thessaloniki, 1991.

Fleischer, Hagen. *Stemma Kai Svastika: E Ellada Tes Katoches Kai Tes Antistases 1941-1944.* Athens: Papazisi, 1995.

Fleming, K. E. *The Muslim Bonaparte: Diplomacy and Orientalism in Ali Pasha's Greece.* Princeton: Princeton University Press, 1999.

Fleming, K. E. "Constantinople: From Christianity to Islam." *The Classical World* 97, no. 1 (Autumn 2003): 69–78.

Fleming, K. E. "The Stereotyped 'Greek Jew' from Auschwitz-Birkenau to Israeli Pop Culture." *Journal of Modern Greek Studies* 25, no. 1 (May 2007): 17–40.

Fleming, K. E. *Greece a Jewish History.* Princeton: Princeton University Press, 2008.

Fotakos. *Apomnimonevmata.* Volume A, Athens: Ekdoseis Vergina, 1996.

Fotakos. *Apomnemonevmata Tou 1821.* Volume B, Athens: Ekdoseis Vergina, 1996.

Fotakos. *Vioi Pelopponision Andron.* Athens: Ekdoseis Vergina, 1996.

Fotiadi, Ioanna. "'Agapo Ten Ellada, Perimeno Karterika Ten Apofase.'" *I Kathimerini,* March 19, 2017, http://www.kathimerini.gr/900970/article/epikairothta/ellada/agapw-thn-ellada-perimenw-karterika-thn-apofash.

Frary, Lucien J. "Russian Consuls and the Greek War of Independence (1821–31)." *Mediterranean Historical Review* 28, no. 1 (2013): 46–65.

Frary, Lucien J. "Russian-Greek Relations During the Crimean War." *Slovo* 21, no. 1 (Spring 2009): 16–28.

Frary, Lucien J. "Russian Missions to the Orthodox East: Antonin Kapustin (1817-1894) and His World." *Russian History* 30 (2013): 133–51.

Frary, Lucien J. *Russia and the Making of Modern Greek Identity, 1821-1844.* Oxford: Oxford University Press, 2015.

Frazee, Charles. "Catholics." In *Minorities in Greece Aspects of a Plural Society,* edited by Richard Clogg, 24–47. London: Hurst & Company, 2002.

Frazee, Charles. *The Orthodox Church and Independent Greece 1821-1852.* Cambridge: Cambridge University Press, 1969.

Frezis, Rafail. *E Israelitike Koinoteta Volou.* Volos: Epikoinonia, 2002.

Friedman, Philip. *Their Brother's Keepers.* New York: Crown Publishers, 1957.

Gallant, Thomas. "The Greek Catholic Islanders and the Revolution of 1821." *East European Quarterly* 13, no. 3 (Fall 1979): 315–26.

Gallant, Thomas. "Peasant Ideology and Excommunication for Crime in a Colonial Context: The Ionian Islands (Greece), 1817-1864." *Journal of Social History* 23, no. 3 (1990): 485–512.

Gallant, Thomas. *Experiencing Dominion. Culture, Identity, and Power in the British Mediterranean.* Notre Dame: University of Notre Dame Press, 2002.

Gallant, Thomas. *Modern Greece, from the War of Independence to the Present.* New York: Bloomsbury, 2016.

Gavrilis, George. "The Greek-Ottoman Boundary as Institution, Locality, and Process, 1832-1882." *American Behavioral Scientist* 51, no. 10 (2008): 1516–37.

Gazi, Effi. "Reading the Ancients: Remnants of Byzantine Controversies in the Greek National Narrative." *Historein* 6 (2006): 144–49.

Gazi, Effi. "Revisiting Religion and Nationalism in Nineteenth-Century Greece." In *The Making of Modern Greece: Nationalism, Romanticism, and the Uses of the Past (1797-1896),* edited by Rodeick Beaton and David Ricks, 95–106. New York: Routledge, 2016.

Geanakoplos, Deno J. "Religion and Nationalism in the Byzantine Empire and After: Conformity or Pluralism?." *Journal of Ecumenical Studies* XIII, no. 4 (Fall 1976): 614–32.

Gekas, Sakis. "For Better or for Worse? A Counter-Narrative of Corfu Jewish History and the Transition from the Ionian State to the Greek Kingdom (1815-1890s)." In *Evraikes*

Koinotetes Anamesa Se Anatole Kai Dyse, 150s-20os Aionas: Oikonomia, Koinonia, Politike, Politismos, edited by Anna Machaira and Leda Papastefanaki. Ioannina: Isnafi, 2016.

Gekas, Sakis. "The Port Jews of Corfu and the 'Blood Libel' of 1891: A Tale of Many Centuries and of One Event." *Jewish Culture and History* 7, no. 1–2 (2012): 171–76.

Gekas, Sakis. *Xenocracy: State, Class, and Colonialism in the Ionian Islands, 1815-1864*. New York: Berghahn Books, 2016.

Gelber, N. M. "An Attempt to Internationilize Salonika." *Jewish Social Studies* 17 (October 1955): 105–20.

Gell, William. *Narrative of a Journey in the Morea*. London: Longman, Hurst, Rees, Orne, and Brown, 1832.

Gellner, Ernest. "The Coming of Nationalism and Its Interpretation: The Myths of Nation and Class." In *Mapping the Nation*, edited by Gopal Balakrishnan, 98–145. London: Verso, 1996.

Gellner, Ernest. *Nations and Nationalism*. Oxford: Blackwell, 1983.

Georgiadou, Vassiliki. "Greek Orthodoxy and the Politics of Nationalism." *International Journal of Politics, Culture, and Society* 9, no. 2 (1995): 295–315.

Georgis, Giorgos. "E Anatolike Politike Tou Kyvernete Ioanni Kapodistria." In *O Kyvernetes Ioannis Kapodistrias*, edited by Giorgos Georgis, 177–96. Athens: Kastaniotis, 2015.

Germanos, Palaion Patron. *Apomnemonevmata*. Athens: Vergina, 1996.

Giakoel, Giomtov. *Apomnemonevmata 1941-1943*. Thessaloniki: Parateretes, 1993.

Giannaras, Christos. *Orthodoxia Kai Dyse Ste Neotere Ellada*. Athens: Domos, 1999.

Ginio, Eyal. "Jews and European Subjects in Eighteenth-Century Salonica: The Ottoman Perspective." *Jewish History* 28 (2014): 289–312.

Ginio, Eyal. "Neither Muslims nor Zimmis: The Gypsies (Roma) in the Ottoman State." *Romani Studies 5* 14, no. 2 (2004): 117–44.

Glencross, Michael. "Greece Restored: Greece and the Greek War of Independence in French Romantic Historiography 1821-1830." *Journal of European Studies* xxvii (1997): 33–48.

Godechot, Jacques. "The New Concept of the Nation and Its Diffusion in Europe." In *Nationalism in the Age of French Revolution*, edited by Otto Dann and John Dinwiddy, 13–26. London: The Hambledon Press, 1988.

Goldwyn, Adam J. "Joseph Eliyia and the Jewish Question in Greece: Zionism, Hellenism, and the Struggle for Modernity." *Journal of Modern Greek Studies* 33, no. 2 (2015): 365–88.

Gordon, Thomas. *History of the Greek Revolution*. Volume II, Edinburgh: William Blackwood, 1832.

Gordon, Thomas. *History of the Greek Revolution*. Volume I, Edinburgh: William Blackwood, 1844.

Goschen, George J. "Despatch from Mr. Goschen Forwarding the Convention for the Settlement of the Frontier between Greece and Turkey," edited by House of Commons. London: Harrison and Sons, 1881.

Gounaris, Basil C. "Emigration from Macedonia in the Early Twentieth Century." *Journal of Modern Greek Studies* 7, no. 1 (1989): 133–53.

Gounaris, Basil C. "National Claims, Conflicts and Developments in Macedonia, 1870-1912." In *The History of Macedonia*, edited by Ioannis Koliopoulos, 183–213. Thessaloniki: Museum of the Macedonian Struggle Foundation, 2007.

Gounaris, Basil C. "Preachers of God and Martyrs of the Nation: The Politics of Murder in Ottoman Macedonia in the Early 20th Century." *Balkanologie* IX, no. 1–2 (2005): 31–43.

Gourgouris, Stathis. *Dream Nation: Enlightenment, Colonization and the Institutions of Modern Greece*. Stanford: Stanford University Press, 1996.

"Grèce—Les Élections législatives." *Paix et Droit* 13, no. 5 (May 1933): 16.

"Grèce—Les Élections législatives." *Paix et Droit* 13, no. 2 (February 1933): 7–8.

"Grece—Les evenements de Mars et les Juifs," *Paix et Droit* 15, no. 3 (March 1935): 12.

"Grece—Le ministre des affairs etrangeres et les Israelites," *Paix et Droit* 8, no. 1 (January 1928): 10–11.

"Grece—Les obligations militaires des Juifs," *Paix et Droit* 7, no. 4 (April 1927): 11.

"Greece.: Extracts from a Letter of Mr. Arnold." *Baptist Missionary Magazine*, November 1845, 282.

"Greece.: Extracts from Letters of Mr. Arnold." *Baptist Missionary Magazine*, September 1845, 240.

"Greece.: Extracts from the Journal of Rev. Eliuas Riggns." *The Missionary Herald*, September 1833, 309.

"The Greek Case." *The Economist*, March 16, 1850, 2–4.

"The Greek Claims and the House of Lords." *The Economist*, June 15, 1850, 1–2.

Greene, Molly. *A Shared World: Christians and Muslims in the Early Modern Mediterranean*. Princeton: Princeton University Press, 2002.

Groen, Basilius J. "Nationalism and Reconciliation: Orthodoxy in the Balkans." *Religion, State and Society* 26, no. 2 (1998): 111–28.

Gross, Jan T. *Neighbors: The Destruction of the Jewish Community in Jedwabne, Poland*. New York: Penguin, 2002.

Hagouel, Paul. "The History of the Jews of Salonika and the Holocaust." *Sephardic Horizons* 3, no. 3 (Fall 2013): 1–43.

Haidia, Elene. "Ellenes Evraioi Tes Thessalonikis: Apo Ta Stratopeda Sygkentroses Stis Aithouses Dikasterion." In *Oi Evraioi Tes Elladas Sten Katoche*, edited by Rika Mpenveniste, 43–52. Thessaloniki: Ekdoseis Vanias, 1998.

Haidia, Eleni. "The Punishment of Collaborators in Northern Greece, 1945-1946." In *After the War Was Over. Reconstructing the Family, Nation, and State in Greece, 1943-1960*, edited by Mark Mazower, 42–61. Princeton: Princeton University Press, 2000.

Hall, John A. "Nationalisms: Classified and Explained." *Daedalus* 122, no. 3 (1993): 1–28.

Hall, Richard C. *The Balkan Wars 1912-1913: Prelude to the First World War*. New York: Routledge, 2000.

Hamilakis, Yannis. *The Nation and Its Ruins: Antiquity, Archaeology, and National Imagination in Greece*. Oxford: Oxford University Press, 2007.

Handzic, Adem. *Population of Bosnia in the Ottoman Period—a Historical Overview*. Istanbul: Organization of the Islamic Conference Research Centre for Islamic History, Art and Culture (IRCICA), 1994.

Hannell, David. "Lord Palmerston and the 'Don Pacifico Affair' of 1850: The Ionian Connection." *European History Quarterly* 19 (1989): 495–507.

Hassiotis, Loukianos I. "Macedonia, 1912-1923: From the Multinational Empire to Nation State." In *The History of Macedonia*, edited by Ioannis Koliopoulos, 245–68. Thessaloniki: Museum of the Macedonian Struggle Foundation, 2007.

Hastaoglou-Martinidis, Vilma. "A Mediterranean City in Transition: Thessaloniki between the Two World Wars." *Facta Univeritatis Archaeology and Civil Engineering* 1, no. 4 (1997): 493–507.

Hatzopoulos, Marios. "From Resurrection to Insurrection: 'Sacred' Myths, Motifs, and Symbols in the Greek War of Independence." In *The Making of Modern Greece: Nationalism, Romanticism and the Uses of the Past (1797-1896)*, edited by Roderick Beaton and David Ricks, 81–93. New York: Ashgate, 2009.

Hekimoglou, E A. "Topoi Egkatastaseos Kai Katoikias Ton Prosphygon Ste Thessalonike 1922-1927." Paper presented at the B' Panellenio Synedrio gia ton Ellenismo tes Mikras Asias, Thessaloniki, 1994.

Hertzberg, Gustav Friedrich. *Istoria Tes Ellenikes Epanastaseos*, translated by Pavlos Karolidis. Volume I, Athens: Georgios D Fexis, 1916.

Hertzberg, Gustav Friedrich. *Istoria Tes Ellenikes Epanastaseos*, translated by Pavlos Karolidis. Volume II, Athens: Georgios D Fexis, 1916.

Hertzberg, Gustav Friedrich. *Istoria Tes Ellenikes Epanastaseos*, translated by Pavlos Karolidis. Volume III, Athens: Georgios D Fexis, 1916.

Hertzberg, Gustav Friedrich. *Istoria Tes Ellenikes Epanastaseos*, translated by Pavlos Karolidis. Volume IV. Athens: Georgios D Fexis, 1916.

Herzfeld, Michael. *Ours Once More: Folklore, Ideology and the Making of Modern Greece*. Austin: University of Texas Press, 1982.

Hesse, Carla, and Thomas W Laqueur. "Orata Kai Aorata Somata: E Exaleipse Tou Evraikou Nekrotafeiou Apo Te Zoe Tes Sygchrones Thessalonikis." In *E Paragoge Tou Koinonikou Somatos*, edited by Martha Mihailidou and Alexandra Halkia. Athens: Katarti, 2006.

Heyberger, Bernard. "Les Chrétiens D'alep (Syrie) À Travers Les Récits Des Conversions Des Missionnaires Carmes Déchaux (1657-1681)." *Mélanges de l'Ecole française de Rome. Moyen-Age, Temps modernes* 100, no. 1 (1988): 461–99.

Heyd, Uriel. "The Jewish Communities of Istanbul in the Seventeenth Century." *Oriens* 6, no. 2 (December 31, 1953): 299–314.

Hicks, Geoffrey. "Don Pacifico, Democracy, and Danger: The Protectionist Party Critique of British Foreign Policy, 1850-1852." *The International History Review* 26, no. 3 (2004): 515–40.

Hirschon, Renee. *Heirs to the Greek Catastrophe: The Social Life of Asia Minor Refugees in Pireaus*. Oxford: Clarendon Press, 1989.

Hobsbawm, Eric J. "Introduction: Inventing Traditions." In *The Invention of Tradition*, edited by Eric J. Hobsbawm and Terence Ranger, 1–14. Cambridge: Cambridge University Press, 1983.

Hobsbawm, Eric J. "Mass-Peoducing Traditions: Europe, 1870-1914." In *The Invention of Tradition*, edited by Eric J. Hobsbawm and Terence Ranger, 263–308. Cambridge: Cambridge University Press, 1983.

Hobsbawm, Eric J. *Nations and Nationalism since 1780: Programme, Myth, Reality*. Cambridge: Cambridge University Press, 1990.

Holland, Henry. *Taxidia Sta Ionia Nesia, Epeiro, Alvania (1812-1813)*. Athens: Afoi Tolidi, 1989.

Holland, Robert, and Diana Makrides. *The British and the Hellenes: Struggles for Mastery in the Eastern Mediterranean 1850-1960*. Oxford: Oxford University Press, 2008.

Hollander, E. J. "The Final Solution in Bulgaria and Romania: A Comparative Perspective." *East European Politics & Societies* 22, no. 2 (2008): 203–48.

Horowitz, Elliott. "'The Vengence of the Jews Was Stronger Than Their Avarice': Modern Historians and the Persian Conquest of Jerusalem in 614." *Jewish Social Studies, New Series* 4, no. 2 (Winter 1998): 1–39.

Horowitz, Donald L. *The Deadly Ethnic Riot*. Berkeley: California University Press, 2001.

Howard-Johnson, James. "Byzantium and Its Neighbours." In *The Oxford Handbook of Byzantine Studies*, edited by Elizabeth Jeffreys, John Haldon, and Robin Cormack, 939–56. Oxford: Oxford University Press, 2008.

Hroch, Miroslav. "From National Movement to Fully-Formed Nation: The Nation-Building Process in Europe." *New Left Review* 198 (1993): 3–20.

Hroch, Miroslav. "Modernization and Communication as Factors of Nation Formation." In *The Sage Handbook of Nations and Nationalism*, edited by Gerard Delanty and Krishan Kumar, 21–32. London: Sage, 2006.

Hroch, Miroslav. "National Self-Determination from a Historical Perspective." In *Notions of Nationalism*, edited by Sukumar Periwal, 65–82. Budapest: Central European University Press, 1995.

Hroch, Miroslav. "Real and Constructed: The Nature of the Nation." In *The State of the Nation: Ernest Gellner and the Theory of Nationalism*, edited by John A Hall, 91–106. Cambridge: Cambridge University Press, 1998.

Hroch, Miroslav. *Social Preconditions of National Revival in Europe: A Comparative Analysis of the Social Composition of Patriotic Groups among the Smaller European Nations*. Cambridge: Cambridge University Press, 1985.

Hupchick, Dennis P. *The Bulgarians in the Seventeenth Century: Slavic Orthodox Society and Culture under Ottoman Rule*. Jefferson: McFarland, 1993.

Iatrides, John O. "Evangelicals." In *Minorities in Greece: Aspects of a Plural Society*, edited by Richard Clogg. London: Hurst & Company, 2002.

Ibn Battuta, Muhammad. *Travels in Asia and Africa 1325-1354*. New York: Routledge, 2005. 1925.

Ilitzak, Soukrou. "O Evraikos Sosialismos Sten Othomanike Thessaloniki." In *Ellenes Kai Evraioi Ergates Ste Thessaloniki Ton Neotourkon*. Ioannina: Isnafi, 2004.

Ioanid, Radu. "The Holocaust in Romania: The Iasi Pogrom of June 1941." *Contemporary European History* 2, no. 2 (July 1993): 119–48.

Ioanid, Radu. *The Holocaust in Romania: The Destruction of Jews and Gypsies under the Antonescu Regime, 1940-1944*. Chicago: Ivan R Dee, 2000.

Iordachi, Constantin. "The Unyielding Boundaries of Citizenship: The Emancipation of 'Non-Citizens' in Romania, 1866-1918." *European Review of History* 8, no. 2 (2001): 157–86.

Iorga, Nikolae. *To Vyzantio Meta to Vyzantio*. Athens: Gutenberg, 1985.

Irshai, Oded. "Confronting a Christian Empire: Jewish Life and Culture in the World of Early Byzantium." In *Jews in Byzantium*, edited by Robert Bonfil, Oded Irshai, Guy G. Stroumsa, and Rina Talgam, 17–64. Boston: Brill, 2012.

Isabella, Maurizio. "Citizens or Faithful? Religion and the Liberal Revolutions of the 1820s in Southern Europe." *Modern Intellectual History* 12, no. 3 (2015): 555–78.

Isabella, Maurizio. "Mediterranean Liberals? Italian Revolutionaries and the Making of a Colonial Sea, Ca. 1800-30." In *Mediterranean Diasporas, Politics and Ideas in the Long 19th Century*, edited by Maurizio Isabella and Konstantina Zanou, 77–96. New York: Bloomsbury, 2016.

Isom-Verhaaren, Christine. "Constructing Ottoman Identity in the Reigns of Mehmed II and Bayezid II." *Journal of Ottoman and Turkish Studies* 1, no. 1–2 (2014): 111–28.

Jacoby, David. "The Jews and the Silk Industry of Constantinople." In *The Jewish Presence in the Greek Territory (4th-19th Centuries)*, edited by Anna Lambropoulou and Kostas Tsiknakis, 17–37. Athens: National Hellenic Research Foundation, 2008.

Jacoby, David. "The Jews in the Byzantine Economy (Seventh to Mid-Fifteenth Century)." In *Jews in Byzantium*, edited by Robert Bonfil, Oded Irshai, Guy G. Stroumsa and Rina Talgam, 219–56. Boston: Brill, 2012.

Jianu, Angela. "Women, Dowries, and Patrimonial Law in Old Regime Romania (C. 1750-1830)." *Journal of Family History* 34, no. 2 (2009): 189–205.

Kabeli, Isaac. *The Resistance of Greek Jews*. Yivo Annual of Jewish Social Science. Volume VIII, New York: Yiddish Scientific Institute—Yivo, 1953.

Kakouri, Athina. *Ta Dyo Veta*. Athens: Ekdoseis Kapon, 2016.

Kaldellis, Anthony. *Hellenism in Byzantium, the Transformations of Greek Identity and the Reception of the Classical Tradition*. Cambridge: Cambridge University Press, 2007.

Kalligas, Pavlos. *Systema Romaikou Dikaiou*. Volume B, Athens: Georgios Fexis kai Yios, 1930.

Kallis, Aristotle A. "To Expand or Not to Expand? Territory, Generic Fascism and the Quest for an 'Ideal Fatherland'." *Journal of Contemporary History* 38, no. 2 (2003): 237–60.

Kallis, Aristotle A. "The Jewish Community of Salonica under Siege: The Antisemitic Violence of the Summer of 1931." *Holocaust and Genocide Studies* 20, no. 1 (2006): 34–56.

Kalman, Julie. "The Unyielding Wall: Jews and Catholics in Restoration and July Monarchy France." *French Historical Studies* 26, no. 4 (2003): 661–86.

Kamouzis, Dimitris. "Elites and the Formation of National Identity: The Case of the Greek Orthodox Millet (Mid-Nineteenth Century to 1922)." In *State-Nationalisms in the Ottoman Empire, Greece and Turkey: Orthodox and Muslims, 1830-1945*, edited by Benjamin C Fortna, Stefanos Katsikas, Dimitris Kamouzis, and Paraskevas Konortas, 13–46. London: Routledge, 2013.

Kampouroglou, Dimitrios Gr. *Istoriai Ton Athenaion*. Volume 2, Athens: Palmos N Antonopoulos & Sia, 1968.

Kandylakis, Manolis. *Efemeridografia Tes Thessalonikis*. Volume C 1923–41. Thessaloniki: University Studio Press, 2008.

Karakasidou, Anastasia. *Fields of Wheat, Hills of Blood: Passages to Nationhood in Greek Macedonia, 1870-1990*. Chicago: University of Chicago Press, 1997.

Karalis, Vrasidas. "In Search of Neo-Hellenic Culture: Confronting the Ambiguities of Modernity in an Ancient Land." *Interactions: Studies in Communication & Culture* 3, no. 2 (2012): 129–45.

Karanikolas, Panteleimonas K. *Evraioi Kai Christianoi*. Corinth: Pnoi, 1980.

Karapidakis, Nikos E. "Gia Ten Evraike Koinoteta Kerkyras." In *E Evraike Parousia Ston Elladiko Choro (4os-19os Ai.)*, edited by Anna Lambropoulou and Kostas Tsiknakis, 149–54. Athens: Ethniko Idryma Erevnon, 2008.

Karatzaferis, Giorgos. "Einai 'Evr(Ai)Os' Gnosto." *AlfAena* January 3–4, 2009, 9.

Kardaras, Christos. *E Voulgarike Propaganda Ste Germanokratoumene Makedonia: Voulgarike Lesche Thessalonikis, 1941-1944*. Athens: Ekdoseis Epikairotita, 1997.

Karolidis, Pavlos. *O Germanikos Filellenismos*. Athens: 1917.

Karyotakis, Minos-Athanasios. "E Apeikonise Ton Evraion Sten Efemerida 'Makedonia' Ten Periodo 1945-1948." Aristotle University of Thessaloniki, 2016.

Kasimatis, Petros. *Aima, Evraioi, Talmoud, Etoi Apodeixeis Threskevtikai, Istorikai Kai Dikastikai Peri Tes Yparxeos Ton Anthropothysion Par' Ebraiois*. Athens, 1891.

Kasumovic, Fahd. "Understanding Ottoman Heritage in Bosnia and Herzegovina: Conversions to Islam in the Records of the Sarajevo Sharia Court, 1800-1851." *Belleten Türk Tarih Kurumu, Atatürk kültür dil ve tarih yüksek kurumu* LXXX, no. 288 (2016): 507–32.

Kates, Gary. "Jews into Frenchmen: Nationality and Representation in Revolutionary France." *Social Research* 56, no. 1 (1989): 213–32.

Katsiardi-Hering, Olga, and Ikaros Madouvalos. "The Tolerant Policy of the Habsburg Authorities Towards the Orthodox People from South-Eastern Europe and the Formation of National Identities (18th-Early 19th Century)." *Balkan Studies* 49 (2014): 5–34.

Katz, Jacob. *From Prejudice to Destruction: Antisemitism, 1700-1933*. Cambridge: Harvard University Press, 1980.

Kavala, Maria. "Aspects of Anti-Semitism in Salonika, During the Nazi Occupation (1941-1944): The Authorities, the Press and the People. An Example of Differentiation and Exclusion." Paper presented at the Croatian Serbian Relations; Minority Rights, fight against discrimination, 6th International Scientific Conference, Novi Sad, 2013.

Kavala, Maria. "Oi Ekteleseis Evraion Ste Thessaloniki Sta Chronia Tes Katoches. Politike Antipoinon Kai Fyletismos." In *Evraikes Koinotetes Anamesa Se Anatole Kai Dyse, 15os-20os Aionas: Oikonomia, Koinonia, Politike, Politismos*, edited by Anna Machaira and Leda Papastefanaki. Ioannina: Isnafi, 2015.

Kavala, Maria. "Epibiose Viologike Kai Pnevmatike." In *O Foros Tou Aimatos Sten Katochike Thessaloniki: Xene Kyriarchia, Antistase Kai Epibiose*, edited by Vasilis K Gounaris and Petros Papapolyviou, 15–40. Thessaloniki: Paratiritis, 2001.

Kavala, Maria. *E Katastrophe Ton Evraion Tes Elladas (1941-1944)*. Athens: Syndesmos Ellinikon Akadimaikon Vivliothikon, 2015.

Kavala, Maria. "Oi Oikonomikes Drasteriotetes Ton Epicheireseon Tes Thessalonikes Sta Chronia Tes Katoches." In *E Epoche Ton Rexeon. E Ellenike Koinonia Ste Dekaetia Tou 1940*, edited by Polymeris Voglis, Flora Tsilaga, Iasonas Chandrinos, and Menelaos Charalampidis, 57–85. Athens: Epikentro, 2012.

Kavala, Maria. "E Thessalonike Ste Germanike Katoche (1941-1944): Koinonia, Oikonomia, Diogmos Evraion." University of Crete, 2009.

Kavala, Maria, and Kostis Kornetis. "O Ellenikos Kratikos Mechanismos Kai E Diacheirise Ton Evraikon Perousion Tes Thessalonikes." In *Ten Epaurion Tou Olokautomatos*, edited by Evaggelos Hekimoglou and Anna Maria Droumpouki. Thessaloniki: Jewish Museum of Thessaloniki, 2017.

Kavsokalybitis, Neophytos. *Ta Ioudaika Etoi Anatrope Tes Threskeias Ton Evraion Kai Ton Ethimon Avton Met' Apodeixeon Ek Tes Agias Grafes*. Zakynthos: Parnassos, 1861.

Kazazis, Neoklis. *To Panepistemion Kai E Ethnike Idea*. Athens: Typografeio tou Kratous, 1902.

Kellas, James G. *The Politics of Nationalism and Ethnicity*. London: Macmillan, 1991.

Kerameos, Konstantinos D. *Nomike Prosopikotes Kai Kratike Epopteia Israelitikon Idrymaton En Elladi: Dyo Gnomodoteseis*. Thessaloniki: 1976. Reprint from Journal Armenopoulos volume 30 issue 10.

Kerem, Yitzchak. "The Influence of Anti-Semitism on the Jewish Immigration Pattern from Greece to the Ottoman Empire in the Nineteenth Century." In *Decision Making and Change in the Ottoman Empire*, edited by Cesar E. Farah, 305–14. Kirksville: Thomas Jefferson University Press, 1993.

Kirmizialtin, Suphan. "Conversion in Ottoman Balkans: A Historiographical Survey." *History Compass* 5, no. 2 (2007): 646–57.

Kitroeff, Alexander. *War-Time Jews. The Case of Athens*. Athens: ELIAMEP, 1995.

Kitromilides, Paschalis. "Republican Aspirations in Southeastern Europe in the Age of the French Revolution." In *Consortium on Revolutionary Europe, 1750-1850: Proceedings*, 275–85. Athens: Consortium on Revolutionary Europe, 1980.

Kitromilides, Paschalis. "On the Intellectual Content of Greek Nationalism: Paparrigopoulos, Byzantium and the Great Idea." In *Byzantium and the Modern Greek Identity*, edited by David Ricks and Paul Magdalino, 25–35. Aldershot: Ashgate, 1998.

Kitromilides, Paschalis. *Enlightenment and Revolution: The Making of Modern Greece*. Cambridge: Harvard University Press, 2013.

Kofos, Evangelos. *Nationalism and Communism in Macedonia*. Thessaloniki: Institute of Balkan Studies and Society for Macedonian Studies, 1964.

Kofos, Evangelos. "Ethnike Kleronomia Kai Ethnike Tautoteta Ste Makedonia Tou 19ou Kai Tou 20ou Aiona." In *Ethnike Tautoteta Kai Ethnikismos Ste Neotere Ellada*, edited by Thanos Veremis, 199–269. Athens: Morfotiko Idryma Ethnikis Trapezis, 1997.

Kofos, Evangelos. *O Ellenismos Sten Periodo 1869-1881*. Athens: Ekdotiki Athinon, 1981.

Kohn, Hans. "Letters from Abroad—New Regime in Greece." *The Menorah Journal* XVI, no. 5 (May 1929): 442–45.

Kokolakis, Michalis. *To Ystero Gianniotiko Pasaliki: Choros, Dioikese Kai Plythysmos Sten Tourkokratoumene Epeiro (1820-1913)*. Athens: Kentro Neoellinikon Erevnon, Ethniko Idryma Erevnon, 2003.

Kolbaba, Tia M. "Byzantine Perceptions of Latin Religious 'Errors': Themes and Changes from 850 to 1350." In *The Crusades from the Perspective of Byzantium and the Muslim World*, edited by Angeliki E. Laiou and Roy Parviz Mottahedeh, 117–43. Washington: Dumbarton Oaks Research Library and Collection, 2001.

Koliopoulos, John S. "The War over the Identity and Numbers of Greece's Slav Macedonians." In *Ourselves and Others: The Development of a Greek Macedonian Cultural Identity since 1912*, edited by Peter Mackridge and Eleni Yannakakis, 39–58. Oxford: Berg, 1997.

Koliopoulos, John S., and Thanos M. Veremis. *Greece the Modern Sequel, from 1821 to the Present*. New York: New York University Press, 2002.

Kolokotronis, Theodoros. *Apomnimonevmata*, edited by Georgios Tertsetis. Athens: Ekdoseis Vergina, 1996.

Konortas, Paraskevas. *Othomanikes Theoreseis gia to Oikoumeniko Patriarcheio*. Athens: Ekdoseis Alexandreia, 1998.

Konstantini, Moysi K. *E Symvole Ton Evraion Eis Ton Apeleftherotikon Agona Ton Ellenon*. Athens: 1971.

Kontogiorgis, Giorgos D. *Koinonike Dynamike Kai Politike Autodioikise*. Athens: Livanis, 1982.

Kontraros, Grigoris D. *Ellenismos-Evraismos (Drase)-(Antidrase) Ellenes Kai Evraioi (Kai Mazi Kai Choria)*. Athens: 2003.

Korais, Adamantios. "Report on the Present State of Civilization in Greece." In *Nationalism in Asia and Africa*, edited by Elie Kedourie, 153–89. New York: World Publishing Company, 1970.

Korais, Adamantios. *Semeioseis Eis to Prosorinon Politevma Tes Ellados Tou 1822 Etous*. Athens: 1983.

Kordatos, Giannis. *Rigas Pheraios Kai I Balkaniki Omospondia*. Athens: Ioan, & P. Zacharopoulos, 1945.

Kostantaras, Dean J. "Christian Elites of the Peloponnese and the Ottoman State, 1715-1821." *European History Quarterly* 43, no. 4 (2013): 628–56.

Kostis, Kostas. *Ta Kakomathemena Paidia Tes Istorias: E Diamorfose Tou Neoellenikou Kratous 18os-21os Aionas*. Vol. Athens: Polis, 2013.

Kostopoulos, Tasos. "Aphaireseis Ithageneias: E Skoteine Pleura Tes Neoellenikes Istorias (1926-2003)." *Sygchrona Themata* 83 (2003): 53–75.

Kostopoulos, Tasos. "Counting the 'Other': Official Census and Classified Statistics in Greece (1830-2001)." *Jahrbücher für Geschichte und Kultur Südosteuropas* 5 (2003): 55–78.

Kostopoulos, Tasos. "How the North Was Won: Épuration Ethnique, Échange Des Populations Et Politique De Colonisation Dans La Macédoine Grecque." *European Journal of Turkish Studies* 12 (2011): 1–61.

Kostopoulos, Tasos. "'Land to the Tiller'. On the Neglected Agrarian Component of the Macedonian Revolutionary Movement, 1893-1912." *Turkish Historical Review* 7 (2016): 134–66.

Kostopoulos, Tasos. *Polemos Kai Ethnokatharse—E Xechasmene Plevra Mias Dekaetous Ethnikes Exormeses (1912-1922)*. Athens: Vivliorama, 2007.

Kostopoulou, Electra. "The Multiple Faces of Autonomy: Ottoman Reform and 19th Century Crete." *Cretica Chronica* 36 (2016): 31–48.

Kotzageorgis, Phokion P. "Conversion to Islam in Ottoman Rural Societies in the Balkans: The Cases of Vallahades and Pomaks." In *Ottoman Rural Societies and Economies*, edited by Elias Kolovos, 131–62. Rethymno: Crete University Press, 2015.

Koukkou, Eleni. *Oi Koinotekoi Thesmoi Stis Kyklades Kata Ten Tourkokratia*. Athens: Istoriki kai Ethnologiki Etaireia tis Ellados, 1980.

Koumarianou, Aikaterini. *E Eleftherofrosyne Tou Theofilou Kairi*. Athens: 1967.

Koumas, Konstantinos. *Oi Ellenes (Istoriai Ton Anthropinon Praxeon Apo Ton Archaiotaton Chronon Eos Ton Emeron Mas)*. Athens: Notis Karavias, 1966. 1832.

Koutsalexis, A. P. *Diaferonda Kai Perierga Tina Istorimata*. Athens: Ekdoseis Vergina, 1996.

Kralova, Katerina. "The 'Holocausts' in Greece: Victim Competition in the Context of Postwar Compensation for Nazi Persecution." *Holocaust Studies* 23, no. 1–2 (2017): 149–75.

Krapsitis, Vasilis. *E Istorike Aletheia Gia Tous Mousoulmanous Tsamedes*. Athens: 1992.

Kremmydas, Vasilis. "E Diakyvernese Kapodistria: Koinonia, Politike, Ideologia." In *O Kyvernetes Ioannis Kapodistrias*, edited by Giorgos Georgis, 46–53. Athens: Kastaniotis, 2015.

Kremmydas, Vasilis. *E Megale Idea: Metamorphoseis Enos Ethnikou Ideologematos*. Athens: Ekdoseis Typotheto, 2010.

Kremmydas, Vasilis. *E Ellenike Epanastase Tou 1821: Tekmeria, Anapselafeseis, Emeneies*. Athens: Gutenberg, 2016.

Kriezis, Antonios Andreas. *Apomnimonevmata*. Athens: Ekdoseis Vergina, 1996.

Kritovoulos. *History of Mehmed the Conqueror*. Westport: Greenwood Press, 1970, 94.

Kyrkini-Koutoula, Anastasia. *E Othomanike Dioikese Sten Ellada: E Periptose Tes Peloponnesou (1715-1821)*. Athens: Ekdoseis Arsenidi, 1996.

"L' accusation de Meurtre Rituel," *Paix et Droit* 1, no. 4 (April 1921): 9–11.

Laiou, Sophia. "The Greek Revolution in the Morea According to the Description of an Ottoman Official." In *The Greek Revolution of 1821: A European Event*, edited by Petros Pizanias. Istanbul: The Isis Press, 2011.

Lamdan, Ruth. "Communal Regulations as a Source for Jewish Women's Lives in the Ottoman Empire." *The Muslim World* 95 (April 2005): 249–63.

Lampropoulou, Anna. "E Evraike Parousia Sten Peloponneso Kata Te Byzantine Periodo." In *Oi Evraioi Ston Elleniko Choro: Zetemata Istorias Ste Makra Diarkeia*, edited by Efi Avdela. Athens: Ekdoseis Gavrilidis, 1995.

Lanicek, Jan. "Governments-in-Exile and the Jews During and After the Second World War." *Holocaust Studies* 18, no. 2–3 (Autumn/Winter 2012): 73–94.

Lappa, Daphne. "Variations on a Religious Theme: Jews and Muslims From the Eastern Mediterranean Converting to Christianity, 17th & 18th Centuries." PhD dissertation, Florence: European University Institute, Department of History and Civilization, 2015.

League, Anti-Defamation. "Adl Global 100: An Index of Anti-Semitism." 2015.

Leake, William Martin. *Historical Outline of the Greek Revolution*. London: John Murray, 1826.

"L' épilogue des désordres De 1931." *Paix et Droit* 12, no. 4 (April 8, 1932).

"Les Désordres Antijuifs De Salonique." *Paix et Droit* 11, no. 6 (June 5–6, 1931).

"Les élections législatives à salonique." *Paix et Droit* 12, no. 8 (October 1932) : 2.

"Lettre De Salonique—La Situation Économique Et La Population Juive 17 Mai 1932."
    Paix et Droit 12, no. 5 (May 7–8, 1932).

Levi, Primo. *Survival in Auschwitz*. New York: Simon & Schuster, 1986.

Levy-Oulmann, Andre. "Les Juifs de Salonique," *L' Univers Israelite* 58, no. 26 (March 20,
    1903): 815–18.

Levy-Oulmann, Andre. "Les Juifs de Salonique," *L' Univers Israelite* 58, no. 29 (April 10,
    1902): 84–85.

Lewkowicz, Bea. "'After the War We Were All Together': Jewish Memories of Postwar
    Thessaloniki." In *After the War Was Over. Reconstructing the Family, Nation, and
    State in Greece, 1943-1960*, edited by Mark Mazower, 247–72. Princeton: Princeton
    University Press, 2000.

Liakos, Antonis. "The Construction of National Time: The Making of the Modern Greek
    Historical Imagination." *Mediterranean Historical Review* 16, no. 1 (2010): 27–42.

Liakos, Antonis. *Ergasia Kai Politike Sten Ellada Tou Mesopolemou. To Diethnes Grafeio
    Ergasias Kai E Anadyse Ton Koinonikon Thesmon*. Athens: Idryma Erevnas kai Paideias
    tes Emporikis Trapezas tis Ellados, 1993.

Liakos, Antonis. *E Italike Enopoiese Kai E Megale Idea 1859-1862*. Athens: Themelio, 1985.

Liata, Eftychia. "The Anti-Semitic Disturbances on Corfu and Zakynthos in 1891 and
    Their Socio-Political Consequences." *The Historical Review/La Revue Historique* 4
    (2007): 147–69.

Liata, Eftychia. *E Kerkyra Kai E Zakynthos Ston Kyklona Tou Antisemitismou. E Sykofantia
    Gia to Aima Tou 1891*. Athens: Institouto Neoellinikon Erevnon Ethnikou Idrymatos
    Erevnon, 2006.

Linder, Amnon. "The Legal Status of Jews in the Byzantine Empire." In *Jews in Byzantium*,
    edited by Robert Bonfil, Oded Irshai, Guy G. Stroumsa, and Rina Talgam, 149–218.
    Boston: Brill, 2012.

Livanios, Dimitris. "'Conquering the Souls': Nationalism and Greek Guerilla Warfare
    in Ottoman Macedonia, 1904-1908." *Byzantine and Modern Greek Studies* 23
    (1999): 195–221.

Lory, Bernard. "1912 Les Hellenes Entrent Dans La Ville." In *Salonique 1850-1918, La
    'Ville Des Juifs' Et Le Reveil Des Balkans*, edited by Gilles Veinstein, 247–53. Paris :
    Editions Autrement, 1992.

Luther, Martin. *The Jews and Their Lies*. Los Angeles: Christian Nationalist Crusade, 1948.

Lyberatos, Andreas. "Unstable Regimes, Strong Consciousness: Eastern Rymelia and Crete
    after the Berlin Congress (1878)." *Cretica Chronika* 36 (2016): 73–92.

Mackridge, Peter. *Language and National Identity in Greece 1766-1976*. Oxford: Oxford
    University Press, 2009.

Magkriotis, Giannis. *Pomakoi E Rodopaioi, Oi Ellenes Mousoulmanoi*. Athens: Ekdoseis
    Risos, 1990.

Makrygiannis, Giannis. *Apomnemonevmata*. Athens: Ekdoseis A. Karavia.

Makrygiannis, Giannis. *Oramata Kai Thamata*. Athens: Morphotiko Idryma Ethnikis
    Trapezis, 2002.

Malakis, Spyridon G. *Apomnemonevmata Epi Tes Sygchronou Istorias, E Istorikon
    Epeisodion Epi Ton Energeion Drasanton Prosopon Pros Epitevxin Tes Megales Ideas*.
    Athens: 1895.

Malesevic, Sinisa. *Identity as Ideology*. New York: Palgrave Macmillan, 2006.

Malkiel, David. "Destruction or Conversion: Intention and Reaction, Crusaders and Jews,
    in 1096." *Jewish History* 15, no. 3 (2001): 257–80.

Mamoukas, Andreas Z., ed. *Ta Kata Ten Anagennesin Tes Ellados Etoi Sylloge Ton Peri Ten
    Anagennomenen Ellada Syntachthenton Politeumaton, Nomon, Kai Allon Episemon*

Praxeon, Apo Tou 1821 Mechri Telous Tou 1832. Volume 9, Pireaus Ilia Christophidou Typografia Agathi Tychi, 1839.

Mansola, A. *Politeiografikai Pleroforiai Peri Ellados*. Athens: Ethniko Typografeio, 1867.

Manuila, Sabin. "Romania's Racial Problem." In *The History of East-Central European Eugenics 1900-1945*, edited by Marius Tudra. New York: Bloomsbury, 2015.

Maragkou-Drygiannaki, Sparti. "E Philorthodoxos Etaireia Kai E Metastrophe Tes Ellenikes Exoterikes Politikes Pros Te Rosia." Panteio University, 1995.

Margaritis, Giorgos. "Ellenikos Antisemitismos: Mia Periegese, 1821, 1891, 1931." Paper presented at the O Ellenikos Evraismos, Athens, 1998.

Margaritis, Giorgos. *Anepithymetoi Sympatriotes*. Athens: Vivliorama, 2005.

Margaroni, Maria. "Antisemitic Rumours and Violence in Corfu at the End of the 19th Century." *Quest Issues in Contemporary Jewish History* 3 (2012): 267–88.

Marketos, Spyros. "E Ensomatose Tes Sepharadikes Thessalonikes Sten Ellada: To Plaisio, 1912-1914." Paper presented at the O Ellenikos Evraismos, Athens, 1998.

Markopoulos, George J. "King George I and the Expansion of Greece, 1875-1881." *Balkan Studies* 9 (1968): 21–39.

Markovich, Slobodan G. "Patterns of National Identity Development among the Balkan Orthodox Christians During the Nineteenth Century." *Balcanica* XLIV (2013): 209–54.

Marrus, Michael R., and Robert O. Paxton. "The Nazis and the Jews in Occupied Western Europe, 1940-1944." *Journal of Modern History* 54, no. 4 (1982): 687–714.

Matsas, Michael. *The Illusion of Safety: The Story of Greek Jews During the Second World War*. New York: Pella, 1997.

Mavrokordatos, Alexandros. *Istoria Iera Etoi Ta Ioudaika*. Bucarest: 1716.

Mavrogordatos, George. "Oi Ethnikes Meionotetes." In *Istoria Tes Ellados Tou 20ou Aiona*, edited by Ch. Chatzeiosef, 9–35. Athens: Vivliorama, 2003.

Mavrogordatos, George. "The Holocaust in Greece: A Vindication of Assimilation." *Etudes Balkaniques* XLVIII, no. 4 (2012): 5–17.

Mavrogordatos, George. *Stillborn Republic: Social Coalitions and Party Strategies in Greece, 1922-1936*. Berkeley: University of California Press, 1983.

Maurer, Georg Ludwig von. *O Ellenikos Laos*. Athens: Afoi Tolidi, 1976.

Mazower, Mark. *The Balkans, a Short History*. New York: The Modern Library, 2002.

Mazower, Mark. *Greece and the Inter-War Economic Crisis*. New York and Oxford [England]: Clarendon Press, 1991.

Mazower, Mark. *Inside Hitler's Greece, the Experience of Occupation 1941-1944*. New Haven: Yale University Press, 1993.

Mazower, Mark. "Minorities and the League of Nations in Interwar Europe." *Daedalus* 126, no. 2 (1997): 47–63.

Mazower, Mark. "Oi Synepeies Tou Diogmou Ton Evraion Gia Ten Pole Tes Thessalonikes." In *Oi Evraioi Tes Elladas Sten Katoche*, edited by Rika Benveniste, 53–61. Thessaloniki: Ekdoseis Vanias, 1998.

Mazower, Mark. "Three Forms of Political Justice: Greece, 1944-1945." In *After the War Was Over. Reconstructing the Family, Nation, and State in Greece, 1943-1960*, edited by Mark Mazower, 24–41. Princeton: Princeton University Press, 2000.

Mazower, Mark. *The Balkans, a Short History*. New York: The Modern Library, 2002.

Mazower, Mark. "Travellers and the Oriental City C 1840-1920." *Transactions of the Royal Historical Society* 12, no. Sixth Series (2002): 59–111.

Mazower, Mark. *Salonica City of Ghosts*. New York: Vintage Books, 2006.

McCarthy, Justin. *Death and Exile, the Ethnic Cleansing of Ottoman Muslims 1821-1922*. Princeton: The Darwin Press, 1995.

Mekos, Zafeirios K. *Mousoulmanoi, Armenioi Kai Evraioi Sympolites Mou Komotenaioi.* Thessaloniki: Ant. Stamoulis Publishing, 2007.

Melammed, Renee Levine. "The Memoirs of a Partisan from Salonika." *Nashim: A Journal of Jewish Women's Studies & Gender Issues* 7, no. 1 (2004): 151–73.

Melo, Vernardos. *Ta Pathe Kai E Exontose Ton Ellenoevraion.* Thessaloniki: Paratiritis, 1998.

Menexiadis, Alexis. "Oi Evraioi Tes Chalkidas Den Xegelastekan Apo Tous Germanous." *Chronika* 201 (February 2006) : 39.

Mengous, Petros. *Apo Te Smyrni Sten Ellada Tou 1821: E Afegese Tou Petrou Meggou.* Ioannina: Isnafi, 2009 (1830).

Miaouli, Antoniou Andrea. *Synoptike Istoria Ton Yper Tes Elevtherias Tes Anagennetheises Ellados Genomenon Navmachion Dia Ton Ploion Ton Trion Neson Ydras, Spatson Kai Psaron.* Athens: Ekdoseis Vergina, 1996.

Michailidis, Iakovos D. "The Statistical Battle for the Population of Greek Macedonia." In *The History of Macedonia,* edited by Ioannis Koliopoulos, 269–83. Thessaloniki: Museum of the Macedonian Struggle Foundation, 2007.

Mikhail, Alan, and Christine M. Philliou. "The Ottoman Empire and the Imperial Turn." *Comparative Studies in Society and History* 54, no. 4 (2012): 721–45.

Minkov, Anton. *Conversion to Islam in the Balkans: Kisve Bahasi Petitions and Ottoman Social Life, 1670-1730.* Leiden: Brill, 2004.

"Missionary Intelligence.: Education in Greece." *Episcopal Recorder,* September 1, 1832, 86.

"Missionary.: Board of Missions of the Protestant Episcopal Church." *Episcopal Recorder,* July 15, 1837, 61.

"Missionary Intelligence.: Evangelism in Greece." *New York Evangelist,* September 30, 1869, 8.

Moissis, Esdra D. *E Evraiki Koinoteta Tes Larisas Prin Kai Meta to Olokautoma.* Larisa: Melanos, 2000.

Moldovan, Iuliu. "The Hygiene of the Nation: Eugenics." In *The History of East-Central European Eugenics 1900-1945,* edited by Marius Tudra. New York: Bloomsbury, 2015.

Molho, Michael. "Le Judaisme Grec En General Et La Communaute Juive De Salonique En Particulier Entre Les Deux Guerres Mondiales." In *Homenaje a Millas-Villicrosa.* Barcelona: Consejo Superior de Investigaciones Cientificas, 1956.

Molho, Rena. "E Avevaioteta Tes Ellenikes Kyriarchias Ste Thessalonike Meta to 1912." *Sygchrona Themata* B 17, no. 52–54 (July-December 1994): 24–32.

Molho, Rena. "The Close Ties between Nationalism and Antisemitism." In *Jahrbuch Für Antisemitismisforschung 24,* edited by Werner Bergmann, Marcus Funck, and Dilek Güven, 217–28. Berlin: Metropol Verlag, 2015.

Molho, Rena. "Popular Antisemitism and State Policy in Salonika During the City's Annexation to Greece." *Jewish Social Studies* 50, no. 3/4 (1988): 253–64.

Molho, Rena. "The Zionist Movement in Thessaloniki 1899-1919." In *The Jewish Communities in Southeastern Europe: From the Fifteenth Century to the End of World War II,* edited by I. K Hassiotis, 327–50. Thessaloniki: Institute of Balkan Studies, 1997.

Molho, Rena. *Oi Evraioi Tes Thessalonikis 1856-1919.* Athens: Themelio, 2001.

Molho, Rena. *Oi Evraioi Tes Thessalonikis 1856-1919.* Athens: Ekdoseis Pataki, 2014.

Morton, Nicholas. "The Saljuq Turks' Conversion to Islam: The Crusading Sources." *Al-Masaq* 27, no. 2 (2015): 109–18.

Moschonas, N. G. "E Evraike Diaspora Sto Ionio (12os—16os Aionas)." In *E Evraike Parousia Ston Elladiko Choro (4os-19os Ai.),* edited by Anna Lambropoulou and Kostas Tsiknakis, 97–121. Athens: Ethniko Idryma Erevnon, 2008.

Moullas, Panagiotis. *O Choros Tou Efemerou, Stoicheia Gia Te Paralogotechnia Tou 19ou Aiona*. Athens: Ekdoseis Sokoli, 2007.

Mouzelis, Nicos. "Nationalism: Restructuring Gellner's Theory." In *Ernest Gellner and Contemporary Social Thought*, edited by Sinisa Malesevic and Mark Haugaard, 125–39. Cambridge: Cambridge University Press, 2007.

Moysis, Aser R. *E Filia Ellenon Kai Israeliton Dia Mesou Ton Aionon*. Athens: Israilitiki Morphotiki Leschi Thessalonikis "I Adelphotis," 1953.

Moysis, Aser R. *Eisagoge Eis to Oikogeneiakon Dikaion Ton En Elladi Israeliton*. Thessaloniki: Triantafyllos M, 1934.

Moysis, Aser R. *Elleno-Ioudaikai Meletai*. Athens: 1958.

Moysis, Esdras D. *E Evraike Koinoteta Tes Larisas Prin Kai Meta to Olokaytoma*. Larisa: Melanos, 2000.

Mpaltsiotis, Lambros. "E Ithageneia Ston Psychro Polemo." In *Ta Dikaiomata Sten Ellada 1953-2003. Apo to Telos Tou Emfyliou Sto Telos Tes Metapolitevses*, edited by Michalis Tsapogas and Dimitris Christopoulos, 81. Athens: Ekdoseis Kastanioti, 2004.

Müller, Michael G. "Poland." In *Nationalism in the Age of French Revolution*, edited by Otto Dann and John Dinwiddy, 113–28. London: The Hambledon Press, 1988.

Myrivilis, Stratis. "E Proelase Tes V Merarchias." In *To Kokkino Vivlio*. Athens: Estia, 2009.

Myrogiannis, Stratos. *The Emergence of a Greek Identity (1700-1821)*. Newcastle upon Tyne: Cambridge Scholars Publishing, 2012.

Naar, Devin E. "Fashioning the 'Mother of Israel': The Ottoman Jewish Historical Narrative and the Image of Jewish Salonica." *Jewish History* 28 (2014): 337–72.

Naar, Devin E. "From the 'Jerusalem of the Balkans' to the Goldene Medina: Jewish Immigration from Salonika to the United States." *American Jewish History* 93, no. 4 (2007): 435–73.

Naar, Devin E. "The 'Mother of Israel' or the 'Sephardi Metropolis'?: Sephardim, Ashkenazim, and Romaniotes in Salonica." *Jewish Social Studies* 22, no. 1 (2016): 81–129.

Naar, Devin E. "Ta Oria Tou Ellenismou: Glossa Kai Afosiose Metaxy Salonikion Evraion, 1917-1933." In *Thessaloniki: Mia Pole Se Metavase, 1912-2012*, edited by Dimitris Kairidis, 205–19. Thessaloniki: Epikentro, 2015.

Naar, Devin E. *Jewish Salonica: Between the Ottoman Empire and Modern Greece*. Stanford: Stanford University Press, 2016.

Nahman, Evtychia. *Giannena—Taxidi Sto Parelthon*. Athens: Talos Press, 1966.

Nar, Albertos. *Keimene Epi Aktes Thalasses.. Meletes Kai Arthra Gia Ten Evraike Koinoteta Tes Thessalonikis*. Thessaloniki: University Studio Press/Ekfrasi, 1997.

Nar, Leon A. *Oi Israelites Vouleutes Sto Elleniko Koinovoulio (1915-1936)*. Athens: Idryma tis Voulis ton Ellinon, 2011.

Nata, Gatenio Osmo. *Apo Ten Kerkyra Sto Birkenau Kai Ten Ierousalem - E Istoria Mias Kerkyraias*. Athens: Gavriilidis, 2005.

Nathans, Eli. *The Politics of Citizenship in Germany: Ethnicity, Utility and Nationalism*. Oxford: Berg, 2004.

Naxidou, Eleonora. "National Identity in the 19th-Century Balkans: The Case of Hatzichristos." *Nationalism and Ethnic Politics* 17, no. 3 (2011): 319–34.

Nehama, Josef. *Istoria Ton Israeliton Tes Salonikes*. Vol. I. Thessaloniki: University Studio Press, 2000.

Nehama, Josef. *Istoria Ton Israeliton Tes Salonikes*. Volume II, Thessaloniki: University Studio Press, 2000.

Nehama, Josef. *Istoria Ton Israeliton Tes Salonikes*. Volume III, Thessaloniki: University Studio Press, 2000.

Neuburger, Mary. "Pomak Borderlands: Muslims on the Edge of Nations." *Nationalities Papers: The Journal of Nationalism and Ethnicity* 28, no. 1 (2010): 181–98.

Nikolopoulos, B. K., and A. I Kakoulidis, eds. *Sylloge Apanton Ton Nomon, Diatagmaton, Egkyklion, Odegion, Kai Eidopoieseon Ton Ypourgeion, Synthekon Tes Ellados Meta Ton Allon Ethnon.* Volume 1, Athens: Typois Ch. Nikolaidoy Filadelfeos, 1859.

Njegos, Petar Petrovic. *The Mountain Wreath.* Chicago: Aristeus Books, 2012.

"O Theodosis Pelegrinis Gia Ten 'Emera Ethnikes Mnemes Gia Ten Katastroge Tou Mikrasiatikou Ellenismou." news release., 2016.

Okey, Robin. *Eastern Europe 1740-1985.* Minneapolis: University of Minnesota Press, 1986.

Oldson, William O. "Alibi for Prejudice: Eastern Orthodoxy, the Holocaust, and Romanian Nationalism." *East European Quarterly* XXXVI, no. 3 (September 2002): 301–11.

O'Leary, Brendan. "Ernest Gellner's Diagnoses of Nationalism: A Critical Overview, or, What Is Living and What Is Dead in Ernest Gellner's Philosophy of Nationalism." In *The State of the Nation: Ernest Gellner and the Theory of Nationalism*, edited by John A Hall, 40–88. Cambridge: Cambridge University Press, 1998.

Osman, Veis. *E Katakteses Tou Kosmou Ypo Ton Ioudaion.* Odessa: Urlich and Sulche, 1874.

Ozkirimli, U., and S. Sofos. *Tormented by History: Nationalism in Greece and Turkey.* London: Hurst and Company, 2008.

Page, Gil. *Being Byzantine: Greek Identity before the Ottomans.* New York: Cambridge University Press, 2008.

Pantazopoulos, Nikolaos I. "Georg Ludwig Von Maurer, E Pros Evropaika Protypa Oloklerotike Strofe Tes Neoellenikes Nomothesias." *Epistemonike Epeteres Scholes Nomikon kai Oikonomikon Epistemon* 13 (1968): 1346–506.

Papademetriou, Tom. *Render unto the Sultan: Power, Authority, and the Greek Church in the early Ottoman Centuries.* Oxford: Oxford University Press, 2015.

Papadopoulos, Chrysostomos. *Istoria Tes Ekklesias Tes Ellados.* Volume A, Athens: P. A Patrakou, 1920.

Papadopoulos, Giannis. "Schedia Epoikismou Prin Apo Ten Ellenotourkike Antallage Plethysmon." *Mnemon* 32 (2012): 151–76.

Papadopoulos, Stefanos I. "Education in Macedonia and Her Contribution in the Development of the Preconditions for the Success of the Macedonian Struggle." In *O Makedonikos Agonas*, 21–27. Thessaloniki: Institute for Balkan Studies, 1987.

Papageorgiou, Spyridon. *Sfazousin Oi Evraioi Christianopaidas Kai Pinousi to Aima Ton?.* Athens: Michail I. Saliveros, 1902.

Papageorgiou, Stephanos P. *Apo to Genos Sto Ethnos: E Themeliose Tpu Ellenikou Kratous 1821-1862.* Athens: Ekdoseis Papazisi, 2005.

Papagiannis, Stavros Asteriou. *Ethnikos Agrotikos Syndesmos Antikomounistikes Drases.* Athens: Ekdoseis Sokoli, 2007.

Paparrigopoulos, Konstantinos. *Istoria Tou Ellenikou Ethnous.* Athens: Eleftheroudakis, 1932.

Papastratis, Sotiris. "Oi Evraioi Tes Chalkidas Sten Katoche." *Chronika* 44 (December 1981): 9–12.

Papastratis, Thrasyvoulos Or. *Oi Evraioi Tes Kavallas.* Athens: "Sylloges" Argyri Vourna, 2010.

Papastratis, Thrasyvoulos Or. *Oi Evraioi Tou Didymoteichou.* Athens: Ekdoseis Tsoukatou, 2001.

Paquette, Gabriel. "An Itinerant Liberal: Almeida Garret's Exilic Itineraries and Political Ideas in the Age of Southern European Revolutions (1820-34)." In *Mediterranean*

Diasporas, Politics and Ideas in the Long 19th Century, edited by Maurizio Isabella and Konstantina Zanou, 43–58. New York: Bloomsbury, 2016.

Patrinelis, Nikolaos V. "Evraioi Kai Ellenes—O Theskevtikos Kai Ylistikos Dogmatismos Choris Maska." 1972.

Paximadopoulou-Stavrinou, Mirada. "Oi Exegerseis Tes Kephallenias Kata Ta Ete 1848 Kai 1849." Panteio University, 1980.

"Pelegrinis: Epicheirei Na Anaskevasei Meta Ten Katakravge." *E Kathimerini*, September 19, 2016.

"Peri Ton Epistemonikon Kai Technologikon Syllogon, Peri Anakalypseos Kai Diatereseos Ton Archaioteton Kai Tes Chreseos Auton." *Efimeris tis Kyverniseos tou Vasileiou tis Ellados*, 22 Navplio: June 16, 1834.

Peters, George F. "'Jeder Reiche Ist Ein Judas Ischariot': Heinrich Heine and the Emancipation of the Jews." *Monatshefte* 104, no. 3 (2012): 209–31.

Petridis, Pavlos B. *Xenike Exartisi Kai Ethniki Politike 1910-1918*. Athens: Parateretes, 1981.

Petrokokkinou, D. P. *Chioi, Evraioi Kai Genovezoi*. Athens: Estia, 1912.

Petropoulos, John Anthony. *Politics and Statecraft in the Kingdom of Greece 1833-1843*. Princeton: Princeton University Press, 1968.

Petropoulos, John Anthony, and Aikaterini Koumarianou. *E Themeliose Tou Ellenikou Kratous 1833-1843*. Athens: Ekdoseis Papazisi, 1982.

Philliou, Christine. "Communities on the Verge: Unraveling the Phanariot Ascendancy in Ottoman Governance." *Comparative Studies in Society and History* 51, no. 1 (2009): 151–81.

Philippis, Dimitris. *Profasimos, Ekfasismos, Psevdofasismos. Ellada, Italia, Kai Ispania Ston Mesopolemo*. Thessaloniki: University Studio Press, 2010.

Pierron, Bernard. *Juifs Et Chretiens De La Grece Moderne, Histoire Des Relations Intercommunautaires De 1821 a 1945*. Paris: Editions L'Harmattan, 1996.

Plaut, Josua Eli. *Greek Jewry in the Twentieth Century 1913-1983*. London: Farleigh Dickinson University Press, 1996.

Plevris, Konstantinos A. *Oi Evraioi. Ole E Aletheia*. Athens: Ilektron, 2006.

Ploumidis, Spyridon G. "To Orama Tou Ioanni Kapodistria Gia to Elleniko Ethnos Kai Ten Koinonia." In *O Kyvernetes Ioannis Kapodistrias*, edited by Giorgos Georgis, 68–87. Athens: Kastaniotis, 2015.

Polyzoidis, Anastasios. *Keimena Gia Te Demokratia 1824-1825*, edited by Filimon Paionidis and Elpida Vogli. Athens: Ekdoseis Okto, 2011.

Potamianos, Nikos. "Moral Economy?: Popular Demands and State Intervention in the Struggle of Anti-Profiteering Laws in Greece." *Journal of Social History* 48, no. 4 (2015): 803–15.

Potamianos, Nikos. "Regulation and the Retailing Community: The Struggle over the Establishment of the Holiday of Sunday in Greece, 1872-1926." *History of Retailing and Consumption* 0, no. 0 (2017): 1–16.

Pouqueville, François Charles Hughes Laurent. *Istoria Tes Ellenikes Epanastaseos Etoi E Anagennesis Tes Ellados*. Translated by Ioannis Th. Zafeiropoulos. Volume III, Athens: A Georgiou, P Tzelatou, G Fexi, 1890.

Pouqueville, François Charles Hughes Laurent. *Istoria Tis Ellinikis Epanastasis*. Volume. 1, Athens: Afoi Tolidi, 1996.

Pouqueville, François Charles Hughes Laurent. *Taxidi Sten Ellada—Epeiros*. Athens: Afoi Tolidi, 1994.

Pouqueville, François Charles Hughes Laurent. *Taxidi Stin Ellada—Sterea Ellada, Attiki, Korinthos*. Athens: Ekdoseis Afon Tolidi, 1995.

"Preliminary Treaty of Peace between Russia and Turkey: Signed at San Stefano, February 9/March 3, 1878." *The American Journal of International Law* 2, no. 4 (1908): 387–401.

"Pros Ti E Epimone Ton Evraion Na Tous .. Timoume Synechos?." *Proinos Logos*, August 4, 2016.

Provatas, Anastasios. *Syntomos Politike Istoria Tou Voreioepeirotikou Zetematos*. Athens: Kentrike Epitrope Voreioepeirotikou Agonos, 1969.

Psallidas, Gregoris. "Social Solidarity on the Periphery of the Greek Kingdom: The Case of the Workers' Fraternity of Corfu." In *Greek Society in the Making, 1863-1913*, edited by Philip Carabott. Aldershot: Ashgate, 1997.

Psarras, Dimitris. "O Antisemitismos Sten Ellada Kai E Aristera." *Efimerida ton Syntakton*, 29 (May 2017), http://www.efsyn.gr/arthro/o-antisimitismos-stin-ellada-kai-i-aristera on 29 May 2017 the day the article was published, no volume or page numbers given.

Psarras, Dimitris. *To Best Seler Tou Misous*. Athens: Ekdoseis Polis, 2013.

Pullan, Brian. "'A Ship with Two Rudders': 'Righetto Marrano' and the Inquisition in Venice." *The Historical Journal* 20, no. 1 (March 1977): 25–58.

Rabbi Benjamin of Tudela. *The Itinerary of Rabbi Benjamin of Tudela*, translated by A. Asher. Volume I, London: A. Asher & Co, 1840.

Rallis, G. A., and M. Potlis. *Oi Ellenikoi Kodikes Meta Ton Tropopoiounton Autous Neoteron Nomon Kai Vasilikon Diatagmaton Eis Prosetethesan to Politiko Syntagma Tes Ellados*. Volume A, Athens: G Chartofylakas, 1844.

Randolph, Bernard. *The Present State of the Morea, Called Anciently Peloponnesus: Together with a Description of the City of Athens, Islands of Zant, Strafades, and Serigo*. London: Will. Notts, 1689.

Ravid, Benjamin. "The Legal Status of the Jewish Merchants of Venice, 1541-1638." *The Journal of Economic History* 35, no. 1 (1975): 274–79.

Redlich, Josef, Baron d'Estournelles de Constant, Justin Godart, Walther Schücking, Francis W. Hirst, H. N. Brailsford, Paul Milioukov, and Samuel T. Dutton. *Report of the International Commission to Inquire into the Causes and Conduct of the Balkan Wars*. Washington DC: Carnegie Endowment for International Peace, 1914.

Riasanovsky, Nicholas V. *Nicholas I and Official Nationality in Russia 1825-1855*. Berkeley: University of California Press, 1969.

Ristovic, Milan. "The Jews of Serbia (1804-1918): From Princely Protection to Formal Emancipation." In *The Jews and the Nation-States of Southeastern Europe from the 19th Century to the Great Depression*, edited by Tullia Catalan and Marco Dogo, 23–50. Newcastle upon Tyne: Cambridge Scholars Publishing, 2016.

Robarts, Andrew. "Imperial Confrontation or Regional Cooperation?: Bulgarian Migration and Ottoman-Russian Relations in the Black Sea Region, 1768-1830s." *Turkish Historical Review* 3 (2012): 149–67.

Rodogno, Davide. "Italiani Brava Gente? Fascist Italy's Policy toward the Jews in the Balkans, April 1941–July 1943." *European History Quarterly* 35, no. 2 (2005): 213–40.

Rodrigue, Aron. "From Millet to Minority: Turkish Jewry in the 19th and 20th Centuries." In *Paths of Emancipation: Jews within States and Capitalism*, edited by Pierre Birnbaum and Ira Katznelson, 238–61. Princeton: Princeton University Press, 1995.

Rothman, Natalie E. "Becoming Venetian: Conversion and Transformation in the Seventeenth-Century Mediterranean." *Mediterranean Historical Review* 21, no. 1 (June 2006): 39–75.

Rothman, Natalie E. *Brokering Empire: Trans-Imperial Subjects between Venice and Istanbul*. Vol. Ithaca: Cornell University Press, 2014.

Rotman, Youval. "Converts in Byzantine Italy: Local Representations of Jewish-Christian Rivalry." In *Jews in Byzantium*, edited by Robert Bonfil, Oded Irshai, Guy G. Stroumsa, and Rina Talgam, 893–921. Boston: Brill, 2012.

Runciman, Steven. *The Great Church in Captivity*. Cambridge: Cambridge University Press, 1968.

Saias, Ioannis. *La Grece Et Les Israelites De Salonique*. Paris: Impremerie de la conference de la Paix, 1919.

Salamanka, Dimitrios. *Kathos Charaze E Levteria*. Ioannina: Ipeirotiki Estia, 1963.

Salamanka, Dimitrios. *Peripatoi Sta Jiannina*. Ioanina: Ekdoseis Etaireias Epirotikon Meleton, 1993.

Saloutos, Theodore. "American Missionaries in Greece: 1820-1869." *Church History* 24, no. 2 (1955): 152–74.

Saltiel, Leon. "Dehumanizing the Dead the Destruction of Thessaloniki's Jewish Cemetery in the Light of New Sources." *Yad Vashem Studies* 42, no. 1 (July 2014): 1–35.

Saltiel, Leon. "Professional Solidarity and the Holocaust: The Case of Thessaloniki." In *Jahrbuch FüR Antisemitismusforschung 24*, edited by Werner Bergmann, Marcus Funck, and Dilek Güven, 229–48. Berlin: Metropol Verlag, 2015.

Saltiel, Leon. "Prospatheies Diasoses Evraiopaidon Thessalonikis Kata Ten Katoche: Ena Agnosto Kykloma Paranomon Yiothesion." *Sygchrona Themata* 36, no. 127 (October–December 2014 2014): 75–78.

Salvanou, Emilia. "The First World War and the Refugee Crisis: Historiography and Memory in the Greek Context." *Historein* 16, no. 1–2 (2017): 120–38.

Schick, Irvin Cemil. "Christian Maids, Turkish Revishes: The Sexualization of National Conflict in the Late Ottoman Period." In *Women in the Ottoman Balkans: Gender, Culture and History*, edited by Amila Buturovic and Irvin Cemil Schick, 273–306. New York: I. B. Tauris, 2007.

Schminck-Gustavus, Christoph U. *Mnemes Katoches II. Italoi Kai Germanoi Sta Giannena Kai E Katastrophe Tes Evraikes Koinotetas*. Ioannina: Isnafi, 2008.

Schorsch, Jonathan. "Blacks, Jews and the Racial Imagination in the Writings of Sephardim in the Long Seventeenth Century." *Jewish History* 19 (2005): 109–35.

Schurman, Jacob Gould. *The Balkan Wars 1912-1913*. Princeton, NJ: Princeton University Press, 1914.

Sciaky, Leon. *Farewell to Salonica*. New York: Current Books, 1946.

Seckendorf, Martin. *E Ellada kato apo ton Agkyloto Stavro*. Athens: Sygchroni Epochi, 1991.

Semerdjian, Elyse. "Armenian Women, Legal Bargaining, and Gendered Politics of Conversion in Seventeenth- and Eighteenth-Century Aleppo." *Journal of Middle East Women's Studies* 12, no. 1 (March 2016): 2–30.

Segeberg, Harro. "Germany." In *Nationalism in the Age of French Revolution*, edited by Otto Dann and John Dinwiddy, 137–56. London: The Hambledon Press, 1988.

Sfetas, Spyros. "Birth of 'Macedonianism in the Interwar Period." In *The History of Macedonia* edited by Ioannis Koliopoulos, 285–303. Thessaloniki: Museum of the Macedonian Struggle Foundation, 2007.

Shaw, Stanford. *The Jews of the Ottoman Empire and the Turkish Republic*. New York: New York University Press, 1991.

Shepkaru, Shmuel. "The Preaching of the First Crusade and the Persecutions of the Jews." *Medieval Encounters* 18 (2012): 93–135.

Sila-Nowicki, Wladyslaw. "A Reply to Jan Blonski." In *My Brother's Keeper. Recent Polish Debates on the Holocaust*, edited by Anthony Polonsky, 59–68. New York: Routledge, 1990.

Simpi, Iakov, and Karina Lampsa. *E Zoe Ap' Ten Arche: E Metanastevsh Ton Ellenon Evraion Sten Palaistini (1945-1948)*. Athens: Ekdoseis Alexandreia, 2010.

Sivan, Hagith. "From Byzantine to Persian Jerusalem: Jewish Perspectives and Jewish/Christian Polemics." *Greek, Roman, and Byzantine Studies* 41 (2000): 277–306.

Skerlj, Bozo. "Eugenics or Racial Hygiene?." In *The History of East-Central European Eugenics 1900-1945*, edited by Marius Tudra. New York: Bloomsbury, 2015.

Skopatea, Elli. *To "Protypo Vasileio" Kai E Megale Idea, Opseis Tou Ethnikou Provlematos Sten Ellada (1830-1880)*. Athens: Polytypo, 1988.

Skoulidas, Ilias G. "Arta: Ena Antiparadeigma." In *Apo Ten Apeiro Chora Sten Megale Epeiro*, edited by Katerina Liampi, Nikolaos Katsikoudis, and Nikolaos Anastasopoulos, 173–84. Ioannina: Kosmeteia Philosophikis Scholis, 2016.

Skoulidas, Ilias G. "Ellenes Proxenoi Se 'Epeiro Kai Alvania' Sta Tele Tou 19ou Aiona: Ideologikoi Prosanatolismoi Kai Kratike Politike." In *To Ethnos Peran Ton Synoron*, edited by Lina Ventoura and Lampros Mpaltsiotis, 83–107. Athens: Vivliorama, 2013.

Smith, Anthony D. *The Ethnic Origins of Nations*. Oxford: Blackwell, 1986.

Smith, Anthony D. "The Geneology of Nations: An Ethno-Symbolic Approach." In *When Is the Nation?*, edited by Atsuko Ichijo and Gordana Uzelac, 94–112. New York: Routledge, 2005.

Smith, Anthony D. *Myths and Memories of the Nation*. Oxford: Oxford University Press, 1999.

Smith, Anthony D. *National Identity*. London: Penguin, 1991.

Smith, Anthony D. "When Is a Nation?." *Geopolitics* 7, no. 2 (2002): 5–32.

Soffer, Yossi. "The View of Byzantine Jews in Islamic and Eastern Christian Sources." In *Jews in Byzantium*, edited by Robert Bonfil, Oded Irshai, Guy G. Stroumsa and Rina Talgam, 845–70. Boston: Brill, 2012.

Solomos, Nikolaos I. *Istoria Ton Evraion Apo Ton Archaiotaton Chronon Mechri Ton Emeron Mas*. Athens: Arg. Drakopoulos, 1893.

Solonari, Vladimir. "Patterns of Violence: The Local Population and the Mass Murder of Jews in Bessarabia and Northern Bukovina, July–August 1941." *Kritika: Explorations in Russian and Eurasian History* 8, no. 4 (Fall 2007): 749–87.

Solonari, Vladimir. *Purifying the Nation: Population Exchange and Ethnic Cleansing in Nazi-Allied Romania*. Baltimore: John Hopkins University Press, 2010.

Sotiriou, Stephanos N. *Meionotetes Kai Alytrotismos*. Athens: Elliniki Evroekdotiki, 1991.

Sotirović, Vladislav B. "Macedonia between Greek, Bulgarian, Albanian, and Serbian National Aspirations, 1870-1912." *Serbian Studies: Journal of the North American Society for Serbian Studies* 23, no. 1 (2009): 17–40.

Soutsos, Dimitrios S. *O Dodekalogos Tou Ethnikiste*. Ethnikistikos Syndesmos Athens: Nik. Sakkoulas, 1946.

Spengler-Axiopoulou, Barbara. "Alleleggye Kai Voetheia Pros Tous Evraious Tes Elladas Kata Te Diarkeia Tes Katoches: 1941-1944." In *Oi Evraioi Tes Elladas Sten Katoche*, edited by Rika Benveniste, 13–28. Thessaloniki: Ekdoseis Vanias, 1998.

Spilioti, Susan-Sophia. "'Mia Ypothese Tes Politikes Kai Ochi Tes Dikaiosynes'. E Dike Tou Merten (1957-1959) Kai Oi Elleno-Germanikes Scheseis." Edited by Rika Mpennveniste., Thessaloniki: Vanias, 1998, 29–42.

Spyropoulos, Giannis. *Othomanike Dioikese Kai Koinonia Sten Proepanastatike Dytike Krete*. Rethymno: Genika Archeia tou Kratous, Archeia N. Rethymnis, 2015.

Stamatopoulos, Dimitris. "Between Middle Classes and Grand Bourgeoisie: Greek-Bulgarian Confrontation and Political Hegemony in Thessaloniki from the Bulgarian Schism (1872) to the Slaughter of the Consuls (1876)." In *Balkan Nationalism(S) and the Ottoman Empire*, edited by Dimitris Stamatopoulos, 101–41. Istanbul: The Isis Press, 2015.

Stamatopoulos, Dimitris. "The Orthodox Church of Greece." In *Orthodox Christianity and Nationalism in Nineteenth-Century Southeastern Europe*, edited by Lucian N. Leustean, 34–64. New York: Fordham University Press, 2014.

Stardelov, Georgi, Cvetan Grozdanov, and Blaze Ristovski, eds. *Macedonia and Its Relations with Greece*. Skopje: Macedonian Academy of Sciences and Arts, 1993.

Starr, Joshua. "The Socialist Federation of Salonika." *Jewish Social Studies* VII (1945): 323–36.

Stathis. "Me Melane Apo Aima." *enikos.gr*, May 10, 2017.

Stavrianos, L. S. "The Jews of Greece." *Journal of Central European Affairs* 8, no. 3 (October 1948): 256–69.

Stavrinos, Miranda. "Palmerston and the Cretan Question, 1839-1841." *Journal of Modern Greek Studies* 10, no. 2 (1992): 249–69.

Stavroulakis, Nicholas. *Salonika: Jews and Dervishes*. Athens: Talos Press, 1993.

St.Clair, W. *That Greece Might Still Be Free: The Philhellenes in the War of Independence*. London: Oxford University Press, 1972.

Stefanou, S. I., ed. *Eleftheriou Venizelou. Ta Keimena: 1909-1935*. Volume C, Athens: Lesche Fileleftheron, 1981.

Stefanou, S. I., ed. *Eleftheriou Venizelou. Ta Keimena: 1909-1935*. Volume D, Athens: Lesche Fileleftheron, 1981.

Stefanovic, Djordje. "Seeing the Albanians through Serbian Eyes: The Inventors of the Tradition of Intolerance and Their Critics, 1804-1939." *European History Quarterly* 35, no. 3 (2005): 465–92.

Stein, Sarah Abrevaya. *Making Jews Modern: The Yiddish and Ladino Press in the Russian and Ottoman Empires*. Bloomington: Indiana University Press, 2006.

Stoianovich, Traian. "The Conquering Balkan Orthodox Merchant." *The Journal of Economic History* 20, no. 2 (June 1960): 234–313.

Stouraiti, Anastasia, and Alexander Kazamias. "The Imaginary Topographies of the Megali Idea: National Territory as Utopia." In *Spatial Conceptions of the Nation: Modernizing Geographies in Greece and Turkey*, edited by Nikiforos Diamandouros, Thalia Dragonas, and Caglar Keyder, 11–34. London: I. B. Tauris, 2010.

Stroumsa, Guy G. "Jewish Survival in Late Antique Alexandria." In *Jews in Byzantium*, edited by Robert Bonfil, Oded Irshai, Guy G. Stroumsa, and Rina Talgam, 257–70. Boston: Brill, 2012.

Svolopoulos, Konstantinos. "O Ioannis Kapodistrias Metaxy Apolytarchias Kai Fileleftherismou." In *O Kyvernetes Ioannis Kapodistrias*, edited by Giorgos Georgis, 29–45. Athens: Kastaniotis, 2015.

Svolos, Alexandros. *Ta Ellinika Syntagmata 1822-1975/1986. I Syntagmatiki Istoria Tis Ellados*. Athens: Stochastis, 1998.

Svoronos, Nikos G. *To Elleniko Ethnos: Genese Kai Diamorphose Tou Newou Ellenismou*. Athens: Polis, 2017.

"Tableaux Des Écoles De L' Alliance." *Paix et Droit* 13, no. 1 (January 8, 1933).

Talhamy, Yvette. "American Protestant Missionary Activity among the Nusayris (Alawis) in Syria in the Nineteenth Century." *Middle Eastern Studies* 47, no. 2 (2011): 215–36.

Tatsios, Theodore George. "Gia Antisemitika Stereotypa Kategorei Ton Pelegrini to Kentriko Israelitiko Symvoulio." *Protagon.gr*, September 21, 2016.

Tatsios, Theodore George. *The Megali Idea and the Greek-Turkish War of 1897: The Impact of the Cretan Problem on Greek Irredentism, 1866-1897*. Boulder: East European Monographs, 1984.

Thanailaki, Polly. "American Schools in Greece in the Nineteenth Century: The Missionary Josiah Brewer and His School on the Island of Syros." *Greek Orthodox Theological Review* 51, no. 1–4 (2006): 91–108.

Theodorou, Theod E. *E Ellenike Topike Autodioikese.* Volume 1, Athens: Afoi Tolidi, 1996.

Thiersch, Friedrich. *E Ellada Tou Kapodistria.* Volume B, Athens: Afoi Tolidi, 1972. Leipzig 1833.

Thiersch, Friedrich. *E Ellada Tou Kapodistria.* Volume A, Athens: Afoi Tolidi, 1972. Leipzig 1833.

Thorne, M. Benjamin. "Assimilation, Invisibility, and the Eugenic Turn in the 'Gypsy Question' in Romanian Society, 1938–1942." *Romani Studies* 21, no. 2 (2011): 177–205.

Tosheff, Andrew. *The Bulgarian-Serbian Debate.* Sofia: The Royal Printing Office, 1932.

Tounta-Fergadi, Areti. *Elleno-Voulgarikes Meionotetes. Protokollo Politi-Kalfof 1924-1925.* Thessaloniki: Institute for Balkan Studies, 1986.

Tozzi, Christopher J. *Nationalizing France's Army: Foreign, Black, and Jewish Troops in the French Military, 1715-1831.* Charlottesville: University of Virginia Press, 2016.

"Treaty between Great Britain, Germany, Austria, France, Italy, Russia, and Turkey for the Settlement of Affairs in the East: Signed at Berlin, July 13, 1878." *The American Journal of International Law* 2, no. 4 (1908): 401–24.

Tricha, Lydia. *Charilaos Trikoupis, O Politikos Tou "Tis Ptaiei;" Kai Tou "Dystychos Eptochevsamen."* Athens: Polis, 2016.

Trikoupis, Spyridon. *Istoria Tis Ellinikis Epanastaseos.* Volume A, Athens: Giovanis, 1978.

Trikoupis, Spyridon. *Istoria Tis Ellinikis Epanastaseos.* Volume B, Athens: Giovanis, 1978.

Tritos, Michael G. *To Tagma Ton Lazariston Kai E Roumanike Propaganda.* Thessaloniki: Kyromanos, 2004.

Tsiknanis, Kostas G. "Metra Kata Tes Kykloforias Evraikon Vivlion Ton 16o Aiona." In *E Evraike Parousia Ston Elladiko Choro (4os-19os Ai.),* edited by Anna Lambropoulou and Kostas Tsiknakis, 155–70. Athens: Ethniko Idryma Erevnon, 2008.

Tsiligiannis, Konstantinos A. *E Evraike Koinoteta Tes Artas.* Athens: Kentriko Israilitiko Symvoulio tes Ellados, 2004.

Tsioumis, Kostis A. *Meionotetes Sten Ellada: Ellenikes Meionotetes Sta Valkania.* Thessaloniki: Ekdotikos Oikos Ant. Stamouli, 2008.

Tsironis, Theodosis. "E Organose Ethnike Enosis 'E Ellas' (E.E.E.) Ste Thessaloniki Tou Mesopolemou (1927-1936). Ta Katastatika Kai E Drase Tes." *Epistemoniki Epeterida tou Kentrou Istorias Thessalonikis tou Demou Thessalonikis* 6 (2002).

Tsormpatzis, Georgios A. *Eos Tes Evraikes Paliggenesias Apo Ellenikes Skopias.* Athens: Eleftheroudakis, 1925.

Tsoutsoumpis, Spyros. "Land of the Kapedani: Brigandage, Paramilitarism and Nation-Building in 20th Century Greece." *Balkan Studies* 51 (2016): 35–67.

Tzedopoulos, Yorgos. "Public Secrets: Crypto-Christianity in the Pontos." *Deltio Kentrou Mikrasiatikon Spoudon* 16 (2009): 165–210.

United Nations. *Convention on the Prevention and Punishment of the Crime of Genocide Adopted by the General Assembly of the United Nations on 9 December 1948.* 1021.

Vakalopoulos, Apostolos E. *Aichmalotoi Ellenon Kata Ten Epanastase Tou 1821.* Athens: Irodotos, 2000.

Vakalopoulos, Konstantinos. *To Makedoniko Zetema: Genese—Diamorphose—Exelixe—Lyse (1856-1912).* Athens: Dimosiographikos Organismos Labraki, 2009.

Varvaritis, Dimitrios. "'The Jews Have Got into Trouble Again.': Responses to the Publication of 'Cronaca Insraelitica' and the Question of Jewish Emancipation in the Ionian Islands (1861-1863)." *Quest Issues in Contemporary Jewish History,* no. 7 (2014): 30–51.

Vasdravellis, Ioannis K. *Oi Makedones Kata Ten Epanastase Tou 1821.* Thessaloniki: 1967.

Vasilikou, Maria. "E Ekpaidevse Ton Evraion Tes Thessalonikes Sto Mesopolemo." In *O Ellenikos Evraismos,* edited by Maria Stephanopoulou, 129–47. Athens: Idryma Moraiti, 1999.

Vasilikou, Maria. "Ethnotikes Antitheseis Sten Ellada Tou Mesopolemou. E Periptose Tou Empresmou Tou Kampel." *Istor* 7 (1994): 153–74.

Vasilopoulos, Charalambos. *Kosmas Aitolos O Ellin Ierapostolos.* Athens: Panellinios Orthodoxos Enosis, 1961.

Vlasidis, Vlasis. "The 'Macedonian Question' on the Bulgarian Political Scene (1919-23)." *Balkan Studies* 32, no. 1 (January 1991): 71–88.

Vogazlis, D. K. *Fyletikes Kai Ethnikes Meionotetes Sten Ellada Kai Te Voulgaria.* Athens: Etaireia Thrakikon Meleton, 1954.

Vogli, Elpida K. *Ellenes to Genos: E Ithageneia Kai E Taytoteta Sto Ethniko Kratos Ton Ellenon (1821-1844).* Irakleio: Panepistimiakes Ekdoseis Kritis, 2008.

Vranousis, I. I. *Rigas.* Athens: I Zacharopoulos, 1953.

Vryonis, Speros. *The Decline of Medieval Hellenism in Asia Minor and the Process of Islamization from the Eleventh through the Fifteenth Century.* Berkeley: University of California Press, 1971.

Walpole, Robert. *Memoirs Relating to European and Asiatic Turkey.* London: Longman, Hurst, Rees, Orme, and Brown, 1818.

Walsh, Robert. *A Residence at Constantinople.* London: 1836.

Weber, Eugen. *Peasants into Frenchmen: The Modernization of Rural France 1870-1914.* Stanford: Stanford University Press, 1976.

Weinberg, Robert. *Blood Libel in Late Imperial Russia: The Ritual Murder Trial of Mendel Beilis.* Indiana-Michigan Series in Russian and East European Studies. Indiana: Indiana University Press, 2013.

Weininger, Otto. *Sex and Character: An Investigation of Fundamental Principles.* Bloomington: Indiana University Press, 2005.

Weiss, James. "Fortress Forever at the Ready: The Jewish Ethos in the Byzantine Mind and Its Ruthenian Translation." *Greek Orthodox Theological Review* 46, no. 3–4 (2001): 287–344.

Weizmann, Chaim. *O Evraikos Laos Kai E Palaistine.* Thessaloniki: Keren Kagiemet kai Keren Agiesod 1937.

Wheaton, Henry. *Elements of International Law.* Boston: Little, Brown and Company, 1866 (1836).

Whitten, Dolphus. "The Don Pacifico Affair." *The Historian* 48, no. 2 (1986): 255–67.

Woodhouse, C. M. *Rigas Velestinlis: The Proto-Martyr of the Greek Revolution.* Limni and Evia: Denise Harvey, 1995.

Yakoel, Yomtov. *Apomnemonevmata 1941-1943.* Thessaloniki: Paratiritis, 1993.

Yerasimos, Stephane. "Les Grecs D'istanbul Apres La Conquete Ottomane. Le Repeuplement De La Ville Et De Ses Environs (1453-1550)." *Revue des mondes musulmans et de la Méditerranée* 107–110 (2005): 375–99.

Yerolympos, Alexandra. "A New City for a New State. City Planning and the Formation of National Identity in the Balkans (1820s-1920s)." *Planning Perspectives* 8 (1993): 233–57.

Yerolympos, Alexandra. "Thessaloniki (Salonika) before and after 1917. Twentieth Century Planning Versus 20 Centuries of Urban Evolution." *Planning Perspectives* 3 (1988): 141–66.

Zanou, Konstantina. "Imperial Nationalism and Orthodox Enlightenment: A Diasporic Story between the Ionian Islands, Russia and Greece, Ca. 1800-30." In *Mediterranean Diasporas, Politics and Ideas in the Long 19th Century,* edited by Maurizio Isabella and Konstantina Zanou, 117–34. New York: Bloomsbury, 2016.

Zavitsianos, Georgios A. *Aktis Photos. Katadiogmos Ton Evraion En Te Istoria. Skepseis.* Kerkyra: N Petsali, 1891.

Zekendorf, Martin. *E Ellada Kato Apo Ton Agyloto Stavro.* Athens: Sychroni Epochi, 1991.

Zens, Robert W. "In the Name of the Sultan: Haci Mustafa Pasha of Belgrade and Ottoman Provincial Rule in the Late 18th Century." *International Journal of Middle East Studies* 44, no. 01 (2012): 129–46.

Zhelyazkova, Antonina. "Islamization in the Balkans as a Historiographical Problem: The Southeast-European Perspective." In *The Ottomans and the Balkans: A Discussion of Historiography,* edited by Fikret Adanir and Suraiya Faroqhi, 223–66. Leiden: Brill, 2002.

Zographakis, Georgios K., ed. *Mordochaios I Frizis: O Protos Anoteros Ellenas Axiomatikos Pou Epese Machomenos Ston Ellenoitaliko Polemo.* Athens: Kentriko Israilitikon Symvoulion, 1977.

Index